# Exploring Creation

## with

# Physical Science

by Dr. Jay L. Wile

# Exploring Creation With Physical Science

Manufactured in the United States of America
Sixth Printing 2004

*Published By*

## Apologia Educational Ministries, Inc.
Anderson, IN

*Printed by*

## The C.J. Krehbiel Company
Cincinnati, OH

# Need Help?

## Apologia Educational Ministries, Inc. Curriculum Support

If you have any questions while using Apologia curriculum, feel free to contact us in any of the following ways.

### By Mail:

Dr. Jay L. Wile
Apologia Educational Ministries, Inc.
1106 Meridian Plaza, Suite 220
Anderson, IN 46016

### By E-MAIL:        help@highschoolscience.com

### On The Web:        http://www.highschoolscience.com

### By FAX:

(765) 608-3290

### By Phone:

(765) 608-3280

## STUDENT NOTES
*Exploring Creation With Physical Science*
Dr. Jay L. Wile

This course will take you on an amazing journey! It will begin with a detailed discussion of the world around you and what makes it work. It will then take you out into the universe so that you may learn the majesty of God's Creation. Like anything worth doing, this course will be hard work, but in the end, you will find it interesting and (hopefully) enjoyable. From the inner-workings of atoms to the grandeur of galaxies, be prepared to be awed and amazed with what the Creator has made for **you!**

### Pedagogy of the Text

There are 16 modules in this course. You can divide the course into 4 quarters, which works out to four modules per quarter. Each quarter should take you 9 weeks to complete, so you should shoot for finishing a module every two weeks or so. If you do that, each quarter will take you 8 weeks. Thus, you have about a week of flexibility time each quarter.

How will you know how much to do in order to spend only 2 weeks per module? Well, start by spending one half hour per day with the course. At the end of 2 weeks, if you have not completed the module, you know that you need to spend more time each day on it. If you finish a module in less than 2 weeks, then you know that you can spend less time per day on it. In the end, then, try to find the pace that will keep you on track.

There are two types of exercises that you are expected to complete: "on your own" problems and an end-of-the module study guide.

- You should answer the "on your own" problems while you read the text. The act of answering these problems will cement in your mind the concepts you are trying to learn. Detailed answers and explanations are provided for you at the end of the module, so that you may check your own work. DO NOT look at the answer to a question until AFTER you have tried to answer it!

- You should complete the study guide in its entirety after you have finished the module. The solutions to the study guides are in a separate volume which your parent/teacher has.

All definitions presented in the text are centered. The words will appear in the study guide and their definitions need to be memorized. Words that appear in bold-face type in the text are important terms that you should know.

The study guide gives you a good feel for what you need to know for the test. Any information needed to answer the study guide questions is information that you must know for the test. Sometimes, tables and other reference material will be provided on a test so that you need not memorize it.  You will be able to tell if this is the case because the questions in the study guide which refer to this information will specifically tell you to use the reference material.

## Experiments

The experiments in this course are designed to be done while you are reading the text.  I recommend that you keep a notebook of these experiments.  As you write about the experiment in the notebook, you will be forced to think through all of the concepts that were explored in the experiment.  This will help you cement them into your mind.  I recommend that you perform your experiments in the following way:

- When you get to the experiment during the reading, read through the experiment in its entirety.  This will allow you to gain a quick understanding of what you must do.

- Once you have read the experiment, start a new page in your laboratory notebook.  The first page should be used to write down all of the data taken during the experiments and perform any exercises discussed in the experiment.

- When you have finished the experiment, you should write a brief report in your notebook, right after the page where the data and exercises were written.  The report should be a brief discussion of what was done and what was learned.  You should write this discussion so that someone who has never read the book can read your discussion and figure out what basic procedure you followed and what you learned as a result of the experiment.

- **PLEASE OBSERVE COMMON SENSE SAFETY PRECAUTIONS. The experiments are no more dangerous than most normal, household activities.  Remember, however, that the vast majority of accidents do happen in the home!**

In order to help you prepare for the experiment in the course, the next few pages list all materials needed to perform the experiments in each module.  You can use this list to make sure that you have everything you need.  That way, when you reach a lab in the reading, you will not be delayed for lack of supplies.  Of all the things listed on the subsequent pages, the only items you might have difficulty finding are the two test tubes needed for Experiment 4.1 (they are shown on page iv in boldface type).  If you cannot get them, you can skip Experiment 4.1.

**Lab Supplies Needed For Module # 1**

- A small glass, like a juice glass
- Baking soda
- Tap water
- A 9-Volt battery (the kind that goes in a radio, smoke detector, or toy.  DO NOT use an electrical outlet, as it will most likely kill you!  A 1.5 Volt flashlight battery will not work.)
- Two 9-inch pieces of insulated wire.  The wire itself must be copper.
- A pair of scissors
- Tape (preferably electrical tape, but cellophane or masking tape will work)
- A long piece of string
- A large table top (like a kitchen table or a big desk)
- A person to help you
- Some cellophane tape
- A pencil
- Vinegar
- 6 TUMS ® tablets  (You can use another antacid tablet, but it must have calcium carbonate as its active ingredient.)
- Measuring cups
- 3 large glasses (They each must be able to hold at least 2 cups of liquid.)
- A spoon

**Lab Supplies Needed For Module # 2**

- Hydrogen peroxide (sold at any drug store)
- Baker's yeast
- Vinegar
- Baking soda
- Two cotton balls
- Tap water
- A small glass, like a juice glass
- A reasonably large glass or jar
- A bottle (A plastic, 1-liter soda bottle, for example)
- A teaspoon
- A bulb thermometer (It must be able to read room temperature and slightly higher, and it must have a bulb at the end.)
- A small piece of plastic such as a ZIPLOC® bag or a square cut from a trash bag.
- A candle  (DO NOT use a lighter or any other gas or alcohol burner.  You must use a candle in order to keep the experiment safe.)
- Matches
- A balloon
- Two clear ZIPLOC® sandwich bags

## Lab Supplies Needed For Module # 3

- Food coloring (any color)
- Ice
- Water
- A tall, clear jar or glass (It should either be straight, or it should be tapered so that the top of the jar is smaller than the bottom.  Do not use a jar that is tapered so that the top is bigger than the bottom, as this will reduce the effect you are trying to see.)
- Plastic bottle (The best volume would be 1 quart or  1 liter, but any size will work.)
- A bowl
- A candle
- A candle holder
- Some matches
- A balloon

## Lab Supplies Needed For Module # 4

- Vegetable oil
- Epsom salts (You can get these at any drug store or large supermarket.)
- Sugar
- Sand
- Table salt
- A stick of butter or margarine  (It must be fresh from the refrigerator so that it is solid.)
- Water
- An ice cube
- Four glasses
- Two small glasses
- A deep bowl (It must be deep enough so that when it is nearly full of water, the battery can stand vertically in the bowl and still be fully submerged in the water.)
- A tablespoon
- A measuring spoon that measures 1/2 of a teaspoon
- A knife  (A serrated one works best.  You will use it to cut the butter.)
- A 9-Volt battery (Newer ones work better.)
- **Two test tubes (You can purchase these at a hobby store.  If you cannot get them, you can skip the experiment that uses them.)**
- A styrofoam or paper cup
- A comb
- A pen
- Stove
- A saucepan
- A spoon
- A sewing needle
- Some thread
- Dish soap

## Lab Supplies Needed For Module # 5

- Water
- Salt
- Ice
- A tablespoon
- A small saucepan
- A saucepan lid or frying pan lid larger than the saucepan used
- A large bowl (It should not be plastic, as it will get hot.)
- Potholders
- A zippered plastic sandwich bag
- Stove
- A measuring cup
- A plastic bowl that holds more than 2 cups of water
- Freezer
- A teaspoon
- A small plate
- A strainer
- A small glass or cup
- A clear plastic 2-liter bottle (the kind that soda pop comes in) with the lid
- A match

## Lab Supplies Needed For Module # 6

- Two metal spoons
- About 3 feet of string (Nylon kite string is ideal, but any reasonably strong string will work. Thread and yarn do not work well.)
- Large sink
- Water
- A 1.5 Volt battery (Any size cell (AA, A, C, or D) will do, just make sure it is nothing other than one of those.  A battery of higher voltage could be dangerous.)
- A steel or iron nail
- A metal paper clip
- Aluminum foil
- A hard-boiled egg
- A dull knife, like a butter knife
- A marker or something else that will make a mark on the egg shell

## Lab Supplies Needed For Module # 7

- Daily local weather information source that contains:
  1. High and low temperatures for yesterday
  2. High and low atmospheric (sometimes called "barometric") pressure for yesterday (It may be hard to find this. If nothing else, find a source with the current atmospheric pressure.)
  3. Amount of precipitation for yesterday

**PLEASE NOTE:** Experiment 7.1 is a 28-day long experiment. Plan your time accordingly

## Lab Supplies Needed For Module # 8

- A balloon
- A dark room

## Lab Supplies Needed For Module # 9

- Four eggs
- Two strips of reasonably strong cardboard (Like the cardboard you find on the back of writing tablets)
- Many books
- A pair of scissors
- Lots of newspaper or paper towels
- Kitchen table
- A large (at least 21 cm by 27 cm), heavy book
- A small (about 3 cm by 3 cm) piece of paper
- A stopwatch (must read hundredths of a second)
- A ball or rock (something heavy so that air resistance won't be a factor)
- A chair or small stepladder
- A tape measure (A meterstick or yardstick will work, if you do not have a tape measure.)

## Lab Supplies Needed For Module # 10

- A coin
- A 3-inch by 5-inch index card (note that I listed the units)
- A small glass (like a juice glass)
- A raw egg
- A hard-boiled egg
- An aluminum pie pan
- A pair of scissors
- A marble or other small ball

- An unfinished board that is at least 2 feet long
- A block eraser
- An ice cube
- A small block of wood
- A relatively flat rock
- Sandpaper
- Many books
- A ruler
- A plastic, 2-liter bottle (like the kind soda comes in)
- A stopper that fits the bottle  (It could be rubber or cork, but you cannot use the screw-on lid.  It has to be something that plugs up the opening of the bottle but can be pushed out by a pressure buildup inside the bottle.  You could also try a large wad of gum, as long as the gum has dried out and has the texture of firm rubber.
- Vinegar
- Baking soda
- Aluminum foil
- Four pencils

## Lab Supplies Needed For Module # 11

- A mechanical pen
- A black marker
- A thin string or thread (preferably white)
- 5 metal washers, all the same size
- A stopwatch
- Something to cover your eyes, such as safety goggles or safety glasses
- A pair of scissors
- A soft seat cushion from a couch (A soft bed will work as well.)
- A bowling ball (A heavy rock will work as well.)
- A marble
- Two balls (Baseball-sized balls are best, but any will do)
- Two people to help you
- A large, open space

## Lab Supplies Needed For Module # 12

- Three balloons  (Round balloons work best, but any kind will do.)
- Some thread
- Cellophane tape
- A glass
- A plastic lid that fits over the glass  (It can be larger than the mouth of the glass, but it cannot be smaller.  The top of a margarine tub or something similar works quite well.)
- A paper clip

- Two 5-cm x 1.5-cm strips of aluminum foil (the thinner the foil the better)
- A pair of pliers
- A 1.5 Volt battery (Any AA, A, C, or D-cell battery will work. Do not use any battery other than one of those, though, because a **higher voltage will make the experiment dangerous**.)
- Aluminum foil

## Lab Supplies Needed For Module # 13

NONE. The nature of the subject precludes experiments.

## Lab Supplies Needed For Module # 14

- Plastic wrap
- A pair of scissors
- Some tape
- A candle (It needs to either be in a candle holder or be able to stand up securely on its own.)
- Some matches
- A plastic 1-liter or 2-liter bottle (the kind soda comes in)
- A large pot
- A wooden spoon
- A large bowl
- Some rice
- Two medium-sized rocks
- A stopwatch
- A 250-meter stretch of sidewalk, pavement, gravel road, or lawn that is relatively straight
- A tape measure, meterstick, or yardstick
- Water
- A glass or plastic bottle (A glass bottle is best, and 2-liter is the ideal size. It must have a narrow neck. A jar will not work.)
- A car with a horn and a parent to drive the car
- If you have access to a stringed instrument such as a violin, guitar, cello, or banjo, that's all you need for this experiment. If you do not have access to such an instrument, you will need a rubber band and a plastic tub like the kind that margarine or whipped cream comes in.

## Lab Supplies Needed For Module # 15

- A flat pan, like the kind you use to bake a cake
- A medium-size mirror (4-inch by 6-inch is a good size)
- A sunny window (A flashlight will work, but it will not be as dramatic.)

- A plain white sheet of paper
- Water
- A flat mirror.  The mirror can be very small, but it needs to be flat.  You can always tell if a mirror is flat by looking at your reflection in it.  If the image you see in the mirror is neither magnified nor reduced, the mirror is flat.
- A white sheet of paper
- A pen
- A protractor
- A flashlight
- Some black construction paper or thin cardboard
- Some tape
- A square or rectangular glass or clear plastic pan  (If you have a flat bottle, that will work as well.  It just needs to be something with clear, flat sides that can hold water.)
- Water
- Milk
- A spoon
- A flashlight with the same cover you used in Experiment 15.2
- A sheet of plain white paper
- A pen
- A protractor
- A ruler
- A quarter
- A bowl that is reasonably deep an not transparent
- Water
- A pitcher or very large glass to hold the water
- Two plain white sheets of paper (there cannot be lines on them)
- A bright red marker (A crayon will also work, but a marker is better.)

## Lab Supplies Needed For Module # 16

- A balloon
- Two colors of markers (You need to be able to write on the balloon with the markers.)

## Module 14: Waves and Sound

## Module 15: Light

## Module 16: An Introduction to Astrophysics

## Module #1: The Basics

### Introduction

In this course, you are going to learn a lot about the world around you and the universe that it is in. We will study things as familiar as the air around you and others as mysterious as radioactivity and distant galaxies. We will learn about the structure of the earth as well as its place in the solar system and the universe. The study of these topics and many others like them are all a part of what we call **physical science**.

In order to make sure that we are both starting on the "same page," I need to discuss some basic concepts with you. It is quite possible that you have learned some (or all) of this before, but it is necessary that we cover the basics before we try and do anything in depth. Thus, even if some of the topics I cover sound familiar, please read this module thoroughly, so that you will not get lost in a later module. In fact, many of the subjects that I will cover in later modules are probably familiar to you on one level or another. After all, most students your age know something about air, the construction of our planet, weather, and astronomy. Nevertheless, I can almost guarantee you that you have not learned these subjects at the depth in which I will discuss them in this course. So, despite how much you might think you know on a given topic, please read the material I present to you carefully. I doubt that you will be disappointed.

If, on the other hand, all of this is completely new to you, don't worry about it. As long as you read the material carefully, perform the experiments thoroughly, and really *think* about what you learning, everything will be fine. Although this course might not be *easy* for you, there are very few things in life that are both easy *and* worthwhile. I promise you that if you *work* at learning this course, you will gain a great deal of knowledge, a solid sense of accomplishment, and a grand appreciation for the wonder of God's Creation!

### Atoms and Molecules

In this course, I am going to illustrate as many concepts as possible with experiments. Hopefully, the "hands on" experience will help bring those concepts home better than any discussion could. In some cases, of course, this will not be possible, so we will have to make due with words and pictures. To start our discussion of atoms and molecules, I want you to perform the following experiment.

---

**EXPERIMENT 1.1**
Atoms and Molecules

Supplies:

- A small glass, like a juice glass
- Baking soda
- Tap water

- A 9-Volt battery (One that goes in a radio, smoke detector, or toy.  DO NOT use an electrical outlet, as it will most likely kill you!  A 1.5 Volt flashlight battery will not work.)
- Two 9-inch pieces of insulated wire.  The wire itself must be copper.
- A pair of scissors
- Some tape (preferably electrical tape, but cellophane or masking tape will work)


Introduction - Atoms and molecules make up everything that surrounds us.  Individually, they are simply too small to see.  However, you can distinguish between different kinds of atoms and different kinds of molecules by examining the substances that they make up, as well as how those substances change.  In this experiment, we will observe molecules changing into atoms and atoms changing into molecules.  By observing these changes, you will learn about the difference between atoms and molecules.

Procedure:

A. Fill your small glass 3/4 full of tap water.
B. Add a teaspoon of baking soda and stir vigorously.
C. Use your scissors to strip about a quarter inch of insulation off both ends of each wire.  The best way to do this is to put the wire in your scissors and squeeze the scissors gently.  You should feel an increase in resistance as the scissors begin to touch the wire.  Squeeze the scissors until you feel that resistance and then back off.  Continue squeezing and backing off as you slowly turn the wire round and round.

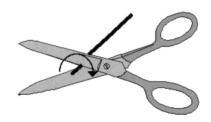

Be careful.  You can cut yourself if you are not paying proper attention!  You will eventually have a cut that goes through the insulation all the way around the wire.  At that point, you can simply pull the insulation off.  It will take some practice to get this right, but you *can* do it.  Make sure that there is at least a quarter inch of bare wire sticking out of both ends of wire.
D. Once you have stripped the insulation off both ends of each wire, connect the end of one wire to one of the two terminals on the battery.  Do this by laying the wire over the terminal and then pressing it down.  Secure it to the terminal with a piece of tape.  It need not look pretty, but it needs to be solidly touching one terminal and not in contact with the other terminal.
E. Repeat step D with the other wire and the other battery terminal.  Now you have two wires attached to the battery, one at each terminal.  Do not allow the bare ends of these wires to touch each other!
F. Now immerse the wires in the baking soda/water solution that is in your small glass so that the bare end of each wire is completely submerged.  It doesn't really matter how much of the insulated portion of the wire is immersed, just make sure that all of the bare end of each wire

is fully submerged.  In the end, your experiment should look something like this:

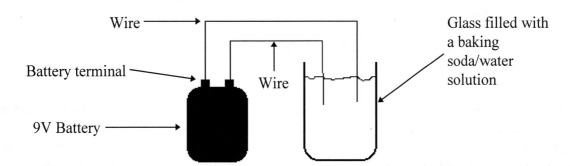

G.  Look at the bare ends of the wires as they are submerged in the baking soda/water solution. What do you see?  Well, if you set everything up right, you should see bubbles coming from both ends.  If you don't see bubbles, the most likely problem is that you do not have good contact between the wires and the battery terminals.  Try pressing the ends of the wire hard against the terminals they are taped to.  If you then see bubbles coming from the submerged ends of the wire, you know that electrical contact is your problem.  If not, your battery might be dead.  Try another one.

H.  Once you get things working, spend some time observing what's going on.  Notice that bubbles are forming on *both* wires.  That's an important point which should be written in your laboratory notebook.

I.  Allow the experiment to run for about ten minutes.  After that time, pull the wires out of the solution and look at the bare ends.  What do you see?  Well, one of the wires should really look no different than when you started.  What about the end of the other wire?  It should now be a different color.  What color is it?  Write that color down in your notebook.

J.  If you really let the experiment run for 10 minutes, it's very possible that your solution became slightly colored.  Write in your notebook whether or not that did happen and what color, if any, the solution became.

K.  Looking at the wire that changed color, trace it back to the battery and determine which terminal (positive or negative) it was attached to.  Write that in your laboratory notebook as well.

L.  **Clean up:** Disconnect the wires from the battery, discard the solution, and wash the glass thoroughly.  Put everything away.

Now, to understand what went on in the experiment, you need a little background information.  Everything that you see around you is made up of tiny little units called **atoms**.

Atom - The smallest stable unit of matter in Creation

Atoms are so small that you cannot see them at all.  They are so small, in fact, that roughly 100,000,000,000,000,000,000 atoms are contained in the head of a pin.  If we can't see them, then how do we know that they exist?  Well, lots of experiments have been done that can only be explained if you *assume* that atoms exist; thus, there is a lot of *indirect* evidence that atoms exist.  All of this indirect evidence leads us to believe that atoms are, indeed, real.

When you stripped the insulation off the ends of each wire, you saw the familiar red-orange color of copper wire. Well, it turns out that copper is a type of atom. Thus, the copper that you observed in the wire was really just a bunch of copper atoms lumped together. You couldn't see the *individual* atoms, but when billions of billions of billions of them are put together, you can see the substance that they make. When you have billions of billions of billions of copper atoms, you get the flexible, electricity-conducting, red-orange metal called copper.

We currently know that there are about 109 basic kinds of atoms in Creation. This number increases as time goes on because, every once in a while, scientists will discover a new kind of atom. In a few years, then, the number of basic kinds of atoms in Creation will probably be a little larger. That's why I say "about" 109 different kinds of atoms in Creation.

If this were the end of the story, Creation would be pretty boring. After all, if everything that you see is made up of atoms, and if there are only about 109 different kinds of atoms in Creation, then there are only 109 different substances in Creation, right? Of course not! Although God used atoms as the basic building blocks of Creation, He designed those atoms to link together to form larger building blocks called **molecules**.

Molecule - Two or more atoms linked together to make a substance with unique properties

It turns out that the water that you used in your experiment is made up of molecules. Although molecules are bigger than atoms, you still cannot really see them. Thus, the water that you see is made up of billions of billions of billions of water molecules, just like the copper wire is made up of billions of billions of billions of atoms of copper. A water molecule is formed when an oxygen atom links together with two hydrogen atoms. When these atoms link together in a very specific way, the result is a water molecule.

Now we are ready to really discuss the results of the experiment. When you filled the glass with water, you were filling it with billions of billion of billions of water molecules. When you placed the wires (which were connected to the battery) into the water, the electricity from the battery began flowing through the water. When this happened, the energy from the electricity flow actually broke some of the water molecules down into hydrogen and oxygen, which began bubbling out of the water because hydrogen and oxygen are gasses!

This is an excellent illustration of atoms and molecules. Each water molecule is made of two hydrogen atoms and an oxygen atom linked together. When these atoms link together in that way, an odorless, colorless, tasteless liquid we call water is formed. When electricity is used to break the water molecules down, hydrogen and oxygen are formed. Hydrogen is an explosive gas with an acrid smell while oxygen is the gas that we breathe to stay alive. Think about that. Oxygen and hydrogen are each gasses with particular properties. When they link together, however, these individual properties are lost and a new substance is formed. If the links between these atoms are broken, then the atoms separate and go back to their original forms!

In the water portion of the experiment, you saw a molecule (water) breaking back down into its constituent atoms (hydrogen and oxygen).  Well, when you pulled the wires out of the water in ten minutes, you saw that the wire connected to the positive terminal of the battery had turned a blueish-green color.  In this case, the copper atoms in the wire interacted with water molecules and baking soda molecules, aided by the energy contained in the electricity.  The result is a blue-green substance called copper hydroxycarbonate (hi drok' see car' buh nate).  Copper hydroxycarbonate is formed when a copper atom links together with oxygen atoms, carbon atoms, and hydrogen atoms.  In this experiment, the hydrogen and oxygen atoms came from both the water and the baking soda, the carbon atoms came from the baking soda alone, and the copper atoms came from the wire.  In this case, then, you observed atoms (copper) linking up with other atoms (oxygen, carbon, and hydrogen) to make a molecule (copper hydroxycarbonate).

Interestingly enough, copper hydroxycarbonate is the same substance that you see on many statues, such as the Statue of Liberty.  You see, if a statue has copper on it and is exposed to weather, a process similar to the one that you observed turns the copper atoms in the statue into copper hydroxycarbonate.  As a result, the statue turns green, just like one of the copper wires did in your experiment.

**FIGURE 1.1**
The Statue of Liberty

*Photo courtesy of the National Libertarian Party*

The Statue of Liberty has turned green over the years because hydrogen, oxygen, and carbon atoms from various substances in the air have combined with the copper atoms in the statue to make copper hydroxycarbonate.

This is how we get all of the incredible substances that you see around you. Some substances (copper, aluminum, and some others) are simply billions of billions of billions of atoms that form the substance. Other substances that we see (water, salt, sugar, and many others) are made up of billions of billions of billions of molecules. Finally, many substances that we see (wood, cereal, plastics, and many others) are actually mixtures of several different substances, each of which is made up of either atoms or molecules. To reinforce this description of atoms and molecules, study Figure 1.2.

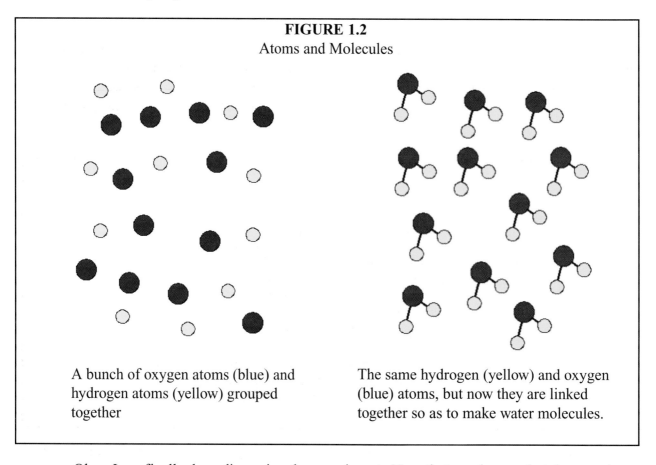

**FIGURE 1.2**
Atoms and Molecules

A bunch of oxygen atoms (blue) and hydrogen atoms (yellow) grouped together

The same hydrogen (yellow) and oxygen (blue) atoms, but now they are linked together so as to make water molecules.

Okay, I am finally done discussing the experiment. Now that you know what the experiment shows, you can write a summary in your laboratory notebook. Write a brief description of what you did, followed by a discussion of what you learned. You will need to do each experiment in this way. Once you have done an experiment and read the discussion that relates to it, you then need to write a summary explaining what you did and what you learned. This will help you get the most from your laboratory exercises.

Now that I am done presenting the concept of atoms and molecules, you need to answer the following "on your own" problems in order to make sure that you understand what you have read. These kinds of problems will show up periodically, and you should answer them as soon as you come to them in your reading.

---

**ON YOUR OWN**

1.1  A molecule is broken down into its constituent atoms.  Do these atoms have the same properties that the molecule had?

1.2  When salt is dissolved in water, it actually breaks down into two different substances.  Is salt composed of atoms or molecules?

---

Before you go on to the next section, I want to dispel a myth that you might have heard. In many simplified science courses, students are told that scientists have actually seen atoms by using an instrument called a "scanning tunneling electron microscope."  Indeed, students are shown figures such as the one below and are told that the conical shapes you see in the picture are atoms.

---

**FIGURE 1.3**

A Scanning Tunneling Electron Microscope Image of the Surface of a Nickel Foil

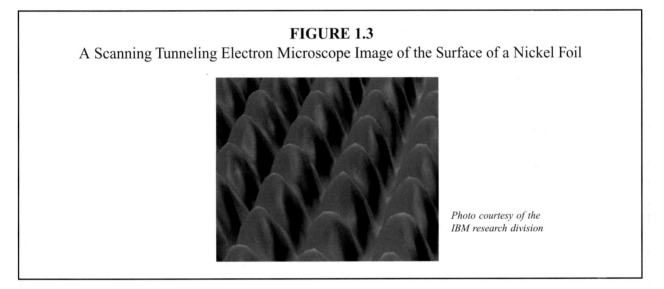

*Photo courtesy of the*
*IBM research division*

---

Is this what nickel atoms really look like?  Are you really seeing a picture of atoms here? Well, although it looks good, it is not really a picture of atoms.  You see, a scanning tunneling electron microscope does not allow you to see things the way a regular microscope does.  Instead, it passes a charged probe across the surface of an object and measures slight changes in electricity that flows through the probe.  It then sends that data to a computer which uses a complicated set of mathematical equations from a theory called "quantum mechanics" to calculate what the surface of the object should look like.  The computer then graphs the results of that calculation. That's what is pictured in Figure 1.3.

So, what you are really seeing in Figure 1.3 is the result of a *calculation* which comes from a *theory* about how electricity flows under certain circumstances.  Thus, *if* the theory is correct, and *if* the computer calculation is correct, *then* you are seeing atoms on the surface of the metal that was examined with the scanning tunneling electron microscope.  Those are two big "ifs," however.  Never be fooled by someone who tells you that we have seen atoms.  We have not.  We have only seen the results of computer calculations that may or may not be right!

## Measurement and Units

Let's suppose I'm making curtains for a friend's windows. I ask the person to measure the window and give me the dimensions so that I can make the curtains the right size. My friend tells me that his windows are 50 by 60, so that's how big I make the curtains. When I go over to his house, it turns out that my curtains are more than twice as big as his windows! My friend tells me that he's certain he measured the windows right, and I tell my friend that I'm certain I measured the curtains right. How can this be? The answer is quite simple. My friend measured the windows with a metric ruler. His measurements were in *centimeters*. I, on the other hand, used a yardstick and measured my curtains in *inches*. Our problem was not caused by one of us measuring incorrectly. Instead, our problem was the result of measuring with different **units.**

When we are making measurements, the units we use are just as important as the numbers that we get. If my friend had told me that his windows were 50 centimeters by 60 centimeters, there would have been no problem. I would have known exactly how big to make the curtains. Since he failed to do this, the numbers that he gave me (50 by 60) were essentially useless. In the end, then, scientists never simply report numbers; they always include units with those numbers, so that everyone knows exactly what those numbers mean. That will be the rule in this course. If you answer a question or a problem and do not list units with the numbers, your answer will be considered incorrect. In science, numbers mean nothing unless there are units attached to them.

Since scientists use units in all of their measurements, it is convenient to define a standard set of units that will be used by everyone. This system of standard units is called the **metric system**.

## The Metric System

There are many different things that we need to measure when studying Creation. First, we must determine how much matter exists in the object that we want to study. We know that there is a lot more matter in a car than there is in a feather, since a car weighs significantly more than a feather. In order to study an object precisely, however, we need to know *exactly* how much matter is in the object. To accomplish this, we measure the object's **mass.** In the metric system, the unit for mass is the **gram**. If an object has a mass of 10 grams, we know that it has exactly 10 times the matter that is in an object whose mass is 1 gram. To give you an idea of the size of a gram, the average mass of a housefly is just about 1 gram. Based on this little fact, we can say that a gram is a rather small unit. Most of the things that we will measure will have masses of 10 to 10,000 grams. For example, when full, a twelve-ounce can of soda pop has a mass of about 375 grams.

Now that we know what the metric unit for mass is, we need to know a little bit more about the concept itself. Many people think that mass and weight are the same thing. This misconception arises because the more an object weighs, the more mass it has. Thus, people tend to think that mass and weight are equivalent. That's not true. Mass and weight are two different things.  Mass measures how much matter exists in an object.  Weight, on the other hand, measures how hard a planet's gravity pulls on that object.

For example, if I were to get on my bathroom scale and weigh myself, I would find that I weigh 170 pounds.  However, if I were to take that scale to the top of Mount Everest and weigh myself, I would find that I only weighed 167 pounds there.  Does that mean I'm thinner on the top of Mount Everest than I am at home?  Of course not.  It means that on the top of Mount Everest, earth's gravity is not as strong as it is in my house.  If I were to weigh myself on the moon, I would find that I only weigh 28 pounds.  That's because the gravity on the moon is very weak.

On the other hand, if I were to measure my mass at home, I would find it to be 76,600 grams.  If I were to measure my mass at the top of  Mount Everest, it would still be 76,600 grams.  Even on the moon, my mass would be 76,600 grams.  That's the difference between mass and weight.  Since weight is a measure of how hard gravity pulls, an object weighs different amounts depending on where that object is.  Mass, on the other hand, is a measure of how much matter is in an object and does not depend on where that object is.

Unfortunately, there are many other unit systems in use today besides the metric system.  In fact, the metric system is probably not the system with which you are most familiar.  You are probably most familiar with the English system.  The unit of pounds comes from the English system.  Now, as I stated before, pounds are not a measure of mass; they are a measure of weight.  The metric unit for weight is called the **Newton**.  The English unit for mass is (believe it or not) called the **slug**.  Although we will not use the slug often, it is important to understand what it means.

There is more to measurement than just grams, however.  We might also want to measure how big an object is.  For this, we must use the metric system's unit for distance, which is the **meter**.  If you stretch out your left arm as far as it will go, the distance from your right shoulder to the tip of the fingers on your left hand is about 1 meter.  The English unit for distance is the **foot**.  What about inches, yards, and miles?  We'll talk about those a little later.

We also need to be able to measure how much space an object occupies.  This measurement is commonly called "volume" and is measured in the metric system with the unit of **liter**.  The main unit for measuring volume in the English system is the gallon.  To give you an idea of the size of a liter, it takes just under four liters to make a gallon.

Finally, we have to be able to measure the passage of time.  When studying Creation, we will see that its contents have the ability to change.  The shape, size, and chemical properties of certain substances change over time, so it is important to be able to measure time so that we can determine how quickly the changes take place.  In both the English and metric systems, time is measured in **seconds.**  Once again, we'll talk about minutes, hours, and days a little later.

Since it is very important for you to be able to recognize what units correspond to which measurements, Table 1.1 summarizes what you have just read. The letters in parentheses are the commonly used abbreviations for the units listed.

## TABLE 1.1
### Physical Quantities and Their Base Units

| Physical Quantity | Base Metric Unit | Base English Unit |
|---|---|---|
| Mass | gram (g) | slug (sl) |
| Distance | meter (m) | foot (ft) |
| Volume | liter (L) | gallon (gal) |
| Time | second (s) | second (s) |

## Manipulating Units

Now, let's suppose I asked you to measure the width of your home's kitchen using the English system. What unit would you use? Most likely, you would express your measurement in feet. However, suppose instead I asked you to measure the length of a pencil. Would you still use the foot as your measurement unit? Probably not. Since you know the English system already, you would probably recognize that inches are also a unit for distance and, since a pencil is relatively small, you would use inches instead of feet. In the same way, if you were asked to measure the distance between two cities, you would probably express your measurement in terms of miles, not feet. This is why I used the term "Base English Unit" in the table above. Even though the English system's normal unit for distance is the foot, there are alternative units for length if you are trying to measure very short or very long distances. The same holds true for all English units. Time, for example, can be measured in seconds, minutes, hours, days, or years.

This concept exists in the metric system as well. There are alternative units for measuring small things as well as alternative units for measuring big things. These alternative units are called "prefix units," and, as you will soon see, prefix units are much easier to use and understand than the English units which you grew up with! The reason that prefix units are easy to use and understand is that they always have the same relationship to the base unit, regardless of what physical quantity you are interested in measuring. You will see how this works in a minute.

In order to use a prefix unit in the metric system, you simply add a prefix to the base unit. For example, in the metric system, the prefix "centi" means one hundredth, or 0.01. So, if I wanted to measure the length of a pencil in the metric system, I would probably express my measurement with the centimeter unit. Since a centimeter is one hundredth of a meter, it can be used to measure relatively small things. On the other hand, the prefix "kilo" means 1,000. So, if I want to measure the distance between two cities, I would probably use the kilometer. Since each kilometer is 1,000 times longer than the meter, it can be used to measure long things.

Now, the beauty of the metric system is that these prefixes mean the same thing *regardless of the physical quantity that you want to measure!* So, if I were measuring something with a very large mass (such as a car), I would probably use the kilogram unit. One kilogram is the same as 1,000 grams. In the same way, if I were measuring something that had a large volume, I might use the kiloliter, which would be 1,000 liters.

Compare this incredibly logical system of units to the chaotic English system. If you want to measure something short, you use the inch unit, which is equal to one twelfth of a foot. On the other hand, if you want to measure something with small volume, you might use the quart unit, which is equal to one fourth of a gallon. In the English system, every alternative unit has a different relationship to the base unit, and you must remember all of those crazy numbers. You have to remember that there are 12 inches in a foot, 3 feet in a yard, and 5280 feet in a mile while at the same time remembering that for volume there are 8 ounces in a cup, 2 cups in a pint, 2 pints in a quart, and 4 quarts in a gallon.

In the metric system, all you have to remember is what the prefix means. Since the "centi" prefix means one hundredth, then you know that 1 centimeter is one hundredth of a meter, 1 centiliter is one hundredth of a liter, and 1 centigram is one hundredth a gram. Since the "kilo" prefix means 1,000, you know that there are 1,000 meters in a kilometer, 1,000 grams in a kilogram, and 1,000 liters in a kiloliter. Doesn't that make a lot more sense?

Another advantage to the metric system is that there are many, many more prefix units than there are alternative units in the English system. Table 1.2 summarizes the most commonly used prefixes and their numerical meanings. The prefixes in boldface type are the ones that we will use over and over again. You will be expected to have those three prefixes and their meanings memorized. Once again, the commonly used abbreviations for these prefixes are listed in parentheses.

### TABLE 1.2
### Common Prefixes Used in the Metric System

| PREFIX | NUMERICAL MEANING |
|---|---|
| micro (μ) | 0.000001 |
| **milli (m)** | **0.001** |
| **centi (c)** | **0.01** |
| deci (d) | 0.1 |
| deca (D) | 10 |
| hecta (H) | 100 |
| **kilo (k)** | **1,000** |
| Mega (M) | 1,000,000 |

Remember that each of these prefixes, when added to a base unit, makes an alternative unit for measurement. So, if you wanted to measure the length of something small, the only unit you could use in the English system would be the inch. However, if you used the metric system, you would have all sorts of options for which unit to use. If you wanted to measure the length of someone's foot, you could use the decimeter. Since the decimeter is one tenth of a meter, it measures things that are only slightly smaller than a meter. On the other hand, if you wanted to measure the length of a sewing needle, you could use the centimeter, because a sewing needle is significantly smaller than a meter. If you wanted to measure the length of an insect's antenna, you might use the millimeter, since it is one thousandth of a meter, which is a *really* small unit.

So you see that the metric system is more logical and versatile than the English system. That is, in part, why scientists use it as their main system of units. The other reason that scientists use the metric system is that most countries in the world use it. With the exception of the United States and Great Britain, almost every other country in the world uses the metric system as its standard system of units. Since scientists in the United States frequently work with scientists from other countries around the world, it is necessary that American scientists use and understand the metric system.

## Converting Between Units

Now that you understand what prefix units are and how they are used in the metric system, you must become familiar with converting between units within the metric system. In other words, if you measure the length of an object in centimeters, you should also be able to convert your answer to any other distance unit. For example, if I measure the length of a pencil in centimeters, I should be able to convert that length to millimeters, decimeters, meters, etc. Accomplishing this task is relatively simple as long as you remember a trick you can use when multiplying fractions. Suppose I asked you to complete the following problem:

$$\frac{7}{64} \times \frac{64}{13} =$$

There are two ways to figure out the answer. The first way would be to multiply the numerators and the denominators together and, once you had accomplished that, simplify the fraction. If you did it that way, it would look something like this:

$$\frac{7}{64} \times \frac{64}{13} = \frac{448}{832} = \frac{7}{13}$$

You could get the answer much more quickly, however, if you remember that when multiplying fractions, common factors in the numerator and the denominator cancel each other out. Thus, the 64 in the numerator cancels with the 64 in the denominator, and the only factors left are the 7 in the numerator and the 13 in the denominator. In this way, you reach the final answer in one less step:

$$\frac{7}{64} \times \frac{64}{13} = \frac{7}{13}$$

We will use the same idea in converting between units. Suppose I measure the length of a pencil to be 15.1 centimeters, but suppose the person who wants to know the length of the pencil would like me to tell him the answer in meters. How would I convert between centimeters and meters?  First, I would need to know the relationship between centimeters and meters. According to Table 1.2, "centi" means 0.01.  So, 1 centimeter is the same thing as 0.01 meters. In mathematical form, we would say:

$$1 \text{ centimeter} = 0.01 \text{ meter}$$

Now that we know how centimeters and meters relate to one another, we can convert from one to another.  First, we write down the measurement that we know:

$$15.1 \text{ centimeters}$$

We then realize that any number can be expressed as a fraction by putting it over the number one. So we can re-write our measurement as:

$$\frac{15.1 \text{ centimeters}}{1}$$

Now we can take that measurement and convert it into meters by multiplying it with the relationship we determined above.  We have to do it the right way, however, so that the units work out properly.  Here's how we do it:

$$\frac{15.1 \;\cancel{\text{centimeters}}}{1} \times \frac{0.01 \text{ meters}}{1 \;\cancel{\text{centimeter}}} = 0.151 \text{ meters}$$

This tells us that 15.1 centimeters is the same as 0.151 meters.  There are two reasons this conversion method, called the **factor-label method**, works.  First, since 0.01 meters is the same as 1 centimeter, multiplying our measurement by 0.01 meters over 1 centimeter is the same as multiplying by one.  Since nothing changes when we multiply by one, we haven't altered the value of our measurement at all.  Second, by putting the 1 centimeter in the denominator of the second fraction, we allow the centimeters unit to cancel (just like the 64 canceled in the previous example).  Once the centimeters unit has canceled, the only thing left is meters, so we know that our measurement is now in meters.

This is how we will do all of our unit conversions.  We will first write the measurement we know in fraction form by putting it over one.  We will then find the relationship between the unit we have and the unit to which we want to convert.  Next, we will use that relationship to make a fraction that, when multiplied by our first fraction, cancels out the unit we have and replaces it with the unit we want to have.  You will see many examples of this method, so don't worry if you are a little confused right now.

It may seem odd to you that words can be treated exactly the same as numbers. Measuring units, however, have just that property.  Whenever a measurement is used in any mathematical equation, the units for that measurement must be included in the equation.  Those units are then treated the same way numbers are treated.

We will be using the factor-label method for many other types of problems as well, so it is very, very important for you to become an expert at using it. Also, since we will be using it so often, we should start abbreviating things so that they will be easier to write down. We will use the abbreviations for the base units that have been listed in Table 1.1 along with the prefix abbreviations listed in Table 1.2. Thus, kilograms will be abbreviated "kg" while milliliters will be abbreviated "mL."

Since the factor-label method is so important in our studies of physical science, let's see how it works in another example:

---

**EXAMPLE 1.1**

**A student measures the mass of a rock to be 14,351 grams. What is the rock's mass in kilograms?**

First, we use the definition of "kilo" to determine the relationship between grams and kilograms:

$$1 \text{ kg} = 1,000 \text{ g}$$

Then we put our measurement in fraction form:

$$\frac{14,351 \text{ g}}{1}$$

Then we multiply our measurement by a fraction that contains the relationship noted above, making sure to put the 1,000 g in the denominator so that the unit of grams will cancel out:

$$\frac{14,351 \text{ g}}{1} \times \frac{1 \text{ kg}}{1,000 \text{ g}} = 14.351 \text{ kg}$$

Thus, 14,351 grams is the same as <u>14.351 kilograms</u>.

---

**ON YOUR OWN**

1.3 A student measures the mass of a book as 12,321 g. What is the book's mass in kg?

1.4 If a glass contains 0.121 L of milk, what is the volume of milk in mL?

1.5 On a professional basketball court, the distance from the three point line to the basket is 640.08 cm. What is this distance in meters?

---

As you may have guessed, the factor-label method can also be used to convert *between systems* of units as well as within systems of units. Thus, if a measurement is done in the English system, the factor-label method can be used to convert that measurement to the metric system, or vice-versa. In order to be able to do this, however, you must learn the relationships between metric and English units. Although these relationships, summarized in Table 1.3, are important, we will not use them very often, so you needn't memorize them. If you need them on a test, they will be given to you.

### TABLE 1.3
### Relationships Between English and Metric Units.

| Measurement | English/Metric Relationship |
|---|---|
| Distance | 1 inch = 2.54 cm |
| Mass | 1 slug = 14.59 kg |
| Volume | 1 gallon = 3.78 L |

We can use this information in the factor-label method the same way we used the information in Table 1.2.

---

### EXAMPLE 1.2

**The length of a tabletop is measured to be 37.8 inches. How many cm is that?**

To solve this problem, we first put the measurement in its fraction form:

$$\frac{37.8 \text{ in}}{1}$$

We then multiply this fraction by the conversion relationship so that the inches unit cancels :

$$\frac{37.8 \text{ in}}{1} \times \frac{2.54 \text{ cm}}{1 \text{ in}} = 96.012 \text{ cm}$$

So, a measurement of 37.8 inches is equivalent to 96.012 cm.

---

Give yourself a little more practice with the factor-label method by answering the following "on your own" problems:

---

### ON YOUR OWN

1.6  A piece of yarn is 3 inches long. How many centimeters long is it?

1.7  How many slugs are there in 12 kg?

1.8  If an object occupies 3.2 gallons of space, how many liters of space does it occupy?

---

The important thing to remember about the conversion system you just learned is that it can be used on *any* system of measurement, whether you are familiar with it or not. To see what I mean, perform the following experiment.

---

**EXPERIMENT 1.2**
Cubits and Fingers

Supplies
- A long piece of string
- Scissors
- A large table top (like a kitchen table or a big desk)
- A person to help you
- Some cellophane tape
- A pencil

Introduction: In the Old Testament, a measurement unit for length called the **cubit** was used. You can find reference to it in Genesis 6:15, for example, where God is telling Noah the dimensions of the ark. Back then, a cubit was defined as the length from a man's elbow to the tip of his outstretched middle finger. There was also a smaller unit of length measurement called the finger. It was defined as the distance from the last knuckle on a man's index finger to the tip of his index finger. You should immediately see a drawback of that measuring system. After all, arm length and finger length changes from man to man. As a result, the cubit that one man used was different than the cubit another man used. The same can be said for the finger. Nowadays, we use precise definitions for our measuring units so that they are the same all over the world. No matter where you go, a meter is a meter. That's not the way it used to be! In this experiment, you will make your own measuring devices for the cubit and the finger, and then you will get some practice converting between these measurement units.

Procedure:

A. Hold your arm so that the elbow is bent but the rest of the arm stretches out horizontally. Open your palm so that your fingers stretch out in the same direction. Have the person helping you hold the end of the string at your elbow.

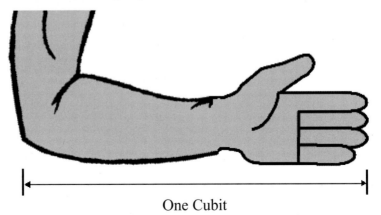

One Cubit

B.  Have your helper stretch the string tightly from your elbow to the tip of your middle finger, and then have him or her cut it so that you have a length of string which runs from your elbow to the tip of your middle finger.  This is your cubit.

C.  Next, point your index finger straight out and have your helper stretch another piece of string so that it stretches from your last knuckle (the one nearest your fingernail) to the tip of your index finger.  Have your helper cut the string so that it runs the length from your last knuckle to the tip of your index finger (not your finger nail).  The string should be less than an inch long.  This is your measurement for the "finger" unit.

D.  Take the string that represents your cubit and tape it down to the table top so that it is stretched out to its full length.

E.  Now, take the string that represents your finger and measure how many of those strings are in your cubit string.  You can do this by simply starting at the beginning of your cubit string and stretching your finger string down next to it.  Use your pencil to mark where the end of the finger string is on the cubit string.  Now pick up the finger string and repeat the process, this time starting at the mark you made.  Count the number of times that you did this, and that will tell you how many fingers are in a cubit.  Most likely, this will not be a whole number.  Try to estimate the fraction of the finger string it took to reach the end of the cubit string on your last measurement.  In other words, if it took 18 finger strings to reach the end of your cubit string, but the cubit string only covered 1/3 of the 18$^{th}$ finger string, then it really took 17.33 fingers to make a cubit.

F.  Record the number of finger strings (including the decimal) it took to reach the end of your cubit string.  Now you know the number of fingers in one cubit.

G.  Unfasten your cubit string from the table top and measure the length of the table top in cubits.  Do this the same way you measured the cubit before, laying the string end-to-end until you reach the end of the table top.  Once again, if the end of the table top only covers a portion of the last cubit string in your measurement, try to estimate the fraction of a cubit that it covered.  Record the length of the table top (including the decimal) in cubits.

H.  Now repeat that measurement, this time using your finger string instead.

I.  Do the same thing with the width of the table top, measuring it in both cubits and fingers.

J.  Now, take your measurement for the length of the table top in cubits and convert it into fingers using the number of fingers in a cubit you determined in step F.  Compare your converted length in fingers to the number of fingers that you actually measured.  If you did the conversion correctly, the answers should be similar.  They won't be exactly the same because of inaccuracies in your measurements.  Nevertheless, they should be close.  If they aren't anywhere close to each other, then you probably did the conversion wrong.  Check the example solution for this experiment that appears after the answers to the "on your own" problems.  This should tell you how to do the conversion.

K.  Do the same thing for your measurement of table width; take your measured width in cubits and convert it to fingers.  Then, compare your answer to the measured length in fingers to check the validity of your conversion.  Once again, the numbers should be close.

Do you see why the factor-label method is so powerful?  Even if you are not familiar with the unit system with which you are working, you can still convert between units as long as you have a conversion relationship.

Before we leave this section, there is one more metric unit I need to bring up.  When we measure temperature, we usually use the **Celsius** temperature scale.  Sometimes called the "centigrade" temperature scale, this temperature scale fits the metric system better than the Fahrenheit scale, with which you are probably more familiar.  When we measure temperature on this scale, we list the unit as "degrees Celsius."  This unit does not have prefixes or anything, degrees Celsius is the only way to use the unit.  The reason we tend to use this temperature scale instead of the Fahrenheit one is because this scale is based on factors of ten.  On this temperature scale, water freezes at 0.00 degrees Celsius and boils at 100.0 degrees Celsius.  This seems to fit right in to the metric system, which is also based on powers of ten.  So, when I talk about temperature in this course, I will always use the degrees Celsius scale.

## Concentration

In the past few sections, we discussed the units used to measure mass, length, and volume.  Although these are very important things to measure, there is one other quantity with which you must be very familiar: **concentration**.

Concentration - The quantity of a substance within a certain volume of space

To get an idea of what concentration means, perform the following experiment.

---

**EXPERIMENT 1.3**
Concentration

Supplies:

- Vinegar
- 6 TUMS ® tablets  (You can use another antacid tablet, but it must have calcium carbonate as its active ingredient.)
- Water
- Measuring cups
- 3 large glasses (They each must be able to hold at least 2 cups of liquid.)
- A spoon

Introduction - Vinegar is a weak acid, a kind of substance you will learn a lot more about when you take chemistry.  TUMS ® are antacid tablets, designed to neutralize acid.  Thus, when TUMS ® are added to vinegar, a chemical reaction occurs.  The TUMS ® tablet disappears as it neutralizes the vinegar.  While this happens, gas (carbon dioxide) bubbles off of the tablet.

That's our conversion relationship.  Since we want to end up with mL, we must multiply the measurement by a fraction that has liters on the bottom (to cancel the liter unit that is there) and mL on the top (so that mL is the unit we are left with):

$$\frac{0.121 \text{ L}}{1} \times \frac{1 \text{ mL}}{0.001 \text{ L}} = 121 \text{ mL}$$

Thus, 0.121 L is the same as 121 mL.

1.5  First, we convert the number to a fractional form:

$$\frac{640.08 \text{ cm}}{1}$$

Next, since we want to convert from centimeters to meters, we need to remember that "centi" means "0.01."  So, one centimeter is the same thing as 0.01 meters.  Thus:

$$1 \text{ cm} = 0.01 \text{ m}$$

That's our conversion relationship.  Since we want to end up with meters in the end, then we must multiply the measurement by a fraction that has centimeters on the bottom (to cancel the cm unit that is there) and meters on the top (so that m is the unit we are left with):

$$\frac{640.08 \text{ cm}}{1} \times \frac{0.01 \text{ m}}{1 \text{ cm}} = 6.4008 \text{ m}$$

The three-point line is 6.4008 m from the basket.

1.6  We use the same procedure that we used in the previous three problems.  Thus, I am going to reduce the length of the explanation.

$$\frac{3 \text{ in}}{1} \times \frac{2.54 \text{ cm}}{1 \text{ in}} = 7.62 \text{ cm}$$

The yarn is 7.62 cm long.

1.7
$$\frac{12 \text{ kg}}{1} \times \frac{1 \text{ slug}}{14.59 \text{ kg}} = 0.822 \text{ slugs}$$

There are 0.822 slugs in 12 kg.  Note that I rounded the answer.  The real answer was "0.822481151," but there are simply too many digits in that number.  When you take chemistry, you will learn about significant figures, a concept that tells you where to round numbers off.  For right now, don't worry about it.  If you rounded at a different spot than I did, that's fine.

1.8
$$\frac{3.2 \ \cancel{gal}}{1} \times \frac{3.78 \ L}{1 \ \cancel{gal}} = 12.096 \ L$$

The object has a volume of 12.096 L.

1.9  Muratic acid is the more powerful cleaner because the active ingredient is more concentrated.  In the same amount of volume, muratic acid has more than 10 times as much active ingredient.  Since the active ingredient is more concentrated, it will clean better.

10.10  Sodium is necessary for the body at a certain concentration.  If you eat too much sodium, then you raise the concentration too much.  In the same way, if you eat too little sodium, you lower its concentration too much.  Either way, your body suffers.  Thus, you need to keep the sodium concentration in your body at the right level.  Too little sodium intake will reduce the sodium concentration to critical levels, while too much sodium intake will raise it to toxic levels.

## SAMPLE RESULTS FOR THE EXPERIMENT

Number of fingers in a cubit:  18.33

Measured length of the table:    2.5 cubits
                                 45.25 fingers

Measured width of the table:     1.67 cubits
                                 31 fingers

Conversions:
    Length of table:

$$\frac{2.5 \ \cancel{cubits}}{1} \times \frac{18.33 \ fingers}{1 \ \cancel{cubit}} = 45.825 \ fingers \quad \text{(a little longer than but close to the}$$

measured value of 45.25  fingers)

    Width of the table:

$$\frac{1.67 \ \cancel{cubits}}{1} \times \frac{18.33 \ fingers}{1 \ \cancel{cubit}} = 30.611 \ fingers \quad \text{(a little shorter than but close to the}$$

measured value of 31  fingers)

Notice that even though the converted lengths in fingers are not equal to the measured values, they are close.  Your answers could be farther off, but they should be within 2.5 fingers.

**STUDY GUIDE FOR MODULE #1**

1. Write out the definitions for the following terms:

a. Atom
b. Molecule
c. Concentration

2. Fifty grams of a carbon disulfide can be broken down into 42.1 grams of sulfur and 7.9 grams of carbon. Is carbon disulfide made up of atoms or molecules?

3. If you put iron near a magnet, the iron will be attracted to the magnet. Rust is made up of molecules which contain iron atoms, oxygen atoms, and hydrogen atoms. Rust is not attracted to a magnet. If rust contains iron atoms, and iron is attracted to a magnet, why isn't rust attracted to a magnet?

4. A statue is made out of copper and displayed outside. After many years, what color will the statue be?

5. Have scientists actually seen atoms?

6. Give the numerical meaning for the prefixes centi, milli, and kilo.

7. If you wanted to measure an object's mass, what metric unit would you use? What English unit would you use?

8. If you wanted to measure an object's volume, what metric unit would you use? What English unit would you use?

9. If you wanted to measure an object's length, what metric unit would you use? What English unit would you use?

10. How many centimeters are in 1.3 meters?

11. If a person has a mass of 75 kg, what is his or her mass in grams?

12. How many liters of milk are in 0.5 gallons of milk? (1 gal = 3.78 L)

13. A meterstick is 100 centimeters long. How long is it in inches? (1 in = 2.54 cm)

14. Ozone is a poisonous gas that can build up in the air in dense cities. Thus, there are many environmental initiatives to lower the amount of ozone in the air. One way you can make ozone, however, is by baking bread. The nice smell that you associate with baking bread is actually due, in part, to ozone. If ozone is poisonous, why is baking bread not considered a dangerous activity?

# Module #2: Air

## Introduction

In this course, we will spend a great deal of time learning about the physical environment that surrounds you. Where better to start than air itself? After all, air completely surrounds you. Even though you cannot see it, you know that it's there. You feel it move when there is a breeze, and you breathe it in and out continuously. Since it is such an important part of our everyday experience, it deserves a close look.

Now you have probably learned a few things about air already. Nevertheless, I am sure that you have not studied air in the detail that I will present it. Do not "turn off," therefore, just because a few of the subjects discussed below sound familiar. There is a LOT to the subject of air, and even though we will study this fascinating mixture of gases in some detail, we will still only scratch the surface of all the things that can be learned about the air which surrounds you.

## The Air and Humidity

In order to begin our study of air, I want to look at its composition. Before I can do that, however, I need to tell you about a very important concept in the study of air: **humidity**.

### Humidity - The moisture content of air

No matter where you are on the planet, the air that you breathe contains some moisture in the form of water vapor. This moisture affects you quite a bit. You see, your body has an ingenious means of cooling off when it is hot. God has designed you to sweat when you are too warm. When you sweat, water is released onto your skin. This water, once exposed to the air, tends to evaporate. Well, the process of evaporation requires energy, which is supplied by the heat on your skin. As a result, when your sweat evaporates, it takes energy (in the form of heat) away from your skin. Since the evaporation of sweat takes heat away from your skin, the net effect is that *your skin cools down!*

Isn't that marvelous? Your body has been designed with its own cooling system! When you get hot, your body releases sweat which evaporates from your skin. In the evaporation process, heat is removed from your skin, cooling it down. You know what's even more amazing? This cooling system in your body is *self-regulating*! You don't sweat when you are cool or comfortable. You only sweat when you need cooling off. Think about that for a moment. It took human science nearly 3,000 years to come up with a thermostat-regulated cooling system. Nevertheless, the human body has had one since it was made! This is just one of the many incredible design features that we see in nature. It is a stirring testimony to the fact that we are "...fearfully and wonderfully made." (Ps 139:14) To see this effect, perform the following experiment.

## EXPERIMENT 2.1
### Evaporation and Temperature

Supplies:

- A small glass, like a juice glass
- Two cotton balls
- Tap water
- A bulb thermometer (It must be able to read room temperature and slightly higher, and it must have a bulb at the end.)
- A small piece of plastic such as a ZIPLOC® bag or a square cut from a trash bag.

Introduction - Everyone knows that water left in the presence of air evaporates. Well, it turns out that the process of evaporation actually takes energy. Thus, when water evaporates, it cools the surface which it is touching. You will see this effect.

Procedure:

A. Fill your small glass 1/4 full of lukewarm tap water. You should just open the tap and fill the glass right away. This will make the water as close to room temperature as possible.
B. Let it sit out for at least 10 minutes. This will ensure that the water is at room temperature.
C. While you are waiting, spread out the piece of plastic on the counter and lay the thermometer on the plastic. Make sure that the thermometer bulb is touching the plastic.
D. Allow the thermometer to sit for a while and then read the temperature. Note that in your laboratory notebook.
E. Once the glass has set for 10 minutes, soak the two cotton balls in the water.
F. Pull the cotton balls out and use them to surround the bulb of the thermometer.
G. Wait 2 minutes and then read the temperature. Compare it to the previous temperature.

What happened in the experiment? Well, when the thermometer was sitting on the plastic, it was reading the temperature of the room. When you surrounded it with the wet cotton balls, it was still being exposed to room temperature, because the water was at room temperature. The thermometer read a lower temperature, however, because water was *evaporating* from the cotton balls. Since water was evaporating from the cotton balls, it was cooling them. Since the thermometer bulb was in contact with the cotton balls, it was cooled as well. Thus, the water was acting like your sweat and the cotton balls were acting like your skin. When the water (representing your sweat) evaporated, the cotton balls (representing your skin) was cooled.

What does all of this have to do with humidity? Well, if there is a lot of moisture in the air already, your sweat does not evaporate as quickly as when there is little moisture in the air. Since the cooling effect of sweat is completely dependent on the sweat evaporating, the process of sweating does not cool you very quickly when the humidity (moisture content of the air) is high. When the humidity is low, however, your sweat evaporates quickly, cooling you off more quickly. Thus, for a given temperature, a high humidity will make you feel warmer. For this reason, many weather reports include a **heat index**, which is a combination of temperature and humidity. It tells you how hot you will feel as a result of humidity's effect on the sweating process.

This effect is further compounded by the fact that since your sweat does not evaporate quickly on a humid day, you tend to notice it more. On a warm day in which the humidity is low, you do not notice your sweat, because it evaporates away soon after it is released onto the skin. When it is humid, however, your sweat does not evaporate readily. It ends up pooling together in little droplets that run across your skin. This makes you even more aware of how hot it is, compounding the misery. This is why people often say, "It's not the heat; it's the humidity."

Before we leave this section on humidity, I need to introduce something that we will discuss again later. When you listen to the weather report, you hear the humidity of the air reported in terms of percent. You need to know what that means. You see, there are two ways of measuring humidity: **absolute humidity** and **relative humidity**. Absolute humidity is easy to understand.

<u>Absolute humidity</u> - The mass of water vapor contained in a certain volume of air

Absolute humidity, therefore, is a measure of the concentration of water vapor in the air.

Relative humidity is a little harder to understand. You see, you cannot put an infinite amount of water vapor in the air. Eventually, the air simply can't hold any more water vapor. As a result, there is a maximum absolute humidity that air can have. When air has that amount of water vapor in it, we say that the air is **saturated** with moisture. Now it turns out that the maximum absolute humidity changes depending on the temperature of the air. When air is warm, it can hold more moisture than when it is cold. Thus, in order to make the reporting of humidity a little easier to understand, weather reports list the humidity as a percentage of the maximum absolute humidity for whatever temperature it happens to be.

<u>Relative humidity</u> - A quantity expressing humidity as a percentage of the maximum absolute humidity for that particular temperature

For example, suppose on a given day, the air holds half as much moisture as it possibly could for that particular temperature. In that case, the relative humidity would be 50%. On the other hand, if the air contained three-quarters of the maximum absolute humidity for that temperature, the relative humidity would be 75%. If you don't completely understand this concept now, don't worry. We will come back to it!

---

**ON YOUR OWN**

2.1 Suppose you were to leave a glass of water outside on two different days. On the first day, it is warm and humid. On the second day, it is the same temperature, but the humidity is low. Each day, you measure how long it takes the water to completely evaporate from the glass. On which day will the time it takes the water to evaporate be the smallest?

2.2  Suppose you did the same experiment that was described in Problem 2.1 when the relative humidity was 100%.  How quickly would the water evaporate from the glass?

## The Composition of Air

Now that we have the concept of humidity out of the way, we can discuss the composition of air.  Why did we need to discuss humidity first?  Well, the first thing we need to do to really analyze the composition of air is to remove the water vapor in it.  Since the humidity of the air changes from place to place as well as from time to time, there is no way to pin down how much water vapor is in the "average" sample of air.  Thus, in order to discuss the composition of air, we will remove all water vapor from it.  So the discussion in this section will focus on dry air, which has a humidity of zero.

The composition of dry air is shown in Figure 2.1

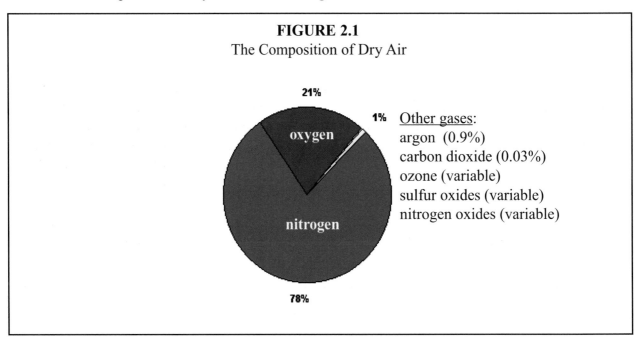

**FIGURE 2.1**
The Composition of Dry Air

21%

1%  <u>Other gases</u>:
argon  (0.9%)
carbon dioxide (0.03%)
ozone (variable)
sulfur oxides (variable)
nitrogen oxides (variable)

oxygen

nitrogen

78%

As shown in Figure 2.1, air is actually a mixture of gases.  The major constituents of this mixture are nitrogen (which makes up 78% of the air we breathe), oxygen (which constitutes 21% of the air), argon (0.9%), and carbon dioxide (0.03%).  Hundreds of other gases make up the remaining 0.07%.  The other gases listed in Figure 2.1 are the ones that we will concentrate on in this module.  Carbon dioxide is a gas that most living creatures exhale.  Ozone is a gas whose concentration in air varies with altitude.  Both of these gases exist in small quantities but are absolutely critical for life to exist on this planet.  We will see why in a moment.  The other gases listed in Figure 2.1 are considered pollutants.  We will discuss them in a moment, also.  For a myriad of reasons, this mixture of gases is perfectly suited for the task of supporting life.  If any of the constituent gases made up significantly more or less of the air than it currently does, earth would suddenly become a planet hostile to all living organisms!

Before we go into that, however, I need to point out something regarding concentration. In the previous module, I spent some time discussing concentration. I then used the concept again to explain humidity. One thing that I have not discussed, however, are the *units* that we use to express concentration. There is a very good reason for this. It turns out that we use many different kinds of units to express concentration. In this figure, for example, we are using the unit of percent. If you think about it, percent is clearly a unit of concentration. Since nitrogen makes up 78% of the air that we breathe and oxygen makes up only 21%, we can say that the concentration of nitrogen is more than three times the concentration of oxygen. Thus, the first unit that we will use to express concentration will be percent. Later on in this module, we will use another unit for concentration. For right now, however, just realize that when I use a percent, I am really talking about concentration.

Now, let's get back to studying the air that we are breathing. In order to live, humans and most other forms of life must take in oxygen. This is because the chemical reactions which supply energy for our bodies are combustion reactions. Combustion is really just another word for burning. Oxygen is necessary for combustion; thus, most living organisms require a steady supply of it. We are, indeed, fortunate that 21% of the air we breathe is made up of oxygen. If there were significantly less oxygen in the air, we could not supply our bodies with the energy necessary to support their various functions, and we would suffocate.

You may not realize, however, that we are also very fortunate that there isn't significantly *more* oxygen in the air, either. If there were significantly more oxygen in the air, then all of the combustion reactions which supply our bodies with energy would speed up. This would result in elevated heart rates, high blood pressure, and hyperactivity, all of which would reduce our lifespan. In addition, elevated oxygen content in the air would result in *significantly* greater risk of natural disaster by fire. For example, the probability that lightning will start a forest fire increases by 70% for every 1% rise in the oxygen concentration of the air. Thus, if oxygen made up 31% of the atmosphere instead of 21%, there would be *seven times more natural forest fires* than there are today! To see the profound effect that oxygen has on combustion, perform the following experiment.

## EXPERIMENT 2.2
Oxygen and Fire

Supplies:

- A reasonably large glass or jar
- A candle (DO NOT use a lighter or any other gas or alcohol burner. You must use a candle in order to keep the experiment safe.)
- Matches
- Hydrogen peroxide (sold at any drug store)
- Baker's yeast
- A bottle (A plastic, 1-liter soda bottle, for example)
- A balloon
- A teaspoon

Introduction - Everyone knows that fire needs oxygen to burn. If you run out of oxygen, there is no fire. What happens, however, when there is more oxygen than usual?

Procedure:

A. Fill your bottle with about 2 cups of hydrogen peroxide. The exact amount is unimportant. Just make it around 2 cups.
B. Quickly add about a teaspoon of yeast to the hydrogen peroxide. Don't worry if you spill some getting it into the bottle. Speed is more important than neatness in this case.
C. Quickly open the balloon and cover the opening of the bottle with it. Be sure it is an airtight seal. The best way to ensure this is to pull as much of the neck of the balloon as possible down the lip of the bottle. If the seal is not airtight, try again.
D. Once you have an airtight seal, gently shake the bottle back and forth. As the yeast and the hydrogen peroxide mix, bubbles should begin to form. Those bubbles are oxygen gas being formed in a chemical reaction.
E. The oxygen gas should continue to form, inflating your balloon. Let this go on for a while.
F. While your balloon inflates, light the candle and then cover it by turning the jar upside down and placing it over the candle. **Be careful at this point. If the glass in the jar is weak, it could crack! Do not get your face close to the jar!** Note what happens in your laboratory notebook.
G. Uncover the candle and light it again, leaving it uncovered.
H. Next, go back to your balloon. It should be partially inflated now. It need not be anywhere near fully inflated. It just needs to have some oxygen in it.
I. Take the balloon off of the bottle, being careful to not let too much oxygen escape.
J. Pinch (do not tie) the neck of the balloon so as to keep the oxygen from escaping.
K. Take your jar and cover the candle again, but this time, tilt the jar so that you can slip the neck of the balloon underneath the jar.
L. Once you have slipped the neck of the balloon under the jar, *slowly* let the oxygen out of the balloon and let it flow into the jar. **Once again, be careful! Do not let your face get too close to the jar, because it might crack from the heat! Also, DO NOT let the oxygen out quickly. Let it SLOWLY fill the jar. If you do it too quickly, the experiment could become dangerous!** Note what happens in your laboratory notebook.

What happened in the experiment? Well, the first part is easy to understand. In fact, you've probably done that part of the experiment before. When you covered the burning candle with the jar, the flame got dimmer and dimmer until it went out. This is because it used up the oxygen in the air surrounding it and, because there was no source of oxygen to replenish that which was used up, the candle burnt out. What about the second part of the experiment, however? When you added oxygen from the balloon, the candle actually burned a lot brighter, didn't it? That's because the *speed* at which fire burns depends directly on the *concentration* of oxygen in the air surrounding it. In the second part of the experiment, you increased the concentration of oxygen in the air. That increased the speed at which the fire burned.

Now, suppose we let the fire in the candle represent the combustion reactions that run our bodies. In fact, the underlying chemistry is really the same, so the representation is reasonable. If the flame represents the combustion reactions in our bodies, then you see what elevated concentrations of oxygen can do to us! It would make the chemical reactions in our bodies run too fast, wreaking all sorts of havoc! Let's now suppose that the candle flame doesn't represent our bodies but instead represents a tiny fire started by a lightning bolt. Most fires like that die out before they have a chance to spread into real forest fires. With elevated oxygen concentrations, however, the tiny fires would burn much faster, greatly enhancing the chance of spreading into real forest fires! Increased oxygen concentration also increases the ferocity of forest fires.

So we see that although the air we breathe must contain oxygen, it cannot contain very much oxygen. The oxygen has to be "diluted" to exactly the right concentration for healthy lives and safe surroundings. It turns out that the gases used to dilute the oxygen in the air are very important as well. Nitrogen and argon, for example, make up the vast majority of the rest of the air we breathe. These gases are relatively inert. In other words, it is very difficult to get them to chemically react with anything else. Thus, when we breathe in nitrogen and argon, neither of them react with our bodies in any way. We simply breathe them in, and then we breathe them right back out again. It turns out that there are, literally, thousands of gases that *could* be used to dilute the air that we breathe. Except for nitrogen, argon, and carbon dioxide, however, *all of the others are toxic to life at any reasonable concentration*! Its a very nice "coincidence" that the principal gases used to dilute the oxygen in the atmosphere are two of the very few gases that do not react with our bodies in any way!

---

**ON YOUR OWN**

2.3 If a scientist were to measure the percentages of nitrogen and oxygen in a sample of air that was not dry, would they be greater than, less than, or essentially the same as the percentages shown in Figure 2.1?

2.4 At high altitudes, the concentration of oxygen in the air is actually lower than that of the air at low altitudes. Would a candle at high altitudes burn dimmer, brighter, or essentially the same as the same candle at low altitudes?

---

Carbon Dioxide in the Air

In addition to nitrogen, oxygen, and argon, there is a small amount of carbon dioxide in the air. This gas is necessary for life to exist on planet earth, but too much carbon dioxide is just as deadly as too little. Carbon dioxide performs two major functions for the maintenance of life on this planet. First, in addition to oxygen, plants need a steady supply of carbon dioxide in order to survive. Through a process called photosynthesis (which you will learn about in biology), plants convert the carbon dioxide they absorb from the air and the water they absorb from the ground into glucose, a sugar. This sugar is used by the plant to provide the energy necessary to sustain its life functions.

Photosynthesis not only produces glucose. It also makes oxygen as a by-product, which is then released into the air. This replenishes the oxygen supply which is continually used by living organisms. Without carbon dioxide, plants would starve and the oxygen content of the atmosphere would slowly decrease to zero.

In addition to providing the means by which plants can synthesize their own food, carbon dioxide also performs another vital function: it helps to regulate the temperature of the earth. The earth's main source of energy is the sun. Every day, the sun bathes the earth with its light. The earth absorbs most of that light and uses it as a source of energy to grow plants, warm the surface of the planet, etc. Interestingly enough, the earth also radiates energy back into space in the form of infrared light. In fact, the earth radiates a significantly large amount of infrared light. If you aren't familiar with the term "infrared light," don't worry. You'll learn more about that in a later module.

Now, the light that the earth absorbs warms the planet. However, when the earth radiates infrared light, that process actually cools the earth. Thus, the earth gets warm when it absorbs light, but it cools down when it radiates light. We know that a significant amount of the light that the earth absorbs gets radiated out again as infrared light. If that were the end of the story, then the earth would be a very, very cold place, far too frigid to support life.

The reason that the earth is not an arctic wasteland is that carbon dioxide (and other gases such as water vapor, methane, and ozone) tend to absorb the infrared light that the earth radiates. This, in turn, heats up the atmosphere, regulating the earth's temperature to near perfect conditions for the maintenance of life. This process, known as the **greenhouse effect**, is illustrated in Figure 2.2.

Greenhouse effect - The process by which certain gases (principally water vapor, carbon dioxide, and methane) trap heat that would otherwise escape the earth and radiate into space

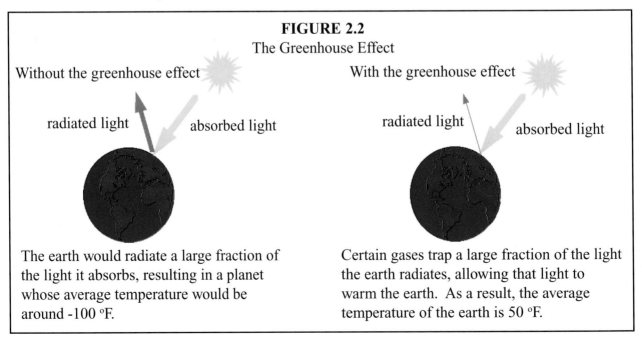

**FIGURE 2.2**
The Greenhouse Effect

Without the greenhouse effect

radiated light          absorbed light

The earth would radiate a large fraction of the light it absorbs, resulting in a planet whose average temperature would be around -100 °F.

With the greenhouse effect

radiated light          absorbed light

Certain gases trap a large fraction of the light the earth radiates, allowing that light to warm the earth. As a result, the average temperature of the earth is 50 °F.

To see how carbon dioxide participates in the greenhouse effect, perform the following experiment:

---

**EXPERIMENT 2.3**
Carbon Dioxide and the Greenhouse Effect

Supplies:

- Thermometer (It can be the same thermometer used in Experiment 2.1. It needs to read from slightly lower than room temperature and to slightly higher than room temperature.)
- Two clear ZIPLOC® sandwich bags
- Sunny windowsill (If it's not sunny today, just wait until it is.)
- Bottle (like the one used in Experiment 2.2)
- Vinegar
- Baking soda
- Teaspoon

Introduction - Carbon dioxide is what environmental scientists call a "greenhouse gas." This means that it traps energy in the form of light. In the greenhouse effect, greenhouse gases trap energy being radiated out from the earth. In this experiment, you will observe carbon dioxide trapping energy that is coming in from the sun.

Procedure:

A. Running the experiment with air

  1. Open your ZIPLOC® bag and fill it with air. Do this by holding the bag wide open with the open side facing down. Then, raise the bag as high as you can and quickly lower it. Zip it locked. You should now have a ZIPLOC® bag that is inflated with air.
  2. Place your thermometer on the sunny windowsill and lay the inflated bag on top of it. Arrange the bag so that it completely covers the thermometer, but so you can still look through the bag and read the thermometer. If the bag is too small to cover the thermometer completely, arrange it so that the bulb of the thermometer is completely covered.
  3. Allow the bag and thermometer to sit for 15 minutes and then read the temperature from the thermometer.

B. Running the experiment with carbon dioxide

  1. Take the thermometer and ZIPLOC® bag off of the windowsill. Open the ZIPLOC® bag and throw it away (or recycle it!). Place the thermometer in a cool area while you prepare the next part of the experiment.
  2. Take the bottle and fill it about one-third of the way full with vinegar.

3.  Measure out 1 teaspoon of baking soda and add it to the vinegar. The contents of the bottle will begin to bubble. Those bubbles tell you that a gas is being formed. The gas is carbon dioxide. Wait for a while. This will allow the carbon dioxide to push the air out of the bottle.

4.  Measure out another teaspoon of baking soda, but this time keep it in the spoon.

5.  Open the ZIPLOC® bag and press it flat to remove any air in it. Keep it handy.

6.  This has to be done quickly. Add the baking soda to the vinegar and then quickly hold the ZIPLOC® bag over the opening of the bottle. Don't worry about making sure all of the baking soda lands in the bottle. In this step, speed is very important. Immediately close the bag around the bottle opening so that the carbon dioxide coming from the bottle inflates the bag. Allow this to continue until the bag is as inflated as the previous bag that you used. If you can't fully inflate the bag the first time, carefully lift it off of the bottle and try again by adding more baking soda. If you are careful enough, you won't lose much carbon dioxide when you lift the bag. Once it is inflated, carefully remove the bag from the bottle and quickly zip it closed. You should now have a bag filled with carbon dioxide.

7.  Go to the windowsill and place the thermometer and your new bag in the same position that you did in part "A" of the experiment. Allow them to sit for 15 minutes again. After the 15 minutes, read the temperature.

C.  Analyzing the data

Look at the two temperatures. They should be different. The temperature that you got in part "A" should be higher than the one you got in part "B." Why? Well, carbon dioxide absorbs energy from sunlight. This is what causes the greenhouse effect. In your experiment, because carbon dioxide absorbed the energy from the sunlight, there was less energy available to the thermometer. As a result, the temperature that the thermometer read was lower.

Since carbon dioxide participates in the greenhouse effect, if the carbon dioxide concentration (and the concentrations of the other greenhouse gases) were significantly lower, then the earth would be colder. In addition, plants would not be able to manufacture enough food via photosynthesis. If the concentration of carbon dioxide (and the other greenhouse gases) in the air were much greater, then the greenhouse effect would warm the earth up too much, turning much of the world into desert wastelands. This is what some environmentalists have termed **global warming**. Now, despite the fact that you usually hear the terms "global warming" and "greenhouse effect" side-by-side, please realize that they are two completely different things. The greenhouse effect is a very good physical process. Without it, life could not exist! Global warming, however, is the result of too much greenhouse effect. In other words, while the greenhouse effect is a good thing, global warming is too much of a good thing!

We are going to study global warming in the next section, but before we do that, I need tell you a little bit about *where* this carbon dioxide comes from. Carbon dioxide is one of the products of fire. When you burn something, carbon dioxide is almost always one of the substances made as a result of the burning process. Remember from the previous section that the chemical reactions which supply us (and almost all of the creatures in Creation) with energy are essentially combustion (burning) reactions. As a result, almost all creatures in Creation produce carbon dioxide continuously, because the chemical reactions that supply living organisms with energy run continuously.

Now most of you know this already. You have already learned that we inhale oxygen and we exhale carbon dioxide. If you examine Figure 2.3, however, you might be a little surprised about what *else* we exhale.

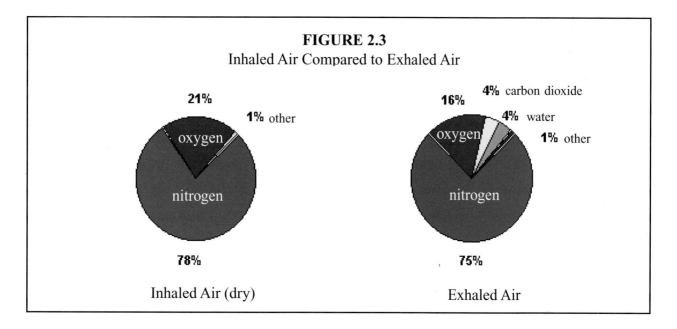

**FIGURE 2.3**
Inhaled Air Compared to Exhaled Air

When most students learn that we inhale oxygen and exhale carbon dioxide, they think that those are the only substances at play. Clearly, this is not the case. As we learned previously, the *majority* of the air we inhale is nitrogen. Less than one-quarter of what we inhale is oxygen. Notice that when we exhale, the majority of what we exhale is also nitrogen. This should make sense. Remember, nitrogen really doesn't interact with our bodies in any way. We breathe it in, and we breathe it right back out. Since it is the majority of what we breathe in, it should also be the majority of what we breathe out.

Notice also that we actually exhale a lot of oxygen as well. That's because under normal circumstances, our bodies do not use all of the oxygen they take in. As a result, there is still a lot of oxygen in a breath of exhaled air. In fact, there is more oxygen in exhaled air than carbon dioxide! Notice also that carbon dioxide and water vapor are of equal concentrations in exhaled air. This is because water is also a product of most combustion reactions. Since exhaled carbon dioxide comes from combustion reactions taking place in our bodies, it makes sense that water will be produced as well.

Thus, carbon dioxide comes from two principal sources: fires and living organisms. Both of these sources have combustion reactions at their root, so they both produce carbon dioxide (and water vapor). When you take biology, you will learn about the "carbon cycle," which is a more detailed means of tracking where carbon dioxide comes from and where it goes. For now, just realize that the two major ways that carbon dioxide gets into the air around us is through fire and the normal life processes of most creatures in Creation.

---

**ON YOUR OWN**

2.5 We know that if the carbon dioxide concentration were too low, then plants would starve. Conversely, experiments indicate that most plants actually flourish when the concentration of carbon dioxide in their vicinity increases. Use this fact to explain why other experiments indicate that houseplants tend to grow better when their caretakers talk to them.

2.6 We know that our bodies do not use the nitrogen that we inhale. Nevertheless, in Figure 2.3, notice that the percentage of nitrogen in exhaled air is *lower* than the percentage of nitrogen in inhaled air. If our bodies do not use nitrogen in any way, why does the percentage decrease?

---

Global Warming

In the previous section, I mentioned that if the concentration of carbon dioxide and other greenhouse gases were to increase too much, the earth would get too warm. This phenomenon is called **global warming**. As you are probably aware, there are those who are worried that this very thing is happening today. Why? Well, as civilization has become more industrialized, people have been burning a lot more than they used to. Before the industrial revolution, we burned wood and coal to heat our homes and businesses, but that was it. As a result of the industrial revolution, however, we are burning coal, wood, natural gas, and gasoline in huge quantities to generate electrical power, run manufacturing engines, and power automobiles. As a result, we have been putting a lot more carbon dioxide into the air than we used to.

At the same time, the population of the earth is greater than it has ever been. Did you know that this century has seen more people living on the earth than the *combined* populations of *all previous centuries*? All of these extra people have been exhaling a lot of carbon dioxide! So, the industrial revolution, combined with the population of the earth, has resulted in a lot of extra carbon dioxide being pumped into the air. As a result, the concentration of carbon dioxide in the air has increased over time, as you will see in a moment.

This is where worries about global warming come from. We know that carbon dioxide is a participant in the greenhouse effect, which warms the planet. We also know that the amount of carbon dioxide in the air has been rising steadily over the last 70 years. Well, increased carbon dioxide means an increased greenhouse effect which will result in global warming, right? Not exactly.

Although the fear that too much carbon dioxide in the air could lead to global warming is based on sound scientific reasoning, reality is just a bit more complex than that. To illustrate what I mean, take a look at the data presented in Figure 2.4. These graphs show both the amount of carbon dioxide in the air and the change in the average temperature of the earth as a function of the year in which those measurements were taken.

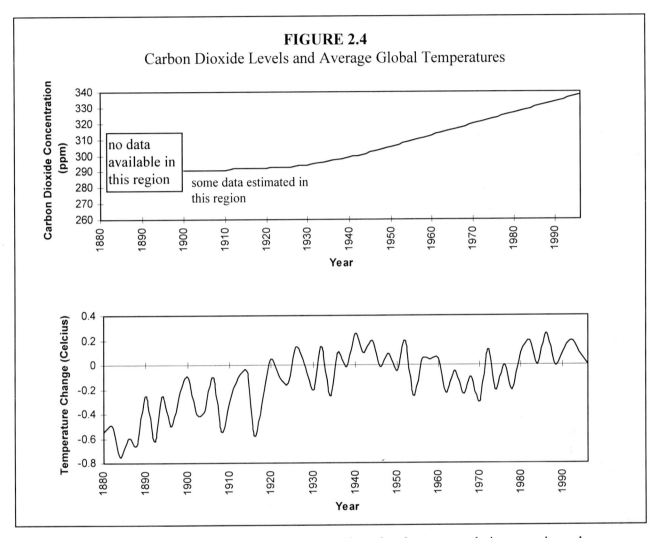

**FIGURE 2.4**
Carbon Dioxide Levels and Average Global Temperatures

What does the figure tell us? It tells us that there has been a steady increase in carbon dioxide levels in the air since about 1920 (see the top graph). If you look at the bottom graph, however, you do not see a corresponding increase in the temperature of the earth. Instead, from about 1880 to 1920, the average global temperature increased in a very shaky pattern by about 0.5 degrees Celsius (0.9 degrees Fahrenheit). After that, however, the temperature change varies up and down quite a bit, but continues to hover around zero. In other words, over the time that the amount of carbon dioxide in the air increased steadily, the average temperature of the earth, on average, did not change!

Does this mean that the amount of carbon dioxide in the air does not affect the temperature of the earth? No, of course not. We know that the greenhouse effect is real, or we wouldn't be here. What these data tell us is that reality is always more complex than theory. First, in order to see a change in the greenhouse effect, there must be a significant change in the amount of carbon dioxide in the air. Unfortunately, scientists do not know what a significant change would be. If the amount of carbon dioxide in the air doubled, would that be significant?

From the standpoint of the greenhouse effect, we really do not know. What we know for sure, however, is that the sum total of all carbon dioxide produced by human activity (both from exhaling as well as from burning fuels) is approximately 3% of the carbon dioxide produced by natural processes on the earth. One could argue, then, that this amount of added carbon dioxide is simply not significant compared to all of the other processes that add carbon dioxide to the air.

Also, the way in which carbon dioxide is added to the air is very important in the greenhouse effect. When humans burn fossil fuels, carbon dioxide is not the only gas that is released. Many other gases are released as well. Some of these gases tend to reflect light rather than absorb it. This actually *reduces* the amount of energy absorbed by the earth, causing a net cooling effect. It could be that any increase in the greenhouse effect due to human-produced carbon dioxide is offset by the cooling caused by the other chemicals associated with human activity.

Another thought to consider is that there are many gases which participate in the greenhouse effect. Methane (often called "natural gas"), water vapor, and ozone are three other gases that trap the heat the earth radiates. It might be that the greenhouse effect is rather sensitive to the concentrations of those gases and rather insensitive to the concentration of carbon dioxide. The fact is, we simply do not know.

We know for sure, however, that right now, all measured data indicates that the greenhouse effect is not being enhanced enough to cause global warming. As a result, the majority of atmospheric scientists (scientists who study the air) do not consider global warming a problem. Now that little fact might surprise you, because you might have heard the television or radio news say that there is a "scientific consensus" that global warming is a big problem today. The scientific consensus, however, is precisely the opposite. In a 1993 Gallup poll conducted for the Institute of Science, Technology, and the Media, only 17% of all atmospheric scientists believed that global warming is a problem. *The majority (53%) said that global warming is not a problem, and the rest (30%) said that there was not enough information to make that decision.* These results are typical of any global warming poll that is taken on atmospheric scientists.

If the data seems to indicate that no global warming has occurred, and if the majority of scientists in the field say that global warming is not a problem, then why does the media seem to say the exact opposite? I have no idea. Perhaps it has something to do with a desire to push an agenda rather than to communicate the truth. Regardless of why, it is very clear that the popular media are ignoring the facts about global warming. Hopefully, the people will be able to learn the facts through some other means.

---

### ON YOUR OWN

2.7 One popular thing to do in American politics is to note that the summers in the United States over the past few years have been very warm. As a result, global warming must be real. What's wrong with this reasoning?

Before we leave this section on global warming, there are two points that I want to make. The first is rather simple. Often times, the impact of scientific data presented in a graph depends on the *way in which* the graph is presented. For example, look at the following graph.

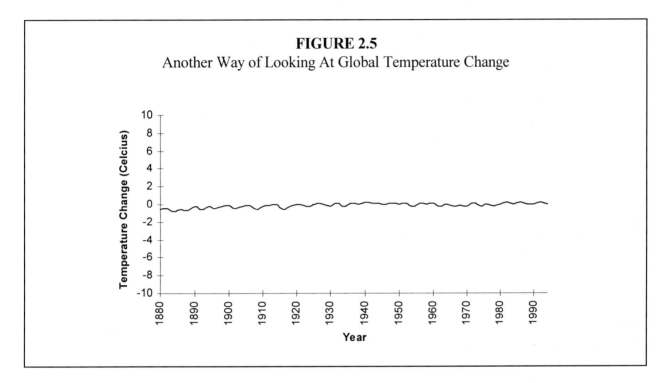

**FIGURE 2.5**
Another Way of Looking At Global Temperature Change

Believe it or not, this is the *same data* as that which was presented in the lower portion of Figure 2.4. What happened to all of the huge ups and downs? What happened to the increase in temperature from 1880 to 1920? Well, it's all still there, but look at the y-axis of the graph and compare that to the y-axis of the graph in the lower portion of Figure 2.4. Do you see the difference? In Figure 2.4, the entire range of the y-axis was a total of 1.2 degrees Celsius (from -0.8 to +0.4 is a range of 1.2). That's a *tiny* range. If the temperature changed 1.2 degrees Celsius, you wouldn't even notice it! Since the graph plots such a tiny range of temperatures, even minuscule changes will be seen. In Figure 2.5, the same data is plotted on a graph whose y-axis spans 20 degrees Celsius (from -10 to +10). This scale is probably a more reasonable one on which to plot the data because a temperature change of 20 degrees Celsius is significant, whereas a temperature change of 1.2 degrees Celsius is not. On this more reasonable scale, the tiny changes in the average temperature of the earth barely even show up!

The point to this discussion is really simple. Whenever you see a graph, look at the scales (both x-axis and y-axis) on it. That way you will know the *range* over which the data is presented. In order to really learn what the data means, you must do this.

The other point I need to bring up comes from the upper part of Figure 2.4. Notice that the graph there shows the concentration of carbon dioxide in the air versus the year. In parentheses, the figure lists the units in which carbon dioxide concentration is measured (ppm). What in the world is ppm? It is an abbreviation for **parts per million**.

<u>Parts per million</u> - The number of molecules (or atoms) of a substance in a mixture for every one million molecules (or atoms) in that mixture

In other words, suppose I had a mixture of argon gas and water vapor. Argon is made up of individual atoms, while water is (of course) made of molecules. Now suppose further that I gathered up enough of the mixture so that the total number of water molecules plus argon atoms was exactly 1,000,000. If, out of those 1,000,000 argon atoms and water molecules, 3,123 of the were argon atoms and the rest were water molecules, then the concentration of argon would be 3,123 parts per million.

Now realize, of course, that ppm can also be expressed as a percentage. After all, percent just tells us how many parts exist per hundred. In other words, if I say that the concentration of nitrogen in air is 78%, it means that for every 100 constituents of air, 78 of them will be nitrogen molecules. Thus, 78% just means 78 parts per hundred. How, then, can we related ppm to percentage? Well, to get 1,000,000 parts of a mixture, you just take 100 parts 10,000 times. In other words:

$$1\% = 10,000 \text{ ppm}$$

If you don't understand the reasoning behind this conversion relationship, don't worry. All you have to do is memorize it, and then you can use it.

For example, think for a moment about the concentrations of carbon dioxide listed in Figure 2.4. In 1900, the graph indicates that the concentration of carbon dioxide in the air was 290 ppm. In percent, that would be:

$$\frac{290 \text{ ppm}}{1} \times \frac{1\%}{10,000 \text{ ppm}} = 0.0290\%$$

That's a really small number percentage. This is why ppm is often used instead of percent. In many people's minds, the unit ppm is easier to visualize when concentrations are small. Thus, small concentrations are often listed in terms of ppm.

To make sure you understand the relationship between ppm and percentage, please study the following example.

**EXAMPLE 2.1**

**The concentration of carbon dioxide in the air today is approximately 340 ppm. What is this concentration in percent?**

Remember, we know the relationship between ppm and percent. We can therefore just use the factor-label method to figure out the answer.

$$\frac{340 \; \cancel{ppm}}{1} \times \frac{1\%}{10,000 \; \cancel{ppm}} = 0.0340\%$$

The concentration of carbon dioxide in the air today is 0.0340%.

**The concentration of oxygen in the air is 21%. What is that concentration in ppm?**

Once again, now that we know the relationship, we can convert using the factor-label method.

$$\frac{21 \; \cancel{\%}}{1} \times \frac{10,000 \; ppm}{1 \cancel{\%}} = 210,000 \; ppm$$

The concentration of oxygen in the air is 210,000 ppm.

---

**ON YOUR OWN**

2.8 The concentration of argon in the air is about 0.9%. What is this in ppm?

2.9 Convert 11 ppm into percent.

---

<u>Ozone</u>

Oxygen and carbon dioxide are not the only gases that play a critical role in supporting life on earth. Life could not exist at all if it weren't for another gas called ozone. As I've mentioned already, the sun provides the earth with almost all of the energy necessary to support life. Thus, the light that comes from the sun is a necessary ingredient for the maintenance of life on earth. Some of the light that comes from the sun, however, is harmful to living organisms. This light is called ultraviolet light, and it is not visible to the human eye.

Ultraviolet light has so much energy that it kills living tissue. If a living organism is exposed to too much ultraviolet light, its cells will die at a very high rate. If the cells are killed by the ultraviolet light faster than the organism can replace them, the organism will die. If the exposure is not too great, the organism might be able to survive, but its increased rate of cellular production might result in various forms of cancer. Thus, in order to support life, the earth must somehow filter out the dangerous, ultraviolet light while still allowing the rest of the light from the sun (visible and infrared light) to reach its surface.

If you think about it for a minute, filtering light is not an easy task. For example, almost everyone has a filter that they place in their furnace. The purpose of this filter is to remove dust from the air in your house. If the filter were really efficient, there would be so little dust in the air that you would never need to dust your furniture. In fact, these furnace dust filters are usually very inefficient and the result is that we must continually pick up the dust that the filter allows to pass. The reason that some dust passes through the filter is simple: dust particles can be smaller than the holes in the filter. Now, think about this: light has neither size nor mass. It is pure energy. How in the world is the earth able to filter out something that has neither size nor mass?

Ozone, a molecule composed of three oxygen atoms, makes up this amazing filter. It turns out that ozone is a molecule which breaks down in the presence of ultraviolet light. The ultraviolet light has just enough energy to break apart one of the bonds that holds the oxygen atoms together. The bond, in order to break, must absorb the ultraviolet light. In other words, when ultraviolet light encounters an ozone molecule, it uses its energy to destroy the ozone molecule instead of destroying living tissue. One truly incredible thing about this wonderful filter is that ozone cannot be broken down by visible or infrared light, so those types of light are allowed to hit the surface of the earth where they are needed by plants and animals!

That's not the end of the story, however. Because each ozone molecule is destroyed when it absorbs ultraviolet light, there must be some way of replenishing the earth's supply of ozone so that the filtering system will stay intact. This is accomplished through a system of four chemical reactions called the "Chapman cycle." Although the Chapman cycle is far too complicated for the purpose of this discussion, suffice it to say that the earth is continually producing more ozone from its supply of oxygen. Thus, not only is there an elegant filtering system that protects us from the sun's harmful rays, but the earth also has a system that ensures the constant renewal of the filter.

The most amazing aspect of the ozone filter hasn't even been presented yet! Although ozone is necessary for life as we know it, ozone is also incredibly poisonous to living organisms. If living organisms breathe in too much ozone, they die. So, we must have ozone to protect us from the sun's ultraviolet rays, but we cannot breathe it in, or it would kill us. Seems like a contradiction, doesn't it? Well it would be, except the *Designer* of our planet is a little smarter than you and I. Earth's air contains plenty of ozone, but the vast majority of it exists in a layer ("the ozone layer") 20 to 30 kilometers (12.4 to 18.6 miles) above sea level where no living organism breathes!

Have you heard about the "hole" that exists in the ozone layer? A large amount of time and money has been spent worrying over this problem. Well, now that you know what ozone in the ozone layers does for us, you might understand why everyone is so worried about it. In the next module, we will look at this ozone "hole" business very thoroughly, and you will find that there is really nothing to be worried about.

---

**ON YOUR OWN**

2.10  A very popular evolutionary theory of how life originated on the planet requires that, at one point, there was no oxygen in the atmosphere.  This theory, of course, assumes that the first life form did not breathe oxygen.  Since there are organisms today that can exist without breathing oxygen, this is not as fantastic as it may first sound.  Based on what you learned in this section, however, what serious objection can you raise against the theory that life originated on an earth with no oxygen in its air?

---

Before we go on, I want you to think about what you have learned for a moment.  Earth just *happens* to have all of the gases necessary for life; it just *happens* to have all the right quantities of those gases; and they just *happen* to be in the right place.  If nearly any other gas than nitrogen or argon diluted the atmosphere, life could not exist.  If too much or too little oxygen was in the air, then life could not exist.  Similarly, if too much or too little carbon dioxide were in the air, life on earth would not be possible.  In addition, not only does life depend on ozone, but it also depends on ozone being far away from the life that it is protecting!  Beyond all of this, the gases in the air are all replenished when they are used, keeping their concentrations relatively constant over time!

Now think about one other thing.  The air that surrounds the earth is just *one aspect* of the physical environment which makes life possible.  There are literally millions and millions of aspects of the earth that make it a haven for life.  If any one of these aspects was wrong, then earth would suddenly be hostile to life.  Do you see how wonderfully God's Creation proclaims His majesty?  The incredible design that exists in the world around us is powerful evidence that this world did not come about by chance.  Accidents do not produce the intricacy that we see in the air around us.  Only intelligent design does!  Truly, anyone who understands the science of air must exercise an *enormous* amount of faith to believe that all of this occurred by chance!

### Air Pollution

Now I can't discuss the air that we breathe without discussing air pollution.  Air pollution has been a major concern in the United States for many, many years; so it is important for us to spend some time studying it.  Of course, the pollutants in the air are all part of that extra 1% that I labeled as "other gases" in Figure 2.1.  In that figure, I list "sulfur oxides" and "nitrogen oxides" as a part of these "other gases."  The term "sulfur oxides" actually refers to two different gas molecules that are made when sulfur is burned.  In the same way, "nitrogen oxides" refers to two different gas molecules that result when nitrogen is burned.  Both of these groups of gases are poisonous, so they are considered pollutants.

In today's air, sulfur oxides, nitrogen oxides, and carbon monoxide make up the majority of pollutants.  There are small quantities of other pollutants, however.  Sulfur oxides and nitrogen oxides are gases that destroy lung tissue, so they are pollutants.  Carbon monoxide is a gas that tends to decrease the amount of oxygen in a person's blood, so it is also a pollutant. Ozone that exists where people can breathe is also a poison and is therefore considered a pollutant.  Finally, airborne lead is a pollutant that we were very worried about in the past, but nowadays is virtually nonexistent in the air around us.

It is important to learn a little bit about each of the major pollutants in the air, so I will discuss each of them briefly. Before I do this, however, I need to stress an important point. Although human activity has increased the concentrations of each pollutant I have discussed, these pollutants were already a part of the air long before human activity began increasing their concentrations. This is because *all* of these pollutants have natural sources as well as human-made sources. Thus, as I discuss each pollutant, I will point out the human-made sources that create more of these pollutants, but I will also discuss the natural sources that create these pollutants regardless of human activity. As the discussion progresses, you will see why it is important to realize that there are natural sources for *all* of these pollutants.

Let's start our discussion of pollutants with **sulfur oxides**. As I said before, sulfur oxides refers to two different gases. These gases, sulfur dioxide and sulfur trioxide, are formed when sulfur burns. So, you might think we can easily get rid of these pollutants in the air if we just stop burning sulfur, right? Well, in principle, that's right. In practice, however, it's a lot tougher to keep from burning sulfur. You see, sulfur is a contaminant in a lot of coal. Since we burn coal both to generate electricity and to generate heat for industry and homes, we cannot help but burn the sulfur that is in the coal right along with the coal. As a result, coal burning is a major human-made source of sulfur oxide pollution.

Now it turns out that there are methods available to reduce the amount of sulfur contamination in coal. We can use a certain chemical process to, in essence, "clean" much of the sulfur contamination out of coal before we burn it. This strongly reduces the sulfur oxides produced when the coal is burned. There is a problem, however. This process is rather expensive. It tends to increase the cost of the electricity produced from the coal or the products that the industry which burns the coal produces. Thus, it is *possible* to clean coal of sulfur, but the process of sulfur-removal is typically used sparingly because of the cost involved.

Although coal-burning is the principal *human-made* source of sulfur oxides in the air, there are natural sources as well. The most important natural source of sulfur oxides pollution is volcanic activity. When volcanoes erupt, they emit an *enormous* amount of sulfur oxides. In 1991, the world witnessed the eruption of Mount Pinatubo. This single volcanic eruption put the same amount of sulfur oxides in the air as three months of worldwide human activity! Thus, although volcanic eruptions do not occur very often, when they do occur, they throw so much sulfur oxides into the air that they remain a major source of sulfur oxides pollution.

**Nitrogen oxides**, like sulfur oxides, are formed when nitrogen burns. Once again, no one purposely burns nitrogen. Nevertheless, nitrogen does get burned as the result of other processes. Automobile, airplane, and lawn mower engines burn gasoline at high temperatures. Since this happens in air, there is a lot of nitrogen surrounding these engines. Although it is hard to burn nitrogen, the heat of these engines burns a tiny fraction of the nitrogen that surrounds them. This results in nitrogen oxides. Thus, engines are a major human-made source of nitrogen oxides. The heat of volcanoes also produces nitrogen oxides, as does the heat of lightning bolts. This latter natural source is considered the most important natural source of nitrogen oxides.

The other important pollutant in the air today is **ozone**. Now remember, ozone is critically important to the survival of life on earth. In order to block the ultraviolet light coming from the sun, ozone *must* be in the air. At the same time, however, ozone is a poison. Thus, we *want* a lot of ozone to be in the air, we just don't want to *breathe* it. Thus, we would like to keep constant or increase the ozone in the ozone layer (where no one is breathing), but we want to *reduce or eliminate* the ozone that exists near the earth's surface. So, ozone is a good thing when it is in the ozone layer, but it is a pollutant when it is near the ground where people are breathing.

Human activities such as driving, mowing lawns, and even baking bread tend to produce ozone. Basically, any activity which involves heat and oxygen will produce some ozone because ozone results from the interaction of three oxygen atoms. Thus, anywhere there is oxygen and the energy necessary to make three oxygen atoms interact, there will be ozone. Automobiles are considered the largest human-made source of ozone near the ground. Lightning is considered the largest natural source of ozone near the ground.

Now I want to ask you a question. Stop and answer this question in your mind before you go on. Is the concentration of pollutants in the air today greater than, similar to, or less than the concentration of those pollutants 25 years ago? What do you think? Well, the answer might surprise you. It turns out that *every pollutant in the air has a lower concentration today than it had 25 years ago!* In fact, there are some pollutants that were a problem 25 years ago which have been basically eliminated today.

Consider, for example, **airborne lead**. Although lead is a solid, small amounts of it can become airborne when it is burned. Well, as automobiles became popular, engineers realized that adding lead to gasoline improved an automobile's performance. As a result, gasoline companies started adding lead to the gasoline. As time went on, scientists suddenly realized that some of that lead, when burned with gasoline, made it into the air as airborne lead. This was a serious problem, as lead is a strong poison that typically destroys brain tissue.

Because of this threat, the U.S. government mandated that cars made after 1976 had to run only on unleaded gasoline. As time went on, fewer and fewer cars were burning leaded gasoline, and, as a result, airborne lead concentrations plummeted. Today, all cars burn unleaded gasoline, and the result is that airborne lead is almost non-existent in the air around us.

The fact that today's air is cleaner than it was 25 years ago is demonstrated not only by the virtual elimination of airborne lead, but also by the fact that all measurable pollutants are less concentrated in the air today than in 1975. Consider the data presented in Figure 2.6. In the top part of the figure, there is a table that lists each pollutant's concentration in both 1975 and 1995. In the lower part of the figure, the decrease in air pollution is illustrated by showing the current air pollution (red bars) concentrations as a percentage of the levels that existed in 1975.

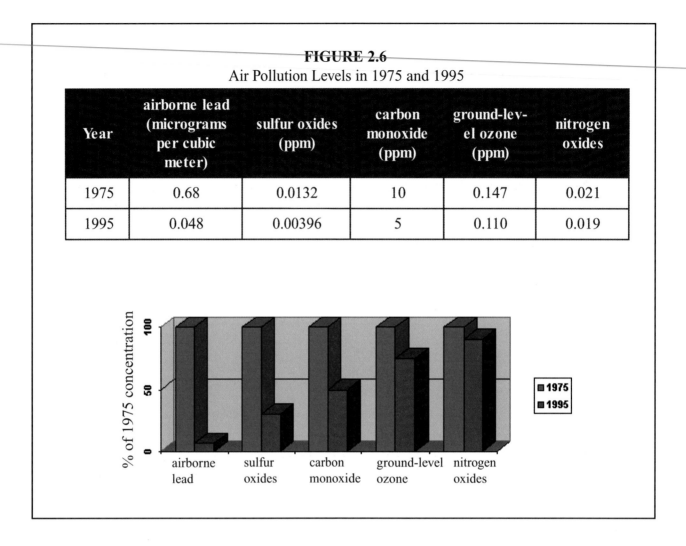

FIGURE 2.6
Air Pollution Levels in 1975 and 1995

| Year | airborne lead (micrograms per cubic meter) | sulfur oxides (ppm) | carbon monoxide (ppm) | ground-level ozone (ppm) | nitrogen oxides |
|------|---------------------------------------------|---------------------|------------------------|--------------------------|------------------|
| 1975 | 0.68 | 0.0132 | 10 | 0.147 | 0.021 |
| 1995 | 0.048 | 0.00396 | 5 | 0.110 | 0.019 |

Notice that no matter what pollutant we consider, the concentration is lower today than it was in 1975. From the table, for example, you can see that sulfur oxides have fallen in concentration from 0.0132 ppm in 1975 to 0.00396 ppm in 1995. The graph illustrates this change in terms of percent. Looking at today's sulfur oxides level (the red bars), you can see that it is about 30% of what it was in 1975!

What was responsible for these dramatic changes? Well, when scientists began studying air pollution in detail, pollutant levels like those shown in the 1975 part of Figure 2.6 rightly caused the U.S. government great concern about the health and safety of the American people. As a result, the government began instituting regulations aimed at reducing pollutant levels. Consider, for example, the pollutant **carbon monoxide**. This gas is a deadly by-product of incomplete combustion. Remember, combustion is fire, and when fire burns, it needs oxygen. When there is plenty of oxygen, fire produces carbon dioxide. When the amount of oxygen available to fire is scarce, the fire begins producing carbon monoxide instead of carbon dioxide. Whenever fire produces carbon monoxide instead of carbon dioxide, we say that the fire is experiencing incomplete combustion. Unlike carbon dioxide, carbon monoxide is a deadly poison which robs your blood of oxygen.

At one time, automobiles were a huge source of carbon monoxide pollution. Automobiles require so much energy that they burn gasoline at a very fast rate. The gasoline is burned so quickly that there is just not enough time to supply it with plenty of oxygen. As a result, incomplete combustion occurs and carbon monoxide is produced. In 1977, however, the U.S. government required car manufacturers to install **catalytic** (kat' uh lih tik) **converters** in all new cars. These devices convert more than 95% of the carbon monoxide produced by automobiles into carbon dioxide. After the government mandated this change in automobile manufacturing, the concentration of carbon monoxide in the air began to decline rapidly, as shown in Figure 2.6.

Now although car exhaust does not produce much carbon monoxide today, it still does produce some. As a result, it is never safe to be in enclosed areas in which an automobile is running. Under those conditions, even the small amount of carbon monoxide produced by the automobile will get more and more concentrated until it becomes deadly.

Other regulations that reduced air pollution levels involved requiring certain electrical power plants and heavy industry to install **scrubbers** in their smokestacks. These devices partially absorb sulfur oxides produced by coal burning, causing fewer sulfur oxides to be emitted. Others had to clean their coal by the expensive process mentioned earlier. In addition, regulations were placed on automobile engines to reduce the ozone and nitrogen oxides that they form.

The results of these regulations were many faceted. First, they dramatically reduced the concentration of pollutants in the air (as is clearly shown in Figure 2.6). Second, they made electricity, manufactured items, and automobiles more expensive. After all, scrubbers on smokestacks cost money. Catalytic converters and engines that use unleaded gasoline efficiently are expensive. As a result, the cost of many things increased significantly over the same period. Finally, there were some unintended consequences as well. In order to meet certain government regulations, automobiles were made lighter. As a result, they were not as safe as their heavier counterparts. In the end, traffic fatalities increased significantly as well.

So, the positive effect of imposed regulations designed to reduce pollution was that, in fact, they did lower pollutant levels. The negative effects were higher prices and more traffic fatalities. Were these negative effects worth the positive effects? I think so. The pollutant levels measured in 1975 were significant. If they continued to grow, widespread health maladies could have resulted. True, some people died as a result of the regulations, but most analysts agree that the increase in traffic fatalities was still less consequential than the deaths that would have resulted from unchecked pollution.

These days, there is still a constant debate as to whether or not we need even more government regulations to reduce pollutant concentrations even further. On the surface, those who want more regulations seem to have a good argument. After all, who can argue with cleaner air? If government regulations resulted in cleaner air from 1975 to 1995, won't more government regulations result in even cleaner air? Isn't that desirable?

Cleaner air is certainly desirable. However, you have to consider two very important questions. First, you must ask yourself how much of a benefit we will get as a result of cleaner air. Second, you have to ask yourself how much cost will accompany that benefit. For example, we can further reduce the carbon monoxide levels in automobiles by having the government raise the average miles per gallon requirement that they impose on the automobile manufacturers. This will raise the price of cars, but it will also force them to become lighter. When cars get lighter, they become more unsafe. Thus, having the government require the automobile manufacturers to raise the gas mileage on their cars will definitely reduce carbon monoxide concentrations in the air that we breathe, but it will also result in higher-priced cars and an increase in the number of people that die as a result of automobile accidents. Is the benefit worth the cost? That's what must be decided.

This kind of reasoning is often called a **cost/benefit** analysis. When the benefit achieved by a certain action is worth the cost involved, then the action should be taken. If the benefit is not worth the cost, however, the action should not be taken. The problem with applying a cost/benefit analysis to air pollution regulations, however, is that there are many things we do not know.

For example, we do not know what pollutant levels are "safe" for people! About the only way to do this is to experiment with people. For example, we could take a bunch of people and put them in a sealed environment and then start varying the concentrations of pollutants to which they are exposed. If we could do enough studies like that over a long, long period of time, we could determine what concentrations of pollutants are considered "safe." Such experiments, of course, are both immoral and illegal, so they cannot be done. The result, then, is that we really have no idea how much air pollution is considered "safe," and cannot, therefore, determine how much of a benefit would be derived from a reduction in air pollution.

Also, we know that there are natural sources for all of these pollutants. What we do not know, however, is what the concentration of these pollutants would be as a result of *only* those natural sources. Thus, we really have no idea of what the "natural" concentrations of these pollutants should be. Sulfur oxides concentrations, for example, are 30% of what they were in 1975. How close are we to the "natural" concentration of sulfur oxides? No one knows. For all we know, we could already be extremely close.

Applying a cost/benefit analysis to air pollution regulations is also difficult from the cost side. Although we can have a pretty good idea of how much *money* any new air pollution requirement will cost, many of the other costs are totally unexpected. For example, when the government began issuing regulations to automobile manufacturers on the average gas mileage of their automobiles, no one had considered the effect these regulations would have on automobile safety. Thus, the tragic loss of life that has been associated with these regulations was a *complete surprise.*

The point of this discussion is twofold. First, you must understand that the air you are breathing now is cleaner than it was 20 years ago. Thus, air pollution is certainly *less* of a problem today than it used to be. Second, you can't simply say that cleaner air is desirable. Instead, you have to do cost/benefit analyses to determine whether or not cleaner air is worth the cost. The problem is, these cost/benefit analyses are rather difficult. Therefore, you must be very careful when you approach the subject of air pollution regulations. Past experience has clearly shown that *some* of these regulations are good. Past experience, however, has also shown that for *some* air pollution regulations, the small benefits have not been worth the immense cost. If we are to ever have sane air pollution regulations in this country, these kinds of issues must be discussed. Unfortunately, they rarely are!

---

**ON YOUR OWN**

2.11 Suppose you could institute regulations that would be targeted at one specific air pollutant. Based on the data in Figure 2.6, which air pollutant would be best to target from a cost/benefit point of view?

---

## ANSWERS TO THE ON YOUR OWN PROBLEMS

2.1 <u>The water will take the least time to evaporate on the second day.</u> Remember, when humidity is high, there is already a lot of water vapor in the air. Thus, water does not evaporate very quickly. On low humidity days, however, there is little water vapor in the air, so water evaporates quickly.

2.2 <u>The water will NOT evaporate.</u> When the relative humidity is 100%, no more water can go into the air, so water cannot evaporate!

2.3 <u>The percentages of nitrogen and oxygen would be less.</u> Think about this one. If there is water in the air, then the total amount of stuff in the air is greater. Well, the percentage of a substance is equal to the amount of that substance divided by the total amount of the mixture times 100. If the total amount in the mixture increases, then the percentage of fixed substances will go down.

2.4 <u>The candle would burn dimmer.</u> As oxygen concentration decreases, things burn slowly.

2.5 <u>Plants grow better when their caretakers talk to them because when someone talks to a plant, he or she exhales carbon dioxide on it. This increases the concentration of carbon dioxide in the plants' vicinity, making them grow better.</u>

2.6 You use the same reasoning here that you used in Problem 2.3. <u>Since exhaled air has more stuff in it (water, extra carbon dioxide), the percentage of nitrogen decreases not because the amount of nitrogen decreases, but because the total amount in the mixture increases.</u>

2.7 <u>The temperature of the summers in the United States is irrelevant to global warming. First of all, you need to consider the temperature *all over the world*, not just the temperature in the U.S. Also, you need to consider the *whole year*, not just the summer. Global warming will affect *all* seasons.</u>

2.8 Remember, we know the relationship between percent and ppm, so we can convert using the factor-label method.

$$\frac{0.9\ \%}{1} \times \frac{10{,}000\ \text{ppm}}{1\%} = 9{,}000\ \text{ppm}$$

The concentration of argon in the air is <u>9,000  ppm</u>.

2.9 Remember, we know the relationship between ppm and percent. We can therefore just use the factor-label method to figure out the answer.

$$\frac{11\ \text{ppm}}{1} \times \frac{1\%}{10{,}000\ \text{ppm}} = 0.0011\%$$

A concentration of 11 ppm is equal to <u>0.0011%</u>.

2.10  <u>No oxygen means no ozone.  With no ozone layer, no life form would be able to exist</u>. Remember, the earth replenishes its ozone supply from its oxygen supply.  With no oxygen, there will be no ozone.

2.11  <u>Nitrogen oxides would be the best pollutant to target</u>, because the concentration of nitrogen oxides is still rather high.  Thus, we could probably derive a lot of benefit from reducing nitrogen oxides.   It turns out that this is rather hard to do, however, because nitrogen oxides come mostly from automobiles, and as of yet, we have no way of reducing them except by reducing the amount of driving that is going on.

**STUDY GUIDE FOR MODULE #2**

1.  Define the following terms:

    a.  Humidity
    b.  Absolute humidity
    c.  Relative humidity
    d.  Greenhouse effect
    e.  Parts per million

2.  The temperature is the same at 1:00 in the afternoon on two consecutive days.  For a person who is outside working, however, the second day feels cooler than the first day.  On which day was the humidity higher?

3.  A child decides to keep his goldfish outside in a small bowl.  He has to add water every day to keep the bowl full.  On two consecutive days, the temperatures are very similar, but on the first day, the relative humidity is 90% while on the second day, it is 60%.  On which day will the child add more water to the goldfish bowl?

4.  If you put a glass of water outside when the relative humidity is 100%, how quickly will the water evaporate?

5.  Why does sweating cool people down?

6.  What is the percentage of nitrogen in dry air?  What about oxygen?

7.  What would be the consequence of removing all of the carbon dioxide in earth's air supply?

8.  What would be the consequence of removing all of the ozone in earth's air supply?

9.  What would be the consequence of a sudden increase in the concentration of oxygen in the earth's air supply?

10. Suppose astronomers found another solar system in which there was a sun just like our sun.  Suppose further that a planet existed in this new solar system which was just as far from its sun as is earth from our sun.  Since the vast majority of energy that planets get comes from their suns, is it reasonable to assume that the new planet would have roughly the same average temperature as that of earth?  Why or why not?

11. What makes up the majority of the air that we exhale?

12. Do we exhale more carbon dioxide or more oxygen?

13. Is global warming happening today?

14. The current concentration of ground-level ozone in the air is about 0.110 ppm. What is that in percent?

15. Suppose you had a sample of air in which the nitrogen oxides concentration is 0.023%. What would the concentration of nitrogen oxides be if you expressed it in ppm?

16. Is the air cleaner today, or was it cleaner 20 years ago?

17. What is a cost/benefit analysis?

18. What does a catalytic converter do in a car?

19. What does a scrubber do in a smokestack?

20. In the U.S., there are many regulations aimed at decreasing the amount of ground-level ozone in the air, because ground level ozone is considered a pollutant. At the same time, there are many regulations aimed at increasing the amount of ozone in the ozone layer. Despite the fact that ozone in the ozone layer is the same as ground-level ozone, ozone in the ozone layer is not considered a pollutant. Instead, it is considered an essential substance. Why?

# Module #3: The Atmosphere

## Introduction

In the previous module, I told you about the wonderful mixture of gases that we call air. In this module, I will continue that discussion. This time, however, we will look at air with a larger point of view. Instead of discussing the makeup, properties, and contaminants in the air itself, we will now look at earth's air supply as a whole. When looked at in this way, we call earth's air supply the **atmosphere**.

<u>Atmosphere</u> - The mass of air surrounding a planet

Since the earth is a planet (of course), the mass of air surrounding the earth is called "earth's atmosphere."

## Atmospheric Pressure

The first thing to realize about the atmosphere is that it presses down on the earth and all of the earth's inhabitants. Remember, air has mass, and that mass is above us. If you put a heavy weight on your shoulders, it presses down on you, doesn't it? Well, the atmosphere can be thought of as a heavy weight, pressing down on us and everything else that it contacts. Believe it or not, the combined weight of all the air surrounding the earth is approximately *6 billion tons*! Now, of course, not all of that weight is sitting on your shoulders! After all, the weight of the atmosphere is distributed across the entire planet. Nevertheless, if you were to measure a square inch of ground at sea level, the atmosphere would exert 14.7 pounds on that one square inch.

Think about that for a moment. At sea level, every square inch of the earth is being pressed down with an average weight of 14.7 pounds. Suppose, for example, you were standing at sea level. Depending on your build, each of your shoulders is about 3 inches wide by 4 inches long. This gives each shoulder an area (length times width) of 12 square inches. This means that on each of your shoulders, the atmosphere is pressing down with a weight of 12 x 14.7, or *176.4 pounds!* This pressure, called **atmospheric pressure**, is exerted on all things that come into contact with earth's atmosphere.

<u>Atmospheric pressure</u> - The pressure exerted by the atmosphere on all objects within it

Now wait a minute, you might think. It certainly doesn't *feel* like I have 176.4 pounds pressing down on each of my shoulders! It doesn't *feel* that way because there is equal pressure pushing on you from all sides, including from within! How does that help? Well, supposed I tied two ropes to a rock and asked two equally strong people to pull on the ropes in opposite directions. Would the rock move? Of course not! The two people pulling in opposite directions would cancel each other out. In the same way, the pressure pushing on you in one direction is canceled by pressure pushing on you in the opposite direction. The net effect is that you do not *feel* any pressure. Nevertheless, the pressure is there. To see that it is there, perform the following experiment.

## EXPERIMENT 3.1
### Air Pressure

Supplies:

- A tall, clear jar or glass (It should either be straight, or it should be tapered so that the top of the jar is smaller than the bottom. Do not use a jar that is tapered so that the top is bigger than the bottom, as this will reduce the effect you are trying to see.)
- A candle
- A candle holder
- Matches
- A clear bowl
- Water
- Food coloring (any color)

Introduction - This experiment will demonstrate the fact that the atmosphere actually does exert pressure on everything that is in it.

Procedure :

A. Take the bowl and fill it with a thin layer of water. This is the real trick to getting the experiment to work. The water should not be very deep in the bowl. To see if you have the right amount of water, invert the jar and set it in the middle of the bowl. The water should cover the lip of the jar, with about 1/8 of an inch to spare. In other words, you should have water in the bowl, but it should not be a lot more than what is necessary to cover the lip on the inverted jar.
B. Once you have the right amount of water, take the jar out of the bowl.
C. Now add a few drops of food coloring and stir it around so that the water is colored. The only reason we do this is to make the water easier to see.
D. Put the candle in the holder and place it in the center of the bowl.
E. Light the candle.
F. While the candle is burning, invert the jar and place it over the candle, letting it stand in the bowl as you did when you were testing the water level. Your experiment should look like this:

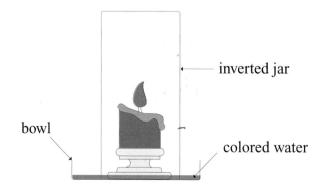

bowl

inverted jar

colored water

G.   As you already know, the candle will eventually burn out.  This is because it will use up all of the oxygen in the jar, and since there is no way for oxygen to get back into the jar (the water keeps the jar sealed), the candle eventually goes out.

H.   Observe what happened to the water level within the jar.  Draw a "before" and "after" picture in your laboratory notebook, indicating what happened.

I.   Clean everything up and put the items back where they belong.

Did nothing happen in your experiment?  Well, if nothing happened, the most likely problem is the water level in your bowl.  It is either too low or too high.  If it is too low, then you will hear a sucking sound or see bubbles near the lip of the jar.  If this is what happened,  then the jar needed more water than you had in the bowl.  Add a little water and try again.  If you did not hear the sucking sound or see bubbles, then your water level was too high.  In that case, there was a change, but it was masked by the water you had in the bowl.  Dump some water out and try again.

Now, what explains the results of the experiment?  Well, if your water level in the bowl was reasonable, you should have seen the water level inside the jar rise, so that it was, in fact, higher than the water level in the bowl.  Why did that happen?  Look at the following "before" and "after" drawings:

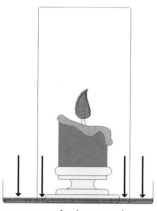

As soon as you put the jar over the candle, the jar had air in it.  That air pushed against the water with the same pressure that the air outside the jar did.  As a result, the water level in the jar stayed the same as the water level in the bowl.

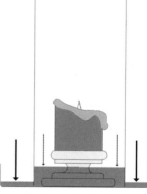

After the candle burned out, there was less air, because the candle had used up all of the oxygen.  As a result, the air in the jar could not exert as much pressure as it used to, and the air outside of the jar pushed water into the jar.  The outside pressure from the air continued to push water into the jar until the additional weight of the water in the jar made up for the loss of pressure due to the lack of oxygen.

Think about this, then.  Air is pressing down on the water in the bowl.  Before you allowed the candle to burn, the air in the jar was essentially the same as the air outside of the jar.  As a result, the water inside the jar was being pressed down with the same pressure (atmospheric pressure) as the water outside the jar.  As the candle burned, however, it used up the oxygen in the jar.  With less oxygen in the jar, there were less molecules in the air inside the jar.  With less molecules, the air in the jar could not exert as much pressure as it did before.  As a result, there was an imbalance.  There was more pressure on the water outside the jar than on the water inside the jar.  As a result, the greater outside pressure began pushing water into the jar.  This increased the water level in the jar.  The water level in the jar did not increase indefinitely, however, because the weight of this extra water added to the force from the air pressure. At some level, the weight of the water "made up" for the lost air pressure so that, in the end, the water inside the jar experienced the same total pressure as the water outside the jar. At that point, the water stopped moving again.

Now, suppose the amount of pressure on the water outside the jar decreased. What would happen? Well, at that point, there would be more pressure inside the jar than outside, so water would be pushed out of the jar until the pressure equalized again. As a result, the water level in the jar would decrease. If, on the other hand, the pressure exerted on the water outside the jar increased, then more water would flow into the jar until the pressure equalized again. In this case, the water level in the jar would increase.

What do we have here, then? We have an instrument that measures atmospheric pressure. Such an instrument is called a **barometer** (buh rom' uh ter).

Barometer - An instrument used to measure atmospheric pressure

Now the experimental setup you had will not really work as a barometer for two main reasons. First, for a barometer to work properly, there should be no air in the jar. That way, all of the pressure being exerted inside the jar is due solely to the weight of the water. This increases the sensitivity of a barometer. In your experiment, you got rid of the oxygen in the air, but since the vast majority of air is made up of nitrogen, there was still a lot of air in your jar. Second, the water in the bowl will evaporate, and that will change the balance of forces.

Typically, a good barometer uses mercury as its liquid. This very heavy liquid is quite toxic, but it works well in a barometer. Instead of a jar, a column of glass is used, and there is absolutely no air in that column when it is placed in a pool of mercury. Besides these details, a good barometer works on the same principle as your experiment. When the atmospheric pressure is large, the height of the mercury in the column is greater than when the atmospheric pressure is small.

At this point, I need to mention the units used to measure atmospheric pressure. It turns out that there are many, many units that we use. When I originally mentioned atmospheric pressure, I gave its "average" value at sea level as 14.7 pounds per square inch. In many applications, the measurement of atmospheric pressure is made based on how much weight it exerts over a certain area. Thus, 14.7 pounds per square inch means that on every square inch that the atmosphere touches, it exerts 14.7 pounds. This number changes based both on altitude and weather conditions, but 14.7 pounds per square inch is a good average at sea level.

Now when you look at a weather report, atmospheric pressure will sometimes be listed as "barometric pressure." In such reports, it is usually not given in pounds per square inch. It is usually reported in terms of inches. How in the world can atmospheric pressure be measures in inches? Well, think about a barometer. When the atmospheric pressure changes, *the height of the mercury in the column changes*. In a really good barometer, even the slightest change in atmospheric pressure results in a change in height of the liquid in the jar. Thus, if we measure the height of the mercury in inches, when that height changes, we would know that the atmospheric pressure has changed.

In a mercury barometer, an atmospheric pressure of 14.7 pounds per square inch will cause a column of mercury to rise 29.9 inches above the pool of mercury in which the glass column is placed. As a result, the average atmospheric pressure at sea level can also be expressed as 29.9 inches. Sometimes, weather reports are a little more descriptive and actually list the unit as "inches of mercury." Now, at least, you know what that means. If, in the weather report, you see that the atmospheric pressure is less than 29.9 inches (or inches of mercury), then you know that the atmospheric pressure is lower than average. If it is greater than 29.9 inches (or inches of mercury), then you know that the atmospheric pressure is greater than the average.

Since we often only worry about the atmospheric pressure in terms of whether it is above or below the average sea-level atmospheric pressure, there is yet another unit we can use to measure atmospheric pressure. This unit, called the **atmosphere** (abbreviated as "atm") is very easy to compare to the average sea-level atmospheric pressure. When the atmospheric pressure is 1.0 atm, then it is at its average sea-level value of 14.7 pounds per square inch. If the pressure is less than 1.0 atm, then you know that the atmospheric pressure is less that its average sea-level value. For example, an atmospheric pressure of 0.9 atm indicates that the atmospheric pressure is only 90% of its average sea-level value. In the same way, a value of 1.1 atm indicates that atmospheric pressure is 110% of the average sea-level value.

---

**ON YOUR OWN**

3.1 In general, should atmospheric pressure increase or decrease as altitude increases?

3.2 The atmospheric pressure is 1.1 atms. Which of the following values for atmospheric pressure would you see in the weather report: 29.9 inches, 32.9 inches, or 28.1 inches?

---

### The Layers of Earth's Atmosphere

One thing you have to realize about earth's atmosphere is that the mixture of gases we discussed in the previous module applies only to a certain region of the atmosphere. You see, the atmosphere can be divided into two general layers called the **homosphere** (hoh' muh sfear) and the **heterosphere** (het' uh ruh sfear).

Homosphere - The lower layer of earth's atmosphere, which exists from ground level to roughly 80 kilometers (50 miles) above sea level

Heterosphere - The upper layer of earth's atmosphere, which exists higher than 80 kilometers (50 miles) above sea level

The air that we breathe, of course, comes from the homosphere. Thus, the mixture of gases that we discussed in Module #2 is the composition of the air in the homosphere. In fact, that's where the term "homosphere" comes from. You see, the air in the homosphere is uniform in its composition. The prefix "homo" means "same;" thus, the homosphere contains air that has the same composition, regardless of where you are in the homosphere.

What about the heterosphere? Well, the prefix "hetero" means "different," so you can bet that the air in the heterosphere is not uniform. In fact, the composition of the air in the heterosphere actually depends on altitude. First of all, there is not nearly as much air in the heterosphere as there is in the homosphere. Whereas the gases that make up the air in the homosphere are reasonably concentrated, the concentration of gases in the heterosphere is very low. As a result, we usually say that the air is "thin" in the heterosphere. Also, there is little nitrogen or argon in the heterosphere. In general, the lower portion of the heterosphere (altitudes of 80 kilometers to 965 kilometers) is predominately made up of oxygen. At higher altitudes (965 kilometers to 2415 kilometers) the heterosphere is dominated by helium, and the highest portion of the heterosphere (2415 kilometers and above) is dominated by hydrogen.

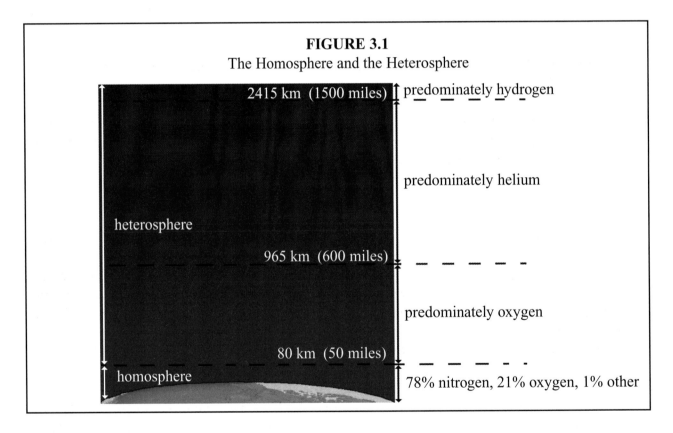

**FIGURE 3.1**
The Homosphere and the Heterosphere

2415 km  (1500 miles)  predominately hydrogen

heterosphere    predominately helium

965 km  (600 miles)

predominately oxygen

80 km  (50 miles)

homosphere    78% nitrogen, 21% oxygen, 1% other

**ON YOUR OWN**

3.3 In chemistry, mixtures are classified as being either *heterogeneous* or *homogeneous*. Based on what you learned about the difference between the heterosphere and homosphere, classify Coca-Cola® as a heterogeneous or homogeneous mixture. What about Italian salad dressing?

3.4 An X-15 fighter jet flies at altitudes in excess of 80 kilometers. If you have ever seen a picture of a pilot flying such a jet, he or she always has a mask covering his or her mouth and nose. What is the purpose of that mask?

## The Homosphere

Although the composition of the air is essentially the same no matter where you are in the homosphere, many other characteristics of the homosphere change with altitude. As a result, we can further divide the homosphere into three regions: the **troposphere** (troh' puh sfear), the **stratosphere** (stra' tuh sfear), and the **mesosphere** (meez' uh sfear).

Troposphere - The region of the atmosphere that extends from ground level to roughly 11 kilometers (7 miles) above sea level

Stratosphere - The region of the atmosphere that spans altitudes of 11 kilometers to 48 kilometers (30 miles)

Mesosphere - The region of the atmosphere that spans altitudes of 48 kilometers to 80 kilometers (50 miles)

The boundaries between these regions and the other regions of the atmosphere are given their own names. The **tropopause** (troh' puh paws) is the boundary between the troposphere and the stratosphere, while the **stratopause** (strat' uh paws) separates the stratosphere and the mesosphere, and the **mesopause** (meez' uh paws) delineates the mesosphere from the heterosphere.

What are the differences between these layers? Well, there are actually many differences, so we will discuss each of these regions individually. However, I can tell you one general difference that exists between these layers. The concentration of the gases that make up the air in these regions decreases significantly as the altitude increases. In other words, the concentration of gases in the air of the troposphere is significantly larger than the concentration of gases in the stratosphere, which is significantly larger than the concentration of gases in the mesosphere. Even *within* a region of the homosphere, the concentration of air decreases with increasing altitude.

As you should have noticed from Experiment 3.1, the concentration of gases affects the air pressure. After all, when the candle used up the oxygen in the jar, the air in the jar could not exert as much pressure. As a result, water was forced into the jar. Well, since the concentration of gases in the atmosphere decreases with increasing altitude, the pressure that the air exerts decreases as well. As a result, air pressure decreases with increasing altitude.

The troposphere, often called earth's "weather layer," is the region of the atmosphere that contains almost all of the weather phenomena such as clouds, rain, snow, storms, lightning, hail, and the like. Because of the fact that the concentration of air decreases significantly with increasing altitude, the vast majority of the earth's air supply exists in this region. In fact, 75% of all of earth's air supply exists within the troposphere. Even within the troposphere itself, the concentration of air varies significantly with altitude. For example, the peak of Mt. Everest is 8.8 kilometers (5.5 miles) above sea level. At that altitude (which is still in the troposphere), the concentration of air is only 21% of that which exists at sea level. In other words, there is 79% less air at the top of Mt. Everest than there is at ground level! Because of this fact, mountain climbers who climb Mt. Everest (and other mountains) must bring their own oxygen supply. If they did not, there would not be enough oxygen to support their life functions!

Even at lower altitudes, there is a noticeable change in the air's concentration. For example, athletes who are used to playing their sport at low altitudes find it much more difficult to play the same sport in cities like Denver, Colorado, where the elevation is approximately one mile above sea level. This is because the concentration of air at that altitude is 90% of the concentration at sea level, so the athletes must breathe harder to get the same amount of oxygen as that to which they are accustomed.

The troposphere is also characterized by a steady drop in temperature as altitude increases. In general, for every kilometer that you increase in altitude, the temperature decreases by about 6.4 degrees Celsius. Since the term "gradient" refers to a steady change, this effect is often called the **temperature gradient** of the troposphere. This temperature gradient is responsible for snow existing on the upper parts of a mountain even in the summer time. By the time you reach altitudes of about 5 kilometers, the temperature is easily 30 degrees Celsius lower than the temperature at sea level. Since summer temperatures are usually in the range of 25-28 degrees Celsius, and since water freezes at zero degrees Celsius, you can see that even on a summer day, the temperature at altitudes of 5 kilometers stays well below the freezing point of water. By the time you reach the tropopause, the air is so thin and cold that an unprotected person would quickly lose consciousness and die.

The stratosphere, which is directly above the tropopause, has completely different characteristics than the troposphere. Virtually no weather phenomena exist there. The very highest clouds might reach the very lowest layers of the stratosphere, but that's about it. In addition, there is virtually no water vapor in this region of the atmosphere (or any higher regions, for that matter). What you do find in the stratosphere are strong, steady winds. In fact, there are well-defined "streams" of wind within the stratosphere called **jet streams**.

Jet streams - Narrow bands of high-speed winds that circle the earth, blowing from west to east

The jet streams are usually found at an altitude of 12.2 kilometers in the winter and 13.7 kilometers in the summer. Winds in the jet streams can blow at speeds of up to 400 kilometers per hour (250 miles per hour)!

One very interesting characteristic of the stratosphere is that, unlike the troposphere, temperature actually *increases* with increasing altitude. In other words, once you reach the stratosphere, it actually starts getting warmer the higher you go. Thus, the stratosphere has a temperature gradient (steady change in temperature), but its temperature gradient is precisely opposite that of the troposphere! Although the temperatures vary with the season, the lower part of the stratosphere is usually somewhere around -65 degrees Celsius (-85 degrees Fahrenheit) and the temperature increases steadily to about 3 degrees Celsius (37 degrees Fahrenheit) by the time you reach the stratopause.

Above the stratopause in the mesosphere, the air is very thin. In addition, the temperature gradient once again reverses itself, and temperature decreases with increasing altitude. By the time you reach the mesopause, the temperature is nearly -100 degrees Celsius (-150 degrees Fahrenheit).

You might be wondering why the temperature gradient reverses in the stratosphere and then again in the mesosphere. Remember, the temperature decreases with increasing altitude in the troposphere; it increases with increasing altitude in the stratosphere; and then it decreases with increasing altitude in the mesosphere. Well, it turns out that there are reasons for this, and we will discuss them in the next section. For right now, review what you have learned by studying Figure 3.2.

On the left-hand side of the figure, the altitudes of the atmospheric layers are shown. On the right-hand side, sample temperatures are given. Notice how the temperature decreases with increasing altitude in the troposphere, then it increases with increasing altitude in the stratosphere, and then decreases again with increasing altitude in the mesosphere. Notice also in the figure that the ozone layer is in the stratosphere. In Module #2, you learned what the ozone layer is. In a little while, I will discuss the "hole" in the ozone layer that concerns many people.

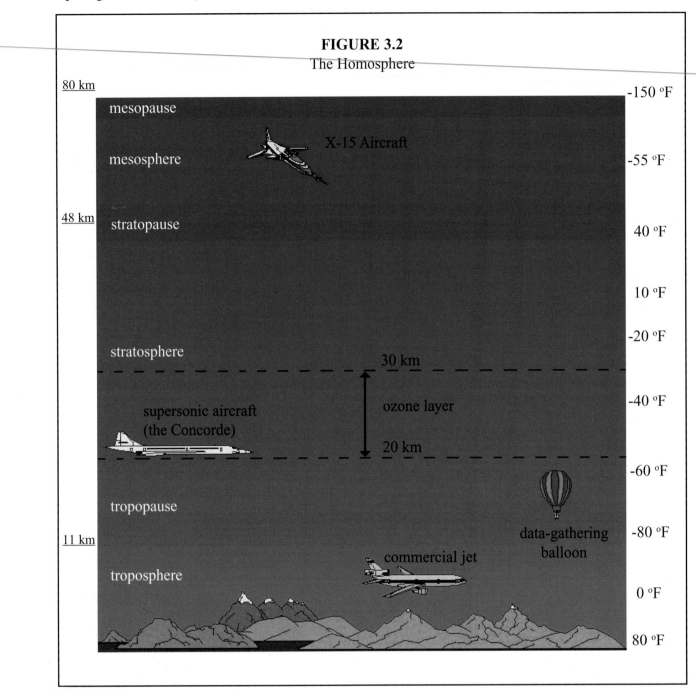

**FIGURE 3.2**
The Homosphere

## ON YOUR OWN

3.5  A supersonic jet travels in the stratosphere.  If such a plane were flying over a region that is experiencing thunderstorms, how would the supersonic jet be affected?

3.6  Water freezes at 32 degrees Fahrenheit.  Suppose you were able to watch a sealed vial of water travel up through the homosphere.  It would freeze once it got 5-7 kilometers high.  Would the frozen water ever melt as the vial traveled farther up?  If so, where would this happen?

## What is Temperature?

Now that you know a little bit about the atmosphere, you need to know why the temperature gradient exists and why it reverses twice in the homosphere. In order to understand that, however, you really need to know what temperature measures. Most people think that temperature measures heat. They think this because as temperature gets higher, we feel hotter. Although that is certainly true, it does not follow that temperature measures heat. To understand what temperature really measures, perform the following experiment.

---

**EXPERIMENT 3.2**
Seeing The Effect of Changing Temperature

Supplies:

- Ice
- Water
- Plastic bottle (The best volume would be 1 quart or 1 liter, but any size will work.)
- Balloon
- Bowl

Introduction - In this experiment, you will see what happens to air when its temperature increases. This will help you understand what temperature really measures.

Procedure:

A. Fill your bowl about 3/4 full with water and ice. There should be enough ice so that there will still be ice left in 5 minutes.
B. Take the lid off of your bottle. Hold your bottle in the icewater for about 5 minutes, so that the bottle gets cold. Try to keep as much of the bottle as possible in contact with the water. You probably can accomplish this best by tilting the bottle so that it lies in the bowl. DO NOT allow any water to get in the bottle, despite the fact that there is no lid on it.
C. Stand the bottle up in the bowl so that at least part of it is still in contact with the icewater.
D. Place the balloon on the opening of the bottle so that the neck of the balloon forms an airtight seal around the top of the bottle. The seal between the bottle and the balloon must be airtight, or this experiment will not work.
E. Take the bottle out of the bowl and sit it on the counter.
F. Empty the bowl of its icewater and let the hot water from the tap run until it gets as hot as possible.
G. Once the water is as hot as it gets, fill the bowl 3/4 of the way full again.
H. Stand the bottle in the bowl so that it is in contact with the hot water. Wait a few minutes. What happens? Draw a "before and after" picture in your lab notebook.
I. Clean everything up and put it away.

---

What does this experiment show?  Well, many science books use this kind of experiment to show that things tend to expand as the temperature increases.  While this is certainly true, it also demonstrates what temperature really measures.  You see, by sealing the bottle with the balloon when it was cold, you trapped a lot of cold air in the bottle.  As the air's temperature was increased by the hot water, the air expanded, inflating the balloon.  To understand temperature, you need to understand *why* the air expanded.

Since you cannot see the atoms and molecules in the air, it may be hard to believe this, but the molecules in the air are actually moving around at very high speeds.  Why do they move around like that?  They do so because they have a lot of energy.  Believe it or not, all substances that you see have molecules which are constantly moving.  In liquids, the molecules move around more slowly than those in the air, but they still move around.  In solid substances, the molecules cannot move around, but they do vibrate back and forth.  Now of course, you do not see this motion because you cannot see the molecules involved.  Nevertheless, the motion is still there.

Now, what are you doing when you heat something up?  You are *adding energy* to it.  So when you placed the bottle in the hot water, the energy in the hot water started flowing into the bottle.  Believe it or not, that's actually what **heat** is.

Heat - Energy that is being transferred

So heat is really energy that flows from one object to another.  As energy flowed from the hot water to the bottle, two things happened.  The bottle's temperature increased, and the water's temperature decreased.

What happened to that energy?  Well, as it flowed into the bottle, it was picked up by the molecules that made up the bottle as well as the molecules that made up the air in the bottle.  What happened when these molecules absorbed this energy?  They began to move faster.  Since the bottle is a solid object, the molecules that make up the bottle began vibrating faster.  The molecules which made up the air in the bottle started moving around faster.

Now what happened as a result of the molecules in the air moving faster?  Well, think about an individual molecule in the air that is inside the bottle.  As the molecule moves, it eventually reaches the wall of the bottle or the balloon.  At that point, the molecule cannot move *through* the bottle's wall or the balloon, so it must bounce off the bottle's wall or the balloon and change direction.  So, on a molecular level, there are billions and billions of molecules bouncing off the walls of the bottle and off of the balloon.  Now, as these molecules get more and more energy, they start traveling faster and faster.  As a result, when they hit the bottle's wall or the balloon, then they start hitting harder and harder.  They also start hitting more and more frequently, because they move from place to place more quickly.

Think about this for a minute.  If the molecules start hitting the bottle's wall and the balloon, harder and faster, what will happen?  Whatever the molecules strike will start to bulge outward because of the increased violence of the collisions.  Well, the balloon can bulge out much more easily than can the walls of the bottle, so the balloon begins to bulge.  Thus, it looks like the balloon is inflating, when in fact, it is simply bulging out as the result of more violent and more frequent collisions by the molecules in the air.

So, the molecules that make up a substance are constantly moving.  As you add energy to those molecules, they start moving around faster and faster.  This is actually why a solid substance will melt as you heat it, and if you continue to heat the liquid, it will eventually become a gas.  Remember, the molecules that make up a solid can only vibrate back and forth.  As you heat up the substance, you add energy to the molecules and they begin to vibrate faster and faster as well as farther and farther back and forth.  The more you heat the solid, the more violent the vibrations become.  Eventually, the vibrations become so violent that the molecules break free of the forces that were keeping them from moving around.  As a result, the molecules begin to move around, and the substance becomes a liquid!  If you keep heating up the liquid, the molecules starting moving faster and faster as well as getting farther and farther apart.  Eventually, the molecules move so quickly and are so far apart that they form a gas!

Thus, the change from solid to liquid to gas (and changes the other way as well) are due to changes in the energy of motion of the molecules involved.  In addition, this is why things tend to expand when they are heated.  The farther and faster a substance's molecules move, the more volume they will occupy.

How does all of this apply to temperature?  Well, when I put a thermometer in a substance, the molecules of that substance begin striking the thermometer.  At the same time, the molecules that make up the thermometer are moving as well.  Thus, collisions will be occurring between the molecules in the thermometer and the molecules of the substance that the thermometer is in.  If the molecules of the substance are moving faster than the molecules of the thermometer, then energy will be transferred from the molecules of the substance to the molecules of the thermometer.  As a result, the liquid in the thermometer heats up and expands.  This causes the column of liquid to rise, and we see a high temperature.

If, on the other hand, the molecules of the thermometer are moving faster than the molecules of the substance, then energy will go from the thermometer to the substance.  As a result, the thermometer cools down, and the liquid in the thermometer contracts.  This causes the liquid column to shrink, and we read a low temperature.  Thus, a thermometer really measures *the speed at which the molecules of a substance are moving.*  Since the speed of the molecules is directly related to their energy, we say that a thermometer measures the energy of the molecules in a substance.  That's what temperature is!

Temperature - A measure of the energy of motion in a substance's molecules

So, in the end, temperature does not measure heat (energy that is transferred); instead, it measures the motional energy of the molecules in a substance.

If you think about it, this explains why you get hot when the temperature is high and why you get cold when the temperature is low.  When the temperature is high, the molecules in the air colliding with your skin have much more energy than the molecules in your skin.  As a result, energy is transferred from the air to you.  This makes you hotter.  When the temperature is low, the molecules in your skin have more energy than the molecules in the air that are colliding with your skin.  As a result, energy is transferred from you to the air, and you end up getting colder.

---

**ON YOUR OWN**

3.7  Two cold bricks are put in contact with one another.  The first one has a temperature of -1.00 degrees Celsius and the other has a temperature of -10.00 degrees Celsius.  Is there any heat in this two-block system?

3.8  A thermometer reads 25.00 degrees Celsius.  Suppose you put that thermometer into a liquid and the thermometer reading increases to 80.17 degrees Celsius.  A bright observer notes that the temperature of the substance was actually a tad higher than 80.17 degrees Celsius the instant the thermometer was placed in it.  Is the observer correct?  Why or why not?

---

### The Temperature Gradient in the Homosphere

Now that you know what temperature really measures, you can finally learn why there is a temperature gradient in the homosphere.  Remember, the concentration of gases in the atmosphere decreases with increasing altitude.  Now the main source of warming for the atmosphere is the greenhouse effect as discussed in Module #2.  As you increase altitude, the concentration of greenhouse gases decreases, so there are fewer molecules absorbing energy.  As a result, the energy content of the troposphere *decreases* with increasing altitude.  Since the energy content of the troposphere decreases with increasing altitude, and since temperature is really a measure of the energy in a substance, the temperature decreases with increasing altitude.

Wait a minute, though.  When you reach the stratosphere, the temperature gradient changes.  Instead of decreasing with increasing altitude, the temperature begins increasing with increasing altitude in the stratosphere.  Why is that?  Does the concentration of gases increase in the stratosphere?  No, not at all.  The concentration of gases in the stratosphere still decreases with increasing altitude.  Something else is responsible for the change in the temperature gradient.  That something else is the ozone layer.  Even though the total concentration of gases decreases with increasing altitude, the ozone layer introduces an increase in the concentration of one particular gas: ozone.

Remember, ozone protects us from the ultraviolet rays of the sun by absorbing them before they reach the planet's surface.  Well, when it absorbs ultraviolet rays, the ozone absorbs the ultraviolet rays' energy as well.  Thus, even though the total concentration of gases decrease with increasing altitude, the concentration of a certain greenhouse gas (ozone) increases in the stratosphere.  As a result, the energy of the gases in the stratosphere is higher than the energy of the gases at the top of the troposphere because the gases in the stratosphere are absorbing more energy from the sun.  As a result, temperature increases with increasing altitude in the stratosphere.  Once you reach the stratopause, however, the ozone concentration falls away again, and the temperature begins to decrease with increasing altitude, as it does in the troposphere.

## The "Hole" in the Ozone Layer

Have you heard or read about the "ozone hole?"  In February of 1992, the National Aeronautics and Space Administration (NASA), shocked the world by reporting that they had conclusive evidence of a hole in the ozone layer.  Since you know what ozone in the ozone layer does for us, you understand why people were worried by such a statement.  As time went on, NASA backed up its claim by showing many graphs of data. The following figure, shows one such graph from October 8, 1993:

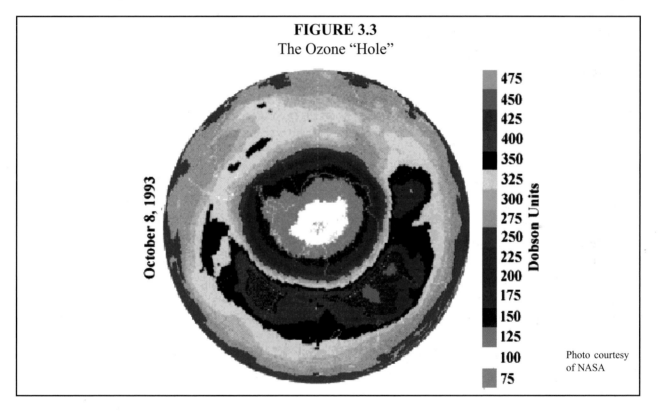

**FIGURE 3.3**
The Ozone "Hole"

Photo courtesy
of NASA

This figure shows the concentration of ozone in the ozone layer over the southern hemisphere of the world on October 8, 1993.  The color bar on the right of the figure is a legend indicating the ozone concentration level represented by the colors that you see in the graph.  Ozone concentration is measured in a unit called the "Dobson unit," named after the scientist who first developed the technique used to measure ozone concentration.

Notice that white and pink area in the middle of the graph.  Centered directly over Antarctica, it represents an area of low ozone concentration.  This is the "hole" that NASA found in the ozone layer.  In a series of very clever experiments, scientists eventually connected this decrease in ozone concentration to chlorine in the stratosphere.  They found that under certain conditions, chlorine atoms can break ozone down into oxygen, and they found such chlorine atoms in the ozone layer above Antarctica.

Well, once scientists connected the "ozone hole" to chlorine, the next question became *where did the chlorine come from*? It turns out that there are many sources that will put chlorine in the stratosphere, but one source that got a lot of attention was a class of substances called **chlorofluorocarbons**, or **CFCs**. These substances are human-made, and they turn out to be incredibly useful. The CFC known as "Freon," for example, is used in refrigeration and air conditioning. Other CFCs are used in surgical sterilizers, and others are used as fire-fighting agents. In all of their applications, these chemicals are *significantly* more efficient than what was used before CFCs were invented.

Not only are CFCs incredibly useful, they are also completely non-toxic. CFCs are so chemically inert that they do not react with our bodies or the bodies of animals. In fact, with the exception of certain microscopic organisms that tend to break CFCs down, these chemicals do not really interact with any living organisms. Since CFCs are so incredibly useful and at the same time non-toxic, they became very widely used in just a few years.

Since scientists linked the "ozone hole" to chlorine, and since they determined that at least some of this chlorine came from CFCs, many people immediately called for the elimination of CFCs. As a result, many world leaders signed a treaty called the "Montreal-London Protocol," which called for the elimination of CFC production by the year 2000 for industrialized countries and the year 2010 for developing countries. President George Bush actually required the U.S. to move ahead of that schedule, and CFC production in the U.S. was halted in 1995. Please note that "production" is different than "use." It is still legal to use CFCs in the U.S., but no one is allowed to make them any more. Eventually, then, we will run out of CFCs, but we have not yet.

Now that CFC production is eliminated in the U.S. and will soon be eliminated in other countries, lives will be saved, right? After all, if CFCs are destroying the ozone in the ozone layer, then the elimination of CFCs will save lives, right? Believe it or not, the elimination of CFCs will, in fact result in a *significantly larger loss of human life* than what would have happened if CFCs were not eliminated. How can I say that? Remember the cost/benefit analysis that we discussed in Module #2? If you do such an analysis on the elimination of CFCs, you will see that the costs far outweigh the benefit!

Let's start with the benefits of CFC elimination. When CFCs are eliminated, the ozone hole will decrease, and lives will be saved, right? Not exactly. Remember, the "ozone hole" is caused by chlorine atoms under certain conditions. The important part of that phrase is "under certain conditions." You see, the "ozone hole" was actually discovered by Dobson (the scientist after whom the ozone concentration unit is named) back in 1956, *before* CFCs were being widely-used. At that time, Dobson noted that the "hole" in the ozone layer appears over Antarctica each year from August to November. The "hole" then fills up again by November, bringing the ozone layer back to full strength.

First of all, it is important to realize that back when Dobson first discovered the "ozone hole," CFCs were not being widely used. Thus, the "ozone hole" itself cannot be traced completely back to CFCs. It seems to be, in part, a natural phenomenon. It is also important to note, however, that over the years, the "hole" has gotten deeper and deeper. In other words, the concentration of ozone in the ozone layer over Antarctica during the months of August to November is significantly (about 20%) lower today than it was when Dobson first discovered the "ozone hole." Obviously, then, something has been happening to make the "ozone hole" worse than it used to be.

At the same time, however, *the concentration of ozone in the ozone layer over Antarctica during the rest of the year (November to August) has not changed.* In other words, even though the "ozone hole" is deeper than it used to be, it is only deeper for about 3 and a half months out of the year. Once November passes, the ozone concentration returns to essentially the same level it has been since ozone levels have been measured. How can this be? Well, remember the phrase "under certain conditions?" That's the key. In early August of every year, a weather phenomenon known as the **Polar Vortex** occurs. In the Polar Vortex, winds blowing around the South Pole prevent warmer air from entering the South Pole region, and the result is constant low temperatures, as low as -90 degrees Celsius (-130 degrees Fahrenheit) and a steady rush of wind blowing upwards.

Under the conditions of the Polar Vortex, water droplets freeze into tiny ice particles and the winds push them up into the stratosphere. If these tiny ice particles happen to have trapped any molecules that have chlorine atoms in them, and if those chlorine-containing molecules survive the trip up to the stratosphere, certain chemical reactions occur on the surface of the tiny ice particles. These chemical reactions remove the chlorine from the chlorine-containing molecules, and the result is chlorine that can destroy ozone. By November, however, the Polar Vortex is gone, and with it these conditions that produce ozone-destroying chlorine in the stratosphere.

In the end, then, the "ozone hole" is a seasonal phenomenon that happens only 4 months out of the year. Also, *the "ozone hole" only appears over Antarctica*, because that's the only place in the world where a strong Polar Vortex exists. A weak Polar Vortex exists in the North Pole, but its effects are very small. Now think about it. How many people are living in Antarctica? Not many! Thus, the CFC ban will reduce the depth of the ozone hole (it won't eliminate the ozone hole because it was there *before* CFCs were really popular) for four months of the year over a region of the world where very few people actually live. As a result, the ban on CFCs will not really save any lives. In fact, not a single malady has ever been linked to the "ozone hole," so the elimination of CFCs will not even *improve* anyone's life!

What about the costs of the CFC ban? As I mentioned before, CFCs are the most efficient refrigerants, surgical sterilizers, and fire-fighting agents in the world. When they are completely banned, refrigeration, surgical sterilizers, and fire-fighting will be less efficient. As a result, *people will die*. There is no question about that. Fires will last longer before they are put out, resulting in loss of property and death. Surgical procedures will be less sterile, causing more infection, which will cause sickness and death. Finally, refrigerators will be so inefficient that third-world food distribution will be reduced, resulting in starvation!  Not only is starvation due to poor food distribution a concern, but so is food spoilage.  Even one of the big supporters of the CFC ban (Robert Watson) has admitted that "... probably more people would die from food poisoning as a consequence of inadequate refrigeration than would die from depleting ozone" (*Environmental Overkill*, Dixie Lee Ray, Regnery Gateway, 1993, p. 45).

So what does our cost/benefit analysis tell us?  The ban on CFCs will result in essentially no lives saved because of less seasonal ozone destruction, but it will certainly result in a significant loss of human life!  Why in the world, then, did the Montreal-London Protocol get signed?  Why have we already banned CFC production?  Mostly because the people who make the laws are completely ignorant about real science.  Unless you hear the whole story, it is very easy to be misinformed.  If you ask any of the legislators who support a CFC ban, you will find that none of them know the details of the "ozone hole."  As a result, they can be easily misinformed by those who are pushing some other agenda.

Please realize that misinformation exists on both sides of the issue.  Those who are against a CFC ban often quote the statistic that only 0.1% of all the chlorine-containing molecules released into the atmosphere come from human-made sources.  This statistic is true, but it is utterly irrelevant in the "ozone hole" debate.  You see, the vast majority of chlorine-containing molecules cannot survive the trip up the Polar Vortex because most chlorine-containing molecules are so chemically-reactive that they tend to react with other substances in the atmosphere long before they reach the ozone layer.  Because CFCs are relatively inert, they tend to survive the trip.  As a result, human sources are responsible for about 81% of the chlorine in the ozone layer.  Since the chlorine in the ozone layer is what is important in terms of ozone-destruction, 81% is the important statistic, not 0.1%.

As a sidelight, the reason that CFCs became so popular was that they were so efficient at certain tasks, and at the same time, they were non-toxic.  The reason CFCs are non-toxic is because they are relatively inert.  Well, what makes it possible for CFCs to survive the long trip up to the ozone layer in the Polar Vortex?  *The fact that they are relatively inert.*  We see, then, an example of an unintended consequence.  CFCs were hailed as the wonder chemical because they were useful *and* non-toxic.  The same property that makes them non-toxic, however, also makes them great ozone destroyers!

In the end, then, the "ozone hole" situation is a great example of how poorly-educated our world leaders are in the sciences.  Anyone with a rudimentary knowledge of science and an ability to do literature research could have easily found out the same facts that I am telling you.  However, because our leaders are so ignorant about these matters, legislation that will result in a tragic loss of life has been enacted.  Hopefully, students like you can change this terrible situation!

Before you leave this section, I want to dispel a very popular myth that is promoted by radical environmentalists.  It is common for certain extremists to link ozone depletion to global warming.  Hopefully, you now see that this is absurd.  Remember, the stratosphere is warmer than the tropopause *because ozone is a greenhouse gas*.  If anything, then, ozone depletion will *cool the earth*, not warm it.  Remember, however that the "ozone hole" effect is so weak and so short-lived that there is really no effect.  Nevertheless, *if* there were an effect, it would be opposite of what environmental extremists claim!

---

### ON YOUR OWN

3.9  Those who are against the CFC ban point out that CFCs are 4-8 times heavier than the nitrogen and oxygen in the air.  As a result, they say, there is no way that CFCs can float up to the ozone layer.  Why are they wrong?

3.10  Those who are for the CFC ban claim that skin cancer rates have increased in Australia as a result of the "ozone hole."  Why are they wrong?

---

### The Heterosphere

I have spent the majority of this module on the homosphere, because it is the most interesting region of the atmosphere.  However, we do need to spend some time on the heterosphere.  The heterosphere consists of two layers, the **thermosphere**(thurm' uh sfear) and the **exosphere** (ecks' uh sfear).

Thermosphere - The region of the atmosphere between altitudes of 80 kilometers and 460 kilometers

Exosphere - The region of the atmosphere above an altitude of 460 kilometers

Now it is important to realize that, for all practical purposes, these two layers of the atmosphere can be considered "outer space."  In the 1960's, we put the first men in outer space, but they never left the thermosphere.  In fact, most space shuttle missions these days occur in the thermosphere.

An interesting effect occurs in the thermosphere.  The concentration of molecules in the air is so small there, that a thermometer would read incredibly low temperatures, because there would be very few collisions between the thermometer and molecules in the thermosphere. Nevertheless, the average energy of the few molecules that are in the thermosphere is very high. Thus, if you define temperature as the average energy of each molecule in the thermosphere, then the temperature of the thermosphere is very high.  If, on the other hand, you measure temperature in the thermosphere, you end up with a very low temperature.  This interesting effect is the source of the name thermosphere.

The exosphere is composed of those atoms and molecules that are actually in orbit around the planet.  Sometimes, the atoms and molecules in the exosphere escape their orbits and go into interplanetary space.  This tends to blur the distinction between the exosphere and interplanetary space.  As a result, it is really hard to say where the exosphere ends and interplanetary space begins.

Between the upper portions of the mesosphere and the lower portions of the thermosphere, there is a region called the **ionosphere** (eye' on oh sfear).

Ionosphere - The region of the atmosphere between the altitudes of 65 kilometers and 330 kilometers where the gases are ionized

Now, of course, this definition does you no good if you don't understand what the word "ionized" means. You will learn more about this in chemistry, but for right now, you need to know that atoms are comprised of protons (which have positive electrical charge), electrons (which have negative electrical charge), and neutrons (which have no electrical charge). Atoms always have the same number of electrons and protons. As a result, they have the same amount of negative charge as positive charge. This means that, overall, atoms have no net electrical charge.

In the ionosphere, powerful radiation called **cosmic rays** collide with the atoms there and rip some of the electrons away from them. This causes the atoms to have an imbalance between positive and negative charges. With an imbalance of negative and positive charges, the atoms in the ionosphere become electrically charged. When an atom becomes electrically charged, it is no longer an atom. Instead, it is an **ion**. When an atom turns into an ion, we say that it has been **ionized**.

The ionosphere is actually a very useful portion of earth's atmosphere, because radio transmitters can use it to increase their range. Radio signals travel in straight lines. Thus, most radio signals (AM and FM radio, for example) can only be received by radios that are relatively close (within a few hundred miles) of the transmitter. Certain radio signals, however, can actually bounce off the ionosphere. As a result, these radio signals can be transmitted a great distance. Short wave radios emit signals with the ideal properties for bouncing off of the ionosphere, so short wave radios can really broadcast around the world.

Have you ever heard of the Northern Lights or the Southern Lights? Scientists call these phenomena **auroras** (uh ror' uhz). If you have never seen them, they appear in the night sky as glowing regions of brilliant, brightly-colored lights. They are the result of high-energy collisions between ionized particles coming from the sun and ionized particles in the ionosphere. The collisions involve a lot of energy, and some of that energy is converted to light, which makes up the auroras.

---

**ON YOUR OWN**

3.11 Sometimes, disturbances in the sun's magnetic field can cause disturbances in the ionosphere. Suppose you were listening to an AM radio at the time of such a disturbance. Would you notice? What about if you were listening to a short-wave radio transmission from another continent?

# ANSWERS TO THE ON YOUR OWN PROBLEMS

3.1 <u>In general, atmospheric pressure decreases with increasing altitude.</u> Think of atmospheric pressure as the weight of air pressing down on what it touches. As you increase altitude, there is less air above you. As a result, there is less weight pressing down on you.

3.2 <u>The atmospheric pressure will be reported as 32.9 inches.</u> Remember, an atmospheric pressure of 1.0 atms means that atmospheric pressure is at its average sea-level value, which is the same as 29.9 inches of mercury. Since the atmospheric pressure is 1.1 atm, we know that it must be higher than its average sea-level value. The only number given that is greater than 29.9 inches of mercury is 32.9 inches of mercury.

3.3 <u>Coca-Cola® is a homogeneous mixture while Italian salad dressing is a heterogeneous mixture.</u> Think about it. The homosphere gets its name from the fact that the air composition is the same throughout. Coca-Cola® has the same composition no matter what part of the bottle or can it comes from. Thus, it must be a homogeneous mixture. Italian salad dressing, however, has all of these herbs and spices that tend to sink to the bottom. Thus, Italian salad dressing pulled from the top of the bottle will be less spicy than that pulled from the bottom of the bottle. Thus, Italian salad dressing does not have the same composition throughout the bottle, and it is therefore a heterogeneous mixture.

3.4 <u>There is very little oxygen up that high because the air is so thin. The mask provides oxygen to the pilot.</u> Without the mask, the pilot would suffocate.

3.5 <u>The supersonic jet will not really be affected.</u> Remember, the earth's weather really occurs in the troposphere. Since the stratosphere is above the troposphere, the supersonic jet will not be affected by the weather.

3.6 <u>The water will melt near the stratopause.</u> Because of the change in the temperature gradient in the stratosphere, the vial will get warmer when it reaches the stratosphere. Near the top of the stratosphere, the temperature does creep above water's freezing point. At that point, the ice will melt.

3.7 <u>There will be heat in this system, because energy will be transferred from the warmer brick to the colder brick.</u> Despite the fact that both bricks are cold, one is warmer than the other. Thus, energy will flow from the warmer brick to the colder brick. Since heat is energy that is being transferred, heat is present!

3.8 <u>The observer is correct. When the thermometer was put into the substance, some energy got transferred from the substance to the thermometer. That's what caused the liquid in the thermometer to rise. Since energy went into the thermometer's liquid, it left the substance. This resulted in some small amount of cooling.</u> In other words, since the thermometer took a little energy from the substance, it cooled the substance slightly.

3.9  Under normal conditions, CFCs cannot rise to the ozone layer.  In the Polar Vortex, however, the steady rush of wind pushes them up to the ozone layer with ease.

3.10  There is no way that ozone depletion could be responsible for cancer in Australia because the "ozone hole" forms only over Antarctica.

3.11  You will not really notice the disturbance while listening to the AM radio, but you will notice it while listening to the short-wave radio. Remember, short-wave radios bounce their signals off of the ionosphere.  A disturbance in the ionosphere will affect the short-wave radio's signal.

# STUDY GUIDE FOR MODULE #3

1.  Define the following terms:

a. Atmosphere
b. Atmospheric pressure
c. Barometer
d. Homosphere
e. Heterosphere

f. Troposphere
g. Stratosphere
h. Mesosphere
i. Jet streams
j. Heat

k. Temperature
l. Thermosphere
m. Exosphere
n. Ionosphere

2.  Suppose the earth's air supply were twice as concentrated as it really is. Would atmospheric pressure be greater than, equal to, or less than it is now?

3.  Two students make two different barometers. The first student uses mercury, while the second uses water. Any volume of mercury is much heavier than an equal volume of water. If both barometers are the same except for the liquid used, which student's barometer will have the highest column of liquid?

4.  The average, sea-level value for atmospheric pressure is 14.7 pounds per square inch, which is the same as 29.9 inches of mercury. If the atmospheric pressure is 0.85 atms, which of the following values would correspond to atmospheric pressure as reported in a weather report?

    31.1 inches of mercury, 29.9 inches of mercury, 25.4 inches of mercury

5.  Two vials contain air samples taken at different altitudes. The first is composed of 21% oxygen, 78% nitrogen, and 1% other. The second is 95% helium, 4% hydrogen, and 1% other. Which came from the homosphere?

6.  You are reading the data coming from a data-gathering balloon as it rises in the atmosphere. You have no idea what altitude it is at, but the balloon is sending a signal from its thermometer, telling you the temperature of its surroundings. How will you know when the balloon enters the stratosphere? How will you know when it enters the mesosphere?

7.  Name the three regions of the homosphere, from lowest to highest.

8.  Although the temperature gradient changes from region to region in the homosphere, there is one gradient that stays the same. It continues to decrease as you increase in altitude, no matter where you are in the homosphere. To what gradient am I referring?

9.  A plane is experiencing a LOT of problems because of a storm in the area. Is the plane flying in the troposphere or the stratosphere?

10. A scientist has two vials of ammonia gas. She tells you that in the first vial, the gas molecules are traveling with an average speed of 20 miles per hour. In the second vial, they are traveling with an average speed of 23 miles per hour. Which vial contains the gas with the higher temperature?

11. As you are outside on a cold, winter night, you begin to shiver from the cold. Your companion says that you are shivering from the heat. Is your companion correct? Why or why not?

12. Suppose there were a layer of carbon dioxide gas in the mesosphere. What would happen to the temperature gradient in that region?

13. Why will a ban on CFCs not really produce any saved or improved lives?

14. Why will a ban on CFCs result in a tragic loss of human life?

15. Even though human civilization is responsible for less than 1% of all chlorine in the atmosphere, it is responsible for 80% of all ozone-destroying chlorine. Why?

16. What makes it possible for CFCs to travel up to the ozone layer and begin destroying ozone?

17. Where is the ionosphere and what makes it useful to us?

# Module #4: The Wonder of Water

## Introduction

Have you ever spent a long, hot day working out in the sun? What makes that kind of work bearable? Tall glasses of ice-cold water! I'm sure at one time or another you've taken a big drink of water and finished with a refreshed "Ahhh!" A drink of water is probably the best all-around thirst-quencher and refresher known to man. As I am sure you already know, we can live for as many as two weeks without food, but if we were to go even a few days without water, we would surely die. Indeed, without water, life as we know it simply cannot exist.

In addition to its necessity for life, water has many other properties that make it a truly remarkable substance. In this chapter, we will study this wondrous substance in some detail. Do you find it surprising that I can spend a whole module talking about nothing but water? You shouldn't. Water has many interesting properties that make it worth a detailed study. In fact, when you are done with this module, you will still not know anywhere near all there is to know about water!

## The Composition of Water

As we know already, water is a molecule. It contains hydrogen atoms and oxygen atoms linked together. In Experiment 1.1, you broke water molecules down into hydrogen and oxygen using the energy from electricity. Such a process is called **electrolysis** (ee leck trawl' uh sis).

Electrolysis - Using electricity to break a molecule down into its constituent elements

If you do such an experiment in a controlled way, you can actually learn something very detailed about water. To see what I mean, perform the following experiment.

---

### EXPERIMENT 4.1
The Chemical Composition of Water

Supplies:
- Water
- A 9-Volt battery (Newer ones work better.)
- Two test tubes (You can purchase these at a hobby store. If you cannot get them, skip the experiment.)
- A deep bowl (It must be deep enough so that when it is nearly full of water, the battery can stand vertically in the bowl and still be fully submerged in the water.)
- Epsom salts (You can get these at any drug store or large supermarket.)
- A tablespoon

Introduction - In Module #1, you observed the electrolysis of water by attaching wires to a battery and placing those wires in a solution of water and baking soda. In this experiment, you will use a slightly different method of water electrolysis to demonstrate the chemical composition of water.

Procedure:

A.  Fill your bowl with water.
B.  Add 3 tablespoons of Epsom salts and stir so that they dissolve. Don't worry if there are some undissolved Epsom salts at the bottom of the bowl.
C.  Stand the battery vertically at the bottom of the bowl. You should immediately see bubbles forming on each terminal. On the positive terminal of the battery, the bubbles are from oxygen gas. On the negative terminal, the bubbles are from hydrogen gas.
D.  Allow the battery to sit like this for 10 minutes. The reason you must do this is that there is air trapped in the battery, and the air escapes in the form of large bubbles. If you watch your battery for a few moments and see some large bubbles coming from the center of the terminals or from the edges of the battery, those are air bubbles that will mess up the results of the experiment.
E.  After 10 minutes, take your test tubes and fill them completely with the solution in the bowl. The best way to do this is to fully immerse the test tubes, tilting them to let all of the air out. In the end, there should be no air bubbles in the tubes.
F.  Now take the two tubes and, while keeping their tops fully immersed in the solution, hold them upside down. You should still see no air bubbles in the tubes. The solution will not pour out as long as you keep the tops of the tubes submerged in the solution at all times.
G.  As simultaneously as possible, place one tube over each terminal of the battery, once again making sure that the tops of the tubes are always submerged in the solution. Your experiment should look something like this:

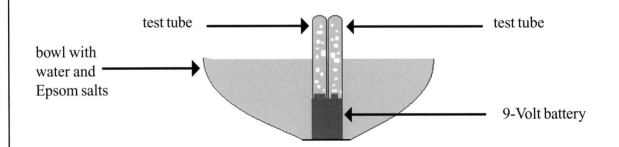

H.  With a little effort, you can make the test tubes balance on the battery so that you do not have to hold them there. If you have trouble doing that, you can tape the test tubes together and then lay two knives across the bowl, sandwiching the test tubes between the knives.
I.  Once you have gotten the test tubes to stand on the battery on their own, watch what's happening. The gases forming at each terminal travel up the test tube until they reach the top. At that point, they fill the top of the test tube, pushing away the water that was there. As time goes on, then, the gases produced at the terminals will be collected at the top of the test tubes.
J.  Let the experiment sit for a while. Go back periodically and check, and you will see that the water level in the test tubes is decreasing. As we learned in Experiment 3.1, this is due to the pressure of the gases being formed in the experiment.

K. The solution will probably turn a nasty color after a while, because substances in the battery will eventually leak into the solution. That's okay, though. It looks ugly, but it does not affect the results of the experiment. **Be sure not to get any of the solution in your mouth! The chemicals coming from the battery are toxic.**

L. When one of the test tubes is filled halfway with gas, draw what the experiment looks like in your laboratory notebook. Be sure to note which terminal is the positive one and which is the negative one. If it is not marked on the battery, the larger terminal is negative while the smaller terminal is positive.

M. Clean up and put everything away. Throw the battery away now; it is useless.

What can we learn from this experiment? Well, look at the amount of gas in each test tube. If your experiment worked correctly, there should be twice as much gas in the test tube that is over the negative terminal of the battery. Remember what I said was forming over the negative terminal of the battery? Hydrogen gas formed there, while oxygen gas formed on the other terminal. Since all of the hydrogen and oxygen gas comes from breaking down water, what can we conclude about the relative number of hydrogen atoms and oxygen atoms in a water molecule? Well, since twice as much hydrogen was formed as compared to oxygen, then there must be twice as many hydrogen atoms in a water molecule as compared to oxygen. In the end, then, this simple experiment gives us insight into the chemical composition of water.

In the next section, we will discuss this result further. Before we do that, however, I need to make a point. Your experiment may not have resulted in twice as much hydrogen as oxygen. Why? Because of experimental error. You see, every experiment has some errors in it. Hopefully, there aren't too many errors, and hopefully those few errors are small. However, sometimes the errors in an experiment are large. For example, remember when I said that air which is trapped in the battery escapes it in large bubbles? Suppose there was still air trapped in the battery despite the fact that you let it sit in the solution for ten minutes before you started collecting the gases. If some of that air escaped into one of your test tubes, you could not tell the difference between it and the gas that was supposed to collect in the test tube. That would throw off the results of the experiment. Suppose, for example, those bubbles got into the test tube that also had oxygen in it. That would make it look like there was more oxygen than what was made by the electrolysis.

Part of being a good scientist is having the ability to recognize all sources of experimental error. Sometimes, the biggest source of experimental error is the experimenter himself! In other experiments, the procedure of the experiment may just lend itself to too many errors, and the results simply cannot be trusted. How do we know, then, when to trust the results of an experiment and when not to trust them? Part of the answer is that a good scientist can recognize which experiments are rife with experimental errors and which experiments are not. The good scientist then trusts only the results of those experiments which are not full of experimental errors. The other part of the answer is what we in the scientific community call **peer review**. When a scientist performs an experiment that seems to lead to a new, interesting conclusion, other scientists in the field look closely at the experimental procedure and try to find sources of error. Sometimes, they actually perform the experiment again, trying to make sure that the original experimenter didn't cause errors in the experiment. When an experimental result passes peer review, then the experiment is considered trustworthy.

An example of how peer review finds experimental errors can be seen in the phenomenon of **cold fusion**. In March of 1989, Dr. Martin Fleischmann and Dr. Stanley Pons shocked the world with the announcement that they had seen cold fusion in one of their experiments. Briefly put, nuclear fusion is a completely clean, efficient, limitless source of energy. Compared to nuclear fission, which is what happens in today's nuclear power plants, nuclear fusion is a scientist's dream! There is no harmful waste produced (as there is in nuclear fission), no possibility of meltdown (as there is in nuclear fission), and no worry of running out of the raw materials needed (as there is in nuclear fission). There is only one problem. Until 1989, the only way to get nuclear fusion going was to use expensive, high energy reactors in a very inefficient way (this is typically called **hot fusion**). The practical upshot is that right now, nuclear fusion is simply too expensive and inefficient to be used as a power source for today's world.

Dr. Fleischmann and Dr. Pons' announcement seemed to change all of that. They claimed to have achieved nuclear fusion under very cheap, low-energy conditions. Compared to "hot fusion," they used so little energy that they called it "cold fusion." Well, the implications were mind-boggling. If this were, indeed, the case, then suddenly the world was faced with a cheap, limitless, and completely safe form of energy. Think what that would mean!

Unfortunately, Drs. Fleischmann and Pons did not submit their experiments to peer review before making their announcement. When other scientists began to examine their work, they found it riddled with experimental errors. They could not do the experiments and produce the same results that Drs. Fleischmann and Pons claimed. In the end, the vast majority of scientists who examined and tried to perform the experiments agreed that the results were from experimental error, not cold fusion. Had Drs. Fleischmann and Pons just submitted their experiments to peer review *before* announcing their results, they would have been saved a lot of embarrassment and the world would not have had its hopes raised just to have them dashed by reality!

---

**ON YOUR OWN**

4.1 Suppose you want a precise measurement of rainfall in your area, so you set a rain gauge outside. After it rains, you measure the level of water in the gauge and record the result. You then empty the rain gauge and wait for the next rain. There are at least two sources of possible experimental error with this procedure. One will lead to a measurement which is too low and the other will lead to a measurement which is too high. What are these sources of error?

## Chemical Formulas

Let's go back and think about the results of Experiment 4.1 for a moment. The experiment (if it worked properly) showed us that there is twice as much hydrogen in a water molecule as oxygen. Now I'm sure you know that the chemical symbol for water is $H_2O$. That's probably the first chemical symbol we learn. Well, our experiment demonstrates what that symbol means. The letter "H" stands for hydrogen while the letter "O" stands for oxygen. The subscript of "2" after the "H" tells us that there are 2 hydrogen atoms in a water molecule. The fact that there is no subscript after the "O" tells us that there is one oxygen atom in a water molecule. Thus, the chemical symbol "$H_2O$" means "two hydrogen atoms and one oxygen atom."

Chemical symbols like this are called **chemical formulas**, because they provide a formula by which you can understand the chemical makeup of any substance. For example, natural gas stoves, water heaters, and furnaces burn a gas called methane, whose chemical formula is $CH_4$. As we already know, the chemical symbol for hydrogen is "H. The chemical symbol for carbon is "C." Thus, this chemical formula tells us that a molecule of methane contains one carbon atom (there is no subscript after the carbon's symbol) and four hydrogen atoms (there is a subscript of "4" after hydrogen's symbol). These atoms, when linked together in those numbers, make a molecule of methane.

Notice what I needed to know to interpret a chemical formula. First, I needed to know the chemical symbols for each atom. Second, I needed to realize that if there is no subscript after a chemical symbol, that means there is only one of those atoms in the molecule. If there is a subscript, then the subscript tells me how many of those atoms exists in the molecule. So, in order to really be able to use chemical formulas, we will need to memorize all of the symbols for all of the atoms out there, right? Of course not. In this course, I will tell you the chemical symbol for any atom that you need to know. Eventually, you will become used to associating the most popular atoms with their symbols.

You need to remember, however, that not all atomic symbols are composed of just one letter. Some atoms have two letters in their symbol. The chemical symbol for neon, an atom that comprises the gas used in neon signs, is "Ne." Notice that even though there are two letters in this symbol, only one of them is capitalized. That is a general rule. All atomic symbols have only one capital letter. If there is a second letter in the symbol, it is always the lower case version of that letter. Also, you must realize that chemical symbols are not always as easily recognized as "C" for carbon and "Ne" for neon. The symbol for an iron atom, for example, is "Fe." Where does that come from? Well, the Latin name for iron begins with the letters "f" and "e." So sometimes we use two letters in an atomic symbol and sometimes we use one. Also, sometimes we base the symbol for an atom on its English name and sometimes we base it on its Latin name. Given all of that, make sure you understand the concept of chemical formulas by solving the "on your own" problems that follow.

**ON YOUR OWN**

4.2  The chemical formula for baking soda is $NaHCO_3$.  How many atoms make up one molecule of baking soda?

4.3  Vinegar's active ingredient is acetic acid, $C_2H_4O_2$.  How many of each atom (see the discussion above if you forget what the symbols are) is present in a molecule of acetic acid?

4.4  The sugar that is in green, leafy vegetables is called glucose.  A molecule of glucose contains six carbon atoms, twelve hydrogen atoms, and six oxygen atoms.  What is the chemical formula of glucose?

## Water's Polarity

Now that we know the chemical formula of water, it is time to investigate some of its very interesting properties.  Perform the following experiment to learn one of those properties.

**EXPERIMENT 4.2**
Water's Polarity

Supplies

- Glass of water
- Vegetable oil
- A Styrofoam or paper cup
- A comb
- A pen

Introduction - In this experiment, you will see how water reacts to static electrical charge and compare it to how vegetable oil reacts under the same conditions.  This will illustrate one of water's interesting properties.

Procedure

A.  First, take the pen and punch a small hole into the bottom of the cup.  The smaller the hole, the better.
B.  While holding it over the sink, pour some water into the cup from the glass.  Water should start running out of the hole in the bottom of the cup.  Make sure that the water is pouring out of the hole in a steady stream, not dripping.  If it is dripping, make your hole just a little bigger.
C.  Once the water is pouring out of the cup in a steady stream, take the comb in your other hand and vigorously comb your hair.  This is meant to make the comb develop an electrical charge.  If your hair is greasy, this may not work too well.

D.  Once you have combed your hair for a few seconds, bring the comb (teeth first) near the stream of water. You should let the comb get very close to, but not actually touch, the water stream. What happens? Write this down in your laboratory notebook.

E.  Repeat this same experiment using vegetable oil instead of water. You may have to make the hole a little bigger this time, because vegetable oil doesn't flow as easily as water does. Once you do the experiment, however, you should observe a major difference between the way oil behaves and the way water behaves when they are both exposed to an electrically charged comb.

F.  Clean up and put everything away.

What did you see in the experiment? You should have seen the stream of water bending towards the comb. Why did that happen? To learn the answer to that question, I first have to show you a model of what a water molecule looks like:

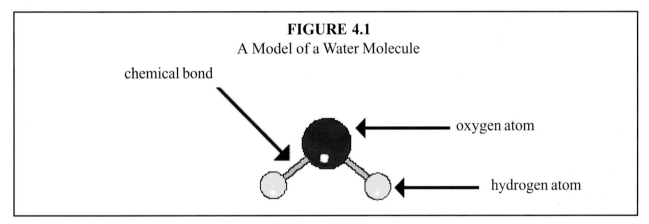

**FIGURE 4.1**
A Model of a Water Molecule

chemical bond

oxygen atom

hydrogen atom

We call this diagram a "model" because we have never actually seen water molecules. Since we can't see water molecules, we need to use pictures like this to model what they look like. Now, of course, we cannot prove that this model is correct. There is a lot of evidence which indicates that this is probably a good model of the real thing, but there is just no way of knowing for sure.

Notice that, indeed, there are two hydrogen atoms in the water molecule as well as one oxygen atom, just like Experiment 4.1 indicated. Also, notice that the blue circle representing the oxygen atom is larger than the yellow circles which represent the hydrogen atoms. Once again, there is a lot of evidence which indicates that oxygen atoms are, indeed, bigger than hydrogen atoms. The colors, of course, are arbitrary. They are just used to distinguish between oxygen atoms and hydrogen atoms. Finally, notice the bars between the oxygen atom and hydrogen atoms. They represent the **chemical bonds** that link the hydrogen atoms to the oxygen atom. Those chemical bonds are the reason for water's behavior in Experiment 4.2.

Remember in Module #3 where I mentioned that atoms are comprised of protons, neutrons, and electrons? Well, protons have positive electrical charge, electrons have negative electrical charge, and neutrons have no electrical charge. As you will learn in detail when you take chemistry, chemical bonds result when atoms within a molecule *share* their electrons. Thus, the bars in Figure 4.1 represent electrons which are shared between the oxygen atom and each hydrogen atom. This sharing of electrons keeps the atoms close together and is responsible for whatever properties that the molecule has.

In the case of water, there is actually a tug-of-war going on between the electrons that are supposedly being "shared" by the atoms. Much like two little children who continually fight over a toy that they are supposedly "sharing," the oxygen atom and each hydrogen atom fight over the electrons that they are supposedly sharing. Continuing our analogy, suppose one of the children is stronger than the other. In the absence of proper adult supervision, the stronger child will end up with the toy more often than the weaker child, right? Well, it turns out that oxygen is stronger at pulling on electrons than is hydrogen so the oxygen atom will end up with the electrons more often than will the hydrogen.

What's the big deal? Sure, oxygen isn't "playing fair," but why worry about it? Remember that electrons are negatively charged. Since the oxygen gets the electrons more often than the hydrogens, it possesses more than its "fair share" of electrons. Since it possesses more than its "fair share" of electrons, it develops a very slight negative electrical charge. In the same way, since the hydrogen atoms get less than their "fair share" of electrons, they have less negative charge than they should. With less negative charge than they should have, they end up having a slight positive charge. In our model, we could illustrate this as follows:

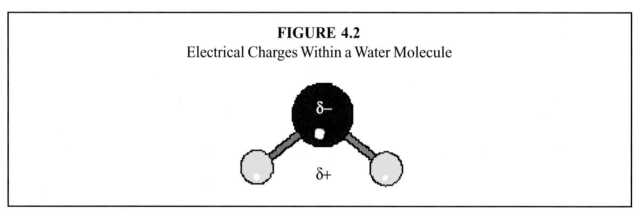

**FIGURE 4.2**
Electrical Charges Within a Water Molecule

The symbol $\delta$ is the lower-case Greek letter delta, and it is used to signify the fact that the electrical charges in the water molecule are very small. When you have positive and negative charges within the same structure, the phenomenon is called polarity (pol' air uh tee). As a result, we call water a **polar molecule**.

Polar molecule - A molecule that has slight positive and negative charges due to an imbalance in
                the way electrons are shared

How does this explain the results of Experiment 4.2? Well, when you combed your hair vigorously, the comb picked up stray electrons in your hair and, as a result, became negatively charged. As you should already know, positive charges are attracted by negative charges and vice-versa. The negative charge on the comb attracted the small positive charges on the hydrogen atoms in the water molecules. Thus, the water molecules all turned around so that their hydrogen atoms pointed towards the comb, as shown below:

Once the water molecules were aligned, the mutual attraction between the small positive charge on the hydrogen atoms and the negative charge on the comb was strong enough to *bend the water stream towards the comb*.

Now, when you did the same experiment with vegetable oil instead of water, did you see the same thing? You shouldn't have. The stream of vegetable oil should not have bent at all. Vegetable oil is not made of polar molecules. As you will learn in chemistry, electrons are shared equally between the atoms in certain kinds of molecules. These molecules, like the ones which make up vegetable oil, are called **nonpolar molecules** and have no net electrical charge. As a result, they are not affected by electrical charges. Thus, the vegetable oil should not have reacted to the charge on the comb. You might have seen a little sputtering from the stream of oil. This is caused by small bits of water or alcohol contaminating the oil. This may not have happened to you, if your vegetable oil had no such contamination.

Before we leave this section, I need to make an important point. Notice that in the previous paragraph, I said that nonpolar molecules have no net electrical charge. You need to know precisely what that means. All substances have electrical charges in them, because all substances are made of atoms which have positive charges (protons) and negative charges (electrons). Individual atoms, however, have equal numbers of protons and electrons, so the positive charges cancel out the negative charges. Thus, we can say that an individual atom has no "net electrical charge." This means that there are positive charges and negative charges all over the place, but they cancel each other out, leaving no overall charge. When atoms form molecules, there will be no net electrical charge as long as all electrons are shared equally. Once again, there are charges all over the molecule, but they cancel each other out, leaving no net charge. When electrons are shared unequally, however, they are concentrated around an atom. At that point, there are more negative charges around the atom than positive charges, and there is a net negative charge on that atom.

So, when I talk about polar molecules, I will say that they have net electrical charge. This simply means that somewhere on the molecule, the positive and negative charges do not cancel each other out, leaving an overall charge on that part of the molecule. When I talk about nonpolar molecules, however, I will say that they have no net electrical charge. This means that while there are electrons and protons everywhere in the molecule, they cancel each other out, resulting in no overall electrical charge.

**ON YOUR OWN**

4.5  Suppose you had something positively charged to hold next to the stream of water in Experiment 4.2.  Would the stream bend the same way as it did with the comb, or would it bend the opposite way?  Why?

4.6  Hydrochloric acid, HCl, is a powerful acid often used in cleaning.  While "H" stands for hydrogen, "Cl" stands for chlorine.  Chlorine atoms can pull on electrons much more strongly than can hydrogen atoms.  Is HCl polar?  If so, where is the small negative charge: on the chlorine atom or the hydrogen atom?

4.7  Chlorine gas, $Cl_2$, is a molecule comprised of two chlorine atoms bonded together with a chemical bond.  Is this molecule polar?  Why or why not?

### Water as a Solvent

The polarity of water is actually responsible for a great many of its properties.  Not the least of which is water's ability to dissolve many substances.  You've experienced this property of water all of your life.  You've probably made a soft drink by mixing a powder in water.  In many of the experiments you've done so far in this course, you've dissolved substances in water.  When you dissolve a substance in a liquid, we say that you have made a **solution**.  When making a solution, you use a **solvent** to dissolve a **solute**.

Solvent - A liquid substance capable of dissolving other substances

Solute - A substance that is dissolved in a solvent

When you dissolve salt in water, for example, water is the solvent, salt is the solute, and saltwater is the solution.

Now while you usually think of solutes as solids, it is important to note that liquids and gases can be solutes as well.  The fizz in soda pop, for example, comes from dissolved carbon dioxide.  The sweet taste comes from a liquid syrup which is also dissolved.  In the end, then, soda pop is a solution in which water is the solvent and carbon dioxide gas as well as a liquid syrup are solutes.

Water is sometimes called the "near-universal solvent," because it seems that water can dissolve nearly anything.  In fact, that's not the case.  As you will learn in the following experiment, water does not dissolve everything!

**EXPERIMENT 4.3**
Water as a Solvent

Supplies:

- Four glasses
- A measuring spoon that measures 1/2 of a teaspoon
- Sugar
- Sand
- Table salt
- Vegetable oil

Introduction - Although water dissolves many things, its does not dissolve everything. Demonstrate that for yourself with the following experiment.

Procedure

A. Take the four glasses and fill them up with warm water.

B. Measure out 1/2 of a teaspoon of sugar and mix it with the water. Write in your laboratory notebook whether or not the sugar dissolved. If the sugar disappears after vigorous stirring, then it dissolved. If you can still see it, it did not dissolve.

C. Repeat the experiment using sand, table salt, and vegetable oil. Use 1/2 of a teaspoon of each in its own glass. Write in your laboratory notebook whether or not each dissolved.

So, does water dissolve everything? Of course not. In the experiment, water should have dissolved sugar and table salt, but not vegetable oil or sand. Of course, the results of the experiment shouldn't have surprised you. Although you were probably able to guess the results of the experiment, you probably don't know the explanation behind those results. Now you can learn that explanation. As you demonstrated a few moments ago, water is made up of polar molecules. Polar molecules, as you learned, have net electrical charge. Well, that electrical charge would like to find other electrical charges to interact with. It turns out that there are two different categories of substances which contain electrical charges. The first is polar molecules. These molecules have small positive and negative charges on the molecule itself, as illustrated in Figure 4.2. There is, however, another category of substances that have electrical charges in them: ionic molecules.

Remember our discussion of ions from Module #3? Ions were once atoms that had equal numbers of electrons (negative charges) and protons (positive charges). As a result, atoms have no net electrical charge. When an atom loses or gains electrons (you'll learn how that happens in chemistry), it has an imbalance of charges. If the atom gains extra electrons, it has more negative charges than positive charges As a result, it ends up with an overall negative charge. If the atom loses electrons, it has more protons than electrons and becomes positively charged. Either way, when that happens, we say that the atom has become an ion.

Ionic molecules are made up of ions. For example, table salt is made up of molecules which contain sodium ions and chloride ions. The sodium ion results when a sodium atom loses an electron. As a result, sodium ions are positive. The chloride ion results when a chlorine atom gains an electron. Chloride ions, therefore, have a negative charge. The positive charge of the sodium ion is attracted to the negative charge of the chloride ion, and the result is that the ions come together to make a molecule.

When an ionic compound like salt is put in water, the electrical charges in the water molecules attract the electrical charges in the ions, pulling the ions away from each other. Eventually, each ion in the solute molecule is surrounded by water molecules and pulled so far away from the other ions that the substance is no longer visible in the solution. It is still there, but its ions are so far removed from each other that they exist on their own. Since the ions are too small to see, the substance seems to disappear. This is illustrated in Figure 4.3.

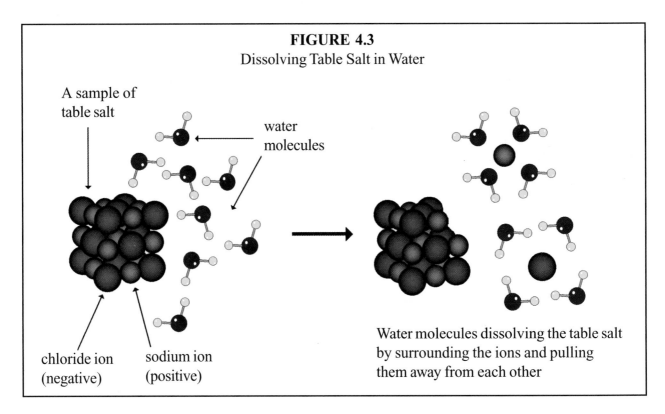

**FIGURE 4.3**
Dissolving Table Salt in Water

A sample of table salt

water molecules

Water molecules dissolving the table salt by surrounding the ions and pulling them away from each other

chloride ion (negative)    sodium ion (positive)

Notice what's happening in this figure. On the left side of the big arrow, the table salt has not dissolved yet. The positive sodium ions and the negative chloride ions are closely-packed, because their opposite electrical charges attract one another. Water molecules, however, are attracted to the ions, so they move in close to the ions. On the right side of the arrow, the table salt is beginning to dissolve. The water molecules have succeeded in pulling a sodium ion and a chloride ion away from the others. Once pulled away, other water molecules can surround each ion. For the positively-charged sodium ion, the water molecules orient themselves so that the small negative charge on the oxygen atom is close to the positive sodium ion. For the negatively-charged chloride ion, however, the water molecules orient themselves so that the hydrogens, which have a small positive charge, are as close as possible to the negative ion.  As time goes on, more water molecules will come in and pull more ions away from each other, eventually dissolving the table salt completely.

Although it is harder to picture, essentially the same thing happens when water dissolves a substance made of polar molecules.  The electrical charges in the water molecules are attracted to the electrical charges in the solute molecules.  The result is that the water molecules pull the solute molecules away from each other, dissolving the solute.

So, water dissolves substances made up of either polar molecules or ionic molecules.  If a molecule is non-polar, however, water will not be attracted to it, since a nonpolar molecule has no net electrical charges in it.  Sand and vegetable oil, for example, are made of non-polar molecules.  As a result, water will not dissolve them.  In the end, then, water dissolves substances made of polar or ionic molecules, and it will not dissolve substances made of nonpolar molecules.  The reason that water seems to dissolve almost everything is that the vast majority of compounds in Creation are either polar or ionic.  Thus, water dissolves a great many substances, but not everything.

Before we leave this section, I want to answer a question you are hopefully asking yourself.  If water cannot dissolve substances made of nonpolar molecules, can anything dissolve those substances?  The answer is yes.  The reason water cannot dissolve nonpolar substances is that water is attracted to molecules with net electrical charges.  Nonpolar molecules do not have net electrical charges, so they are only attracted to *other* nonpolar molecules.  Thus, substances made of nonpolar molecules can only be dissolved in other substances made of nonpolar molecules!

---

**ON YOUR OWN**

4.8  Water does not dissolve gasoline.  Is gasoline made up of ionic, polar, or non-polar molecules?

4.9  Suppose you did Experiment 4.3 with gasoline instead of water.  (Don't actually do it, the fumes are very dangerous!)  Would table salt dissolve in gasoline?  What about vegetable oil?

---

Hydrogen Bonding in Water

Did you think that we were done studying the polar nature of water molecules?  If so, you were sadly mistaken!  It turns out that the polar nature of water leads to its most interesting property: hydrogen bonding.  In order to really understand hydrogen bonding, we need to think about a group of water molecules together.  Remember, each water molecule has a small negative charge around its oxygen atom and a small positive charge around its hydrogen atoms.  Now, if we have a whole lot of water molecules sitting around together, what do you think will happen?  Well, since the positive charge on one molecule is attracted to any other negative charges, the water molecules will tend to align themselves so that the positive charge on the hydrogens of one molecule will be as close as possible to the negative charge on the oxygen of another molecule. In the end, it would look something like this:

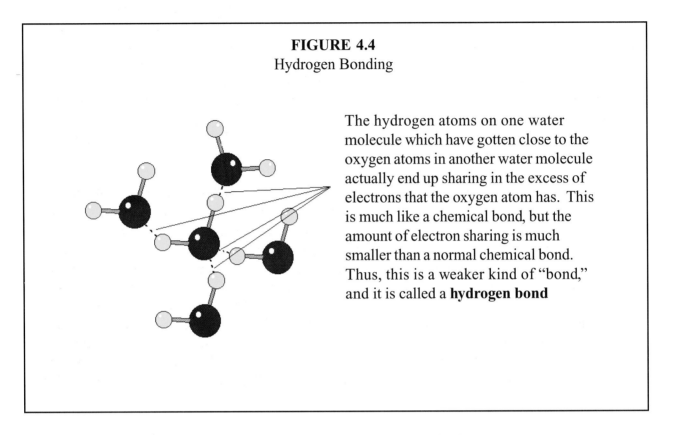

**FIGURE 4.4**
Hydrogen Bonding

The hydrogen atoms on one water molecule which have gotten close to the oxygen atoms in another water molecule actually end up sharing in the excess of electrons that the oxygen atom has. This is much like a chemical bond, but the amount of electron sharing is much smaller than a normal chemical bond. Thus, this is a weaker kind of "bond," and it is called a **hydrogen bond**

When the water molecules get close to one another in this way, the hydrogen atoms on one water molecule get very close to the oxygen atom on another water molecule. Now remember, the hydrogen atoms have less than their fair share of electrons, while the oxygen atom has more than its fair share. As a result, the hydrogen atoms on one water molecule try to make up for their lack of electrons by sharing some of the extra electron charge found on the oxygen atom of the other water molecule. If you think about it, this is like a chemical bond. Remember, you already learned that a chemical bond is made up of shared electrons. Since the oxygen has only a small excess of electrons, there is not a lot to share. Nevertheless, some sharing goes on, and as a result, a weak bond is established between the hydrogens on one water molecule and the oxygens on another. This weak bond is called a **hydrogen bond**.

Notice what hydrogen bonds do. They link *molecules* together. Chemical bonds link atoms together to form molecules. Hydrogen bonds, on the other hand, bring individual molecules close together, linking them. Thus, while a chemical bond forms between atoms, a hydrogen bond forms between molecules. Also, since hydrogen bonds are weak, they can be easily broken. For example, if you boil water, you are adding enough energy to the water to pull the water molecules far apart, breaking the hydrogen bonds. Despite the fact that the hydrogen bonds break, the chemical bonds which hold the two hydrogen atoms to the oxygen atom do not break.  Water vapor is still $H_2O$, so the chemical bonds still hold.  The molecules are so far apart, however, that the hydrogen bonds are eliminated.

So, what's the big deal?  Why is hydrogen bonding so special?  Well, there are a couple of reasons.  First, because water molecules want to hydrogen bond to each other, and because they need to get close to one another to do that, water molecules tend to stick much closer together than do other molecules.  For example, consider the following molecules: $H_2S$, $H_2Se$, and $H_2Te$.  Those chemical formulas look a lot like $H_2O$, don't they?  In fact, the only real difference is that the other molecules have a different atom in place of the oxygen atom.  From a chemistry point of view, those three molecules are very similar to water.  In fact, they are the chemicals most like water in all of Creation.  Guess what, though?  All three of those molecules are *gases at room temperature*!

Why is it that water is a liquid at room temperature, while other chemicals similar to water are gases?  The answer is hydrogen bonding.  Remember from Module #3 that the major difference between a liquid and a gas is how far apart the substance's molecules are and how quickly they move around.  Well, hydrogen bonding keeps the water molecules close together and limits their movement somewhat.  As a result, water is a liquid at room temperatures when other chemically similar substances are gases.  We are, in fact, very "lucky" that this is the case.  Water is one of the basic needs of life.  All biochemists agree that if water were not liquid at room temperature, life as we know it could not exist!  Despite the fact that *all chemically similar molecules* are gases at room temperature, water is a liquid, as it must be for life.  The chemical explanation for this is hydrogen bonding, but the real explanation, of course, is the Creator.  He designed the world and its physical laws, and hydrogen bonding was a special provision that He made in order to make life possible!

Hydrogen bonding actually gives water another unique property.  To learn about that property, perform the following experiment.

---

**EXPERIMENT 4.4**
Comparing Solid Water to Solid Butter

Supplies:

- A stick of butter or margarine  (It must be fresh from the refrigerator so that it is solid.)
- Two small glasses
- Water
- An ice cube
- A Stove
- A Saucepan
- A Knife  (A serrated one works best.  You will use it to cut the butter.)
- A Spoon

Introduction - You should have already learned that when most things are heated, they expand, and when they are cooled, they contract. This is not always the case with water. This experiment demonstrates that fact.

Procedure:

A. Take a stick of butter and look at the tablespoon markings on the foil which covers the stick of butter. Using those markings as a guide, cut 1/2 of a tablespoon off of the end of the stick with the knife so that you have a small square of butter.
B. Unwrap both the piece you cut off and the rest of the stick.
C. Put the stick into the saucepan, and put the 1/2 tablespoon of butter you cut off of the end back in the refrigerator until it is needed in step G.
D. Heat the butter in the saucepan over low heat until it is completely melted. Stir it with the spoon to keep it from boiling.
E. When the butter is completely melted, carefully pour it into the small glass. You will then have a glass of liquid butter.
F. Now fill the other glass with water.
G. Go to the refrigerator and get the 1/2 tablespoon of butter that you put there, and also get an ice cube from the freezer.
H. Drop the ice cube in the water.
I. Drop the 1/2 tablespoon of butter in the liquid butter.
J. Note in your laboratory notebook what happened to the ice cube and what happened to the solid square of butter.
K. Clean up and put everything away.

What was the difference in behavior between the ice cube and the square of butter? Well, when you dropped the ice cube into the water, it should have floated. When you dropped the square of butter in the liquid butter, it should have sunk. Why the difference? Well, in nearly every substance in the world, the molecules get closer when the substance turns solid and get farther apart as the substance turns into a liquid. Butter is an example of such a substance. Thus, the molecules which made up the solid butter were closer together than the molecules which made up the liquid butter. As a result, the solid butter pushed its way through the liquid butter and sank. For water, however, precisely the opposite is true. When water is a solid, its molecules must stay in a rigid arrangement that reduces the strength of its hydrogen bonds. When water is a liquid, however, its molecules are free to move close enough together to hydrogen bond strongly. As a result, *water molecules are closer together when water is a liquid compared to when water is a solid.* Because of this, the ice cube could not push its way through the water molecules, and the ice cube stayed afloat.

So, unlike almost any other substance in Creation, when water is a solid its molecules are actually farther apart than when it is a liquid. As a result, solid water (ice) floats in liquid water. Once again, we are quite "lucky" that this is the case. After all, what happens to lakes in the winter? They freeze don't they? Does all of the water in the lake freeze? Of course not. If that were the case, then all living things in that lake would die. Instead, as the water freezes, it *floats to the top of the lake* because of water's unique property. As a layer of ice builds up on top of the lake, it insulates the water below, and at some point, no more water will freeze! Because of this, the living organisms in the lake survive the winter. Think about all of the food that we get from lakes or from other creatures that depend on the living organisms in a lake. Without water's unique property, lakes could not support life, and most likely, we would not be able to survive! This is more striking evidence for the awesomeness of our Creator!

---

**ON YOUR OWN**

4.10  Water has a very high boiling point (the temperature at which it boils) compared to most other substances which are liquid at room temperature. Use hydrogen bonding to explain why this is the case.

4.11  Butane is a gas at room temperature but is stored under pressure as a liquid in a butane lighter. The chemical formula is $C_4H_{10}$. Isopropyl alcohol (commonly called rubbing alcohol) is another liquid that you might have around the house. Its chemical formula is $C_3H_8O$. One of these liquids participates in hydrogen bonding. Which one?

---

### Water's Cohesion

The polarity of water molecules, combined with hydrogen bonding, tends to keep water molecules close together when it is a liquid. Once they are close, they tend to want to stay close. Although the water molecules will move around, as all molecules do in liquid form, they still stay close together. This phenomenon is often called **cohesion** (coh he' shun).

Cohesion - The phenomenon that occurs when individual molecules are so strongly attracted to
          each other that they tend to stay together, even when exposed to tension

What does this definition mean? Perform the following experiment to find out.

---

**EXPERIMENT 4.5**
Water's Cohesion

Supplies:

- Water
- A bowl
- A sewing needle
- Thread
- Dish soap
- Someone to help you

Introduction - Water molecules are attracted to one another by hydrogen bonds as well as the electrical charges that are the result of polarity. Because they are attracted to one another, they do not like to be pulled apart, as this experiment will demonstrate.

Procedure

A. Fill the bowl with water.
B. Cut two equal lengths of thread and hold them parallel to one another about an inch apart.
C. Have your helper lay the needle on those two lengths of thread so that the needle is cradled by the threads.
D. Using the threads, gently move the needle over the center of the bowl and slowly lower it onto the top of the water. Continue to lower the threads, and you will eventually see that the needle is floating on the water. Let go of the threads and allow them to sink.
E. Now add a few drops of dish soap to the water, away from the needle. What happens?
F. Clean up and put everything away.

What happened in the experiment? The needle floated on the water. Despite the fact that the needle is heavy enough to sink in the water, it did not. Why not? The answer is water's cohesion. You see, the water molecules are close together. In order for the needle to sink, it needs to push them out of the way. The water molecules fight that push, however, because they are attracted to one another due to hydrogen bonding and their own polarity. The sewing needle, then, was exerting pressure on the water molecules. The water molecules, however, did not want to move apart, so they fought that pressure. That's cohesion.

What happened when you added the dish soap? Well, most likely, the needle was shoved directly opposite of where you placed the dish soap, and then it probably sank suddenly. Why? Well, the active ingredient in dish soap (sodium stearate) is composed of long molecules which are strongly attracted to water. When you added the dish soap, those long molecules got in between the water molecules and forced them apart. Once they got so far apart that they could not hydrogen bond to one another effectively, they lost their cohesion, and the needle was able to sink.

The phenomenon demonstrated in the experiment is called **surface tension**. Although that is an adequate term for the effect in the experiment, it is a rather specific term. It refers to the effect of cohesion at the surface of a liquid. The best way to think about this is to realize that cohesion causes surface tension. Because of cohesion, the surfaces of most liquids resist tension. Water has one of the greatest tendencies towards cohesion, so it also has one of the largest surface tensions in all of Creation. Even though water has a large surface tension, you have to realize that compared to most of what you and I are familiar with, that surface tension is still pretty small. After all, you had to be very careful in how you laid the needle in the water. If you had tried to put it on the water's surface with your hands, it would have sunk. So don't think that the surface tension of water is so great that it can keep most things from sinking. Nevertheless, the surface tension is real, as was demonstrated in the experiment.

Water's cohesion is a very important property in plants. As you will learn in biology, water travels up through plants in small tubes called **xylem** (zy' lum). Water's cohesion is what makes that possible. Without its cohesion, water could not travel upwards in plants, and thus plants could not exist. Once again, this is great testimony to the creative genius of God.

---

**ON YOUR OWN**

4.12 Water's cohesion is a necessary property in order for plants to survive. The surface tension caused by that cohesion is used by another organism in nature: a pond-dwelling insect. To what insect am I referring?

---

## Hard Water and Soft Water

Have you ever heard of "hard" water? If you live in a city, you might have hard water coming out of your faucets. What is hard water? Well, water that comes into our houses was, at one time or another, in a lake, stream, or underground reservoir. For most people, that water goes through some sort of treatment process before it comes into their home. In the treatment process, the water is filtered to get rid of foreign particles, and then chlorine is usually added to kill the microscopic organisms that thrive in the water. Most water treatment plants also add fluoride to the water for good dental hygiene.

Many people think that hard water is a result of the treatment process I just described. This is not the case. In fact, if you get your water from a freshwater well with no treatment process at all, you are just as likely to have hard water as is someone who gets their water from a water treatment plant. Hard water is the result of the *source from which the water is taken*. Some areas of the world (especially the midwestern United States) have rocks (like limestone) which are rich in calcium. This calcium is usually in molecules that make up ionic compounds. Limestone, for example, is made up of ionic molecules of calcium oxide, or CaO. This molecule is comprised of a positive calcium ion and a negative oxygen ion.

What does water do to ionic substances? It dissolves them. Water from regions of the world which are rich in limestone and other calcium-containing rocks tends to have calcium ions dissolved in it. That's what hard water is.

Hard water - Water that has certain dissolved ions in it, predominately calcium ions

Just like salt dissolved in water makes water taste bad, calcium ions dissolved in water also makes the water taste differently. Some people who are used to the taste actually think it makes water taste better, but most people think it tastes worse. Also, when hard water evaporates, it leaves a film behind. This film is the result of the calcium-containing ionic compounds that cannot evaporate with the water. This film builds up in sinks, bathtubs, and toilets to make the stains referred to as "hard water stains." When you shower or bathe in such water, you often do not feel as clean as you would like because the film tends to remain on your skin and hair. Also, a chemical reaction occurs between most laundry detergents and calcium ions dissolved in hard water. This chemical reaction makes the laundry detergent less effective at cleaning. Although the calcium ions in water pose no health risks, most people simply would rather not have them in the water due to these other concerns.

Some detergent manufactures actually have a special formulation of their laundry detergent designed to get rid of the calcium ions in hard water. This makes the detergent much more effective at cleaning. However, many people get rid of hard water completely by "softening" it with a water softener. In a water softener, a chemical process called "ion exchange" removes the calcium ions from the water. In this process, however, the calcium ions must be replaced with something else. That something else is usually sodium ions. If you have a water softener, or if you know someone who does, you probably know that in order for the water softener to work, salt must be added to it. Recall that salt is made up of sodium ions and chloride ions. In a water softener, the sodium ions from the salt are exchanged with the calcium ions in the water.

This water-softening process works very well because sodium ions are not well-detected by our taste buds. As a result, the "funny" taste of hard water is removed. Also, sodium ions do not form the ionic compounds that leave a film behind after water evaporates. As a result, you feel cleaner when bathing in soft water and there are fewer hard water stains left behind in sinks, bathtubs, and toilets. Also, sodium ions do not react with laundry detergents, so laundry detergents work more effectively.

Although soft water is more pleasant than hard water, there is actually a health risk for some people. Sodium ions can cause heart troubles in certain people. The amount of sodium ions you get by drinking soft water is relatively small compared to the amount of sodium ions you get through your diet. Nevertheless, people who are on strict sodium-control regimes should either not soften their water or use more expensive, sodium-free water softener salts.

# ANSWERS TO THE ON YOUR OWN PROBLEMS

4.1  <u>There will be a length of time between when it stops raining and when you measure the amount of water in the gauge.  During that time, water will evaporate, causing your result to be too low.  The second source of error occurs when you dump the water out.  Unless you dry the gauge thoroughly, there will be water droplets left in the gauge.  If the next rain falls before these water droplets have a chance to evaporate, your next measurement will be too large.</u>  There could be more errors as well.  These are the two that I thought of.

4.2  The Na is one atom since the second letter is lower case.  The other letters each represent an atom since they are all capitals.  There are no subscripts after the Na, H, or C, so there is only one each of them.  There is a subscript of 3 after the O, indicating 3 oxygen atoms.  This makes <u>6</u> total.

4.3  The C stands for carbon and there is a subscript of 2, indicating <u>2 carbon atoms</u>.  The H is for hydrogen, and there is a subscript of 4 after the H, making <u>4 hydrogen atoms</u>.  Finally, the O represents oxygen and there is a subscript of 2, indicating <u>2 oxygen atoms</u>.

4.4  Carbon is represented by C, the symbol for hydrogen is H, and oxygen is represented by O.  You put subscripts after each to indicate the number.  Thus, the chemical formula is <u>$C_6H_{12}O_6$</u>.

4.5  <u>The stream will bend the same way it did before: towards the comb.</u>  If you thought it should bend the other way because of the opposite charge, think about it for a moment.  The water molecules are originally all jumbled around, pointing in no particular direction.  The reason the stream bends is that in the presence of a charged object, the water molecules re-orient themselves so that the opposite charge is facing the object.  Thus, the water stream will always be attracted to the charged object, because the water molecules can point whichever way they want to, and they will always want to point so that the charge opposite the charged object is pointed towards the object.

4.6  <u>HCl is polar.  The chlorine will have the small negative charge.</u>  After all, if the chlorine can pull on the electrons with more strength, it will win the battle and get the electrons.

4.7  <u>Chlorine gas is not polar, because the only two atoms in the molecule are the same.  Thus, they pull on electrons with equal strength</u>.  Since they pull with equal strength, neither one of them will win more than its fair share of electrons.

4.8  <u>Gasoline is made up of nonpolar molecules.</u>  The only substances that water cannot dissolve are nonpolar substances.

4.9  <u>Table salt would not dissolve, but vegetable oil would.</u>  After all, nonpolar substances dissolve only other nonpolar substances.  Since table salt is ionic, it will not dissolve in a nonpolar substance.  Since vegetable oil is nonpolar, it will dissolve in a nonpolar substance.

4.10  <u>Water has a high boiling point because the hydrogen bonds hold the molecules together.  In order to turn into a gas, the water molecules need to get far apart from one another.  When you heat something, you are giving it energy.  Because the hydrogen bonds hold the molecules together, it takes a lot of energy (thus a high boiling temperature) to pull them apart.</u>

4.11  <u>The isopropyl alcohol participates in hydrogen bonding.</u>  Remember, hydrogen bonding in water takes place between the hydrogen and oxygen atoms.  There are plenty of hydrogen atoms in butane, but no oxygen atoms.  The other way you can tell is that butane is a gas at room temperature, thus the molecules are not held together tightly.  Isopropyl alcohol is a liquid at room temperature, indicating that its molecules are held more tightly together.  Between the two, then, the alcohol is the more likely one to have hydrogen bonds.

4.12  <u>The water strider, which is sometimes (incorrectly) called the water spider</u> is the pond-dwelling insect to which I am referring.  This insect "walks on water," because the pressure that it exerts with its legs is less than the surface tension brought about by cohesion.

**STUDY GUIDE FOR MODULE #4**

1. Define the following terms:

a.  Electrolysis
b.  Polar molecule
c.  Solvent
d.  Solute
e.  Cohesion
f.  Hard water

2.  Suppose you did an electrolysis experiment like Experiment 4.1 on hydrogen peroxide, whose chemical formula is $H_2O_2$. Which of the following results would you expect: (a) same as with water, (b) equal amounts of hydrogen and oxygen, or (c) twice as much oxygen as hydrogen.

3.  Suppose you performed Experiment 4.1 with a test tube which had a crack in it. Gas could slowly leak out that crack, but not nearly as quickly as it was being made in the experiment. Suppose further that the crack was in the test tube which held hydrogen gas. Which chemical formula might result from such a botched experiment: HO or $H_4O$?

4.  Epsom salts, which you used in Experiment 4.1, have the chemical formula of $MgSO_4$. If Mg is the symbol for magnesium, S stands for sulfur, and O represents oxygen, how many of each atom are in a molecule of Epsom salts?

5.  Calcium carbonate is an ionic substance that is commonly called "chalk." If this molecule has one calcium atom (Ca), one carbon atom (C), and three oxygen atoms (O), what is its chemical formula?

6.  One of the most common household cleaners is ammonia, whose chemical formula is $NH_3$. How many atoms are in a molecule of ammonia?

7.  A molecule is comprised of atoms that all pull on electrons with the same strength. Will this molecule be polar?

8.  Baking soda dissolves in water. Will it dissolve in vegetable oil, which is a nonpolar substance?

9.  Carbon tetrachloride will not dissolve in water. Is it made of ionic molecules, polar molecules, or nonpolar molecules?

10.  Suppose you were able to count the molecules in a substance. Which would have more molecules, 1 liter of liquid water or 1 liter of ice?

11.  If the substance in question #10 were virtually any other substance, what would the answer be?

12.  What is responsible for water being a liquid at room temperature as well as water's cohesion?

13.  What causes surface tension?

14.  Why is water harder in certain regions of the world than in others?

# Module #5: The Hydrosphere

## Introduction

Have you ever wondered what it would be like to travel in outer space? I confess that I dreamed of being an astronaut when I was young. Well, if I ever were to travel in outer space, I expect that one of the most breathtaking sights I would see would be one of my first: a look back at our planet. Astronauts have said that there are simply no words to describe that sight, and although no picture can do it justice, many have been taken. Figure 5.1 is one such picture.

**FIGURE 5.1**
The Earth as Viewed From Outer Space

*Photo from the
MasterClips collection*

Isn't God's Creation marvelous? As you should be able to tell from its shape, the brown object in the picture is the continent of Africa as well as the Arabian Peninsula. The white stuff is, of course, cloud cover. What color really dominates, however? The blue. In fact, blue dominates the picture so much that astronomers and astrophysicists call earth "the blue planet." What causes the blue color? The *water*. The earth is predominately water. In fact, 71% of the surface of the earth is covered with water in the form of oceans, lakes, ponds, rivers, creeks, and streams. But that's not the end of the story! Some of the water on our planet isn't visible from above because it is underground. Even the white parts of Figure 5.1 are really water, because

~~clouds are made up mostly of water.  Finally, there are icebergs and glaciers, made up of water in~~ its solid phase.  In short, our planet is "overflowing" with water.

Collectively, all of these water sources are called the **hydrosphere** (hi' droh sfear), and they are essential for life's existence.

<u>Hydrosphere</u> - The mass of water on a planet

As I said in the introduction to the previous module, people can live for two weeks or more with no food, but without water, we would die in a day or two.  That's why statesman and scientist Benjamin Franklin said, "When the well's dry, we know the worth of water."

As you know, water exists as liquid (what we usually call "water"), gas (which we call "water vapor"), and solid (known as "ice").  Did you know that of all the planets in our solar system, earth is the *only one* that has water in its liquid form?  It's one of the main reasons that life cannot exist on any of the other planets and does exist here on earth.  Liquid water, a necessity for life, can only be found in one place: the planet earth.  Does that mean there isn't water on the other planets?  No.  It means that on the other planets, water is either a gas or a solid, not a liquid.  Why is earth so special?  There are many reasons.

First of all, water is only a liquid in a certain temperature range (above 0 $^{\circ}$C [32 $^{\circ}$F] and below 100 $^{\circ}$C [212 $^{\circ}$F]).  Thus, in order for a planet to have liquid water, there must be regions that are within that temperature range.  Well, the vast majority of the earth is in that temperature range, so the vast majority of the water on the earth is liquid!  What controls the temperature of a planet?  There are two important factors: the distance from the sun and the atmosphere.  As you have already learned, the greenhouse effect that is caused by earth's unique atmosphere keeps the average temperature of the earth at a balmy 50 $^{\circ}$F.  As you have already seen, if the mixture of gases in the atmosphere were to change even slightly, the temperature would go up or down, potentially out of the range necessary for water to exist as a liquid.  In addition, scientists have estimated that if the earth were only 2% closer to the sun, it would be so warm that the vast majority of its water would exist as a gas.  Similarly, if the earth were a mere 2% farther away from the sun, most of its water would exist as ice.  Thus, earth has *just the right mixture of gases in its atmosphere* and *just the right distance from the sun* to ensure that the vast majority of its water is liquid.  No other planet we know of is like this!

Do you see what I'm trying to say here?  In the previous module, you learned that unlike the molecules most chemically similar to water, it is naturally a liquid at room temperature.  Now you have learned that earth's temperature is quite unique, because of its atmosphere and its distance from the sun.  That's an awful lot of coincidences, don't you think?  If earth were just a little closer to or farther away from the sun, water would not be a liquid on earth, and as a result, life could not exist.  If the earth's atmosphere were slightly different than it is now, we would have the same result.  If water didn't participate in hydrogen bonding, then it would not be liquid at the earth's temperature.  In the end, it seems that water, earth, and life were all *designed* for each other, doesn't it?  That should not surprise any scientist that believes in a supreme Designer, but it should certainly astound any scientist that does not!

<u>The Parts of the Hydrosphere and the Hydrologic Cycle</u>

Since the hydrosphere is actually the sum total of all water (gas, liquid, and solid) that exists on the planet, it is important to take a look at all of the sources of water on the earth. The vast majority (97.25%) of earth's water is found in the oceans. Since the oceans contain saltwater, most of earth's water supply isn't even drinkable! Only 2.75% of earth's water supply is freshwater and therefore at least potentially drinkable. Where is the majority of earth's supply of freshwater? Most people think it is contained in the lakes, ponds, rivers, streams, and creeks on the planet, but they are wrong! It turns out that almost three-quarters of the freshwater on the earth exists in the glaciers and icebergs of the planet. A large fraction of the remaining freshwater is underground. Scientists call this water **groundwater**. In the end, less than 1% of the earth's freshwater supply is in the lakes, ponds, rivers, streams, and creeks of the planet. This water, called **surface freshwater**, is what we typically think of when we think of earth's freshwater supply. However, it represents only a tiny, tiny fraction of the freshwater that the earth really holds, and even a tinier fraction of all of earth's water. Table 5.1 summarizes the sources of water on the planet.

**TABLE 5.1**

| Water Source | Type of Water | Percent of Hydrosphere |
|---|---|---|
| Oceans | saltwater | 97.250% |
| Glaciers and Icebergs | freshwater | 2.050% |
| Groundwater | freshwater | 0.685% |
| Surface Water (not oceans) | mostly freshwater | 0.009% |
| Soil Moisture | freshwater | 0.005% |
| Atmospheric Moisture | freshwater | 0.001% |

Although you do not need to memorize this table, there are a few facts that I would like you to remember:

1. **The vast majority of earth's water supply is contained in the oceans as saltwater.**
2. **The vast majority of earth's freshwater supply is stored in icebergs and glaciers.**
3. **The largest source of *liquid* freshwater is groundwater.**

If you remember these facts, there is no need to memorize the table.

I am going to discuss each water source in the table individually as I go through this module. Before I do that, however, I want to show you that these sources are *not isolated from each other*. Even though we can list them as different water sources and account for how much water is in each of them, they do interact with one another, which makes for some very interesting science.

The interaction between these sources of water is described by the **hydrologic** (hi droh loj' ik) **cycle**.

<u>Hydrologic cycle</u> - The process by which water is continuously exchanged between earth's various water sources

The hydrologic cycle is best illustrated by a figure.

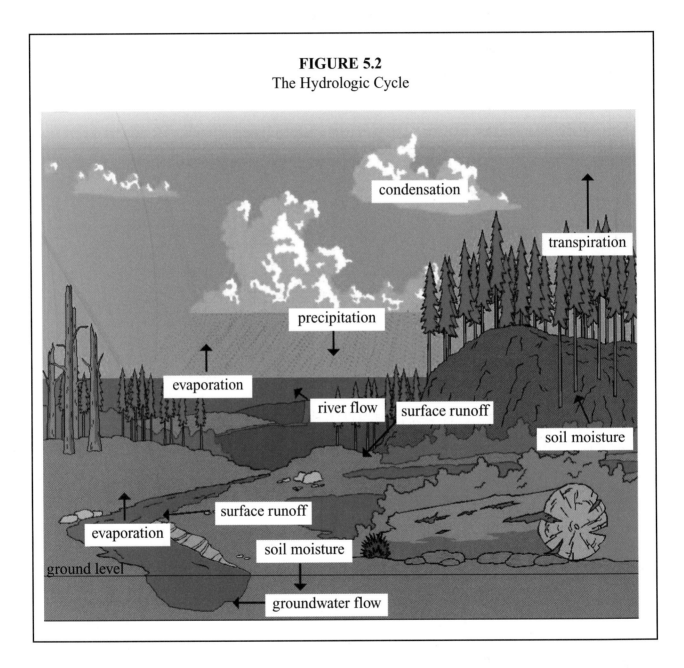

**FIGURE 5.2**
The Hydrologic Cycle

There are many ways of viewing and discussing the hydrologic cycle, but for the purposes of this course, Figure 5.2 covers the major concepts. Water gets into the atmosphere predominately by **evaporation** and **transpiration**. Although you probably know what evaporation is, you might not be familiar with the other term:

<u>Transpiration</u> - Emission of water vapor from plants

As a part of a plant's natural life processes, it emits water vapor. We call that process transpiration. If you think about it, evaporation takes water out of the oceans, lakes, rivers, and streams, while transpiration takes water from the soil. After all, plants absorb water from the soil, so any water that they emit must have originally come from there. Thus, transpiration depletes **soil moisture**. Soil moisture can also be depleted when it soaks down into the groundwater sources and feeds into lakes, rivers, and streams by the process of **groundwater flow**.

When evaporation and transpiration take place, water vapor goes into the atmosphere. It then forms clouds by a process which we call **condensation**.

<u>Condensation</u> - The process by which water vapor turns into liquid water

I will discuss cloud formation in more detail a bit later. Eventually, the oceans, lakes, rivers, streams, and soil moisture all get replenished when the water in the clouds falls out of the atmosphere as **precipitation**.

<u>Precipitation</u> - Water falling from the atmosphere as rain, snow, sleet, or hail

Some of the precipitation falls directly into the oceans, lakes, rivers, streams, and some of it falls onto land. That water can replenish the soil moisture, or it can run along the surface of the land into an ocean, lake, river, or stream as **surface runoff**.

Now don't get bogged down in the details so much that you miss the big picture here. It is important to know all of the processes in the hydrologic cycle, but it is also important to step back and look at the cycle as a whole. Look at what's happening. Water that started in the ocean can evaporate and form clouds. When those clouds finally cause precipitation, that water might very well fall into a lake, river, or stream. It also might become surface runoff or groundwater which eventually feeds a river, lake, or stream. As a result, water that starts out in the ocean can very easily be transferred to one of the freshwater sources in the hydrosphere. In the same way, a freshwater river might dump into the ocean, allowing freshwater to be transferred to the ocean via **river flow**. Alternatively, water that evaporates from a freshwater source might eventually precipitate in an ocean, once again transferring water from a freshwater source to an ocean, which is a saltwater source. The point is that the hydrologic cycle constantly exchanges water between all of the sources in the hydrosphere. Think about that. Because of the hydrologic cycle, the next drink that you take might contain water which was once at the bottom of the ocean!

If you think it odd that water can be transferred from the ocean to a freshwater source, perform the following experiment.

## EXPERIMENT 5.1
Evaporation, Condensation, and Precipitation

Supplies:

- Water
- Salt
- Ice
- A tablespoon
- A small saucepan
- A saucepan lid or frying pan lid larger than the saucepan used
- A large bowl (It should not be plastic, as it will get hot.)
- Potholders
- A zippered plastic sandwich bag
- Stove

Introduction - In the hydrologic cycle, water can be transferred from a saltwater source (the ocean) to a freshwater source through the process of evaporation, condensation, and precipitation. This experiment will show you how that works.

Procedure:

A. Fill the saucepan about three-quarters full with water.
B. Add three tablespoons of salt to the water and stir to make as much salt dissolve as possible. Do not be concerned if you can't get it all to dissolve.
C. Taste the saltwater you have made. Please note that you should **NEVER** get into the habit of tasting things in an experiment unless someone who knows a lot more chemistry than you do (like me) says to do so. In this case, I know that you are not at risk of poisoning yourself by tasting the saltwater you have just made. However, there may be times when you make something in an experiment which *you* think will not hurt you, but is, in fact, quite toxic. So **DO NOT TASTE THINGS IN AN EXPERIMENT UNLESS I TELL YOU TO DO SO!**
D. Tastes bad, doesn't it? Now set the pan of saltwater on the stove and start heating it up. Your goal is to have vigorously boiling water, so turn up the heat!
E. While you are waiting for the saltwater to boil, take your zippered sandwich bag and fill it full of ice. Zipper it shut so that no water from the ice can leak out.
F. Once the saltwater has started boiling vigorously, place the bowl next to the saucepan. The bowl should not be on a burner. You do not want to heat the bowl. You just want it close to the boiling water.
G. Now use the potholder to hold the saucepan lid and put the zippered sandwich bag full of ice on top of the lid. You may have to use a finger or two from the hand holding the lid to make sure that the bag of ice stays on top of the saucepan lid.

H. Take the lid and hold it so that one end (the one with the most ice on it) is over the saucepan and the other end is over the bowl. Tilt the lid so that it tilts toward the bowl. In the end, your setup should look like this:

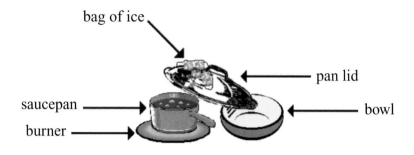

I. Hold the lid there for a little while and watch what happens on the underside of the lid. **BE CAREFUL! EVERYTHING HERE IS HOT!** Notice that water droplets are forming on the underside of the lid over the saucepan and they slowly drip down the lid towards the bowl.

J. If your arm gets tired, you can set the lid down so that part of it rests on the saucepan and the rest sits on the bowl. Make sure that the bowl is lower than the saucepan so that the lid still tilts towards the bowl.

K. Eventually, you will see water dripping off of the pan lid and into the bowl. Wait until there is enough water in the bowl to be able to take a drink. Once that happens, turn off the burner and wait a moment.

L. **Using potholders**, take the lid away and put it in the sink. Pour the half-melted ice out of the bag and throw the bag away (or recycle it). **Still using potholders**, take the bowl away from the stove and set it on the counter. Empty the saucepan and put it in the sink as well.

M. Allow the bowl to cool down completely, and then taste the water in the bowl. Once again, you can only do this because I am telling you to!

N. Does the water in the bowl taste like saltwater?

What happened in the experiment? Well, the water in the saucepan was supposed to represent ocean water. When you tasted it, it tasted salty. If you allowed the pan of saltwater to sit out long enough, eventually the water would all evaporate away. It would take a while for that to happen, however, so in the experiment, we accelerated things by heating the pan until the water started boiling. Thus, boiling the saltwater was just a way to speed up the rate at which the water would evaporate from the pan. When the steam (the water vapor) hit the pan lid, the coolness of the ice caused the water to turn from vapor back into liquid. This process is condensation, and it is basically the same thing that happens to form a cloud. Thus, the cool pan lid was supposed to represent the clouds that are formed when ocean water evaporates into the atmosphere. Eventually, so many drops of water formed that they trickled down the pan lid into the bowl. This, of course, represents precipitation. In the end, when you tasted the water in the bowl, there was no salt taste at all. The bowl, therefore, represents a freshwater source.

The point of the experiment was to show you that even though water might start out as a part of a saltwater source, through the process of evaporation, condensation, and precipitation, it can very easily be transferred to a freshwater source. How can this happen? Water evaporates but salt does not. So in a mixture of saltwater, when the water evaporates, the salt stays behind. This keeps the salt in the ocean but allows the water from the ocean to be exchanged with the many other water sources of the hydrosphere.

The experiment that you performed is actually a very standard technique in chemistry. It is called **distillation** (dis tuh lay' shun).

Distillation - Evaporation and condensation of a mixture to separate out the mixture's individual components

When a chemist does a distillation, he or she typically has a mixture of two or more substances that need to be separated. When the mixture is boiled, the substances tend to evaporate one at a time, allowing the chemist to separate them. In the distillation that you performed, you could have allowed all of the water to boil away and condense into the bowl. In the end, you would have had freshwater in the bowl and nothing but salt in the saucepan; thus, the saltwater mixture would have been separated into its components, salt and water.

Now that you have an easier time believing that water can, indeed, be exchanged between all of the water sources in the hydrosphere, I want to introduce one more concept. Since water is continually being exchanged between the water sources of the hydrosphere, a given molecule of water can only stay in a given water source for a certain amount of time. For example, if a water molecule is in a river that eventually flows into the ocean, then the water molecule will be in the river until it either evaporates away or follows the flow of the river and ends up in the ocean. Either way, the water molecule will eventually be transferred from the river to another water course in the hydrosphere.

This tells us that a given molecule of water will only stay in a given water source for a certain length of time. Scientists call that time the **residence time** of the water source.

Residence time - The average time a given molecule of water will stay in a given water source

The residence time of a water molecule depends on the source in which it resides. For example, the oceans hold a LOT of water, and there is really only one way a molecule of water in the ocean can be transferred to another water source in the hydrosphere. It must evaporate from the ocean. As a result, the residence time for a molecule of water in the ocean is rather long. Most calculations of residence time indicate that the average water molecule spends as many as 4,000 years in the ocean before being transferred to another water source. Water in rivers, however, tends to be transferred to other water sources rather quickly. After all, there isn't nearly as much water in a river as compared to an ocean. Also, rivers tend to flow and dump their water somewhere. As a result, the average residence time for water in a typical river is about 2 weeks. In order to get some idea of residence times throughout the hydrosphere, look at Table 5.2.

**TABLE 5.2**
Residence Times for Different Water Sources

| Water Source | Residence Time | | Water Source | Residence Time |
|---|---|---|---|---|
| Ocean | 4,000 years | | Atmosphere | 10 days |
| Glaciers and Icebergs | 1000 years | | Lakes | 10 years |
| Groundwater | 2 weeks - 1000 years | | Rivers | 2 weeks |
| Soil moisture | 2 weeks - 1 year | | Swamps | 1 - 10 years |

Now the first thing you have to realize when looking at Table 5.2 is that they are only approximations. After all, there is no way to *measure* residence time. These numbers are based on calculations that make a lot of assumptions and use current theories of how the processes in the hydrologic cycle work. Only if the assumptions and theories used in the calculation are good will these numbers be accurate. If not, then you cannot rely on them. Nevertheless, the numbers at least illustrate what I am trying to say. The nature of the water source determines the length of the residence time.

The next thing you need to realize is that these numbers are averages. The residence time in a small lake will be much shorter than the residence time in a large lake. Averaged over all lake sizes, however, the typical residence time for water in a lake is 10 years. Finally, you need to realize that I don't want you to memorize this table. Instead, I want you to look at the numbers and understand *why* the residence times are so different. Water in the atmosphere, for example, has a short residence time. Why? Well, the water in the atmosphere is constantly forming clouds and precipitating. Thus, a drop of water doesn't spend much time there. That's the kind of thinking I want you to develop in reference to residence times.

**ON YOUR OWN**

5.1 Suppose you are given a sample of water taken from somewhere in earth's hydrosphere.

    a. Would it most likely be saltwater or freshwater?

    b. If it were freshwater, where did it most likely come from?

    c. If the person who collected the sample tells you it is freshwater that originally came from a liquid source, where did it most likely come from?

5.2 Water that was originally in a plant ends up in a cloud. What two processes of the hydrologic cycle caused it to be transferred in that way?

5.3 Rain that hits the land can travel as a liquid into a lake, river, stream, or ocean in two different ways. What are they?

5.4  Suppose a scientist were studying two groundwater sources.  The first is an underground river that flows quickly into a large lake.  The second is a large basin of underground water that moves at a much slower rate towards a small pond.  Which groundwater source has the largest residence time?

### The Ocean

Since the ocean is the largest source of water in earth's hydrosphere, it seems only natural to look at it first.  Water in the ocean is mostly made up of table salt (called sodium chloride) and water, as illustrated in Figure 5.3.

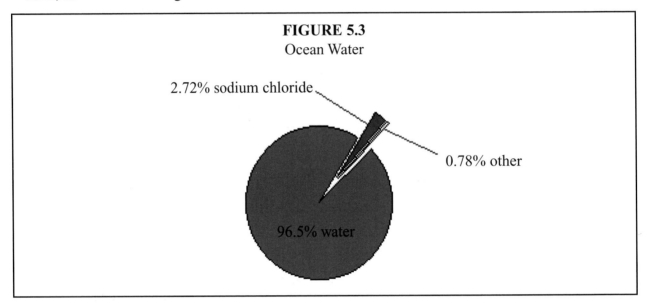

**FIGURE 5.3**
Ocean Water

2.72% sodium chloride

0.78% other

96.5% water

It is important to realize that scientists use the term "salt" differently than we do.  When you and I speak of "salt," we are referring to a specific substance, table salt.  Scientists call this substance sodium (so' dee uhm) chloride (klor' eyed).  When scientists speak of "salt," they are actually talking about a *large class* of substances, of which sodium chloride is a member.  There are many other substances that fall within the classification of "salt," however.  Have you ever heard of someone soaking their feet in a mixture of Epsom salt and water?  Epsom salt is another member of the "salt" class; its specific name is magnesium (mag nee' see uhm) sulfate.  To a scientist, then, many of the substances I lumped into the "other" category are considered "salts" as well.  Thus, you might hear someone say that ocean water is about 96.5% water and about 3.5% salt.  That's true, but the person saying that is obviously using the term "salt" to mean a class of substances, not just table salt.

This brings me to the term **salinity** (suh lin uh tee').

<u>Salinity</u> - A measure of the quantity of dissolved salt in water

In this definition, I am using the term "salt" in its broad sense, as I will throughout the rest of this module.  In chemistry, you will learn how to tell whether or not a substance is a salt.  For right now, however, you can think of most solids that dissolve in water as salts.  Thus, salinity can be thought of as a measure of how much solid matter is dissolved in water.

The salinity of ocean water is about 35 grams per 1,000 grams, or 35 g  per kg.  What does that mean?  It means that in every kilogram (1,000 grams) of ocean water, there are 35 grams of dissolved salts.  As Figure 5.3 illustrates, the majority of the salinity comes from one substance, sodium chloride, but you can't forget the other salts that account for the rest of the salinity.  Of course, the salinity of the water varies from place to place in the ocean.  In places where freshwater rivers are dumping into the ocean, the freshwater dilutes the saltwater, so the salinity is decreased in those regions.  In other regions, the salinity is higher due to a variety of conditions.  In the end, then, the figure of 35 grams per kilogram is really just the average salinity of ocean water.

With all of the talk about the salinity of ocean water, you might wonder why ocean water is salty while freshwater is not.  Well, the answer to that lies in the hydrologic cycle.  Remember that one of the ways water gets into the ocean is by surface runoff.  As this surface runoff passes over the rocks and soil of the land, it tends to dissolve the salts that are contained therein.  As a result, salts are constantly being added to the ocean.  Some of these salts get used by organisms in the ocean, so they don't build up there.  For example, a lot of calcium is dumped into the ocean, but most of it is used by shellfish to make their shells.  As a result, even though a lot of calcium gets dumped into the ocean, there isn't a lot of calcium in ocean water.  Sodium chloride, however, is not used much by the organisms of the ocean, so it tends to concentrate in the ocean.

Now wait a minute, you might be thinking.  Lakes, rivers, and streams receive water from surface runoff as well.  Why aren't they salty?  Well, first of all, there is salt in every lake, river, and stream in the hydrosphere.  The water is still considered freshwater because, as you learned in Module #1, the *concentration* of a chemical is as important as its presence.  In most lakes, rivers, and streams, the salt concentration is so low that it is not really noticeable.  In some lakes, however, the salt concentration is high.  You will learn about that in an upcoming section of this module.  For right now, the proper way to ask the question is, "Why is the salt concentration so high in the ocean and so low in freshwater sources?"

The answer to that question lies in the way in which the ocean participates in the hydrologic cycle.  The ocean's principal way of putting water into the hydrologic cycle is through evaporation.  Since, as Experiment 5.1 showed you, salt gets left behind when that happens, the salt in the ocean stays in the ocean.  This concentrates the salt in the ocean, making ocean water very salty.  Most lakes, rivers, and streams not only put water into the hydrologic cycle via evaporation, but they also tend to exchange water directly with other sources.  For example, lakes tend to feed rivers that tend to dump water into the ocean.  The net result is that the salts in most lakes, rivers, and streams never have a chance to concentrate, because they tend to leave whenever water leaves by any mode except evaporation.  Thus, since the ocean keeps getting salts and never loses them, the result is salty water.  Lakes, rivers, and streams get salts as well, but they tend to get rid of them through the hydrologic cycle.  The result is water which has such a low salinity that it is considered freshwater.

The amount of salt in the oceans actually provides an argument for the fact that the earth is not nearly as old as what some scientists would like you to believe. You see, we have studied the hydrologic cycle enough to know how much salt gets put into the ocean every year. In addition, we have a pretty good idea of how much salt is removed from the ocean every year. In the end, then, we can actually "add up" the amount of salt going into the ocean and "add up" how much is being removed. As you might expect, this inventory leads us to the conclusion that more salt is going into the oceans than what is being removed. In the end, then, the oceans are getting saltier and saltier. Suppose we assume that the oceans originally had *absolutely no salt in them*, and that *all* of the salt in them today came from the hydrologic cycle. Well, based on the inventory that scientists have done, you can actually determine how long it would take for freshwater oceans to become as salty as they are now. The most careful estimates indicate that it would take just over 1 million years to go from freshwater oceans to oceans with the salinity that we see today.

What does this tell us about the age of the earth? Well, first of all, it makes it awfully hard to believe that the earth is billions of years old as some scientists want you to believe. After all, if it really were billions of years old, then why aren't the oceans *a lot* saltier than they are now? No one who believes that the earth is billions of years old has any detailed answer to this question. Secondly, the times that one calculates this way are, in fact, only upper limits to the real age of the earth. God certainly created the oceans with salt in them, since the organisms in the ocean are designed to live with salt. Thus, the assumption that the oceans were, at one time, completely freshwater is pretty silly. Also, careful analysis of the hydrologic cycle tells us that the rate of salt being dumped into the ocean most likely decreases as time goes on. As a result, the rate that we measure now is probably lower than what it was a few thousand years ago. Thus, the salinity of the oceans really tells us that the earth is *significantly* younger than 1 million years old.

---

### ON YOUR OWN

5.5  Suppose you analyzed the salinity of three samples of ocean water. One was taken from deep in the ocean, one was taken from near the surface, and one was taken from a place near to where a large river emptied into the ocean. If the salinities of samples 1, 2, and 3 were 37 grams per kilogram, 25 grams per kilogram, and 35 grams per kilogram, which sample was taken near the river?

5.6  If a lake were completely isolated from all rivers and streams so that the only way it could get rid of water was by evaporation, would it most likely be a freshwater or saltwater source?

---

### Glaciers and Icebergs

As I mentioned before, glaciers and icebergs hold the vast majority of the hydrosphere's freshwater. It is therefore important to spend some time studying these vast reserves of drinkable water. Begin your study by performing the following experiment.

**EXPERIMENT 5.2**
Ice and Salt

Supplies:

- An ice cube
- Table salt
- A measuring cup
- Water
- A plastic bowl that holds more than 2 cups of water
- Freezer
- A teaspoon
- A small plate
- A strainer
- A small glass or cup

Introduction - Saltwater freezes at a lower temperature than does freshwater. You will see that fact demonstrated in this experiment. Additionally, this experiment will shatter a myth that seems to be quite popular among science students.

Procedure:

A. Fill your plastic bowl with 2 cups of water and then add 2 teaspoons of salt. Stir to dissolve as much of the salt as possible.
B. Keeping in mind that you should **NEVER** do this unless I explicitly tell you, taste the saltwater.
C. Place the bowl of saltwater in the freezer. While you are there, get an ice cube. Close the freezer.
D. Put the ice cube on the small plate and put a small pile of salt on one spot near the middle of the top of the ice cube. Do not cover the whole ice cube with the salt. Instead, make a small pile on top of the ice cube near the middle.
E. Watch the ice cube for a few minutes. It will be rather dull at first, but as time goes on, you should see something interesting happening. Make a drawing of what you see.
F. Go back to the freezer and take a look at the saltwater you put there. Continue to check on it periodically while you do other things, like more schoolwork! Wait until about half of the saltwater has frozen. Do not wait so long that it all freezes.
G. Once the contents of the bowl are about half ice and half saltwater, remove the bowl and pour the entire solution into the strainer, allowing the ice to separate from the saltwater. Rinse the ice in the strainer with *cold* water to remove any saltwater that might be clinging to it. You will re-melt a lot of ice in the process, but enough should survive so that you can take a drink.
H. Pour the ice into a small glass and allow the ice to melt. Once it has melted, taste the water that results. What does it taste like?

What happened in the experiment? Well, let's start with the obvious part first. When you placed salt on the ice cube, you should have seen the part of the ice cube under the pile of salt melt faster than the rest of the cube, so that the salt "burrowed" a hole in the ice cube. The reason this happened (as you probably already guessed) is that saltwater freezes at a lower temperature than does pure water. Thus, the part of the ice cube that had salt on it melted, because the ice cube was not cold enough to keep saltwater frozen. This technique, of course, is used to help melt snow and ice on roads and sidewalks. When salt (either sodium chloride or calcium chloride) is spread on snow and ice, the snow and ice melt due to the fact that saltwater freezes at a lower temperature than does pure water.

Now what about the second part of the experiment? Did the result surprise you? When students taste the melted ice in part (H) of the experiment, they usually expect the water to taste like freshwater. After all, they reason, if saltwater freezes at a lower temperature than does freshwater, then as a solution of saltwater freezes, the salt should be removed, leaving only freshwater. Sounds reasonable, doesn't it? The problem with this explanation is that it neglects what you learned back in Module #3.

When I talked about solids, liquids, and gases, I said that the major difference between them had to do with the motion of their constituent molecules or atoms. In a solid, the molecules or atoms are only allowed to vibrate back and forth, whereas in a liquid they can move around with a fair amount of freedom. In order for a liquid to freeze, then, enough energy must be removed to slow the motion of all of the constituent molecules. In the case of saltwater, this means that the water molecules *and the dissolved salt* must be slowed down. As a result, the salt and the water freeze together. They freeze at a lower temperature than that of pure water, but they both still freeze together.

Water and salt do not freeze as saltwater. They typically separate out as they freeze, making solid water and solid salt mixed together. Thus, a cube of frozen saltwater contains solid water with specks of solid salt mixed in. When the cube melts, the salt re-dissolves, making saltwater again.

Why did I go through all of this? Well, I need to dispel a myth that is common among students these days. Many students seem to think that icebergs are the result of ocean water freezing. This is simply *not true*. Icebergs are composed of freshwater. There is no salt in them. They *do not* form as a result of ocean water freezing! After all, in your experiment, the mixture of salt and water was actually very close to the salinity of sea water. Nevertheless, when you allowed part of the saltwater to freeze, the frozen portion still contained salt! The same thing happens when sea water freezes. In certain polar regions, the water in the ocean does freeze to form **sea ice**, but sea ice is not composed of freshwater. It is a mixture of solid water and solid salt. Sometimes, it is actually composed of ice that surrounds pockets of very concentrated saltwater, usually called **brine**. If icebergs don't come from ocean water freezing, where do they come from? Believe it or not, icebergs come from mountains!

You see, every iceberg starts as a glacier, so that's where I have to start in order to tell you about icebergs. As you learned in Module #2, the temperature of the troposphere decreases with increasing altitude. As a result, the upper portion of many mountains contain snow year round. Each winter, new snow falls, adding to the snow that is already there. As time goes on, more and more snow piles up, and the accumulated weight of the snow begins pressing the snow near the bottom of the pile into a thick, hard-packed layer called **firn**.

<u>Firn</u> - A dense, icy pack of snow

After a while, the whole mass of ice and snow gets so heavy that it starts to slowly slide down the mountain. The speed at which glaciers slide is rather slow, usually about 1 meter (a little more than 3 feet) per day. Glaciers have been recorded moving more rapidly, however. In 1937, the Black Rapids Glacier in Alaska was observed moving more than 30 meters (more than 100 feet) per day. Figure 5.4 is a satellite photo of a glacier moving down a mountain near the northern Atlantic ocean:

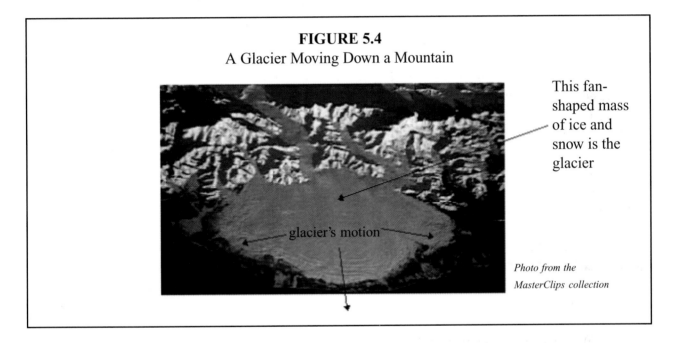

**FIGURE 5.4**
A Glacier Moving Down a Mountain

This fan-shaped mass of ice and snow is the glacier

glacier's motion

*Photo from the MasterClips collection*

As a glacier moves, it tends to sculpt the earth over which it is traveling, plowing earth and rocks out of the way, often making valleys where there were none before. As the glacier travels down the mountain, it will often reach an altitude where the snow and ice begin to melt faster than new snowfall can replenish it. At that point, the glacier starts to melt, feeding many freshwater sources in the hydrosphere. Glaciers in the polar regions of the earth, however, never reach that point, and they continue to flow into the sea, forming huge sheets of ice. The continent of Greenland, for example, is almost entirely covered in a huge sheet of ice that comes from two glaciers! The entire Antarctic continent is covered by a glacier which occupies an area of more than 13 million square kilometers (5 million square miles)!

At some point, such glaciers move so far out into the sea that they end up in water deeper than they are thick. At that point, since ice floats in water (remember Experiment 4.4), the glacier begins to float. Typically, large chunks of the end of the glacier break away, forming **icebergs**. As you probably know, the vast majority (about 90%) of an iceberg exists below the surface of the water, so what we can see of an iceberg is really only about 10% of the total. This is easy to understand if you look at an ice cube floating in a glass of water. We know that ice floats in water, but not very well. Since the mass of ice is only slightly smaller than the mass of an equal volume of water, only a small portion of the ice cube can actually float above the surface of the water. The same is true for an iceberg. This is what makes them dangerous to ships. As a ship travels, it might see the tip of an iceberg and steer clear of it. However, since 90% of the iceberg is under water, it is very possible that even though the ship steers clear of the portion of the iceberg that can be seen, the bottom of the boat can still collide with the other 90% of the iceberg that is under water!

Sometimes the glaciers do not break apart as they float, and they end up forming vast **ice shelves** that extend out into the ocean. One such ice shelf is called the *Ross Ice Shelf*, and it covers a portion of the Antarctic ocean that is about the size of Texas.

In the end, then, an iceberg is really a portion of a glacier that has broken off and floats in the ocean. Ice shelves are simply the ends of glaciers that float in the ocean. A glacier is the result of heavy snowfall in the mountains that does not melt away during the summer. So the largest sources of freshwater on the planet (icebergs and glaciers) are really the result of precipitation. After all, without snowfall in the mountains, none of this would ever happen!

---

**ON YOUR OWN**

5.7 A sailor brings you a chunk of ice from what he thinks was an iceberg. Based on the description of what he saw, however, you think that it might just have been a large chunk of sea ice. How could you tell whether the ice is from an iceberg or from sea ice?

---

## Groundwater and Soil Moisture

Next to glaciers and icebergs, the largest source of freshwater is the groundwater that flows beneath us. Since soil moisture is one of the main ways that groundwater gets renewed, I think that it is only natural to discuss these two sources of freshwater together. Much like glaciers, the story of groundwater and soil moisture begins with precipitation.

When it rains on land, the water is absorbed by the soil. Some of that water is used by plants and gets put back into the atmosphere through transpiration, and some of the water runs over the surface of the land and feeds another water source as surface runoff. Some of that water, however, soaks into the soil and continues to travel deeper into the earth, eventually becoming part of the groundwater. The way all of this works is best illustrated by a figure.

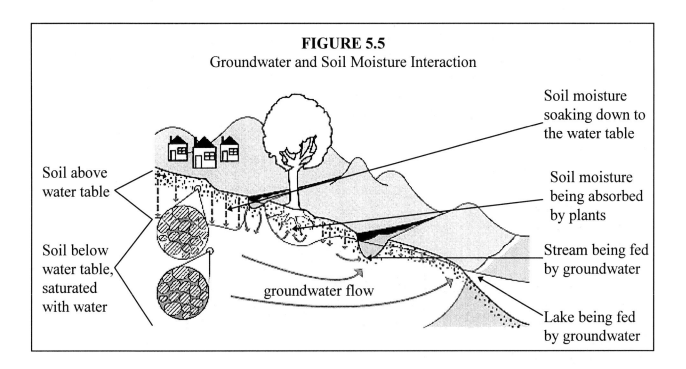

**FIGURE 5.5**
Groundwater and Soil Moisture Interaction

Soil moisture soaking down to the water table

Soil moisture being absorbed by plants

Stream being fed by groundwater

Lake being fed by groundwater

Soil above water table

Soil below water table, saturated with water

groundwater flow

As you can see from the figure, there is a region of soil that is completely saturated with water. This means that there is no way that any more water can be put in the soil. This water is considered **groundwater** and flows towards bodies of water such as lakes, rivers, oceans, and streams in order to feed them with new water. Above that region, the soil is not saturated, so it can hold more water. The water in this region is considered **soil moisture**. Some of the soil moisture goes into plants and is then ejected into the atmosphere through **transpiration**. Some of it can filter all the way down into the saturated soil to become part of the groundwater. The imaginary line that exists between the saturated and unsaturated soil is called the **water table**.

Water table - The imaginary line between the water-saturated soil and the soil not saturated with water

The depth of the water table changes based on how much water is available. After all, when water is scarce, soil that used to be saturated with water will eventually not be saturated any longer. Thus, if you wanted to find soil that was saturated with water, you would have to go deeper into the ground. The depth of the water table, therefore, increases under those conditions.

When soil moisture flows through the water table to become a part of the groundwater, we say that it has experienced **percolation**.

Percolation - The process by which water passes from above the water table to below it

Since the water below the water table is saturated, percolation occurs only when some of the groundwater has flowed out of the region. At that point, there is some room for new groundwater, and soil moisture quickly percolates through to re-saturate the soil.

As I stated before, groundwater is our largest source of liquid freshwater. In fact, 95% of all of the water used in the United States comes from its groundwater supply. Typically, we access this groundwater by digging wells or by draining lakes and ponds whose main water source is groundwater discharge. Most groundwater flows quickly, at rates of up to 50 feet per day. Some groundwater moves slowly, however. Rates as slow as 1 foot every ten days have been observed for certain groundwater sources.

---

**ON YOUR OWN**

5.8  You are studying a sample of soil and want to know if the water in it is groundwater or soil moisture. What could you do to determine this?

5.9  In a certain region, the depth of the water table is measured. If there is a lot less rain than usual over the summer, what will happen to the depth of the water table?

---

## Surface Water

In addition to icebergs, glaciers, and groundwater, lakes, rivers, ponds, and streams are sources of freshwater in the hydrosphere. It is very important to note, however, that *not all* lakes and ponds are sources of freshwater. In fact, some lakes have a larger salinity than the oceans! How is that possible? Well, remember why the oceans have salt in them. Salts get dissolved in the surface runoff and groundwater that feed the oceans, so salt is continually being dumped into the oceans. The only way that any significant amount of water leaves the oceans is by evaporation, which leaves the salt behind. Thus, lots of salt goes into the oceans and very little leaves them. As a result, the oceans are salty.

If a lake has a similar situation, the result would be pretty much the same. In fact, there are many lakes like this around the world. Most likely, you have heard about the **Great Salt Lake** in northern Utah.   This lake is about 75 miles long and 30-50 miles wide, with an average depth of about 6 feet. It has three rivers that feed into it, and it gets a lot of its water from surface runoff. All of these sources carry small concentrations of dissolved salts. Unlike most lakes, however, the Great Salt Lake has no rivers or streams that it feeds. As a result, the only way that it can get rid of water is through evaporation. This concentrates the salts in the lake, giving it a salinity of about 23 grams per kilogram, which is only slightly smaller than the average salinity of the ocean (about 35 grams per kilogram). No fish live in the Great Salt Lake, but scientists have found other forms of water life, such as several species of shrimp.

Another salty lake you have probably heard of is the **Dead Sea**. Unlike its name implies, the Dead Sea is not an ocean. It is a lake about 47 miles long and 10 miles wide, bordered on the west by Israel and the West Bank and bordered on the east by Jordan. It is actually the lowest body of water in the world, and as a result, gets water from many sources. Like the Great Salt Lake, however, water only leaves this lake by evaporation, so all of the salts brought into the Dead Sea never leave. The influx of water (mainly by the Jordan river) is large, but because evaporation occurs so quickly in the arid climate, the Dead Sea gets rid of water just as quickly as it comes in. This rapid filling and evaporation just increases the concentration of salts in the lake, so that its average salinity is 240 grams per kilogram! This number varies a lot by depth, but it makes clear the fact that the Dead Sea is *significantly* more salty than the oceans. This salinity makes it impossible for all life (except a few species of microscopic organisms) to exist there.

## Atmospheric Moisture

The last water source I want to discuss is that which resides in the atmosphere. Once water enters the atmosphere through evaporation or transpiration, it can reside there in one of two forms. It can either exist as water vapor, making the **humidity** that you learned about in Module #2, or it can condense and form clouds. To learn a little bit about how clouds form, perform the following experiment.

---

**EXPERIMENT 5.3**
Cloud Formation

Supplies:

- A clear plastic 2-liter bottle (the kind that soda pop comes in) with the lid
- Water
- A match

Introduction - Cloud formation involves the condensation of water vapor. This experiment will show how water vapor in the atmosphere condenses to form clouds.

Procedure:

A. Clean your plastic bottle out and remove any labels or wrapping so that you can see through the entire bottle.
B. Fill the bottle about 1/8 of the way with warm water.
C. Put the lid on the bottle tightly and squeeze the bottle with both hands. Hold it like that for a moment and then release the pressure, still holding on to the bottle. Do you see anything happening? Probably not.
D. Open the bottle. If necessary, re-shape it so that it is back to its original shape. Now light a match and allow it to burn for a moment.
E. Drop the match into the bottle. It will extinguish (of course) when it hits the water. Now cap the lid and repeat step (C). Did you see something this time? Make a "before" and "after" drawing in your lab notebook.
F. Repeat step (C) several times. Record your observations.

---

What happened in the experiment? Essentially, you formed a cloud. As you already know, when water vapor turns into water liquid, we say that it has condensed. Typically, water vapor condenses as it gets cooler. If you leave a glass of ice-water out on the counter, for example, water droplets will form on the outside of the glass. This is because water vapor in the air contacts the cold surface of the glass and condenses into water liquid. In the same way, atmospheric water vapor condenses to form clouds.

The predominate way this happens was demonstrated in the experiment. When you squeezed the bottle, you put the air under pressure, containing it in a small volume. When you released, the air inside expanded back to its original size. Now think about the energy required to do this. While the air was in the bottle under pressure, it was moving about randomly, as you learned back in Module #3. This motion is responsible for the temperature of the air. When you released the pressure, the air had to expand outwards.

Now think about that from a temperature point of view for a moment. In Module #3, you learned that a substance has a certain temperature because its atoms or molecules are moving about in a random manner. The atoms and molecules of solids vibrate back and forth while those of liquids and gases actually move about in a random fashion. When these atoms or molecules strike a thermometer, they either transfer energy to the thermometer or take it away from the thermometer, depending on whether the thermometer's molecules are moving faster or slower than the substance's molecules. Well, suppose I had a certain number of gas molecules, and I suddenly let those gas molecules expand to fill up a much larger volume. What would happen to the temperature of the gas?

If you think about it, the collisions between the gas molecules and a thermometer would decrease in frequency. After all, if the same number of gas molecules fills a much bigger space, it would take a lot longer for each molecule to reach and collide with the thermometer. This would reduce the amount of energy that the molecules could give to the thermometer and, as a result, the thermometer would read a *lower* temperature. Thus, when a gas expands (and everything else stays the same), the gas cools. We call this **adiabatic** (aye die uh ba tik') **cooling**.

Adiabatic cooling - The cooling of a gas that happens when the gas expands

When you released the pressure on the bottle, the air inside expanded. This caused adiabatic cooling, which caused some of the water vapor in the bottle to condense. This made the cloud that you saw in the bottle.

The vast majority of clouds that you see are formed via adiabatic cooling. In the first part of your experiment, you probably did not see a cloud form, because even though the air cooled, there was nothing for the water vapor to condense on. That's why I had you use the match in the second part of the experiment. The match put small particles of smoke into the bottle. The water then could condense onto those smoke particles, forming a cloud. Most clouds in Creation form around small particles in the atmosphere, like the smoke particles left by the match in your experiment.  We call these particles **cloud condensation nuclei** (new' klee eye), because they form the "center" of water condensation.

<u>Cloud condensation nuclei</u> - Small particles that water vapor condenses on to form clouds

Cloud condensation nuclei come from sources such a volcanoes, fires, and dust blown up by the wind.  Human industrial activity also contributes to the amount of cloud condensation nuclei in the atmosphere.

I will be talking a lot more about clouds in an upcoming module on weather, so I only want to say a couple more things about them in this module.  First of all, the clouds that you see in the sky usually have ice in them as well.  After all, they are far enough up in the troposphere that the temperature is cold enough for the water in the clouds to freeze.  The ice crystals formed are so small, however, that they still stay suspended in the air.  Second, when you see **fog**, what you are really seeing is a cloud that has formed on the ground.  Fog usually forms when the humidity is very high and the temperature on the ground cools quickly.  This causes a large amount of condensation in the air near the ground, forming a cloud.

A very thick fog is usually the result of a fog forming in very dirty or dusty air.  Such air is filled with a lot more cloud condensation nuclei, and can result in very thick fog.  Thus, when fog happens in a dusty or dirty place, it is usually quite thick.  London, especially after the Industrial Revolution, is famous for such thick, often foul-smelling fogs.  This mixture of dirt (or dust) and fog used to be called **smog**, but nowadays that term is usually reserved for the brownish haze you see hanging around a city due to large amounts of industrial and automobile pollution.  To be completely correct, a thick fog brought on by dust and dirt in the air making a normal fog more visible is still called smog.  The brownish haze from large amounts of industrial and automobile pollution, however, is called **photochemical smog**.

Before I finish this topic, I need to make sure that you do not confuse a couple of effects.  We all know that as you heat things, they expand.  In Experiment 3.2, for example, you partially inflated a balloon by heating the air in a bottle.  So, when you heat up air, it expands.  Wait a minute, however.  I just told you that when air expands, it cools.  Isn't that a contradiction?  No, it is not.  The thing you have to think about is *energy*.  When I heat up a substance, I am giving it energy.  As a result, it can expand without cooling.  After all, If I heat up a gas, its molecules move more quickly.  Thus, even when it expands, it will still be warm, because despite the fact that the molecules have more room to move, they move more quickly.  Thus, they still hit the thermometer with a reasonably large frequency.  Also, since they are moving faster, they transfer more energy to the thermometer with each collision.  Thus, *because I give the substance energy*, it expands without cooling.

In the adiabatic cooling that I talked about in this section, energy is not being given to the gas.  Thus, it expands, but its molecules do not move any quicker.  They therefore hit the thermometer with less frequency and no extra violence.  This results in a lower temperature.  In the end, then, a gas will expand without cooling when it is heated because the process of heating gives it extra energy.  Adiabatic cooling, however, happens when a gas is expanded *without* adding any extra energy to it. That's the distinction you must keep in mind if you want to understand why air expands when it is heated but also cools when it adiabatically expands.

---

**ON YOUR OWN**

5.10 Suppose you had a balloon whose volume you could change. You inflate it to 1 liter and measure the temperature of the gas inside. You then very quickly change the balloon's volume to 0.5 liters. What happens to the temperature?

---

Before I leave this section, I want to make a practical point. The correct answer to the "on your own" question is that the gas temperature would be higher. After all, if a gas cools when it expands, it must warm when it contracts. That's why the cloud disappeared in step (F) of Experiment 5.3 each time you squeezed the bottle. The gas warmed when it was compressed, evaporating the water in the cloud. The fact that a gas cools on expansion and heats up on compression is the principle behind a refrigerator! In a refrigerator, there is a reservoir of gas, usually a CFC. The gas is allowed to expand, thus cooling it. The cool gas then runs through coils of pipe, cooling the interior of the refrigerator.

On the other side of those pipes, the gas must be compressed again so that the process can start all over. When that happens, of course, the gas heats up. In order to keep that heat from warming up the refrigerator, there is an insulating wall between the hot place where the gas is compressed and the cold place where the gas is expanded. The hot portion of the refrigerator is then cooled by the air behind the refrigerator. So a refrigerator works by simply allowing a gas to expand, and the resulting adiabatic cooling then cools the interior of the refrigerator. On the other side of an insulating wall, that same gas is compressed again so that the cycle can start over, and the resulting heat is dissipated into the room that contains the refrigerator. In a way, then, a refrigerator "pumps" heat out of the refrigerator and simply dumps it into the room. Since the volume of the room is usually huge compared to the refrigerator, you never really notice the heat. If you put a refrigerator in a small room, however, you will notice the heat that it generates! This same principle governs air conditioning as well, but the heat from the gas compression in air conditioners is usually released outside.

## Water Pollution

Since this module is devoted to the hydrosphere, I cannot end it without mentioning one of the real environmental problems that exists today: water pollution. As you have hopefully learned in this course already, some of the environmental "crises" that exist today are really not problems at all. Instead, they are mostly media hype with little science attached to them. Such is the case with global warming and ozone depletion, for example. Water pollution, however, is a real problem, and one that gets precious little media attention.

Industries dumping waste into rivers or medical waste being thrown into the ocean is often what we think of when we think of water pollution. Although these problems are real and do exist, the more damaging water pollution today is happening in our groundwater supply. Pesticides, fertilizers, gasoline, and common industrial chemicals seep into the soil moisture and end up in the groundwater. From there, they feed all of the other water sources in Creation. The reason groundwater pollution is so damaging today is that it is very hard to control. After all, in most industrialized nations, there are laws about what can be dumped into rivers, oceans, and lakes. These laws are easily enforced because water in a river outside an industrial plant can be tested to see if the plant is dumping pollutants into it. The groundwater is a bit more difficult to test, however.

Because of the nature of groundwater flow, pollutants that an industry allows to seep into the soil may show up in a lake 100 miles away! How will we know what industry to blame? Industry isn't the only culprit, either. Pesticides and certain fertilizers that are fine on land can be devastating to a lake or river. If a farmer overuses such chemicals, they make their way into the groundwater as well. Also, underground storage vessels at gasoline stations are notorious for leaking. When they leak, gasoline filters into the groundwater and makes its way into our lakes and rivers, as well as our drinking water. Finally, when the wrong kind of trash is put in a landfill or dump, toxic chemicals can seep from them into the soil, eventually percolating into the groundwater supply. In 1994, 41% of surveyed public water systems were contaminated by pesticides, gasoline, and industrial chemicals. There was no precise way to determine who the culprits were.

Other types of water pollution exist as well. In many non-industrialized nations, human waste has so contaminated water sources that it is deadly to even drink from the lakes and rivers that once provided water for massive populations. In industrialized nations, water is often pulled from a lake or river to cool hot machinery. This cooling water gets hot in the process, and when it is returned to the water source, it changes the temperature of the water. This affects what kinds of organisms can live there, and if the temperature change is too severe, the entire balance of the lake's organisms can be thrown off. This kind of pollution, often called **thermal pollution**, can essentially result in total destruction of a local ecosystem.

Needless to say, water pollution is a very big problem today and should be addressed in several ways. Now I don't mean to imply that nothing is being done about water pollution. There is legislation that has been enacted over the years which really has resulted in cleaner water. There is a lot of ongoing research into how to better address groundwater pollution. It is just frustrating to see so much attention devoted to issues that are absolutely not problems, when more time could be spent on real environmental problems!

## ANSWERS TO THE ON YOUR OWN QUESTIONS

5.1  a.  It would most likely be <u>saltwater</u>.  After all, more than 97% of the earth's water is ocean water, so the most likely source for water is the ocean.

b.  If it is freshwater, then it most likely came from <u>an iceberg or glacier</u> since that's the largest source of freshwater on the planet.

c.  If the person tells you it is from a liquid source, then it is most likely <u>groundwater</u> because groundwater is the largest source of *liquid* freshwater.

5.2  <u>Transpiration and condensation</u> put the water into the cloud.  Since it was in a plant, the only way to get it into the atmosphere is by transpiration.  At that point, however, it is water vapor, not in a cloud.  To be in a cloud, the water vapor must condense.

5.3  Rain on the land can get into another water source via <u>surface runoff or groundwater flow</u>.  If the rain never really gets absorbed by the soil, it becomes surface runoff.  If it gets absorbed by the soil and enters into the groundwater, it will get to another water source by groundwater flow.

5.4  Residence time measures how long a single molecule of water stays in a water source.  The slower the water source exchanges water with other sources, the longer the residence time.  Thus, the <u>slow-moving groundwater source will have the longest residence time</u> because groundwater must flow into another source.  If it flows slowly, it will take a long time to transfer water.

5.5  <u>Sample 2 was taken from the place near the river</u>.  The other two salinities are at or above the average salinity of the oceans.  Sample 2's salinity, however, is significantly lower.  This means it must be near a place where freshwater dilutes the salt concentration.

5.6  <u>It would be saltwater</u>.  If evaporation is the only way the lake loses water, then it can never get rid of any salt that it gets.  So salts keep building up, making the lake a saltwater lake.

5.7  <u>Melt the ice and taste the water.  If it is salty, it came from sea ice.  If it is not salty, it comes from an iceberg</u>.

5.8  <u>Add some additional water to the soil.  If the soil absorbs the water, then the water in the soil is soil moisture.  If the soil cannot absorb the water, then the water in the soil is groundwater</u>.  Remember, groundwater is in soil that is saturated.  Soil moisture is in unsaturated soil.  If the soil absorbs water, then it cannot be saturated.

5.9  <u>The depth of the water table will increase</u>.  The water table separates saturated soil from unsaturated soil.  With little rain, groundwater flow will deplete the saturated soil faster than percolation will replace it, and soil that used to be saturated will become unsaturated.

5.10  <u>The temperature will increase</u>.  Since air cools when it expands, it will warm when compressed.

# STUDY GUIDE FOR MODULE #5

1. Define the following terms:

a. Hydrosphere
b. Hydrologic cycle
c. Transpiration
d. Condensation
e. Precipitation

f. Distillation
g. Residence time
h. Salinity
i. Firn
j. Water table

k. Percolation
l. Adiabatic cooling
m. Cloud condensation nuclei

2. What kind of water makes up the majority of earth's water supply?

3. What is the largest source of freshwater on the planet.

4. What is the largest source of *liquid* freshwater on the planet?

5. In the hydrologic cycle, name the ways that water can enter the atmosphere.

6. When a raindrop hits the ground, name three ways it can eventually end up in a river.

7. What process in the hydrologic cycle puts soil moisture into the atmosphere?

8. In which body of water would the residence time be shorter: a quickly-moving river or a lake that has no river outlets?

9. What must a lake have in order for it to contain freshwater?

10. Why is the salinity of the ocean evidence that the earth is not billions of years old?

11. If you tasted melted sea ice, would it taste like freshwater or saltwater?

12. Where do icebergs come from?

13. Where do glaciers come from?

14. The captain of a ship sees an iceberg and steers clear of it. Why is the captain still worried about a collision?

15. Suppose you studied two areas of land close to one another. In the first, there are a lot of trees. In the second, there are almost no trees at all. Other than that, the two areas seem identical. They have the same kind of grass and experience the same weather. Which one has the deeper water table?

16. If no energy is added to air, what happens to the temperature when the air expands?

17.  Will fog be thicker in a dusty area or an area free of dust and dirt?

18.  What kind of cooling is responsible for most cloud formation?

19.  What kind of water pollution is the hardest to track back to its source?

## Module #6: Earth and the Lithosphere

### Introduction

In physical science, the earth is typically viewed as being made up of five sections. We have already talked about the first two: the **atmosphere** and the **hydrosphere**. In this module, we will cover the other three sections (illustrated in Figure 6.1): the **lithosphere** (lith' uh sfear), the **mantle**, and the **core**.

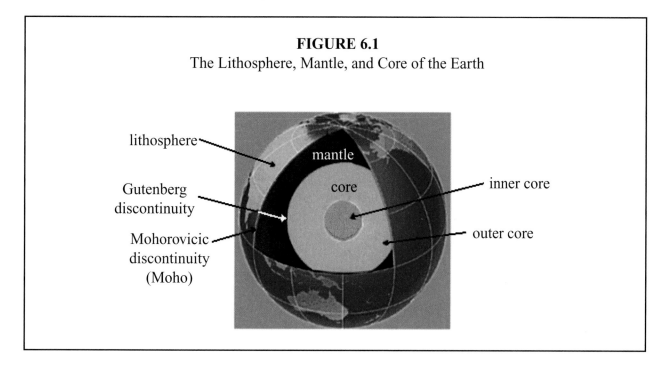

**FIGURE 6.1**
The Lithosphere, Mantle, and Core of the Earth

As you can see from the figure, the lithosphere is the top portion of the earth. Underneath the lithosphere we find the mantle. Underneath the mantle is the core, which is split into two regions: the inner core and the outer core.

In this module, I will spend the majority of time discussing the lithosphere because scientists understand that section of the earth better than the others. There is a very good reason for this. We have never directly observed any part of the mantle or the core. You see, no drill has come anywhere close to penetrating even the topmost part of the earth's mantle. As a result, all information that we have been able to learn about the mantle and the core come from *indirect* observation.

What do I mean by indirect observation? Well, in science, we often want to learn about things that we cannot see. For example, we want to know everything we can about atoms. Nevertheless, we cannot see them. The way we learn about atoms, then, is to do experiments that "disturb" them in some way and then watch what happens as they react. For example, when a glass tube is filled with neon gas and electricity is passed through it, the tube will glow with an orange-yellow light. We call this a "neon light." The reason the tube glows is that the neon atoms in the tube are disturbed by the electricity. In response, they emit the orange-yellow light. It turns out that the color of light changes if you put different kinds of gas in the tube.

Well, that little fact tells us something about atoms. It tells us that they are disturbed by electricity and that each atom reacts to this disturbance differently. Scientists developed several theories to try and learn more from this little fact, and in the end, a scientist named Niels Bohr came up with a theory that could actually predict the color of light emitted by an atom when it is disturbed by electricity. It turns out that this theory, called the "Bohr Model," was actually quite successful at predicting these colors. As a result, the Bohr Model was accepted as a good theory because it could explain some indirect observations of atoms. You will learn about the Bohr Model in a future module, so I don't want to go into it here. The point that I want to make is that even though we cannot see atoms, we have a good idea of what they look like because of indirect observation. The same can be said of the earth. We cannot directly observe any part of the earth except the lithosphere. However, because of indirect observation and some theories that have tried to explain these observations, we have a good idea of what all sections of the earth look like.

What kind of indirect observation can be made of the earth? Well, just like when scientists study atoms, an indirect observation of the earth's interior involves "disturbing" the earth and watching how it reacts. We can disturb the earth ourselves with explosives, or we can wait for times when the earth gets disturbed by earthquakes and other such events. If we observe how the earth reacts to these disturbances, we can learn about the parts of the earth that we cannot study directly. I will discuss this further in another section of this module.

## The Lithosphere

As I said before, the lithosphere is the only section of the earth that we really know well because it is the only section of the earth that we can actually observe directly. The thickness of the lithosphere varies depending on where you are. The majority of the lithosphere ranges in thickness from about 100 km (60 miles) to about 35 km (22 miles). There are very thin layers of the lithosphere (only 5 km thick), but they only exist beneath the deepest parts of the ocean. Now you know why we have not observed any section of the earth other than the lithosphere. The deepest that any drill has ever penetrated the lithosphere is 15 kilometers. Since drilling does not take place in the deep ocean, you can see that drilling has not come close to penetrating through the lithosphere.

The lithosphere is usually divided into three sections: **soil, sediments**, and **crust**. Even in the deep oceans, there is a thin layer of soil that rests on top of the lithosphere. Under that soil layer, there is a layer of sediment.

Sediment - A deposit of sand and mineral fragments, usually laid down by water

Sometimes, heat, pressure, and chemical reactions turn those sediments into rock, which is (not surprisingly) called **sedimentary** (sed i men' tuh ree) **rock**.

<u>Sedimentary rock</u> - Rock formed when heat, pressure, and chemical reactions cement sediments
        together

Sediments and sedimentary rock form a layer whose thickness ranges from about 1 km (3300 feet) to 6 km (4 miles).

Finally, underneath the soil and sediment lies the thickest part of the lithosphere, the earth's crust.

<u>Earth's crust</u> - Earth's outermost layer of rock

The rock that composes the earth's crust is a mixture of sedimentary rock and **igneous** (ig' nee us) **rock**.

<u>Igneous rock</u> - Rock that forms from molten rock

Volcanoes emit lava, which is molten rock, or **magma**. Once the magma cools, it solidifies, forming igneous rock. The main component of the crust is a substance known as silica. You have probably had some experience with silica, because it is also the principal component of sand and glass.

---

**ON YOUR OWN**

6.1 Consider the three sections of the lithosphere. Are all three of them present everywhere on the earth? If not, which section or sections might be missing? Which is the most likely to be missing?

---

<u>The Mantle</u>

Directly under the earth's crust, we find the earth's mantle. As I mentioned before, we have never made direct observations of the earth's mantle, but we have learned a great deal about it by indirect observation. To see what I mean, perform the following experiment.

---

**EXPERIMENT 6.1**
How Sound Travels Through Different Substances

<u>Supplies</u>:

- Two metal spoons
- About 3 feet of string (Nylon kite string is ideal, but any reasonably strong string will work. Thread and yarn do not work well.)
- Large sink
- Water

Introduction - Study of the mantle and core makes use of the fact that waves travel differently in different substances. In this experiment, you will make use of sound waves in order to "see" this effect.

Procedure:

A. Fill up the sink with water. While you are waiting, take about three feet of string and tie the two spoons to the center of it. Tie them individually right next to each other so that when you hold the string by both ends and let the spoons dangle, they bang against each other making a dull ringing sound.
B. Once the sink is reasonably full, turn off the water.
C. Hold the string by both ends and bounce it up and down, allowing the spoons to jingle, to get an idea of what they sound like when they bang into each other. Write a description of the sound in your notebook.
D. Now stick each end of the string into your ears, and hold them there with your fingers. In order for the experiment to work, the ends of the string must be pushed into your ear and held there tightly with your fingers, so that you can only hear sounds that travel through the string.
E. Lean forward so that the spoons dangle in front of you. Both sides of the string should be held taut by the weight of the spoons. If not, adjust the way you are leaning or the way you are holding the string in your ears in order to make sure that both sides of the string are taut.
F. With one of your free fingers, flick one side of the string near your ears so that the spoons jangle together. What kind of sound do you hear? Write a description of that in your notebook, comparing it to the sound you heard in step (C).
G. Now take the ends of the string out of your ears and dangle the spoons so that they are under water in the sink. Bounce the string up and down again to get an idea of what they sound like banging together under water. Once again, write a description of the sound.
H. Once you have an idea of what they sound like, tilt your head and lay it sideways in the water, so that one of your ears is completely under water. Now repeat part (G), listening to how the spoons sound when your ear is under water with them. Write a comparison between this sound and the one you heard in part (G).
I. Finally, pull your head out of the water and repeat steps (D) through (G), this time keep the spoons under water when you flick the string to make them jingle. Compare the sound you hear to the sounds you heard in (G) and (H). What are the differences? Write them down.

What did you hear? In the first part of the experiment (before you put the spoons under water), the spoons should have sounded much different when you had the string in your ears. This is because sound travels as a wave. I haven't really talked about waves yet, and I really don't want to go into detail about them until a much later module. In brief, then, a wave is really just a vibration that passes through a substance. When sound travels through air, the air vibrates back and forth, eventually hitting a vibration sensor in your ear. The vibration sensor then sends signals to the brain, and the brain interprets those signals. That's how you hear.

For the purpose of this experiment, all you have to understand is that sound travels as a vibration in the substance through which it is moving. Before you put the ends of the string in your ears, you heard the sound vibrations as they traveled through air. When you put the ends of the string in your ears, however, you heard the vibrations that traveled through the string. Which was louder? The spoons should have sounded much louder when you listened to the sound traveling through the string. That should make sense. After all, if sound really does travel as a vibration, the more matter there is to vibrate, the better the sound should travel, right? Well, the string has a lot more mass than the same amount of air, so there is more matter in the string to vibrate. Thus, the sound travels better in the string.

Now think about the second part of the experiment. In the second part, you listened to the spoons bang together under water. First, you listened with your ears in air. Next, you put your ears in the water, and finally, you listened through the string. They sounded different in each case, right? That's because the substances through which the vibrations traveled were different in each case. In the end, then, the experiment should definitely prove to you that vibrations travel differently depending on the substance through which they travel.

Scientists make use of this fact in order to study the portions of the earth that they cannot observe directly. When earthquakes occur, they emit vibrations called **seismic** (size' mik) **waves**. These seismic waves travel through the earth, eventually reaching the surface. If enough vibration detectors, called **seismographs** (size' mo grafs), are used to analyze the vibrations at different points of the earth, scientists can determine the speed at which the seismic waves travel, how much energy they lose as they travel, and how their course changes in different parts of the earth. All of these things are affected by the type of substance through which the waves travel.

The first scientist to really make use of this fact was a Croatian scientist named Andrija Mohorovicic. By careful study of seismic waves over a period of several years, he came to the conclusion that around 20 miles beneath the surface, there is a drastic change in the makeup of the earth. In 1909, he proposed that the earth was not the same throughout its interior. He postulated that roughly 20 miles beneath the surface, there was a border beyond which the composition of the earth was much different than that of the earth's crust. That border became known as the **Mohorovicic discontinuity**, or **Moho** (mo' ho) for short. We now know that Moho marks the boundary between the earth's crust and the beginning of the earth's mantle.

As time went on and the study of seismic waves became more detailed, scientists began proposing models of the earth's mantle. They would make calculations of how seismic waves should travel through the earth's mantle if it really was composed the way theory said, and then they would compare studies of seismic waves to these calculations. As scientists learned more, the models were refined, and eventually, the calculations based on the models were in excellent agreement with the data. Thus, even though we have never directly seen the mantle, we think we know its composition and its general properties simply because we have analyzed how seismic waves travel through it.

Now before I actually tell you what the mantle is thought to be like, I want to make a couple of points. The majority of real science going on in this day and age involves trying to understand things we cannot really see: atoms, the earth's interior, distant galaxies, the origin of life, etc. Since we cannot observe these things (or at least their details) directly, we are forced to perform indirect observations. We then come up with a theory that "guesses" at the nature of what we are studying and predicts what the results of certain experiments should be. If the experiments agree with the theory's predictions, we consider the theory to be a good one. If not, we refine the theory or come up with another one until the predictions of the theory match the experimental results.

The second point I want to make is very important. Although indirect observations are used all of the time in science, the conclusions to which they lead *may be completely wrong*. After all, it might be pure coincidence that a theory correctly predicts the results of an experiment. There might be a completely different explanation for the results. Alternatively, the experiments which confirm the theory's predictions might be fatally flawed in some way that no one has thought of. We have no way of knowing for sure without direct observation. The history of science is littered with theories that we now know are wrong, even though they had a lot of experimental confirmation at one time. Thus, it is important to understand that a lot of scientific knowledge today most likely will be proven wrong later on. Nevertheless, until direct observation is possible, indirect observation at least tells us *something*, so it is worth trying to understand what we can.

So what do the indirect observations of the earth's mantle tell us? Well, they tell us that the rock of the mantle is still mostly silica, but the properties of that rock are incredibly different. First of all, the matter in the mantle is more densely-packed than that of the crust. As one travels deeper into the core, matter becomes even more tightly-packed. At the same time, the temperature of the rock in the mantle increases the deeper one goes. At the Moho, the temperature is about 930 $^{\circ}$F (500 $^{\circ}$C), while the lower portion of the mantle gets as hot as 4000 $^{\circ}$F (2200 $^{\circ}$C). That's some *hot* rock! As you might expect, the pressure that the rock is under increases with increasing depth as well. After all, the more rock that's above, the more weight that's pressing down. By the time you reach the bottom of the mantle, the pressure is about 1.4 *million* times that of atmospheric pressure!

The high temperature and pressure of the mantle causes the rock that makes it up to have some very interesting properties. Unlike the rock that makes up the crust, the rock in the mantle is not completely solid. It behaves more like a very thick syrup, flowing very slowly around in the mantle. When subjected to an abrupt force, however, the "syrup" hardens into a firm solid. After the force passes, the rock returns to its syrupy, flowing state. Scientists call this state of rock **plastic rock**, because it has some properties of a solid and other properties of a thick liquid.

Plastic rock - Rock that behaves like something between a liquid and a solid

Most theories that describe the earth's mantle actually have this plastic rock constantly moving about in huge currents under the Moho.

---

**ON YOUR OWN**

6.2 Suppose you had a long, steel rod, and you stood at one end of it while a friend stood at the other end. Consider the following experiment: Your friend hit his end of the rod with a hammer and you listen for the sound. You then press an ear against the rod, and your friend hits it with the hammer again. In which case would the sound be the loudest?

6.3 Suppose you were able to remove a sample of the plastic rock from the mantle and take it into a laboratory. How would it behave differently as compared to a rock sample that you took from earth's crust?

---

### The Earth's Core

In 1913, a German geologist, Beno Gutenberg, used seismic wave experiments to demonstrate that there is another drastic change in the makeup of the earth about 2900 km (1800 miles) below the surface. The boundary which marks that change is now known as the **Gutenberg discontinuity** and signals the beginning of the earth's core. The core is, indeed, remarkably different than the mantle. First, it is composed mostly of iron, not silica. Second, below the Gutenberg discontinuity, the core is actually *a liquid,* not a solid. It is a liquid because, at the depth of the Gutenberg discontinuity, the temperature is hot enough to melt iron.

Interestingly enough, in 1936, Inge Lehmann's work with seismic waves led to the realization that the core actually has an inner region that is *solid.* This leads us to separate the core into two sections: the **inner core** and the **outer core**. The outer core lies just below the Gutenberg discontinuity and is most likely molten iron. The inner core starts about 5150 km (3200 miles) below the earth's surface and is most likely solid iron. The exact distance from the surface to the beginning of the inner core was not well known until 1960. At that time, underground nuclear tests were performed, and the resulting seismic waves were so well-suited to indirect observation of the earth that many interesting facts about the earth's core and mantle were learned. The precise beginning of the inner core was one of those facts.

"Now wait a minute," you should be saying, "how can the outer core be hot enough to be molten and yet the inner core still be a solid? Is the inner core that much cooler than the outer core?" No. Actually, the inner core is *hotter* than the outer core. How, then, can the inner core be a solid? Well, remember from Module #4 that in almost all substances (except water), the molecules and atoms are close together when the substance is a solid, and they are farther apart when it is a liquid. The reason substances melt is that as you heat them up, you are giving them more energy. This allows the atoms or molecules that make up the substance to travel far apart from one another, turning the solid into a liquid. That effect can be counteracted by pressure. Think about it. With a lot of pressure pushing against a substance, its atoms or molecules will actually be pushed close together.

In the outer core, the temperature is high enough that the iron atoms in the core are given plenty of energy to stay far apart from one another and therefore remain liquid. Even though the iron is under high pressure, the pressure is not strong enough to counteract the effect of high temperature. Deeper in the core, however, the pressure increases due to all of the rock pressing down from above. At the inner core, the force of that pressure is great enough to counteract the effect of high temperature, and the atoms actually get pushed closer together again, causing the inner core to be solid! This effect is known as **pressure freezing**. In the end, then, the physical pressure caused by the great mass of rock above the inner core is enough to keep the atoms that make it up close together, making the inner core solid, despite its high temperature.

Probably the most interesting (and at the same time controversial) aspects of the earth's core is the magnetic field that it generates. Most of you probably already know that the earth has a magnetic field. In some ways, the earth acts like a big magnet, as illustrated in the following figure.

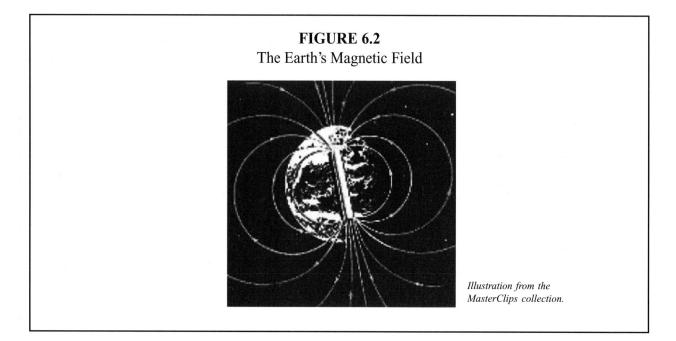

**FIGURE 6.2**
The Earth's Magnetic Field

*Illustration from the MasterClips collection.*

The lines in the figure are called **magnetic field lines**, and you will learn a lot more about them when you take a detailed physics course. For the purposes of this course, you just need to realize that these lines map out how the earth's magnetic field interacts with other magnets. For example, we know that a compass always points to the north. This is because the earth's magnetic field exerts a force on the magnet in the compass, turning that magnet towards the north, no matter where you are on the planet.

Now it is important to note that even though the earth *behaves* as if it is a big magnet like the one drawn in the figure, that's not the reason earth has a magnetic field. Earth doesn't have some huge bar magnet inside of it. Why does the earth have a magnetic field, then? Well, the short answer to that question is, "We don't really know." The long answer, however, is a little more interesting.

Almost all scientists agree that the magnetic field is caused by something that goes on in the earth's core.  To get an idea of what that "something" is, perform the following experiment.

**EXPERIMENT 6.2**
Making An Electromagnet

Supplies:

- A 1.5 Volt battery (Any size cell (AA, A, C, or D) will do, just make sure it is nothing other than one of those.  A battery of higher voltage could be dangerous.)
- A steel or iron nail
- A metal paper clip
- Aluminum foil

Introduction - Some materials are naturally magnetic and generate their own magnetic field.  It is possible, however, to create a magnetic field with electricity.  This experiment shows you how that is done.

Procedure:

A.  Lay the paper clip out on a table or desk.
B.  Take the nail and touch it to the paper clip, then pull it away.  Did the paper clip stick to the nail as if the nail was a magnet? No, of course not.  The nail is not a magnet.  We can, however, make it a magnet.
C.  Take a thin strip of aluminum foil that is about 3 times the length of the nail.  Roll the aluminum foil up so that you have a long, snake-like roll of aluminum foil.  Next, wrap the aluminum foil around the nail several times, leaving about 4 cm of foil on each end.  Your nail and aluminum foil should look something like this:

D.  Now use your thumb and forefinger to touch the ends of the foil to the ends of the battery.  That way, electricity will flow through the foil.  The aluminum foil will get hot, because the flow of electricity results in energy.  You can wear gloves if the heat gets too uncomfortable.
E.  Wait a few moments, and then, with the electricity still flowing, touch the nail to the paper clip.  What happens this time?

In the experiment, you took a non-magnetic substance (the nail) and made it into a magnet by forcing electricity to flow around it. The motion of the electricity caused the nail to become a magnet. That is basically the same way that scientists think the earth gets it magnetic field. Most scientists think that the core has enormous electrical current running through it. It is that electrical current which most scientists think is responsible for the earth's magnetic field. Just as the electrical current in your experiment caused the nail to become a magnet, the electrical current in the earth's core is thought to make the earth a big magnet.

If most scientists agree that electrical current in the earth's core is responsible for the earth's magnetic field, where is the controversy? I said that the earth's magnetic field is one of the most controversial things about the earth's core. What is controversial about it? Well, if electrical current in the earth's core is responsible for the earth's magnetic field, it is only natural to ask, "Where does that electrical current come from?" *That's* where the controversy lies.

There are basically two theories that try to explain where this electrical current in the earth's core comes from. The first theory, called the **dynamo theory**, is believed by the majority of geologists today. This theory says that the rotation of the earth, along with other, random currents that naturally occur in the liquid core of the earth, cause the liquid core to move in one general, overall direction. This motion causes the motion of electrical charges in the core, which in the end creates electrical current, just like electricity running through a wire. Just like Experiment 6.2, then, this would cause the earth to be magnetic.

The second theory, which is believed by a minority of geologists, is called the **rapid decay theory**. This theory states the electrical current of the earth is a consequence of how it was formed. If one makes a few assumptions about how the earth was formed, it is possible to actually calculate how much electrical current would be generated as a result. That electrical current would then begin to slow down over time, because electrical flow is resisted by all matter through which it flows. That is why the aluminum foil in the experiment got so hot. The aluminum foil resisted the flow of electricity, and a lot of heat was generated as the aluminum foil caused the electricity to slow down. In the end, then, just as the flow of electricity is resisted by the wire in which it moves, the flow of the electrical current in the earth's core would be resisted as well. This would cause the current to slow down, eventually stopping.

Do you see the difference between the two theories? The dynamo theory says that the motion of the earth and the random motion of the core work together to keep the electrical current in the core going. The rapid decay theory says that the earth's inner core is actually slowing down the flow of electricity that was started as a consequence of how the earth was formed. Well, since the majority of geologists believe the dynamo theory, it must be the correct one, right? Not necessarily. Science is not done by majority rule. It is done by experiment. We cannot directly observe the core of the earth to see whether it is helping the electrical current or slowing it down, but we can observe it indirectly.

How do we observe the inner core indirectly?  We determined its size and composition by examining the way it responded to seismic waves.  Another way to examine it indirectly is to make careful measurements of the magnetic field that it produces.  Now remember how we try to determine the validity of a scientific theory when we are making indirect observations.  We use the theory to make predictions, and then we compare those predictions to data that we collect.  In the end, the theory that is most consistent with the data is the one that we should believe.

The first thing that we can observe about the magnetic field is that its strength is decaying.  Over the past 150 years, scientists have been making careful measurements of the strength of earth's magnetic field, and these measurements tell us that over time, the earth's magnetic field is getting weaker.  Which theory best explains this fact?  Well, they both do, but the rapid decay theory does a slightly better job.  The rapid decay theory predicts a rather steady decay in the earth's magnetic field, and that's what's been observed over the last 150 years.  The dynamo theory predicts a *changing* magnetic field, because the random currents in the inner core will sometimes add to and sometimes take away from the movement caused by the earth's rotation.  It could be that during the past 150 years, this is what has been occurring.  Thus, both theories predict changes in the earth's magnetic field, but the rapid decay theory explains the data more directly.

The next thing we can observe about the magnetic field is that throughout the history of the earth, it has most likely *reversed* a few times.  What this means is that during certain times in earth's past, there is evidence to indicate that the field actually pointed in the *opposite* direction.  How do we know this?  Well, there are certain materials in the lithosphere that are naturally magnetic.  These materials always tend to point north, like a compass.  In certain rock layers of the lithosphere, however, those natural magnets imbedded in the rock are pointed in the *opposite* direction.  This would indicate that when those rock layers formed, the earth's magnetic field was actually pointed in the opposite direction, as compared to the direction in which it is pointed today.

Which theory explains this fact?  Well, they both do.  Once again, however, one theory has the edge.  This time, it is the dynamo theory.  The dynamo theory predicts such reversals, because it predicts that the random currents in the inner core will, every now and again, overpower the motion caused by the rotation of the earth.  This will cause the electrical current to flow in the opposite direction, causing the magnetic field to reverse.  The rapid decay model allows for magnetic field reversals, too, but only in the event of cataclysmic volcanic and geological activity.  If such activity happened in the past, then the rapid decay theory allows for several magnetic reversals as well.

The final thing that we can observe is the magnetic fields of other planets.  After all, any theory that explains the earth's magnetic field should be able to explain the magnetic fields of the other planets that have them, right?  It should also be able to explain why certain planets do not have magnetic fields.  Which theory best fits the data in this case?  *Only the rapid decay theory.* The rapid decay theory has correctly calculated the magnetic field of every planet that has one.  In addition, the dynamo theory predicts a magnetic field on the planet Mars, while the rapid decay theory says there should not be one.  The data indicate that Mars has no magnetic field.

Conversely, the dynamo theory predicts no magnetic field on Mercury, while the rapid decay theory predicts that Mercury should have a magnetic field. It turns out that Mercury does have a magnetic field. Even more convincing, years before the Voyager spacecraft measured the magnetic fields of Uranus and Neptune, scientists used both the rapid decay theory and the dynamo theory to make predictions of the strength of both planets' magnetic fields. The rapid decay theory correctly predicted the results of Voyager's measurements, while the dynamo theory was off by a factor of 100,000!

In the realm of science, a theory that attempts to explain a phenomenon we cannot observe directly must be consistent with any indirect measurements we make. In the case of a planet's magnetic field, only the rapid decay theory is consistent with all measured data. Why, then, do the majority of scientists believe in the dynamo theory? Well, it turns out that the rapid decay theory has two consequences that the majority of scientists don't want to believe. First, in order to be consistent with the idea of magnetic field reversals, the rapid decay theory must rely on a global, cataclysmic event. Most geologists don't believe that such an event ever occurred. Geologists that believe in Noah's Flood, however, know that such an event did happen. Rapid decay theorists say that an event such as Noah's Flood explains these magnetic field reversals in the context of their theory.

The other consequence makes even more geologists uneasy. If you use the rapid decay theory to predict what the magnetic field was like in earth's past, you find out that the earth had to have been formed less than 10,000 years ago. Otherwise, the electrical current necessary to sustain the magnetic field would have been so large that it would cause the earth to explode! This makes many geologists uneasy, because they want to believe that the earth is much older than that! Thus, since the rapid decay theory assumes that a world-wide, cataclysmic event such as Noah's Flood occurred sometime in earth's past, and since the rapid decay theory concludes that the earth must be less than 10,000 years old, most geologists reject it. They reject it *despite the fact that it is the only theory consistent with all of the data collected!*

Bible-believing Christians, of course, have no problem with assuming that Noah's Flood really happened and that the earth is less that 10,000 years old. Thus, it is easy for them to accept the consequences of the rapid decay model, and thus most of the scientists who believe the rapid decay model are Bible-believing Christians.

This brings me to one of the most important points you will ever learn when it comes to science: **There is no such thing as an unbiased scientist**. People seem to have the view that scientists are unbiased observers who look at the facts and draw conclusions only from those facts. Although this is the ideal scientist, such a scientist does not exist. A scientist's preconceived notions will strongly affect the way he or she does science! The two theories that try to explain the earth's magnetic field is a great illustration of this point. Scientists whose preconceived notions rule out Noah's Flood and a young earth refuse to believe the most scientifically valid theory for the earth's magnetic field. Instead, they rely on a theory that has been demonstrated to go against one of the major observables related to a planet's magnetic field! They go against the dictates of science solely because of bias caused by preconceptions. Scientists who do not have those preconceptions are free to choose the more scientifically valid theory.  This is not to say that Bible-believing scientists are unbiased.  They have their preconceptions as well.  In this case, though, their preconceptions aid in following the dictates of science.

Before I leave this section, I want to point out that life on earth would not be possible without the earth's magnetic field.  You see, there are certain high-energy electrically-charged particles that are emitted from the sun and travel towards our planet.  These particles are called **cosmic rays**.  If they were allowed to strike the earth, they would kill all life on the planet.  Lucky for us, however, the earth's magnetic field deflects the vast majority of these particles, keeping them from hitting the planet.  As a result, life can flourish.  If the earth's magnetic field were too small, it would not deflect enough of these cosmic rays.  If it were too strong, it would deflect the cosmic rays, but the electrical current required to keep the field going would be too large, and the core would explode!  Thus, the earth has a magnetic field at *just the right strength*.  This is just one more piece of evidence that the earth was *designed* for life and did not occur by chance!

---

**ON YOUR OWN**

6.4  Would water be subject to pressure freezing?  Why or why not?

6.5  Regardless of whether the dynamo theory, the rapid decay theory, or some as yet unknown theory is correct in explaining the earth's magnetic field, we are reasonably certain that substances in the core of the earth are in motion.  Why?

---

Plate Tectonics

It is now time to discuss a theory related to earth's lithosphere.  It is called **plate tectonics** (tek tahn' iks).  This theory relies on the idea that the earth's crust is not one big, unbroken slab of rock.  Instead, it is comprised of several "plates" of rock that all move about on the plastic rock of the upper mantle.  These plates are illustrated in Figure 6.3.

**FIGURE 6.3**
The Plates in the Crust of the Earth

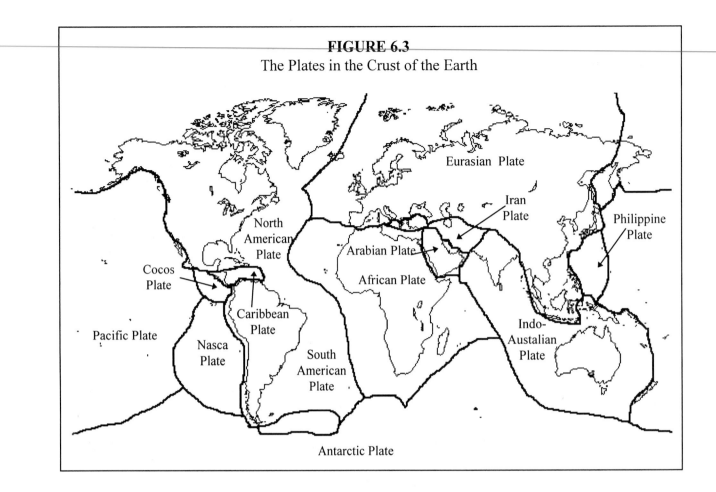

According to plate tectonics, these plates are like islands of rock that "float" on the upper portion of the mantle, which is often called the **asthenosphere** (uh sten' uh sfear).  The plates supposedly move independently of one another, and tend to push up against each other.  This results in some rather interesting geological effects.  Before I tell you about these effects, I want you to try an experiment in which you will simulate plate tectonics yourself.  Hopefully, you will see the effects that I will then discuss.

**EXPERIMENT 6.3**
A Model of Plate Tectonics

Supplies:

- A hard-boiled egg (You might want a second in case you mess up the first time.)
- A dull knife, like a butter knife
- A marker or something else that will make a mark on the egg shell

Introduction - A hard-boiled egg can be used to model the idea of plate tectonics.  The shell represents the crust of the earth, while the rubbery egg white represents the plastic rock of the mantle.  If you cut out a "plate" on the egg and move it around, you will get an idea of what plate tectonics is all about.

A. Take your hard-boiled egg and draw a circle somewhere on the shell. The circle should be about three times the diameter of the end of your thumb.
B. Use the dull knife to cut the circle out of the egg shell. Do this by simply pushing the knife through the shell along the circle's edge. If the knife penetrates the egg white, that's fine. Just make sure the circle is completely cut away from the rest of the shell. Portions of the egg shell will crack. That's okay, too.
C. Once you have cut the circle out of the shell, do not remove the circle. Instead, place your thumb on the circle and use your thumb to move the circle around. Push it back and forth, allowing it to collide with the shell that it was cut away from.
D. The circle of egg shell represents a plate of the earth's crust, while the egg white represents the plastic rock of the mantle. As you move the egg shell circle back and forth, you are simulating a plate moving back and forth on the mantle. When the circle of egg shell collides with the rest of the egg shell, you are simulating that plate running into another plate. Draw pictures of the different things that happen when your circle of egg shell collides with the rest of the shell .

What kind of interactions did you find between your plates? Most of the time, you probably saw that both plates cracked and broke when they ran into each other. When two plates of the earth collide and grind with each other, an earthquake is usually the result. You should have seen other interactions as well. For example, when one plate runs into another, they will often buckle, producing mountains. On your egg shell, you would have seen the shell cracking and then piling up to make a small mountain. Another interaction that occurs between plates happens when one plate actually slides under another one. When this happens, a trench is formed.

Plate tectonics, then, says that the continents (and all things in the lithosphere) are moving around on little islands of rock. When these islands crash into each other, earthquakes can occur, mountains can form, or deep trenches can be dug. Why would anyone believe such an outlandish theory? Because there is a lot of evidence to back it up! A lot of our observations of earthquakes and mountains seem to support the theory. We have also found deep trenches at the bottom of the oceans, the characteristics of which are well-described by the plate tectonics theory. In the end, then, most geologists do believe that the plate tectonics theory is correct and that the lithosphere is, indeed, composed of many independently moving plates.

There is an interesting possibility regarding earth's past that becomes apparent if you believe that the continents are not really fixed but can move about. If you look at the continents, they seem to fit together like a jigsaw puzzle. This has led some scientists to speculate that years ago, all of the continents were connected in a giant supercontinent, which has been called **Pangaea** (pan gee' uh). Since plate tectonics says that the continents can move on their plates, it is possible, then, that the continents moved apart from each other, destroying Pangaea, and taking the positions that we see them in today. This hypothetical scenario is illustrated in Figure 6.4.

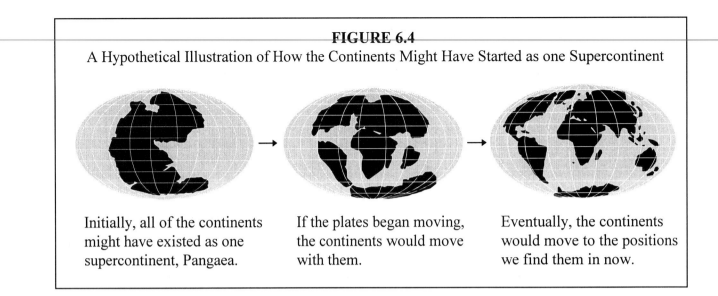

**FIGURE 6.4**

A Hypothetical Illustration of How the Continents Might Have Started as one Supercontinent

Initially, all of the continents might have existed as one supercontinent, Pangaea.

If the plates began moving, the continents would move with them.

Eventually, the continents would move to the positions we find them in now.

Now this is all just conjecture, of course. First of all, we aren't even sure that plate tectonics is really true. There is a lot of evidence that tends to support it, but many theories that had evidence in their favor were later proven wrong. Furthermore, even if plate tectonics is true, that doesn't mean that Pangaea ever existed. It is possible that the plates are quite limited in their movement. Thus, the continents might not be able to move very far at all. Clearly, then, the whole process in Figure 6.4 might never have happened. Plate tectonics does make it possible, however. Additionally, if something like that really happened, it might explain a few things that otherwise might be hard to understand. For example, how did land-living creatures get to Australia? They were made in the Garden of Eden, and there is no way they could swim to Australia. If all of the continents were connected back then, the animals could have easily migrated there. Then, when the continents began to separate, they would simply ride away with the continent of Australia. Also, it would explain why the continents tend to look like they could fit together in a giant jigsaw puzzle. Thus, there are certain questions that could be answered if this process really did happen back in earth's past.

Let me point out something really important here. Most geologists who believe in plate tectonics believe that the plates move very slowly. Thus, if Pangaea really did exist, they think it must have existed billions of years ago. That's the only way the plates would have time to drift as far as they have. Since this is the prevailing thought behind plate tectonics, many Bible-believing scientists refuse to consider plate tectonics as a valid theory, since most of its proponents seem to think that it requires the earth to be billions of years old. This is another example of unscientific bias; but in this case, it is on the part of the Bible-believing scientists. If you really look at the evidence, there is simply too much data in support of plate tectonics to dismiss it. The theory has a *lot* of scientific merit. Thus, we cannot reject it out of hand and still remain good scientists.

We can, however, quarrel with the geologists about the time scale. It is true that plates move very slowly right now. There is no reason to believe, however, that the plates *always* moved slowly. In fact, if a global cataclysm (like Noah's Flood) happened, the plates would probably react by moving very quickly. In the end, then, the whole concept of plate tectonics, even the existence of Pangaea, is not contrary to Scripture!  It is quite possible that Pangaea did exist and the flood was the cause of its breakup.  Under such cataclysmic conditions, the continents could have easily moved to their present locations in a very short time.

The last thing I need to mention about plate tectonics is that this theory is not a full explanation of the geological features of the earth.  Many mountains are *not* caused by plates buckling against each other.  Not all earthquakes are caused by plates grinding against each other.  Many trenches are not the result of one plate sliding under another.  Nevertheless, plate tectonics does a good job of explaining some of these phenomena.

---

**ON YOUR OWN**

6.6  Would plate tectonics work if the mantle were made out of normal, solid rock?

6.7  Look at Figure 6.3.  Assuming plate tectonics is true, where would you expect the majority of the earthquakes in the United States to occur?

---

### Earthquakes

Since I've already talked about how earthquakes can be used to indirectly observe the interior of the earth, it only seems natural to spend some time talking about how earthquakes occur and what the results of earthquakes are.  Let's start with a definition:

Earthquake - A trembling or shaking of the earth as a result of rock masses suddenly moving along a fault

That's quite a definition.  What does it mean?  The "trembling or shaking of the earth" part is pretty self-explanatory, but what does the rest of the definition mean?  Well, scientists know that portions of the earth's surface move relative to each other.  We already discussed plate tectonics, which theorizes that the entire crust of the earth is composed of islands of rock that move relative to each other.  Even *within a plate*, however, there can be great masses of rocks that move due to forces at play underneath them.  The boundary between a moving mass of rock and a stationary mass of rock is called a **fault**.

Fault - The boundary between a section of moving rock and a section of stationary rock

Wherever such a fault exists, there is the possibility of an earthquake.

You see, the moving rocks on one side of a fault do not move smoothly relative to the stationary rocks, because the fault is rough and jagged.  As a result, the masses of rock tend to get hung up on each other.  As the one mass of rocks moves, it gets caught on the rough, jagged fault, and the stationary rocks then resist the motion.  As time goes on, the mobile rocks keep trying to move and the stationary rocks keep holding them back. This builds up great forces, eventually "bending" the rocks. This bending occurs very slowly, so it is not really noticeable. At some point, however, the forces become too great, and the moving rock finally breaks free of the jagged fault edges. When this happens, the two masses of rock "unbend," returning to their original shapes. This results in vibrations, which we observe as an earthquake.

It is hard to prove that the scenario I described is really what causes an earthquake, but there is a lot of indirect evidence indicating that it does. As a result, the whole idea I just described to you is a theory that we call the **elastic rebound theory**. Figure 6.5 is an illustration of this theory.

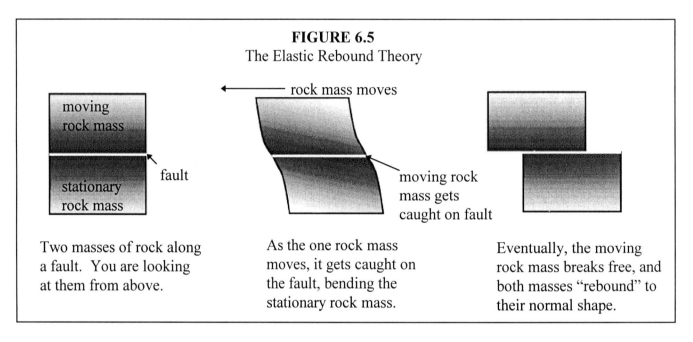

**FIGURE 6.5**
The Elastic Rebound Theory

rock mass moves

moving rock mass

stationary rock mass

fault

moving rock mass gets caught on fault

Two masses of rock along a fault. You are looking at them from above.

As the one rock mass moves, it gets caught on the fault, bending the stationary rock mass.

Eventually, the moving rock mass breaks free, and both masses "rebound" to their normal shape.

Hopefully, you can now see how this theory gets its name. The term "elastic" comes from the fact that the rock masses act a bit like a rubber band, deforming as a result of stress and then "rebounding" back into place.

One of the places that scientists can actually observe this activity is in California. Along a 600 mile stretch from the Imperial Valley in southern Californian to Point Arena in the northern part of the state, there is a well-known fault called the "San Andreas Fault." This fault is most likely a portion of the border between the North American plate and the Pacific plate (see Figure 6.3). Along this fault, the western edge of California is moving at a rate of about 5 cm (2 inches) per year. The movement is halting, however, because the western edge keeps getting caught on the fault. As a result, the motion stops, the rocks bend, and eventually the rocks release, rebounding back into place. Each time this happens, an earthquake occurs. Sometimes the earthquake is mild and can only be detected by the most sensitive equipment. At other times, the vibrations are severe, causing massive damage.

Now it is important to realize that even though I discussed a fault that exists between two plates, that's not the only kind of fault that exists. There are many small faults located within a plate that can result in severe earthquakes.  When these earthquakes happen, many interesting geological events can occur.  For example, suppose a rock mass is moving vertically rather than horizontally as shown in Figure 6.5.  When the elastic rebound occurs, the moving rock mass will thrust upwards, while the stationary rock mass will rebound back into place.  What will result? A cliff!  Right along the fault, there will be a cliff, because the moving rock mass moves higher than the stationary rock mass.  If the moving rock mass continues to move, the cliff might get so high that a mountain forms!  Alternatively, suppose someone were to build a road or building over a fault.  When the elastic rebound occurs, the road or buildings would be in sad shape!

An earthquake will always begin somewhere below the surface of the earth along a fault. The place at which the earthquake begins is called the **focus** of the earthquake.

Focus - The point along a fault where an earthquake begins

Since we live on the surface of the earth, however, the actual point at which the earthquake begins is not all that interesting.  Instead, we would like to know where the vibrations first hit the surface of the earth.  This will occur at the earthquake's **epicenter**, which is the point on the surface of the earth directly above the earthquake's focus.

Epicenter - The point on the surface of the earth directly above an earthquake's focus

The effects of an earthquake are most severe at its epicenter.

The study of earthquakes, called **seismology** (size mol' uh gee), has developed quite a bit over the past few decades.  Seismologists have delicate instruments called **seismographs** that can measure vibrations which are too small for us to notice.  This has led to a scale that classifies earthquakes based on their strength.  The **Richter** (rik' ter) **scale** was developed by a seismologist named Charles Richter.  It measures the strength of an earthquake based on the nature of the seismic waves that it produces.  The Richter scale runs from 1 to 10.  Each step along this scale is an increase of 32 in the energy of an earthquake.  This means that an earthquake measuring 2 on the Richter scale releases 32 times more energy than an earthquake that measures 1 on the Richter scale.  In the same way, an earthquake that measures 3 on the Richter scale releases 1,024 (32x32) times more energy than an earthquake that measures 1.

Typically, earthquakes that measure 4.5 or more on the Richter scale are powerful enough to damage buildings and roads.  If the earthquake measures much less than 3 on the Richter scale, then it can hardly be noticed by us without the aid of seismographs.  Most seismologists consider any earthquake over 7 to be a major earthquake.  The San Francisco earthquake of 1989, for example, caused enormous damage, even to some structures that were considered "earthquake safe."  This earthquake measured 7.1 on the Richter scale.  The most powerful recorded earthquake occurred in Chile in 1960 and measured 8.9 on the Richter scale.  Since this is almost 2 units higher than that of the San Francisco earthquake, it released almost 1,024 times more energy!

Since earthquakes occur along faults, areas with a lot of geological faults will have a lot of earthquakes. If you think about it, the biggest faults will always occur along the boundaries between plates of the earth. Thus, if plate tectonics is right, the majority of earthquakes should occur along the boundaries shown in Figure 6.3. In fact, that's exactly what we see today. The vast majority of earthquakes have epicenters directly above the boundary between the plates of the earth. This is one of the many pieces of evidence indicating that the theory of plate tectonics is a valid scientific theory. I must stress again, however, that earthquakes will occur at places other than the boundaries between plates, because there are other faults that exist on the planet. Nevertheless, places like southern California will always be prone to earthquakes because they rest on the boundaries between the plates in the earth's crust.

---

**ON YOUR OWN**

6.8 Suppose you found a fault where, instead of one moving rock mass and one stationary rock mass, both rock masses were moving. Could an earthquake happen there? Why or why not?

6.9 A seismologist is studying a region near a fault. She measures two earthquakes. One measures 2 on the Richter scale and the next measures 5. How many times more energy does the second earthquake release as compared to the first?

---

## Mountains and Volcanoes

One of the more prominent features of earth's lithosphere is its mountains. How do mountains form? There are actually several different ways. One of them I have already mentioned briefly. If a fault exists in which one rock mass is moving up and the other is stationary or moving down, then the upward-moving mass of rock will form a mountain which rises up from the stationary or downward-moving rock, as illustrated in Figure 6.6. This kind of mountain is called a **fault-block mountain**.

**FIGURE 6.6**
Fault-Block Mountain

fault

Rock mass that moves upwards against the fault

Stationary rock mass

The Sierra-Nevada mountains in California and Nevada and the Grand Teton mountain range in Wyoming are examples of such mountains. Typically, the most spectacular mountains in Creation are fault-block mountains.

When two moving plates push against each other with extreme force, the crust can bend in an up and down, rolling pattern. This forms mountains which we call **folded mountains**. This process is illustrated in Figure 6.7.

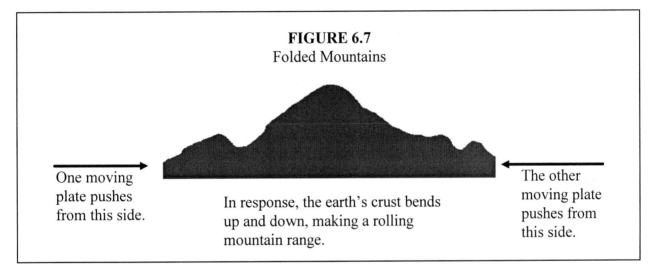

**FIGURE 6.7**
Folded Mountains

One moving plate pushes from this side.

In response, the earth's crust bends up and down, making a rolling mountain range.

The other moving plate pushes from this side.

There are two other main ways that mountains form, but they are not the result of movement in the earth's crust. Instead, they are formed when a hole is torn in the earth's crust. When this happens, the plastic rock from the mantle rises up through the hole. Remember, the rock from the mantle is hot enough to melt, but the extreme pressure of the mantle keeps the rock in its plastic form. When the rock is released from the mantle, a large amount of that pressure goes away, and the rock is free to liquefy, forming molten rock, or **magma**. This magma pushes against the crust of the earth. When that happens, the crust heaves upwards, forming a mountain. The crust can then crack, forming a vent through which the magma can escape, and the result is a **volcano**. Mountains formed by volcanoes are called (not surprisingly) **volcanic mountains**. Mount St. Helens in southwestern Washington state is a volcanic mountain.

Sometimes, magma escapes from the mantle of the earth but does not travel directly upwards. Instead, it flows underground. When this happens, the overlying rock is still pushed upwards, but a vent is not formed. Thus, the magma is never released through the mountain, and a volcano does not form. Because the rock is pushed upwards, a mountain that often looks similar to a volcanic mountain is formed. Typically, this kind of mountain, called a **domed mountain**, is rounder and more sloping than a volcanic mountain, which usually has a rather conical shape. The Black Hills in South Dakota are domed mountains. The difference between a volcanic mountain and a domed mountain can be seen in Figure 6.8.

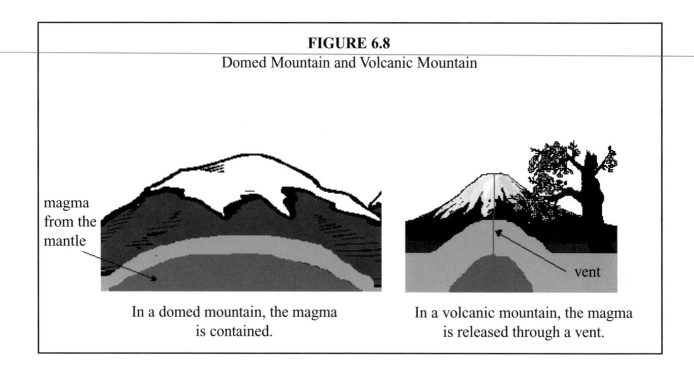

**FIGURE 6.8**
Domed Mountain and Volcanic Mountain

magma from the mantle

vent

In a domed mountain, the magma
is contained.

In a volcanic mountain, the magma
is released through a vent.

Volcanic mountains tend to be more cone-shaped than domed mountains, but (as you might expect), both kinds of mountains tend to be found in the same general area, since they are both formed by magma escaping the mantle of the earth.

Volcanoes are scientifically very interesting for a number of reasons. First of all, the magma that is released comes from the mantle, so it allows us to learn more about the nature of the interior of the earth. Secondly, scientists are just now beginning to realize how much a volcanic eruption can affect the landscape of the volcano's surroundings. Detailed studies from the 1980 eruption of Mount St. Helens seem to indicate that a *lot* of the geological features of the earth might have been formed rapidly as the result of volcanic eruptions. For example, scientists found a huge canyon that formed *overnight* as the result of the violent activity that accompanied the Mount St. Helens eruption!

In the next two modules, I want to try and bring the concepts from this module and the past four together. In Modules 2 and 3 you studied air and the atmosphere. In Modules 4 and 5 you studied water and the hydrosphere. In this module, you studied earth and the lithosphere. In the next two modules, I will put all of that together in the study of weather. Until then, study what you have learned in this module so you will be ready for what lies ahead.

**ON YOUR OWN**

6.10 List the kind or kinds of mountains you would expect in a region that:

a. sits on the boundary between two of the plates in earth's crust
b. is in a region of high volcanic activity
c. is not very near a fault or volcanic activity

# ANSWERS TO THE OWN YOUR OWN PROBLEMS

6.1  The lithosphere is made of soil, sediment, and crust.  <u>Not all three need to be present in a given region of the earth.  Soil and sediment can be missing</u>.  For example, they might be washed away by heavy rains.  Of these two, <u>soil is the most likely to be missing</u> because it is easiest to wash away.

6.2  <u>The sound would be loudest when you put your ear to the rod</u>.  The experiment showed you that sound travels better through substances in which the matter is more tightly-packed.  Steel is a lot denser than air, so sound will travel better through it.

6.3  <u>It would not behave differently than any other rock</u>.  Remember, the plastic nature of the rock in the mantle is due to the extreme heat and pressure found there.  As soon as you remove the rock from the mantle and take it to the lab, that heat and pressure are gone.  It will then behave just like any other rock.

6.4  <u>No it would not</u>.  Water is one of the few substances in Creation that has its molecules closer when it is a liquid compared to when it is a solid.  Thus, if I press water molecules closer together, they become more liquid.  In fact, if you exert pressure on ice, it will melt, because you are pushing the molecules closer together, like they are in liquid water.

6.5  <u>The earth has a magnetic field which must be caused by the motion of electricity</u>.  Thus, something in the core must be moving, or there would be no electrical flow and thus, no magnetic field.

6.6  <u>No, it would not work</u>.  If the mantle were normal, solid rock, the plates would not be able to move.  The plastic nature of the mantle's rock (like the interior of the hard-boiled egg you used in the experiment) makes it possible for the plates to move.

6.7  <u>The majority of earthquakes should occur in California, Oregon, Washington, and Alaska</u>.  Those are the places in the U.S. which rest on a plate.  Since earthquakes can be caused by plates moving against each other, a lot of earthquakes should occur in these states.  This is another piece of evidence in favor of plate tectonics.

6.8  <u>Yes, it could</u>.  After all, an earthquake happens as a result of motion along a fault.  If both rock masses are moving, there is all the more motion.

6.9  Since the Richter scale says that every unit corresponds to a 32 times increase in energy, an earthquake that measures 3 will release 32 times more energy than the one that measures 2.  An earthquake that measures 4 will release 32x32 = 1,024 times more energy than the one that measures 2.  Finally, the one that measures 5 will release 32x32x32= <u>32,768  times more energy</u> than the one that measured 2.

6.10    a.  You would expect <u>fault-block mountains</u>, because there is motion along a fault there.

b.  You would expect <u>volcanic and domed mountains</u>, because of all the magma.

c. You would expect  <u>folded mountains</u>, because without fault motion or volcanic activity, these are the only kind that can form.

**STUDY GUIDE FOR MODULE #6**

1.  Define the following terms:

a.  Sediment
b.  Sedimentary rock
c.  Earth's crust

d.  Igneous rock
e.  Plastic rock
f.  Earthquake

g.  Fault
h.  Focus
i.  Epicenter

2.  Scientists often separate the earth into five distinct sections.  Name those sections.

3.  Of the five sections listed in problem 2, which can we observe directly?

4.  What two regions of the earth does the Moho discontinuity separate?  What about the Gutenberg discontinuity?

5.  What three sections make up the lithosphere?

6.  What is the difference between the ways that igneous rock and sedimentary rock form?

7.  What is unique about the rock in the mantle?

8.  What is the main thing scientists observe in order to learn about the makeup of the earth's interior?

9.  Which is solid, the inner core or the outer core?  Why is it solid when the other is liquid?

10.  Where is the magnetic field of the earth generated?

11.  What causes the magnetic field of the earth?

12.  Give a brief description of the two main theories that attempt to explain the earth's magnetic field.

13.  What makes the rapid decay theory more scientifically valid than the dynamo theory?

14.  Why is a catastrophe like Noah's Flood an essential part of earth's history if the rapid decay theory is true?

15.  What two reasons make otherwise good scientists ignore the more scientifically valid rapid decay theory?

16.  Why would life cease to exist without the earth's magnetic field?

17.  What are the "plates" in plate tectonics?

18.  What can happen when plates collide with one another?

19.  What is Pangaea?

20.  Why do otherwise good scientists ignore the plate tectonics theory, despite the evidence that exists for it?

21.  What causes earthquakes?

22.  Briefly describe the elastic rebound theory of earthquakes.

23.  A seismologists detects an earthquake that measures 4 on the Richter scale.  Later, he detects one that measures 8.  How many times more energy does the second earthquake release as compared to the first?

24.  Name the four kinds of mountains.  What is required for the formation of each?

# Module #7: Factors That Affect Earth's Weather

## Introduction

What's the weather going to be like tomorrow? How many times have you asked yourself that question? People want to know what the weather is going to be so that they can plan their activities, determine what to wear, even decide what mood they will be in. Gorgeous weather can make an otherwise dull day pleasurable or make a good day even better. Bad weather can put us in a bad mood, cancel our plans, or, in some cases, cause great amounts of damage to both property and life. Humankind has always searched for a deeper understanding of the weather. You will start your search in this module.

Before I start my discussion of weather, however, it is important to define a couple of terms. Many people use the words **weather** and **climate** interchangeably, but they are two completely different things. The term "weather" refers to the condition of the earth's atmosphere at any particular time. The current temperature, humidity, precipitation, and wind speeds are all part of today's weather. Climate, on the other hand, is a steady condition that prevails day in and day out in a particular region of Creation. For example, southern California is known for its warm, sunny climate. That's because the *general* atmospheric conditions are warm and sunny. Despite what the song says, however, it *really does* rain in southern California. Whether it is raining or sunny on a particular day is a question of that day's *weather*, whereas the general expectation to experience warm and sunny days when you travel to southern California is a question of climate. The Scripps Institute of Oceanography in San Diego, CA, puts it this way: "Climate is what you expect, but weather is what you get." Keep that distinction in your mind.

## Factors That Influence Weather

A region's weather is influenced by many, many factors. Principal among these factors are **thermal energy, uneven distribution of thermal energy**, and **water vapor in the atmosphere**. I have already talked a bit about thermal energy. Earth's thermal energy comes from the sun. You have already learned how the makeup of the atmosphere affects this energy. In this module, you will learn about other factors that affect the thermal energy that the earth receives. Once the thermal energy hits the earth, it is distributed across the planet through an incredibly complex set of interconnected systems. I will talk a little about that. Finally, the water vapor in the atmosphere exists either as humidity, or it condenses into clouds. I have talked a bit about each of those subjects, but you will learn more about them here. I will start with a detailed discussion of clouds, because you need to know a bit more about clouds before you perform an important experiment.

## Clouds

When water vapor condenses out of the atmosphere onto cloud condensation nuclei, the result is clouds. You have already had some experience with clouds, having formed one in a plastic bottle during Experiment 5.3. In this module and the next, I hope to give you a good understanding of how clouds affect the weather. I need to start by telling you about the different kinds of clouds that can form.

Meteorologists separate clouds into four basic groups: **cumulus** (kyoum' you lus), **stratus** (stra' tus), **cirrus** (sear' us), and **lenticular** (len tik' you lar). These basic cloud types are shown in the figure below.

**FIGURE 7.1**

*Photos from the MasterClips collection*

The Four Basic Cloud Types

7.1a  Cumulus Clouds

7.1b  Cirrus Clouds

7.1c  Stratus Clouds

7.1d  Lenticular Clouds

You generally find each type of cloud at a characteristic altitude. There are exceptions to this rule, however. As a result, a prefix of "alto" might be added to one of those four group names if a cloud is found at a higher altitude than what is typical for other members of its group. For example, altocumulus clouds are cumulus clouds that are found higher in the atmosphere than the vast majority of cumulus clouds. Finally, a prefix of "nimbo" or a suffix of "nimbus" will be added if the cloud is dark.  Dark clouds are the ones that bring precipitation.  For example, dark cumulus clouds are called cumulonimbus clouds and are the most common type of rain cloud.

**Cumulus clouds** (Figure 7.1a) are named from the Latin word "cumulus," which means "a pile."  Their name describes them well.  They are fluffy clouds that look like piles of cotton in the sky.  They form just as the cloud in your bottle (Experiment 5.3) formed.  As air rises, it fans out in all directions, increasing the volume in which it is occupied.  This is one means of adiabatic expansion, which causes the same cooling effect and condensation that you observed in your experiment.  Unusually large upward-moving wind currents can produce huge, towering **cumulonimbus clouds** that most people call "thunderclouds."  Cumulonimbus clouds are usually dark at the bottom and whiter at the top.  Some of them are so tall that they stretch from a few thousand feet above the ground all the way to the top of the troposphere!

Speaking of the top of the troposphere, that's where you can find **cirrus clouds** (Figure 7.1b).  The name for these clouds is derived from a Latin word that means "wisp" or "curl."  Since the air is so cold at the top of the troposphere, these clouds are made completely of tiny ice crystals.  This gives the clouds their feathery appearance.  In addition, the winds at the top of the tropopause tend to spread these clouds out, making them look thin and flowing.  If you think it's odd that ice can stay suspended in the air, remember that for the same volume, ice is actually lighter than water (remember Experiment 4.4).  If water droplets can stay suspended in the air, then ice crystals of the same size can as well!

At the other extreme, **stratus clouds** (Figure 7.1c) typically form low in the sky.  They are formed when a mass of warm air is lifted slowly upwards.  I will explain how this happens in a later section of this module.  For right now, you just need to know that as the warm air is being lifted, the vapor in it will condense and form clouds when it reaches the higher, cooler air.  This forms a flat layer of clouds relatively close to the ground.  Indeed, the name "stratus" comes from the Latin word for "layer."  Because there can be a lot of water in warm air, stratus clouds can easily turn into dark, rain and snow-producing **nimbostratus clouds**.  Like cumulonimbus clouds, nimbostratus clouds get darker and darker until they start precipitating.

The last family of clouds, **lenticular clouds** (Figure 7.1d), are generally formed in mountainous regions.  In these areas, there can be pockets of low pressure in the sky.  When air encounters these low-pressure regions, it expands.  As you know from Experiment 5.3, this causes the air to cool.  If the air cools enough, it will condense to form clouds.  The name "lenticular" actually means lens-shaped, because these clouds usually form an oval.

As is the case in virtually all of Creation, these four broad groups, along with the "alto" and "nimbus" prefixes and suffixes are just not enough to classify every cloud in Creation.  You can often go out and see clouds that seem to be crosses between two of the groups I mentioned here.  **Cirrocumulus clouds**, for example, have the feathery appearance of cirrus clouds because they are made of ice crystals, but they are not blown apart by the wind.  Instead, they form thin puffs that look like a cross between cirrus clouds and cumulus clouds.  In the same way, some stratus clouds do not end up forming in a flat layer, but end up forming puffs and looking very similar to cumulus clouds.  Because they form so low in the sky, however, they are clearly formed in the same way that stratus clouds are formed, so they are called **stratocumulus clouds**. Finally, some clouds have the feathery appearance of cirrus clouds, but they form flat layers like that of stratus clouds. They are too high to be formed in the way that stratus clouds are formed, however, so they are called **cirrostratus clouds**.

**FIGURE 7.2**
A Summary of Cloud Types

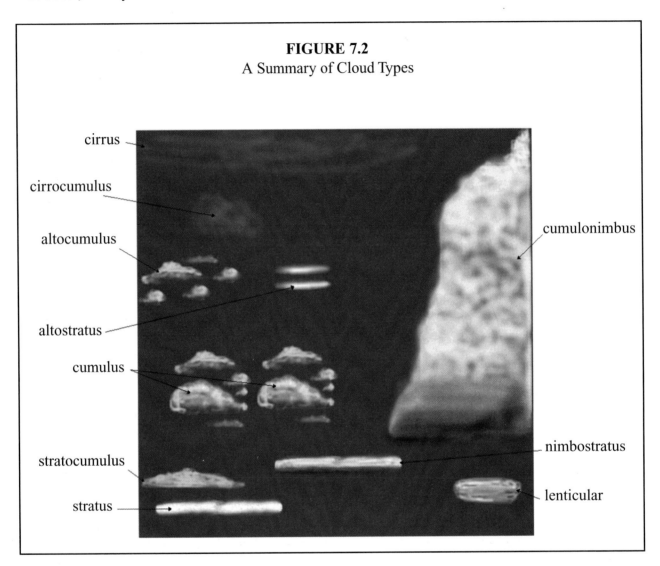

**ON YOUR OWN**

7.1 Is it possible to have altocirrus clouds? Why or why not?

7.2 If a group of cumulus clouds were higher than typical cumulus clouds but were also dark, what would they be called?

Now that you can identify certain types of clouds, start the following experiment:

**EXPERIMENT 7.1**
A Long-Term Weather Experiment

Supplies:
- Daily local weather information source that contains:
  1. High and low temperatures for yesterday
  2. High and low atmospheric (sometimes called "barometric") pressure for yesterday (It may be hard to find this. If nothing else, find a source with the current atmospheric pressure.)
  3. Amount of precipitation for yesterday


Introduction - This is a long-term experiment. Over the course of this module and the next, you will get an in-depth look at weather and what causes it. The purpose of this experiment is to help you correlate the information you learn with some observations you make. In addition, you will get some experience with long-term data gathering and interpretation. Stick with this experiment. It is important for you to learn how to do long-term projects like this one.

Procedure:

A. Find a weather information source that contains all of the data mentioned in the supplies list above. If you cannot find a listing of the high and low atmospheric pressure, try and find at least one atmospheric pressure reading for each day. At the end of the solutions to the study guide (in the solutions and tests guide of the course), there are some suggestions of where you should look. In order to get some practice doing research, I recommend that you try to find this information on your own first. If you spend some time searching and cannot come up with anything, then check with your parent/teacher for the suggestions listed in the solutions and tests guide.

B. Choose two times during the day (one in the morning and one in the early evening) that are convenient for you to make an observation of the types of clouds in the sky. Go outside at each of those two times and identify the type of clouds that you see and the amount of cloud cover. For example, if the entire sky is covered in clouds, it is "cloudy." If there are a lot of clouds but they don't cover the whole sky, it is "mostly cloudy." If somewhere between 1/4 and 1/2 of the sky is covered in clouds, it is "mostly sunny." Finally, if less than 1/4 of the sky is covered in clouds, it is "sunny."

C. Make a record in your notebook that lists each day, the high and low temperature, the high and low (or single if that's all you could find) atmospheric pressure, precipitation, and early and late cloud observations. Remember to put the data with the appropriate day. For example, you will be getting yesterday's temperatures, precipitation and (hopefully) low and high atmospheric pressures. Put those with yesterday's date. Your cloud cover observations, however, and the current atmospheric pressure reading (if that's all you could get) should go with today's date. In the end, your table should look like this:

| Date | High Temp | Low Temp | High Pressure | Low Pressure | Precip | Early cloud cover | Late cloud cover |
|------|-----------|----------|---------------|--------------|--------|-------------------|------------------|
| 11/1/98 | 55 °F | 38 °F | 30.1 in | 29.8 in | 0.10 in | N/A | N/A |
| 11/2/98 | | | | | | Cumulonimbus and cumulus, mostly cloudy | Stratus and cirrus, mostly sunny |

Notice how the first day has no cloud cover observations. This is because 11/2/98 was the first day I started the experiment. Thus, I got all of the other data for yesterday and filled it in on yesterday's date (11/1/98), but my cloud cover observations were for today, so they went in today's date. On 11/3/98, I would fill in all of the data for 11/2/98 from my weather information source, and then I would start a new line for 11/3/98 and put my cloud cover observations in there.

D. Continue recording these facts throughout the rest of this module and the next. That's almost 4 weeks worth of data. Do not give up on this! What you learn from this experience will be well worth it. In Module #8, I will discuss how you should interpret the results of your experiment.

## Earth's Thermal Energy

Thermal energy is another big factor that affects earth's weather. As I mentioned in the introduction, earth's thermal energy comes from the sun in the form of light. Now remember from Module #2 that light comes in many different forms (infrared, ultraviolet, visible, etc.). The light that we see is really just a tiny fraction of the light that comes from the sun. In order to be more precise, scientists call the sum total of all the light that comes to the earth **insolation** (in so lay' shun), which is an abbreviation of "incoming solar radiation." Although you might have heard the term "radiation" in the context of radioactivity, it is important to realize that the term "radiation" is actually a general term scientists use for light and certain other forms of energy you will learn about in later modules.

Now it turns out that the earth has been placed *perfectly* in space to absorb *just the right* amount of insolation from the sun. The amount of insolation earth gets from the sun as affected primarily by two factors: earth's **distance from the sun** and earth's **axial** (ax' ee uhl) **tilt**. As you have already learned from Module #5, the earth has been placed at *exactly the right distance from the sun*. If earth's average distance from the sun were different by as little as 2%, life as we know it could not exist. Why do I say "average" distance from the sun? I say this because the earth does not orbit the sun in a perfect circle. Instead, the earth's path as it travels around the sun is a slight oval, which mathematicians call an **ellipse** (ee lips').

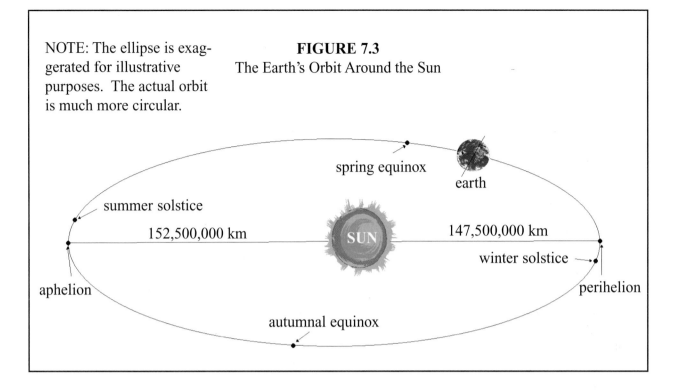

NOTE: The ellipse is exaggerated for illustrative purposes. The actual orbit is much more circular.

**FIGURE 7.3**
The Earth's Orbit Around the Sun

spring equinox

earth

summer solstice

152,500,000 km

SUN

147,500,000 km

winter solstice

aphelion

perihelion

autumnal equinox

Notice also from the figure that earth does not hang in space completely vertically. Instead, earth is "tilted" in space by about 23.5 degrees. This is what scientists call earth's axial tilt, and together with the elliptical nature of earth's orbit, it is responsible for earth's seasons.

How does this work? When the earth is at its **aphelion** (uh fee' lee uhn), it is the farthest that it will ever be from the sun. At that point, the earth receives 3.5% less than its average amount of insolation. When it is at its **perihelion** (pear uh he' lee uhn), the earth is closest to the sun, and it gets about 3.5% more insolation that it does on average.

Aphelion - The point at which the earth is farthest from the sun

Perihelion - The point at which the earth is closest to the sun

This means that it is summer when the earth is near its perihelion and winter when it is near its aphelion, right? Well, not exactly. The earth's axial tilt also plays a role in all of this.

Because the earth is tilted, insolation hits it in different ways depending on which **hemisphere** you are looking at. Remember, the earth can be split into equal halves (hemispheres), above and below the equator. Thus, the Northern Hemisphere is comprised of all regions of the earth north of the equator, and the Southern Hemisphere is comprised of all regions of the earth south of the equator.

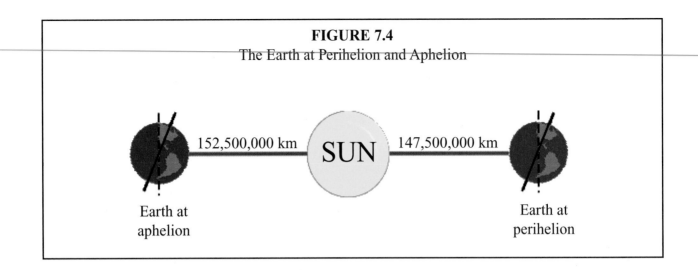

**FIGURE 7.4**
The Earth at Perihelion and Aphelion

152,500,000 km     SUN     147,500,000 km

Earth at
aphelion

Earth at
perihelion

Notice that at perihelion, the Southern Hemisphere of the earth tilts towards the sun and the Northern Hemisphere points away from the sun. Because of this, the sun's light shines more directly on the Southern Hemisphere than it does on the Northern Hemisphere. As a result, the sun's light warms the Southern Hemisphere more effectively, which results in summer for the *Southern Hemisphere*. At the same time, however, the sun's light is not heating the Northern Hemisphere nearly as effectively because it shines less directly on the Northern Hemisphere. This makes it winter in the Northern Hemisphere. Thus, even though the earth receives more insolation at perihelion, only the Southern Hemisphere benefits from that. Conversely, at aphelion, the Northern Hemisphere points towards the sun. Thus, even though the earth receives the least insolation at that point, it is still summer in the Northern Hemisphere, because that's when the sun's light shines most directly on the Northern Hemisphere, heating it up the best. Of course, the Southern Hemisphere is pointed away from the sun at that time, so when it is summer in the Northern Hemisphere, it is winter in the Southern Hemisphere.

You see, then, that the earth's orbit around the sun, combined with its axial tilt, is responsible not only for the seasons that we have, but also for the fact that the seasons are reversed from the Northern to the Southern Hemisphere. There is more to this discussion, however. While the earth is orbiting around the sun, it is also spinning on its axis, turning day into night and night into day. When a region of the earth is pointed towards the sun, it receives light, and it is therefore daytime. When it is pointed away from the sun, it receives no light from the sun, and it is nighttime. During the day, then, it is typically warmer because insolation is hitting that region of the planet. During the night it is typically cooler, because that region of the planet is getting little or no insolation.

Our practical experience tells us that the days get longer in the summer and shorter in the winter. As you might expect, this is also due to the way that the earth orbits the sun and its axial tilt. Because the earth is tilted, it usually exposes more of one hemisphere to the sun than the other. As a result, the days are longer in the hemisphere that points more directly to the sun, and they are shorter in the hemisphere that points away from the sun. June 21 or 22 (depending on the year) is called the **summer solstice** (see Figure 7.3). This is the time when the earth's path around the sun has forced the Northern Hemisphere to start pointing directly at the sun. At that point, every part of the Northern Hemisphere sees the sun for more than 12 hours and every part of the Southern Hemisphere sees the sun for less than 12 hours.  On December 21 or 22 (depending on the year), the **winter solstice** (see Figure 7.3) occurs, in which the Southern Hemisphere becomes pointed directly at the sun.  At that time, the situation is exactly reversed, and every part of the Northern Hemisphere has daylight for less than 12 hours while every part of the Southern Hemisphere has daylight for more than 12 hours.

There are two points in earth's orbit around the sun where, because of the position of the earth relative to the sun, the axial tilt is no longer relevant.  It is still there, of course, but the way the earth is positioned relative to the sun cancels its effect.  At that point, neither hemisphere is tilted towards the sun, and all points on the earth have a day length of 12 hours and a night length of 12 hours.  These are called the **spring equinox** (ee kwuh' nahks) and the **autumnal** (aw tum' nuhl) **equinox**.  They occur (see Figure 7.3) on  March 20 or 21 and September 22 or 23, respectively.  From the summer solstice to the winter solstice, then, the length of the day decreases in the Northern Hemisphere and increases in the Southern Hemisphere.  The autumnal equinox marks the halfway point between those two events.  In the same way, from the winter solstice to the summer solstice, the length of the day increases in the Northern Hemisphere and decreases in the Southern Hemisphere, with the spring equinox marking that halfway point.

All four of these particular events in earth's orbit used to be celebrated as holidays by different pagan religions because the pagans did not understand how all of these things worked together according to God's plan.  For example, pagan sun worshipers in the Northern Hemisphere used to celebrate December 25th as the "birthday of the sun."  Despite the fact that the days in the Northern Hemisphere start getting longer after the winter solstice, these pagans didn't actually notice it happening until December 25th, a few days later.  Since they noticed the day length decreasing every day before the winter solstice and noticed them increasing again on December 25th, they actually thought that the sun was "reborn" on that day.  They celebrated the sun's supposed new birth as a religious holiday.  When Christians came to witness to these people, they changed that holiday into the "birthday of the *Son*," to try and make Christianity a little more directly relevant to their culture.  That's why we celebrate Christ's birth (Christmas) on December 25th even though Christ was almost certainly born in early April.

Although earth's axial tilt makes the seasons and the length of the day much harder to keep track of, we are very "lucky" that the tilt is there.  Because the earth tilts, it exposes a larger amount of its surface area to the sun.  As a result, the sun shines on a larger portion of the earth than it would without the axial tilt.  This is fortunate for us because, as I have already mentioned, the earth cools off when it is not exposed to the sun and warms up when it is exposed to the sun.  If the earth were not tilted, less of earth's area would be exposed to the sun at any given time.  As a result, the difference between daytime and nighttime temperatures would increase substantially.  If this were to happen year-round, it would result in huge temperature imbalances that would make the earth very hostile to life.

Think about all of this for a moment.  The earth is just the right average distance from the sun, and it has just the right axial tilt.  The slightly oval nature of its orbit around the sun, combined with its axial tilt, makes for the wonderful changes in the seasons.  If the earth's orbit or axial tilt were even slightly different, life would not be possible on the planet.  All of this is so complex that it took nearly 3,000 years of human science to figure it out!  These are just two more factors that indicate we are not here by chance!  All of this is the work of an incredibly awesome Designer!

There are factors other than the earth's distance from the sun and its axial tilt that influence that amount of insolation the earth receives from the sun.  One such factor is **cloud cover**.  Clouds reflect insolation, keeping it from hitting the earth.  On an extremely cloudy day, the amount of insolation that hits the earth can be reduced by as much as 65%. As you have already learned, the makeup of earth's atmosphere affects the amount of insolation that the earth retains.

---

**ON YOUR OWN**

7.3  Suppose the earth were tilted opposite of the way it is now.  Would the Northern Hemisphere experience summer at the earth's aphelion or perihelion?

7.4  Between what dates is the length of the day less than 12 hours in the Southern Hemisphere and at the same time decreasing from day to day?

7.5  Suppose the earth's orbit around the sun were circular rather than elliptical.  If that were true, the earth would always be the same distance from the sun.  Under these conditions, would there still be seasons?

---

Latitude and Longitude

Before I discuss the uneven thermal energy distribution of the earth, I need to get some terminology squared away.  In order to make referring to different regions of the earth a little easier, geographers have divided the earth into two groups of imaginary, lines called **lines of longitude** and **lines of latitude**.

Lines of longitude - Imaginary lines that run north and south across the earth

Lines of latitude - Imaginary lines that run east and west across the earth

These lines are illustrated in Figure 7.5.

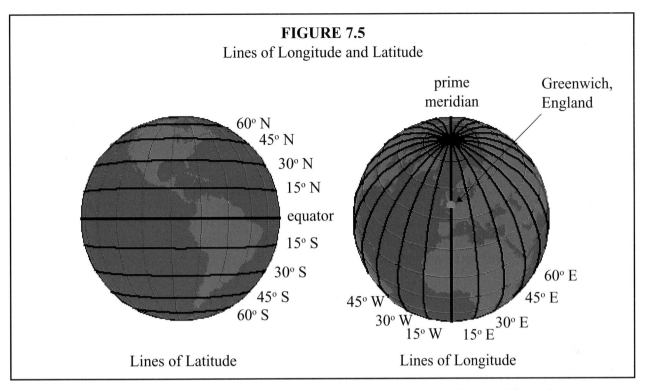

**FIGURE 7.5**
Lines of Longitude and Latitude

Lines of Latitude

Lines of Longitude

Notice that the lines of latitude are labeled in angles that are referenced from the equator. The latitude lines, then, essentially tell you how far north or south you are from the equator. Thus, it is an easy system to reference your north/south position on the globe. If you are at a latitude of 60° N, for example, you know that you are north of the equator, relatively near the North Pole. A position of 15° N, on the other hand, tells you that you are still north of the equator, but not by much.

In the same way, the lines of longitude are a convenient way to determine your east/west position on the earth. The reference line of longitude is an imaginary line, called the **prime meridian**, that runs through Greenwich (gren' itch), England. Any longitude line east of Greenwich is labeled as an eastern line and any line west of Greenwich is labeled as a western line. Thus, if you are at 15° E, you know that you are close to but still east of Greenwich, England. If you are at 60° E, however, you are far east of Greenwich, England.

I will use latitude references in my discussion of uneven thermal energy distribution, so you need to be familiar with this terminology before you proceed into the next section.

<u>Uneven Thermal Energy Distribution</u>

By far, the most complex factor that influences earth's weather is the uneven distribution of thermal energy that comes from the sun. As you have already learned, earth's axial tilt causes the sunlight to shine differently on different parts of the earth. The more directly the sun's light shines on the earth, the better it heats the planet. Well, the sun's light shines most directly on the **equator**, which is the imaginary line that runs directly between the Northern and Southern Hemispheres of the earth. That's why it is always warm at the equator. Above and below the

So you see that because the circumference of the earth is different at different latitudes, the speed at which a point on that latitude of the earth rotates is different than that of points on other latitudes.

How does this relate to wind? Well, consider a mass of air sinking at the North Pole. Because it starts there, it is rotating around the earth at the speed of everything else that sits on the North Pole. As Figure 7.7 indicates, things at the poles rotate around the earth slowly. As the air starts to move towards the equator, however, the ground below starts moving faster, because things closer to the equator rotate around the earth faster than things closer to the pole. Thus, the ground beneath this air mass starts "outrunning" the air above it. This makes the wind bend away from the rotational motion of the earth. I am sure this is a bit confusing, so I will explain it again with a figure.

---

**FIGURE 7.8**
The Coriolis Effect

Suppose you fired a missile from somewhere near the North Pole and aimed it due south.

Without the Coriolis effect, the missile would travel straight down this line of longitude.

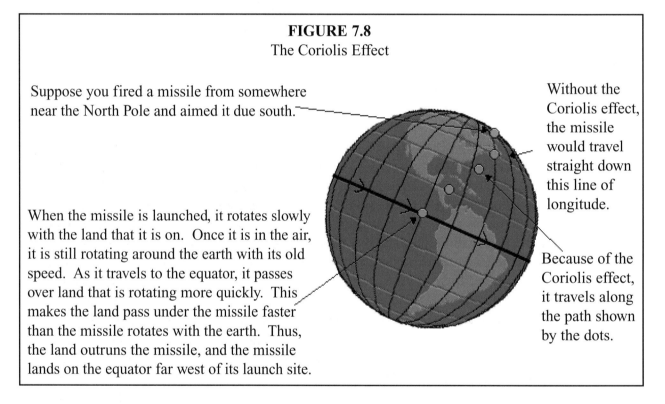

When the missile is launched, it rotates slowly with the land that it is on. Once it is in the air, it is still rotating around the earth with its old speed. As it travels to the equator, it passes over land that is rotating more quickly. This makes the land pass under the missile faster than the missile rotates with the earth. Thus, the land outruns the missile, and the missile lands on the equator far west of its launch site.

Because of the Coriolis effect, it travels along the path shown by the dots.

---

As the figure indicates, the apparent bending of the winds due to the rotation of the earth is called the Coriolis effect. This same effect alters currents in the sea as well.

Coriolis effect - The way in which the rotation of the earth bends the path of winds, sea currents, and objects that fly through different latitudes

When you add the Coriolis effect to the effect of changing air temperature discussed above, you get the following global wind patterns.

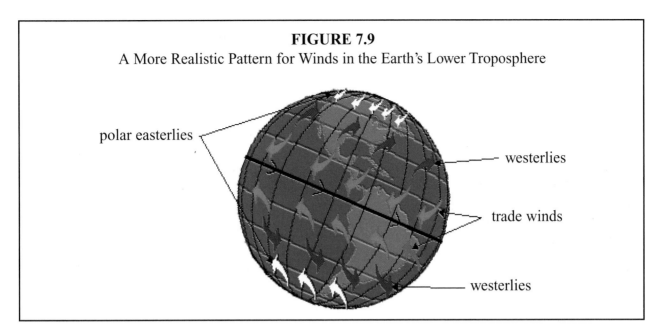

**FIGURE 7.9**
A More Realistic Pattern for Winds in the Earth's Lower Troposphere

polar easterlies

westerlies

trade winds

westerlies

Please realize that these wind currents are only those found in the lower troposphere. The wind currents in the upper troposphere are even more complicated. Thankfully, I will not discuss them in this course!

Look at Figure 7.9 for a moment and try to understand *why* the air currents are bent in the way that they are bent. Begin by looking at the air currents near the North Pole. As Figure 7.7 indicates, things near the poles rotate rather slowly around the earth, because in the space of a day, they travel a shorter distance around than things closer to the equator. As a result, the winds that start out at the North Pole are rotating at a slow speed. As they travel south, they pass over land which is traveling faster. Figure 7.8 gives you the direction of earth's rotation, so the land will "outrun" the wind in that direction. This makes the wind look like it bends in the opposite direction. Thus, the winds near the poles bend opposite the direction of the earth's rotation. Between the latitudes of 30° N and 60° N, however, the winds travel from south to north. Thus, they start out rotating quickly and end up passing over land that is rotating more slowly. As a result, they "outrun" the land. This makes them look like they bend in the direction of the earth's rotation. In the end, then, winds traveling towards the equator get "outrun" by the land they are passing over and end up bending opposite the direction of the earth's motion. Winds that travel towards the poles "outrun" the earth they are passing over, so they bend in the direction of the earth's rotation.

Now please realize that Figure 7.9 shows the *general* wind patterns that exist on the planet. At any given time, however, there is no reason to believe that you can predict the way the wind is blowing by looking at Figure 7.9. Why? Well, remember that temperature imbalances are the driving forces for these winds, and that the temperature of a region is affected by several factors. For example, if the cloud cover over a region of the equator is high, then that portion of the earth will not receive as much insolation as another portion of the equator. This will make the cloudy region of the equator cooler, and the global winds in that area of the planet will be weakened. At the same time, another region near the equator might not be at all cloudy, causing temperature imbalance between different regions along the equator. This will set up a different wind pattern, interfering with the global wind patterns. In addition to all of this, local winds can dominate the global wind patterns completely, or they can just interfere a bit. In the end, then, Figure 7.9 shows us a general rule for global wind circulation, but the real picture is infinitely more complex!

Since local winds can affect the global wind patterns in Figure 7.9, it is important to know how local winds develop. Just like the global winds, they start as a result of temperature imbalance. Consider, for example, a region of the earth near a large lake. During the day, the sun's light warms the area. Water, however, does not warm up as quickly as soil and sediment. As a result, the **land gets warmer than the sea when the sun's light shines on them both equally**. This temperature imbalance causes a low to form over the land and a high to form over the lake. This results in a **sea breeze**, shown in Figure 7.10a. At night, the **land cools faster than the water**. This eventually causes the opposite temperature imbalance, and the breeze blows the other way, as a **land breeze** shown in Figure 7.10b.

**FIGURE 7.10**
Sea Breeze (a) and Land Breeze (b)

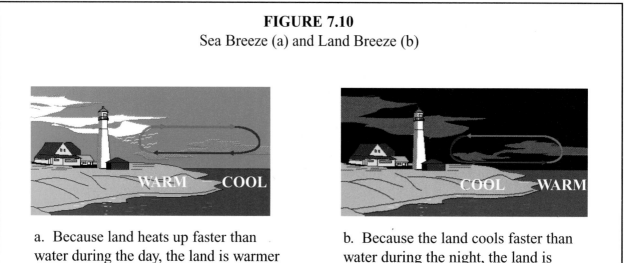

a. Because land heats up faster than water during the day, the land is warmer than the water. This temperature imbalance causes a breeze.

b. Because the land cools faster than water during the night, the land is cooler than the water. This temperature imbalance causes a breeze.

Wherever regions of the earth have areas that warm up and cool off faster than other areas, local temperature imbalances will occur. This will result in local winds that will interfere with the global winds shown in Figure 7.9. How does all of this affect the weather? Well, I want to start to answer that question in the next section.

**ON YOUR OWN**

7.6 On a day at the beach, you notice that the sand is so hot that it is hard to walk on it with bare feet. At the same time, however, the ocean is quite cool. When you left your hotel, you noticed no breeze at all, but when you got to the beach, you noticed a reasonably strong breeze. Is the wind blowing from the ocean to the shore or vice-versa?

7.7  Suppose you want to fire a missile from southern California to a point in northern Canada that is due north of your location in California.  Ignoring the effects of wind and weather,  would you aim the missile due north, northwest, or northeast?

7.8  The global patterns of wind circulation in Figure 7.9 indicate that in Mexico, the winds should be blowing basically east to west.  Does this mean that in Mexico the wind will never blow from west to east?

## Air Masses

When the factors that I discussed in the previous section cause a stillness in the wind in a particular region of the earth, the air which occupies that region tends to pick up the region's temperature, humidity, and pressure.  When this happens, we call the result an **air mass**.

Air mass - A large body of air with relatively uniform pressure, temperature, and humidity

Because an air mass is relatively uniform throughout, it tends to stay together, moving as a unit.

When an air mass moves into a region, it brings with it the weather characteristic of the region in which it was formed.  Wherever the air mass stays, the weather in that region of the earth is the same from day to day, until the air mass moves away and another takes its place.  By tracing the movements of air masses across the earth's surface, **meteorologists** (scientists who study weather) can predict the kind of weather a region will have by predicting what air mass will be moving over the region.

There are three basic types of air masses: **arctic, polar,** and **tropical**.  As their names imply, arctic air masses are very cold, polar air masses are cold, and tropical air masses are warm.  Polar and tropical air masses can further be divided into **maritime** (formed over the ocean) or **continental** (formed over a continent).  **Maritime tropical** (abbreviated as **mT**) air masses, for example, are warm air masses that form over the ocean.  These air masses tend to have high humidity, so we typically say that they are warm and moist.  Likewise, **maritime polar (mP)** air masses are cold and moist.  Since continental air masses form over continents, they are considerably less humid than their maritime counterparts.  Thus, **continental tropical (cT)** air masses are warm and dry while **continental polar (cP)** air masses are cold and dry.  Arctic air masses are always low in humidity, so we say that they are very cold and dry.

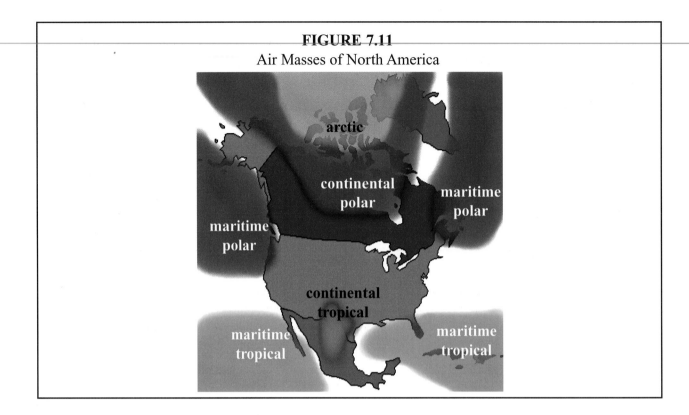

**FIGURE 7.11**
Air Masses of North America

　　　As air masses move, they can encounter other air masses.  As I mentioned before, air masses stay together as a unit because of their uniform characteristics.  Thus, when one air mass encounters another, it does not mix with the other air mass.  Instead, it collides with the other air mass and "fights" to "take over" the region.  When two air masses collide like that, it is called a **weather front**.

<u>Weather front</u> - A boundary between two air masses

There are four basic types of weather fronts: **cold fronts, warm fronts, stationary fronts,** and **occluded fronts.**

　　　In a **cold front**, a cold air mass is trying to move in on a region of warmer air.  Since cold air tends to sink, the cold air mass wedges under the warm air mass and lifts it up off the ground, pushing it back.  This situation is illustrated in Figure 7.12.

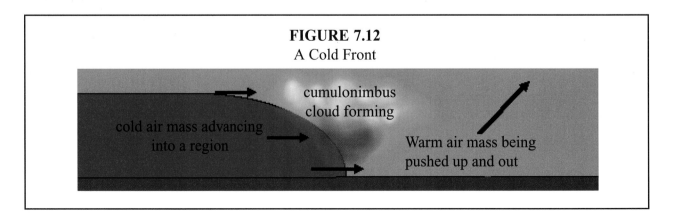

**FIGURE 7.12**
A Cold Front

cumulonimbus
cloud forming

cold air mass advancing
into a region

Warm air mass being
pushed up and out

As a cold front lifts up the warm air in its way, moisture in the warm air condenses into clouds. If the warm air is really moist, then thick, severe weather clouds can form. Since the warm air gets lifted up, the clouds tend to pile up. Usually, cumulus clouds form first, and as the warm air continues to rise, altocumulus clouds can form. If the warm air is particularly moist, cumulonimbus clouds can form. In fact, if the cold front moves in fast enough, you can often see the curved shape of the cold front in the edge of the clouds that form.

Cold fronts are usually the cause of the most severe weather systems. The violent upheaval of a warm air mass, especially a warm air mass that is high in humidity, can result in the rapid formation of thunderclouds with little warning. A storm can come just as quickly. As you might expect, the temperature drops as the cold front moves in. This is actually a good thing, however. Once the cold air mass moves in, the sky generally clears within a few hours.

A **warm front**, on the other hand, results when a warm air mass moves into a region that is occupied by colder air. Since warm air tends to rise, a warm front usually moves over a cold front. This flattens the cold air below and forms an upwardly-sloping front that can stretch for several hundreds of miles, as illustrated in Figure 7.13.

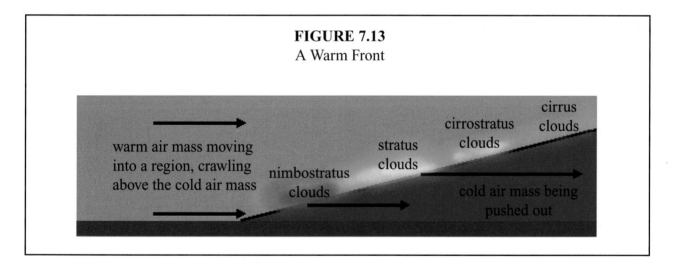

**FIGURE 7.13**
A Warm Front

This is a less violent collision than what I described for a cold front, so the resulting weather is usually less violent. The end result is still warm air rising, so clouds do form as the warm air cools. In a warm front, this usually starts out with cirrus clouds, followed by cirrostratus clouds. Then altostratus clouds are formed, and finally, nimbostratus clouds appear. The rain that results from this kind of front is typically less heavy than that formed by cold fronts, but it usually lasts longer.

When two air masses collide and neither moves, the result is a **stationary front**. As you can see from the figure, a stationary front looks much like a warm front.

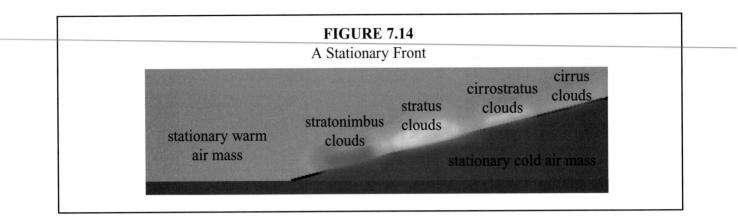

**FIGURE 7.14**
A Stationary Front

The main difference between a warm front and a stationary front is that winds typically blow along a stationary front in opposite directions up and down the front rather than against the front. Also, since neither mass makes headway in a stationary front, the weather tends to stick around longer than that produced by a warm front. Stationary fronts often turn into warm fronts or cold fronts when one of the air masses actually begins to make some progress.

The last kind of major front is called an **occluded** (uh clue' did) **front**. It arises when two air masses traveling in the same direction collide. How can two air masses traveling in the same direction collide? Well, it turns out that **cold air masses travel faster than warm air masses**. So, it is possible for cold air masses to overtake and collide with warm air masses. When that happens, an occluded front forms.

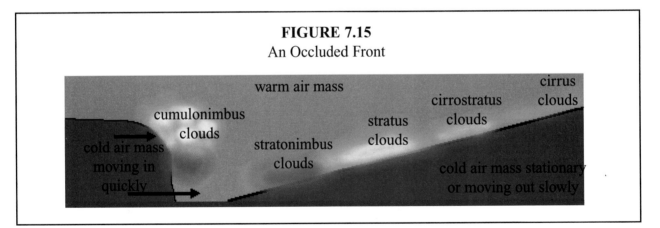

**FIGURE 7.15**
An Occluded Front

Usually, an occluded front forms when a warm front is traveling over a cold front. Another, fast-moving cold air mass comes in from behind the warm front and lifts the warm air mass up and away.

Because an occluded front starts out as a warm front and ends up much like a cold front, the weather produced is a combination of that produced by each type of front. First, the clouds that herald a warm front form. They are then followed by the cumulus and cumulonimbus clouds of a cold front. As you might expect, the weather starts out as the slow, light rain of a warm front, and then the severe weather typical of a cold front moves in behind it.

Hopefully this chapter has given you a glimpse at the incredibly complex nature of earth's weather. Now that you know the basics of the factors that influence weather, you can move on to the next module, which will cover weather and how we try to predict it. As you might expect from the complexities you have already learned, our attempts at weather prediction are sometimes not very good!

**ON YOUR OWN**

7.9  Suppose you were to observe a long, light rain. After the rain is over and the sky is clear, would you expect warmer temperatures or colder temperatures?

7.10 Why can't an occluded front start out with the weather typical of a cold front and then end with the weather typical of a warm front?

Even though this module has come to an end, do not stop performing Experiment 7.1! I will be discussing the results towards the end of the next module, and you will need a *lot* of data in order to really learn from the experiment. Therefore, you need to keep taking the data.

## ANSWERS TO THE ON YOUR OWN PROBLEMS

7.1. <u>Altocirrus clouds cannot exist because cirrus clouds are the clouds at the highest altitudes</u>. Since the prefix "alto" means "higher than usual," it just doesn't apply to these kinds of clouds.

7.2. Dark clouds have the "nimbus" suffix or the "nimbo" prefix, and higher than expected clouds have the "alto" prefix. Thus, they would be called <u>altocumulonimbus clouds</u>. Although altonimbocumulus is technically right, nimbus is usually used as a suffix with cumulus clouds.

7.3. If earth were tilted opposite of what it is now, then the Northern Hemisphere would be pointed toward the sun during perihelion. Since summer occurs when the hemisphere receives the most direct sunlight, <u>summer in the Northern Hemisphere would occur at perihelion</u>.

7.4. The days decrease in length in the Southern Hemisphere from the winter solstice to the summer solstice. At the spring equinox, the days in both hemispheres are 12 hours long. This tells us that from the winter solstice to the spring equinox, the length of the day in the Southern hemisphere is more than 12 hours. After all, the length of the day must decrease from the winter solstice to the summer solstice. Since the spring equinox is in between the two, then the length of the day in the Southern Hemisphere is decreasing up until the spring equinox. If the day length must be 12 hours at the spring equinox, and it had to be decreasing up to that point, then it must have been longer than 12 hours to begin with. After the spring equinox, though, the day length keeps decreasing, so it becomes less than 12 hours. Thus, from the spring equinox to the summer solstice, the day length decreases and at the same time is less than twelve hours. This means the date range is <u>March 20 or 21 to June 21 or 22</u>.

7.5. <u>Yes, there would still be seasons</u>. Remember, the most important factor in the seasons is the earth's axial tilt. That determines when a hemisphere is pointed at the sun or away from the sun, which determines winter and summer. If the earth's orbit were perfectly circular, then the dates for the season changes would be slightly different.

7.6. <u>The wind is blowing from the ocean to the shore</u>. Since you notice no breeze at the hotel, the breeze at the beach is a local wind. Near the surface of the earth, wind blows from cold (the high) to warm (the low), so the wind must be blowing from the ocean to the shore.

7.7. Since we are not considering wind at all, the only thing we have to worry about is the Coriolis effect. Like the winds, the missile will be rotating with the earth when it is fired. As the speed at which the earth rotates changes, this will bend the missile's path. Since the missile starts in southern California, it is near the equator. This means it starts out rotating quickly. As it travels north, it passes over land that is rotating more slowly. Thus, the missile's path is bent in the direction of the earth's rotation. Based on the rotation of the earth in Figure 7.7, then, if you aimed the missile due north, it would end up hitting east of the target. Thus, you must <u>aim the missile northwest</u>. This will correct for the Coriolis effect.

# MODULE #8: Weather and Its Prediction

## Introduction

In this module, I want to tell you about weather and how to predict it. Now you have already learned a lot about weather. You know what causes the seasons, what causes wind, the major types of clouds, the major types of weather fronts, the different types of air masses, and the general patterns of wind in Creation. I will now build on that knowledge so that you have a good handle on how weather occurs.

## Precipitation

As you learned in Module #5, water vapor enters the atmosphere as a result of evaporation. In fact, 14.6 trillion tons of water are evaporated from the lakes, rivers, and oceans of earth each year. That's a lot of water! Eventually, all of that water falls back to earth, mostly in the form of **precipitation**. Precipitation can be **rain, sleet, snow, drizzle**, or **hail**. Besides precipitation, water can leave the atmosphere and return to the earth in the form of **dew** or **frost**.

By far, the most common form of precipitation is **rain**. We all know that rain comes from clouds, but do you actually know *how* this happens? I doubt that you do. Meteorologists have two theories that they think do a pretty good job of describing how clouds produce rain. These theories do not compete with each other. Instead, they describe how rain forms in two different situations.

The first theory, called the **Bergeron process**, deals with how rain is formed in cold clouds. Cold clouds are clouds whose temperatures remain below freezing. Thus, these clouds are composed entirely of ice crystals. As more water condenses out of the atmosphere, the ice crystals grow larger. Eventually, the ice crystals grow too large to remain suspended in the air, and they begin to fall through the cloud. As they fall, they typically pick up more ice, growing even heavier. Eventually, these ice crystals become so big that they fragment. This results in several ice crystals falling through the cloud, each growing bigger and eventually fragmenting as well. This process goes on and on until there are billions of ice crystals falling from the cloud.

As these ice crystals fall out of the cloud and descend to the lower portions of the troposphere, they encounter the warmer air of the lower troposphere. If the temperature of the air is above freezing, then the ice crystals begin to melt, forming rain. If not, they remain the tiny ice crystals that we call snow. This theory has a lot of evidence in its favor. In mountainous country, for example, snow can be observed falling on a mountain while rain is falling in the valley below, despite the fact that all of the precipitation is coming from just one cloud.

Not all rain is formed in the Bergeron process, however. In warm clouds, meteorologists think that rain forms according to a process called the **collision-coalescence** (ko uh less' ents) **process**. In this theory, each cloud contains certain cloud condensation nuclei that are abnormally large. These form abnormally large water droplets, which eventually begin falling through the cloud. As a water droplet collides with other water droplets, the other water droplets stick to the falling droplet, making the falling droplet even bigger. Often, updrafts of air blow the water droplet back into the cloud, allowing it to grow even bigger. Eventually, billions of raindrops are formed in the process, and the result is rain.

Another less prevalent form of precipitation is **drizzle**. Drizzle usually forms in stratus clouds. It consists of tiny droplets of water. In fact, the size of the water droplets is all that sets drizzle apart from rain. Raindrops typically have a diameter of about 2 mm, while drizzle drops have diameters of less the 0.5 mm. Because they are so small, drizzle drops do not fall very quickly. They tend to drift downwards, staying close together and evenly spaced. This makes drizzle seem more like a fog that is slowly moving downwards.

If raindrops fall through a layer of cold air, they can freeze, forming **sleet**. Because raindrops are large (as these things go), when they freeze they form solid ice pellets. These ice pellets hit the ground and either pile up or melt, depending on the temperature. Now please realize that sleet is much different than **freezing rain**. In freezing rain, the raindrops fall through a layer of air that is just at or slightly below the freezing point of rain. When this happens, the raindrops do not freeze until they hit something solid. As soon as they do, however, they freeze almost instantaneously. Freezing rain in *much* more dangerous than sleet because freezing rain causes a smooth glaze of ice to form over all solid surfaces. This makes roads very hazardous. Also, power lines can be destroyed due to the extra weight of the ice that forms on them.

**Hail** is similar to sleet but a lot more destructive. It starts out as a raindrop or an ice crystal that is blown back into the cloud by an upward gust of wind. If blown high enough, the raindrop will freeze or the ice crystal will pick up more ice and get larger. Either way, the end result is a larger than normal ice crystal. Depending on the wind conditions, that ice crystal might be blown back up into the clouds several times. On each successive trip back up, the ice crystal grows bigger. Eventually, it gets so big that the upward gusts of wind are no longer strong enough to push it back up into the clouds, and it falls to the earth as a hailstone.

Hail usually forms in the strong thunderstorms of summer and spring. Remember, most thunderstorms result from a cold front that is lifting a warm air mass. This produces the strong upward gusts of wind necessary for hailstones to form. The stronger the winds, the larger the hailstone produced. The largest hailstone on record weighed 1.67 pounds and had a diameter of 5.6 inches!

The last form of precipitation is, by far, the most beautiful. I am talking, of course, about **snow**. Snow starts out as cold-cloud precipitation. As the ice crystals fall from the clouds, they absorb more water, freezing and growing into bigger ice crystals. This process is responsible for the intricate design of snowflakes. Both the design and the size of the snowflake depend on the temperature. When the temperature is close to the freezing point of water, snowflakes can get quite large. Surprisingly enough, when the temperature is well below freezing, the snowflakes formed are small and powdery.

You may have heard that no two snowflakes are alike. That's not really true, but it's a close approximation. The formation of a snowflake involves several random processes which happen over and over again. Since there are several of these processes, and since they each occur several times, there is a *huge* number of possible shapes and patterns for a snowflake formed under a given set of circumstances. Because there is such a huge number of possible shapes, sizes, and patterns for a snowflake, the probability of two snowflakes coming out exactly the same is very small. Nevertheless, the odds do not preclude two identical snowflakes forming every thousand years or so!

Although not considered forms of precipitation, **dew** and **frost** are two other means by which water can leave the atmosphere and make it back to the earth. Dew forms when air near the surface of the earth gets cool. As this happens, the water vapor in the air will tend to condense into liquid. The problem, however, is that water vapor will not condense unless it can do so *onto* something. That's why clouds need cloud condensation nuclei in order to form. Near the surface of the earth, water will condense onto plants and soil, forming water droplets. These water droplets are called dew. The temperature at which dew forms, called the **dew point**, depends on the pressure and humidity of the air. The higher the pressure and humidity, the higher the dew point.

During autumn or winter, the air near the surface of the earth may get colder than the freezing point of water. When this happens, water vapor skips the liquid stage and immediately freezes on any surface with which it can come into contact, covering the surface with frost. Like dew, however, frost can only form on a surface. The temperature at which this occurs is called the **frost point**. The low temperatures which cause frost can be deadly for certain plants, so gardeners often cover their plants during cold nights to try and keep the cold air away from them.

---

**ON YOUR OWN**

8.1  If a thunderstorm is not accompanied by strong, upward gusts of wind, will the thunderstorm produce hail?

8.2  How can you tell the difference between sleet and freezing rain?

---

## Thunderstorms

Now that you know how rain forms, I want to spend some time looking at the more severe weather in Creation. I will start out with something with which you are rather familiar: thunderstorms. Thunderstorms are localized weather phenomena that involve thunder (of course), lightning, heavy winds, driving rains, and sometimes hail. Although you might not think it at first, they are very common. Meteorologists estimate that more than 4500 thunderstorms occur on the earth *every day*!

All thunderstorms start in the same way. They begin with a strong **updraft** of air.

<u>Updraft</u> - A current of rising air

Usually, this updraft is caused by a cold front moving in on a warm front. As you learned in the previous module, the cold air mass tends to get under the warm air mass and lift it up, making an updraft. Updrafts can occur in other ways, however. For example, storms can be frequent in some mountainous regions because air must rise to pass over the mountains. This can result in a storm-producing updraft.

When a strong updraft occurs, the current of air rises, causing it to cool. As you already know, when air cools, water vapor tends to condense out of the air and form clouds. What you may not know, however, is that when water condenses, it actually releases energy. This might be hard to believe at first, but look at it this way. In Module #2, you did an experiment to show that when water evaporates, it absorbs energy, cooling whatever surface it evaporated from. Now think about it. Water condensing is essentially the opposite of water evaporating, isn't it? Well, if evaporating water tends to *absorb* energy and *cool* the surface off which it evaporated, then condensation should *release* energy and *warm* the surface on which it occurs. In a cloud, this surface is the cloud condensation nuclei. So condensation tends to heat up the cloud condensation nuclei. This makes the updraft even stronger! As the updraft pulls more and more warm, moist air into the atmosphere, a rapidly-growing cumulus cloud begins to form. This is the **cumulus stage** of the thunderstorm.

The cumulus stage does not last very long. In less than 20 minutes or so, the updraft has pushed so much moist air high into the troposphere that a tall, cumulonimbus cloud has formed. These cumulonimbus clouds can get so tall that they actually reach the tropopause and begin to flatten out against it. This typically gives the cumulonimbus cloud the shape of an anvil.

Eventually, the water droplets and/or ice crystals in the cloud become too large for the updraft to support. At that point, one of the processes I discussed in the last section takes over, and it begins to rain. This marks the **mature stage** of the thunderstorm, which consists of heavy rain, thunder, lightning, strong winds, and sometimes hail.

As the rain falls during the mature stage of a thunderstorm, it causes winds that blow downwards, hitting the land and spreading out in strong gusts of wind. These downward rushes of air are called, reasonably enough, **downdrafts**. These downdrafts can be quite severe if concentrated in a small enough area. Winds of up to 170 miles an hour can be caused by local downdrafts in a thunderstorm. Often, they are as destructive as a tornado!

As time goes on (typically less than thirty minutes), the downdrafts caused by the rain overpower the updrafts that started the storm, and the entire area is full of only downdrafts. This marks the final stage of the thunderstorm, the **dissipation** (dis uh pa' shun) **stage**. During this stage, the rain gets lighter and lighter, and the downdrafts get less and less powerful. Eventually, the storm runs its course and the rain stops. Figure 8.1 illustrates the stages I just described.

**FIGURE 8.1**
The Formation of a Thunderstorm

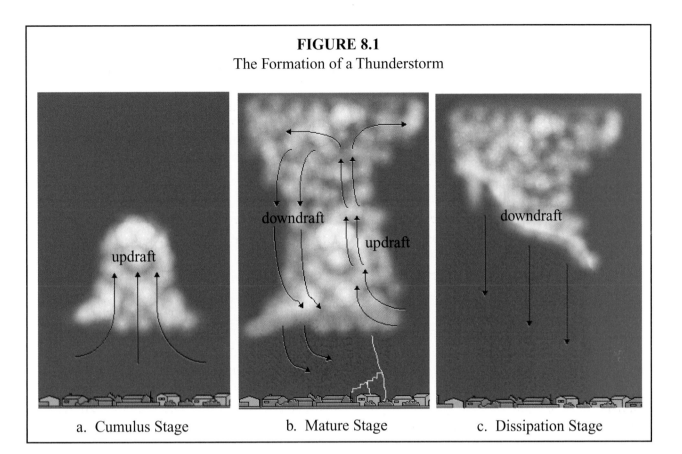

a. Cumulus Stage          b. Mature Stage          c. Dissipation Stage

What I just described to you is called a **thunderstorm cell**. In a thunderstorm cell, there is one updraft system and one resulting thundercloud. Most thunderstorms consist of several such cells. Figure 8.2, for example, is an aerial shot of a thunderstorm system that consists of several cells.

**FIGURE 8.2**
Multiple Thunderstorm Cells in one Thunderstorm System

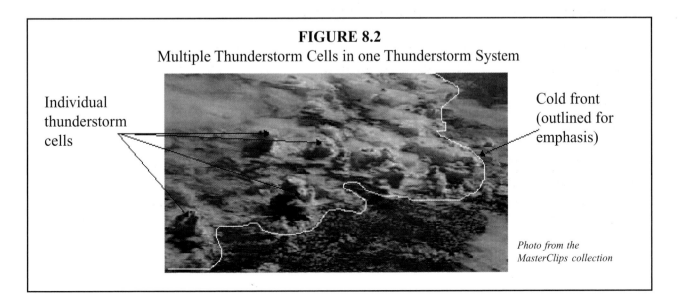

Individual thunderstorm cells

Cold front (outlined for emphasis)

*Photo from the MasterClips collection*

Although a single thunderstorm cell usually lasts for less than an hour, a thunderstorm composed of several cells can last a *lot* longer.

Thunderstorms, of course, are best known for their **thunder** and **lightning**. These two effects always accompany one another. I am sure you have wondered where thunder and lightning come from. Perform the following experiment to find out. Remember, you should still be doing Experiment 7.1. Don't stop doing it just because there is another experiment to do!

---

**EXPERIMENT 8.1**
Making Your Own Lightning

<u>Supplies</u>:
- Balloon
- Dark Room

<u>Introduction</u> - Thunder and lightning are produced as a result of electrical imbalances between a cloud and the ground. In this experiment, the balloon will represent the cloud and your hand will represent the ground.

<u>Procedure</u>:

A. Blow up the balloon and tie it off.
B. Go into a dark room and allow your eyes to get accustomed to the lack of light.
C. Hold the balloon with one hand and rub it back and forth against your hair. This will cause the balloon (and your hair) to become electrically charged.
D. Now form a fist with the other hand and put it 6-12 inches from your face at eye level. Hold your fist so that your knuckles point straight up.
E. Slowly use your other hand to pass the balloon over your fist and look at your fist carefully. You should not be able to see your fist because of the darkness. Just look where you know that your fist is. The balloon should pass by close to your knuckles, but *do not allow the balloon to touch them*. You may have to do this several times, but you will eventually see an effect. If you try several times and see nothing, the humidity might be too high. Try this on a drier day.
F. Note in your laboratory notebook what your fist felt like as the balloon passed over it and what you eventually saw and heard.
G. Do the experiment again, this time holding your hand flat instead of in a fist. Hold it palm-up at eye level and see if you can duplicate the effect you saw. You probably will not be able to see anything, but your hand should feel roughly the same as your fist did in the first part of the experiment.

---

In your experiment, you should have seen a bluish-purple spark leap from the balloon to your hand. Believe it or not, that was a small lightning bolt. Obviously it did not have the power of the lightning that accompanies a thunderstorm, but it was produced in an almost identical way.

The snap that you heard when the spark formed was actually thunder; it just didn't have the power of the thunder in a storm.

How did your lightning form? Well, when you rubbed the balloon against your hair, the balloon picked up some negative electrical charges from your hair. Remember from Module #4 that all matter (including your hair, the balloon, and your fist) contains positive and negative electrical charges. When the balloon picked up those charges, it became negatively charged. Since your hair lost those electrical charges, it became positively charged. This explains why your hair tends to stand up when you rub a balloon in it. Your positively-charged hair is attracted to the negatively-charged balloon, and it stands up to get closer to the balloon.

Once you got the balloon to be negatively charged, you passed it near your fist, which has just as many positive charges as negative charges in it. When the negatively-charged balloon came close to your fist, the positive charges in your fist were attracted to it. Thus, they moved in your fist to be as close to the negatively-charged balloon as possible. When they reached your skin, however, they had to stop because electrical charges do not move well in air. Because of this, air is called an **insulator**.

Insulator - A substance that does not conduct electricity very well

Since the positive charges could not pass through the air, they built up on the surface of your skin and on the hairs of your skin. The strange feeling you felt as the balloon passed over your hand was that electrical charge buildup.

Eventually, the electrical charge buildup became so strong that the air was forced to allow some of the positive charges to move towards the balloon. Even though the electrical charges began to move in the air, they had a hard time traveling through it because air is an insulator. Thus, they lost a lot of energy. That energy was transformed mostly into light. The light, obviously, was the spark that you saw. The rest of the energy heated the surrounding air. The heat was rather substantial, and it happened very quickly. As a result, the hot air began to rush outwards, forming waves of air. In Module #6, what did you learn about sound? It moves as a wave through air and other substances. Thus, the motion of the hot air actually forms sound waves. Those sound waves created the crackle that you heard.

Now why didn't you see the lightning when you held your hand out flat? Well, remember that in order for the charges to travel from your hand to the balloon, they need to build up enough to overcome the insulating properties of the air. When you had a fist formed, the positive charges moved as close as they could to the balloon, so they built up in your knuckles, since they are higher than the rest of your fist. Since this concentrated the positive charge, the charge was able to overcome air's insulating properties, making the spark. When you had your hand flat, the charge did not concentrate anywhere. Instead, it spread out along your hand. Thus, you probably felt the electrical buildup over a larger area, but you never saw a spark because it was not concentrated enough at any one spot to overcome air's insulating properties.

Lightning forms in almost an identical way as did the spark in your experiment. In a large cumulonimbus cloud, the heavy ice crystals near the top of the cloud eventually are too heavy to be supported by the updraft that formed the cloud in the first place. The ice crystals therefore begin to fall through the cloud, starting the Bergeron process you learned about in the first section of this module. Since a thunderstorm cloud is so large, the ice crystal makes several collisions with water droplets and other ice crystals on the way down. When those collisions are glancing collisions rather than head-on collisions, electrical charges can be transferred, much like what happened when the balloon rubbed up against your hair in the experiment.

This transfer of charge that occurs in glancing collisions results in an imbalance of electricity within the cloud. The bottom of the cloud starts building up negative charge (like the surface of the balloon in the experiment), and the top of the cloud starts building up positive electrical charge (like your hair in the experiment). The negative charges attract the positive charges in the ground (like the positive charges in your hand were attracted to the balloon). This causes a buildup of positive electrical charge on the ground. This positive electrical charge causes some of the negative charge in the cloud to move in a jerky, stepwise fashion towards the earth. This jerky movement of negative charges towards the earth is called a **stepped leader**.

Since the negative charges are moving through air, they lose a lot of energy due to the insulating properties of the air. Thus, a stepped leader is often accompanied by a dim spark. As the negative charges get closer to the ground, however, the positive charges build up more force, eventually overcoming the insulating properties of air and rushing up to meet the negative charges that are moving down. This **return stroke**, as it is called, is responsible for most of the light and sound of a lighting strike. This process is illustrated below.

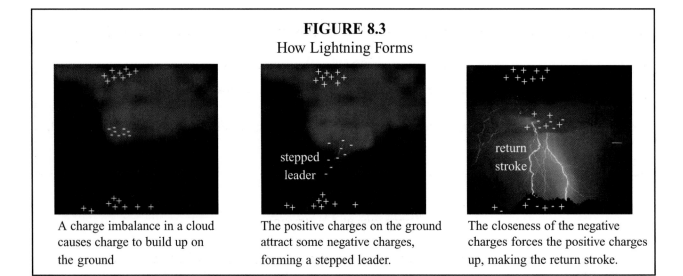

**FIGURE 8.3**
How Lightning Forms

| A charge imbalance in a cloud causes charge to build up on the ground | The positive charges on the ground attract some negative charges, forming a stepped leader. | The closeness of the negative charges forces the positive charges up, making the return stroke. |

Notice where the lightning bolts are striking in the figure. They are striking two tall trees. Just like the spark in the experiment tended to hit your knuckle because it was closest to the balloon, lightning tends to hit things that are tall. That's because the positive charges concentrate on those things, trying to get as close to the negatively-charged cloud as possible. That's why it's dangerous to stand under trees during a thunderstorm. The tree may shield you from rain, but it tends to attract lightning bolts!

Just as the spark in the experiment causes a snapping sound, the return stroke in lightning causes the booming sound we call thunder. This is caused by the intense heating that results when the charges push their way through the air. The charges lose so much energy fighting their way through air that a single lightning bolt can heat the surrounding air to temperatures in excess of 50,000 °F! This superheated air quickly rushes outwards in waves, forming sound waves that our ears detect as thunder.

The lightning that I just described to you is called **cloud-to-ground** lighting. Although this is what we usually think of when we hear the word "lightning," it is not the most common type of lightning that occurs in thunderstorms. The typical lightning that accompanies thunderstorms is called **cloud-to-cloud** lightning and is commonly referred to as "sheet lightning." This kind of lightning is caused by the same process, but the electrical building and charge transfer occurs between two clouds, not between the ground and a cloud. This kind of lightning lights up the sky in big sheets, rather than striking the ground in a bolt. Since the air is still heated as a result of the charges moving, however, there is still thunder. A form of cloud-to-cloud lightning can actually occur between cirrus clouds without the benefit of a thunderstorm. Typically called **heat lightning**, it occurs because of motion within cirrus clouds high in the troposphere. Sometimes, heat lightning can be seen on relatively clear nights during the summer.

---

### ON YOUR OWN

8.3  If a thunderstorm produces hail, in which stage of the thunderstorm would it come?

8.4  A thunderstorm begins and rains heavy sheets of rain for more than an hour before the rain begins to lighten. Was this thunderstorm composed of one cell or many cells?

8.5  Survivors of lightning strikes say that just before the lightning hit, their hair stood up on end. Why does this happen?

---

### Tornadoes and Hurricanes

Although the winds and lightning in a thunderstorm can do a lot of damage, there are no weather phenomena more devastating than tornadoes and hurricanes. Figure 8.4 provides an example of each.

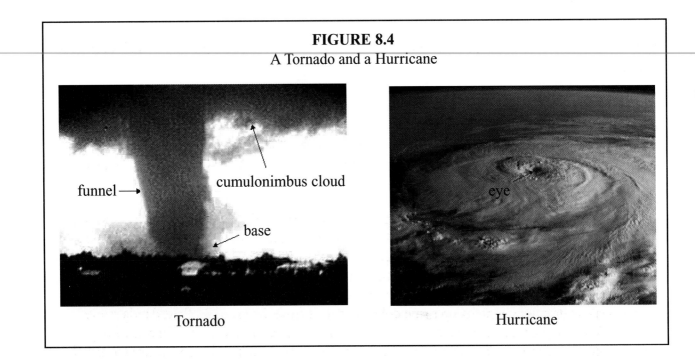

**FIGURE 8.4**
A Tornado and a Hurricane

funnel ⟶          cumulonimbus cloud

base

eye

Tornado                    Hurricane

Although tornadoes have been studied extensively, the details of how they form are still a great mystery to us. There are currently 22 theories that attempt to explain the formation of a tornado, so I will not try to explain them to you. Even though the details of their formation are not well known, there are certain things that we know for sure. First of all, tornadoes start as the result of updrafts that form thunderstorms. In the first stage of their development, known as the **whirl stage**, the updraft of air that is forming a cumulonimbus cloud begins being hit by winds blowing in a different direction at higher altitudes. The origin of these winds is one of the mysteries related to tornado development. These winds cause air to begin rotating horizontally. Combined with the updraft, this causes a funnel of air to form, with air whirling both around and up. This is often called a **vortex**.

The funnel of air then touches the ground, starting the **organizing stage** of the tornado. Once the funnel touches the ground, it forms a solid base, and the upward, whirling motion of the vortex sucks debris up into the funnel. This darkens the tornado, marking the fact that it has reached the **mature stage**. It is in this stage that the tornado is most destructive. Eventually, the forces that hold the vortex together begin to dissipate, and the tornado begins to get smaller. This is called its **shrinking stage**. Finally, the tornado weakens to the point that it is no longer visible, and it slowly dies out in its final stage, the **decaying stage**. Because a tornado starts as a result of the updrafts that form a thunderstorm, you always see thunderstorm-like conditions before a tornado, and a tornado always "hangs" from a cumulonimbus cloud.

Tornadoes can form anywhere, but the conditions that make tornado formation ideal seem to exist in the Mississippi Valley and Eastern Great Plains of the U.S. These areas make up "Tornado Alley," so called because tornadoes form there more frequently than anywhere else in the U.S. Wind speeds within a tornado are often over 100 miles per hour, but rarely exceed 250 miles per hour. Compared to hurricanes, tornadoes are relatively small. They are typically 400 to 500 feet in diameter at their base and might travel 4 to 5 miles before they enter their decaying stage.

When tornadoes form over the water, the result is called a **waterspout**. For reasons that are still relatively difficult to understand, waterspouts are not nearly as strong as tornadoes. If a waterspout is strong, it is usually the result of a tornado that formed over land and then moved into the water. Even though waterspouts are typically weaker than tornadoes, they are a great danger to boats!

An even weaker version of a tornado is called a **dust devil**. It forms as the result of an updraft, but the updraft is not the powerful kind that you find in a cumulonimbus cloud. Instead, a dust devil will typically form in the afternoon when the ground has reached its maximum temperature. Under the proper conditions, this will heat the air above the ground relatively quickly. Since the warm air rises, an updraft occurs. Horizontal winds might form that updraft into a weak vortex, which picks up some debris and dust from the ground. Dust devils rarely exceed 15 feet in diameter and usually do not last longer than a minute or so. They are quite weak. Although some have been known to be powerful enough to knock down a cat or a small dog, they are generally considered harmless.

Hurricanes, on the other hand, are significantly more destructive than tornadoes. The wind speeds in a hurricane (74 - 200 mph) are somewhat lower than those of a tornado (85 - 250 mph), but the size of a hurricane is immense! Hurricanes usually have diameters of 100 miles or more and can be as high as 9 miles! Although commonly called hurricanes, these destructive giants are properly called **tropical cyclones** because they always start in the tropics.

A hurricane begins as a thunderstorm over a tropical sea. If the sea is warm enough, there will be a lot of moisture in the air. As the updraft begins to form thunderclouds, the rate of condensation into the cloud will be very high because of the warm, moist air being lifted up. This causes a pocket of low pressure in the cloud. As winds blow along this low-pressure pocket, they begin to rotate due to the Coriolis effect. This causes a vortex of whirling winds to form, which meteorologists call a **tropical disturbance**. The warm, moist air of the tropical sea continues to feed the vortex, increasing the strength of the wind.

If the rotating winds reach a sustained speed of 23 miles per hour, the tropical disturbance is "upgraded" to a **tropical depression**. As the warm sea continues to feed the tropical depression, its winds might increase in strength. If they reach a sustained speed of 39 miles per hour, the depression is "upgraded" again to a **tropical storm**. Finally, if the winds reach 74 miles per hour, it becomes a full-fledged hurricane and is called by meteorologists a **tropical cyclone**. Once a storm system has become a tropical cyclone, there are 5 categories that tell how strong a hurricane it is. Reasonably enough, they are simply called category 1 through category 5. The category of a hurricane depends on its wind speeds. Category 1 hurricanes have wind speeds of 74-95 miles per hour while category 5 hurricanes have wind speeds in excess of 155 miles per hour or more. As the category of a hurricane increases, so does its destructive power. Hurricane Andrew, which wrecked the coast of Florida in 1992, was a Category 4 hurricane.

As you can see in Figure 8.4, the most pronounced feature of a hurricane is its **eye**. This is an area of low pressure that originally formed the vortex which led to the hurricane. Typically 10 miles or so in diameter, the eye of a hurricane is a calm area, with calm winds and often a sunny sky! At the edge of the eye, however, things are not nearly as pleasant. Meteorologists call this the **eye wall**, and it is a cylinder of whirling clouds and rain that can be as much as 9 miles high. As the clouds and rain rise up through the eye wall, they exit at the top and are thrown into a spiral that spins counterclockwise in the Northern Hemisphere and clockwise in the Southern Hemisphere.

Why do hurricanes spin in opposite directions in opposite hemispheres? Well, look at Figure 7.9 in the previous module. Notice how the winds just north of the equator are bent one way, but those just south of the equator are bent the other way? That's the result of the Coriolis effect. So the hurricanes rotate differently in the Northern Hemisphere and the Southern Hemisphere because the wind is bent differently in each hemisphere by the Coriolis effect.

Have you ever heard that when toilets are flushed they swirl the opposite way in the Northern Hemisphere as compared to the Southern Hemisphere because of the Coriolis effect? Although this sounds reasonable, it is actually a myth. Although the Coriolis effect can bend winds on a large scale, its force is small on a small scale. The way a toilet swirls when it flushes or the way a sink drains is due entirely to the way in which the basin is filled, the irregularities in the shape of the basin, and the way in which the water was disturbed prior to draining.

Surrounding the eye wall are **rain bands**. These are lines of thunderstorm cells that rotate around the eye, spiraling slowly inward as they go. Winds in the rain bands peak near the eye and become less severe as the rain band is farther from the center. A hurricane moves as a whole in the direction of the prevailing winds. As the hurricane leaves the tropics, it weakens because it loses its supply of warm, moist air. If it reaches land, it quickly dissipates into several thunderstorm systems.

Now if you think about it, a hurricane really needs two things in order to form. It needs a warm ocean to continually feed it warm, moist air, and it needs to be formed in a place where the Coriolis effect is most pronounced. Where can both of these conditions be found? Well, the earth rotates most quickly at the equator, which is also the warmest spot on the earth. This is why hurricanes always form in the tropics, usually between $10^{\circ}$ and $20^{\circ}$ north or south of the equator.

Although the winds of a hurricane can cause severe damage, most of the devastation of a hurricane comes in the form of floods. The low pressure of the eye causes the ocean beneath the hurricane to bulge upward. In addition, the winds in a hurricane tend to push water along in the direction of its motion, causing huge waves. The waves, combined with the bulge, cause the ocean to rise as much as 25 feet higher than it otherwise would. This front, called a **storm surge**, can devastate low-lying shoreline communities.

---

**ON YOUR OWN**

8.6 The early warning stage of a tornado is called a "funnel cloud." This is a cloud that has the distinct shape of a tornado but is not touching the ground. What stage is the tornado in at this point?

8.7 Suppose you are unfortunate enough to be caught in a hurricane. The winds are blowing, the rain is coming down, and water is everywhere. Suddenly, it is sunny and calm. Is the hurricane over?

---

## Weather Maps and Weather Prediction

The heart of predicting the weather is taking measurements of the factors that influence weather. Temperature, atmospheric pressure, wind direction and speed, humidity, amount of precipitation, cloud cover, cloud type, and conditions in the upper atmosphere all play a role in determining the weather. By measuring and recording these phenomena, we can put together a picture of the weather that will allow us to predict what will happen in the near term. Of course, since we really don't understand a lot about the weather, these predictions are shaky, at best!

In the experiment you are still conducting (Experiment 7.1), you have been recording the temperature, pressure, cloud cover, cloud type, and amount of precipitation for several days in a row. In the next section of this module, you will look at all of that data and see trends that will help you understand how the data you collected allow you to predict certain trends in the weather. Meteorologists have a lot of other data at their disposal to help them in trying to understand and predict weather.

**Radar** (**ra**dio **d**etection **a**nd **r**anging), for example, provides meteorologists with a lot of data regarding cloud cover and the types of clouds that are currently forming in the atmosphere. In a radar unit, a transmitter emits radio waves at a rate of about 500 per second. As those waves encounter objects, they bounce off of them and head back towards the radar unit. A receiver in the radar unit then records when the bounced signals return. The time that it takes for the radio waves to travel to an object and then bounce back indicates how far away the object is. In addition, differences between the outgoing and returning waves provide information about the makeup of the object. Weather radar, for example, can determine whether a cloud is made up of ice crystals (a cold cloud) or water droplets (a warm cloud). If the radar unit is slowly turned in a circle so that it sends out waves in all directions, it can provide a good view of the surrounding area.

**Doppler radar** is relatively new for meteorologists, but it is a well-known tool in law enforcement. This radar uses the **Doppler effect**, which you will learn about in a later module. The Doppler effect says that by analyzing a specific kind of difference (the wavelength) between the outgoing and returning waves, the speed of the object being observed can actually be determined.  Traffic police use Doppler radar to determine the speed of automobiles, while meteorologists use it to measure the speed of distant winds.

Meteorology probably made its greatest step forward when satellites were deployed for weather-related measurements.  The first weather satellite, TIROS I, was launched in 1960. Today, there are close to 50 weather satellites circling the globe, taking constant measurements of the kinds of data I mentioned above.  They give us an accurate, global picture of the weather fronts and patterns that exist on a day-to-day basis.

As a brief sidelight,  weather satellites have given us the best evidence yet that global warming is *not* happening.  Weather satellites take data continuously all over the world.  Thus, when satellite data is used to measure the average temperature of the earth, a <u>very</u> accurate number - the most accurate possible - is determined.  Courtesy of NASA, here are the average global temperature changes since 1979 based on satellite data.  The line at zero indicates no change in temperature.  Any data above that line indicates warmer weather, anything below that line indicates colder weather.

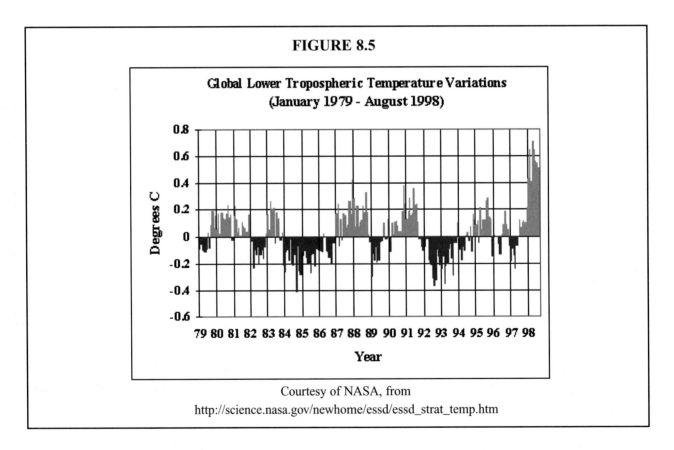

Courtesy of NASA, from
http://science.nasa.gov/newhome/essd/essd_strat_temp.htm

Notice first that the y-axis plots a range of 1.4 degrees (-0.6 to 0.8), telling you that all variations are quite minor.  Notice also that there are just as many colder temperatures as warmer temperatures, once again showing that global warming is simply not happening.  Now this data is different than that shown in Figure 2.4, where I first discussed global warming. That's because the data in Figure 2.4 come from land-based measurements, whereas these are from satellites. This data is more accurate than that shown in Figure 2.4, but the conclusion is the same from both graphs.

Since satellites can take measurements over the entire world, the network of weather satellites augment the data being taken on the ground. This data can all be compiled in something called a **weather map**. An example of a weather map is given below.

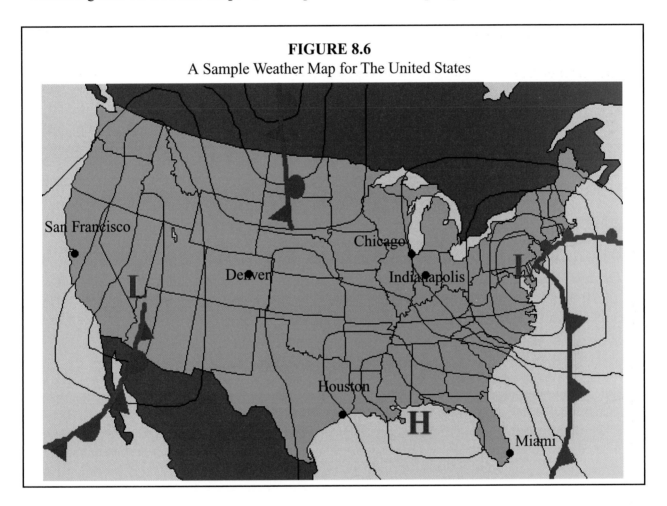

**FIGURE 8.6**
A Sample Weather Map for The United States

There are many different kinds of weather maps. Some have detailed information while others have less detailed, more general information. This weather map is one of the less detailed ones. Notice the thin black lines that are drawn all around the map. These lines are **isobars** and represent regions of equal atmospheric pressure. If you travel along a single isobar, the atmospheric pressure does not change. Notice how between Houston and Miami the isobars form irregular ovals and at the center is a large "H." That "H" tells you that the isobar surrounding it represents high pressure. As you move away from the "H," each isobar represents a lower pressure. Thus, the atmospheric pressure in Miami is *higher* than the atmospheric pressure in Houston because Miami is between the first and second isobar away from the "H," while Houston is just past the second isobar. Thus, Houston is more isobars away from the "H" and therefore has lower atmospheric pressure. Chicago and Indianapolis, however, have similar atmospheric pressures because they are very near the same isobar.

Look at the "L" centered over the New England area. This tells us that the isobar surrounding the "L" represents the lowest atmospheric pressure. Each isobar moving outward from that "L" represents areas with increasing atmospheric pressure. Thus, we can tell the general atmospheric pressure of a region by looking at such a map and reading the isobars.

Now look at the heavier, colored lines on the map. These lines represent the weather fronts in the region. The blue line with triangles represents a cold front. The triangles tell us the direction in which the cold front is traveling. The red line with the ovals represents a warm front, and the ovals tell us which direction the lines are moving. The purple line towards the north with ovals on one side and triangles on the other is a stationary front. Finally, the purple line in the west that has ovals and triangles on the same side represents an occluded front. The ovals and triangles indicate the direction of motion.

The fronts on the map give us a great deal of information about the weather. After all, we already know the weather characteristic of each front. Thus, we can predict that the area to the east of Miami will probably experience storms because of the cold front. The New England area will probably experience long, wet days due to the warm front. The northern United States and Canada will be experiencing similar weather due to the stationary front. Finally, the southwestern United States will experience long, wet days followed by storms due to the occluded front.

Depending on how detailed you want to get, there are many other different kinds of weather maps. Some weather maps plot **isotherms** instead of, or in addition to, isobars. Isotherms are lines that represent constant temperature. In addition, there are special maps that plot the wind speed, cloud cover, and other data related to weather.

In weather forecasting, all of that information gets put into a computer and mathematical models predict where weather fronts will move and how quickly. The people interpreting the results decide, based on the characteristics of the weather fronts, what kind of weather is likely. Since we know so little about weather, these forecasts are not able to predict the weather accurately. Instead, they predict the percentage chance of weather events. For example, a weather forecast might say that there is a 30% chance of rain tomorrow. This forecast means that most likely, there will not be rain tomorrow. Nevertheless, it is *possible* for it to rain. Not very accurate, is it? Nevertheless, today's weather forecasting is significantly more accurate than it used to be!

---

**ON YOUR OWN**

8.8 Ground-based temperature measurements tend to be made near places where people live, whereas satellite temperature measurements cover essentially the whole earth. Would you expect the average temperature of the earth, as calculated by ground-based measurements, to be greater than or less than that calculated by satellite measurements?

8.9 Based on Figure 8.6, would you expect to experience higher or lower atmospheric pressure if you left San Francisco and started heading east?

8.10 Based on Figure 8.6, where will the occluded front be in the next few days: Mexico or Denver?

---

### Interpreting the Results of Experiment 7.1 and Making Your Own Weather Predictions

Now that you have been taking weather-related data for about 3 weeks, it is time to learn from it. First of all, take the table of data that you have collected and look through it for days that had precipitation. Get an idea of what constitutes a lot of precipitation over this time span and what constitutes a little. Next, use markers or colored pens or pencils to mark those days. If there was a lot of precipitation in a day, mark it with one color. If there was only a little, mark it with another color. If there was no precipitation, don't mark it at all.

Once you have finished doing that, find the first day that was marked and look at the cloud cover, temperature, and pressure in the few days leading up to the day of precipitation. Was there a progression of clouds typical of a warm front? Did the clouds rush in quickly, typical of a cold front? Was there precipitation several days in a row, perhaps indicating a stationary or occluded front? What about temperature? Was there a progression from warm to cold or vice-versa, or did the temperature stay constant for a long time, indicative of a stationary front? What about atmospheric pressure? Was there a steady rise or fall?

Think about the data in terms of weather fronts. If a cold front moves in, for example, you expect reasonably quick, heavy rain or snow. After the rain or snow is finished, the temperature should be cooler than before. The atmospheric pressure should be lower during the storm, but it should rise again once the storm is done. So, if you see a single day of precipitation that is preceded by warmer temperatures and followed by cooler temperatures, then the weather was probably caused by a cold front.

On the other hand, a progression of clouds from cirrus to stratus before a day of precipitation most likely means a warm front. If the precipitation lasts only a day or two, this is more evidence of a warm front. Once the precipitation ends, warmer temperatures as compared to the day before the precipitation began give even more evidence of a warm front. If the precipitation lasted for two or more days and there was no appreciable change in temperature, the weather was probably caused by a stationary front. Finally, light precipitation followed by heavy precipitation can be indicative of an occluded front. A progression of temperatures from cold to warm back to cold would be more evidence for such a front.

Analyze each of the days with precipitation using these questions. Try to determine the weather front that caused the precipitation you experienced. Once you have done that, you should see some patterns emerging. Based on those patterns, it is time to do some weather predictions with the following experiment. I have purposely made this module short in order to give you time to do this because it is important for you to learn to apply knowledge. Thus, please do the experiment and check your results!

---

### EXPERIMENT 8.2
#### Turning Experiment 7.1 Into a Weather Prediction Tool

Supplies:

- The data table from Experiment 7.1
- The same source of weather data you used before

Introduction - It is time to take the knowledge that you gained from Experiment 7.1 and try to use it to predict the weather. You will use the patterns that you recognized in analyzing Experiment 7.1 to predict the weather for the next few days.

Procedure:

A. Add another column to your table, and in that column, make a general prediction about tomorrow's weather. Based on the weather data for yesterday and before, and based on the cloud cover you see today, try to determine if a weather front is moving in or not.
B. If there is no indication of a weather front, then you can expect no change in the weather, and that's your prediction. If you do think that the data indicate a weather front, predict whether there will be precipitation, predict the cloud type and cover, and predict whether the temperature will be warmer or cooler.
C. The next day, check your prediction to see how accurate it is. Make a mark to indicate whether you were right, partially right, or dead wrong.
D. Continue this for at least a week. See if you get any better as time goes on. Perhaps you will get some idea of how hard a meteorologist's job really is!

# ANSWERS TO THE ON YOUR OWN PROBLEMS

8.1 <u>Without strong, upward gusts of wind, there will be no hail.</u> In order for hail to form, it must be recycled through the cloud by strong, upward gusts of wind.

8.2 Sleet falls to the ground as ice, while freezing rain falls to the ground as water and then freezes. To tell the difference, <u>catch some in your hand. If it is frozen when it touches your hand, it is sleet. If it is liquid when it touches your hand, it is freezing rain.</u> Another answer would be to look at the ground. Sleet piles up like tiny chunks of ice while freezing rain makes a glassy glaze over everything.

8.3 <u>It would be in its mature stage.</u> Hail is the result of precipitation recycled by a strong updraft. Thus, there must be both precipitation and an updraft. Both of those conditions exist only in the mature stage of a thunderstorm.

8.4 <u>The thunderstorm was composed of many cells.</u> Strong, heavy sheets of rain are indicative of the mature stage of a thunderstorm, which lasts only 30 minutes or less. Thus, there must have been several cells to make the heavy rain go on so long.

8.5 <u>Their hair stood on end because of the positive charges on the ground trying to rise to the negative charges in the sky. Some of them traveled up the person and into his or her hair.</u> Remember the effect you felt in the experiment. Imagine that effect all over your body. That's what a lightning strike victim feels an instant before the stroke.

8.6 <u>The tornado is still in its whirl stage.</u> The next stage (organization) does not occur until the funnel touches the ground.

8.7 <u>The hurricane is not over.</u> You are currently in the eye of the hurricane. When the eye passes, you will be back into the thick of things.

8.8 <u>Ground-based temperature measurements are, on average, warmer than satellite measurements.</u> After all, people tend to live where it is warm or moderate, not where it is very cold. Thus, the measurements on the ground are biased towards warmer areas. As a result, the average temperature of the earth as calculated by ground-based measurements is always higher than that calculated by satellites.

8.9 San Francisco is past the second isobar from a low pressure minimum. As you travel east, you will get closer to the low pressure minimum. <u>This means your atmospheric pressure will decrease as you travel east.</u>

8.10 <u>Mexico will get the occluded front.</u> The ovals and triangles clearly indicate that the front is moving to Mexico.

**STUDY GUIDE FOR MODULE #8**

1. Define the following terms:

a. Updraft
b. Insulator

2. Both the Bergeron process and the collision-coalescence process explain precipitation, but they each begin with a different kind of cloud. With what kind of cloud does each theory begin?

3. Which of the two theories of precipitation governs the fall of rain from the tops of a cumulonimbus cloud? What about a nimbostratus cloud?

4. What is the difference between drizzle and rain?

5. What are the differences between sleet, hail, and freezing rain?

6. A meteorologist measures the dew point on two different mornings. The first morning is very humid and the atmospheric pressure is high. The second morning is not nearly as humid and the atmospheric pressure has fallen. On which day will the dew point be coldest?

7. Name the three stages of a thunderstorm cell in the order that they occur. At each stage, indicate whether an updraft, downdraft or both are present. Also, indicate whether or not precipitation occurs.

8. If the heavy rain of a thunderstorm lasts for more than 30 minutes, what can you conclude about its makeup?

9. Lightning forms as a result of electrical charge imbalance. Where does that charge imbalance originate and why does it occur?

10. Which is responsible for most of the light and sound in a lightning bolt: the stepped leader or the return stroke?

11. Where does the thunder in a thunderstorm come from?

12. Why do lightning bolts tend to strike targets that are high?

13. What is the difference between sheet lightning and a lightning bolt?

14. What kind of cloud is necessary for tornado formation?

15. List the five stages of a tornado in order. At which stage is the tornado most destructive?

16. What are the four classifications that lead to a hurricane? What is used to determine which classification a storm fits in?

17. What are the conditions in the eye of a hurricane?

18. What causes a hurricane in the Southern Hemisphere to rotate in a different direction than a hurricane in the Northern Hemisphere?

Given the following weather map, answer questions 19-24.

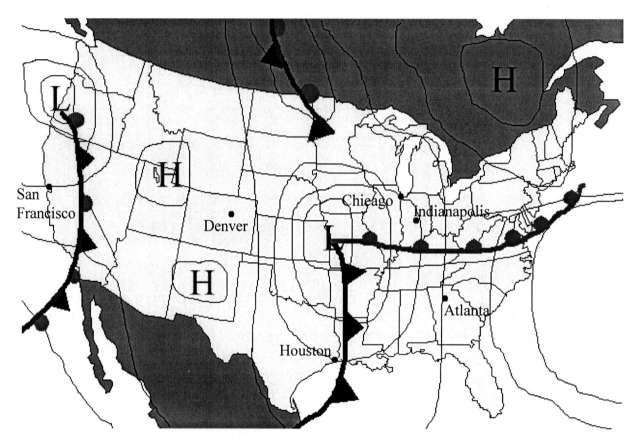

19. Is the atmospheric pressure in Houston, TX higher, lower, or equivalent to that of Chicago, IL?

20. Is the atmospheric pressure in Houston, TX higher, lower, or equivalent to that of Atlanta, GA?

21. Is the occluded front nearer to San Francisco, CA or Canada?

22. Will Atlanta or Indianapolis be in for some warmer weather soon?

23. At the time this map was drawn, what city might be experiencing thunderstorms?

24. What city probably experienced long rains followed by thunderstorms recently?

# MODULE #9: An Introduction to the Physics of Motion

## Introduction

Over the previous semester, I gave you a basic introduction to earth's physical environment. You have (hopefully) learned about the atmosphere, hydrosphere, lithosphere, and cores of the earth. You have also seen how those "regions" of the physical environment interact to form weather phenomenon and other physical effects in our daily experience. Now it is time to take a *deeper* look into your physical environment. In this semester, I want to give you an introduction to the most fundamental of all sciences: physics.

What do I mean when I say "fundamental?" Well, physics lies at the root of all other sciences. For example, in the previous semester, you learned about weather. The study of weather is a science unto itself. Called **meteorology**, this science analyzes weather fronts, winds, humidity, cloud cover, etc. in an attempt to better understand weather and the factors which cause it. The science of physics, however, describes how all things, including weather fronts, move. It describes how water evaporates to form humidity and then condenses again to form clouds. It also describes how the temperature imbalances which cause wind actually form. In the end, then, *every* science relies on the science of physics. As a result, we call physics the most fundamental of all sciences.

Before I begin introducing the science of physics to you, there is one important thing that you must realize. Even though I will spend a lot of this semester on physics, please understand that what you learn here is just a bare-bones introduction to this fascinating field. I cannot go into nearly enough detail because you do not have the mathematical skills necessary. Physics is an inherently mathematical science. You may not fully appreciate that fact as a result of taking this course, because I have had to weed out a great deal of the mathematics. In high school, however, you will (hopefully) spend a whole year on physics. At that point, you will develop a deep appreciation for the mathematical nature of the science!

## Mechanics - The Study of Motion

If you look around, you will see many things in motion. Trees, plants, and sometimes bits of garbage blow around in the wind. Cars, planes, animals, insects, and people move about from place to place. In Module #3, you learned that even objects which appear stationary are, in fact, filled with motion because their component molecules or atoms are moving. In short, the world around us is alive with motion.

In fact, St. Thomas Aquinas listed the presence of motion as one of his five arguments for the existence of God. He said that in all of our experience, humans have found that motion cannot occur without a mover. In other words, in order for something to move, there must be something else that moves it. When a rolling ball collides with a toy car, the car will move because the ball gives it motion. But, of course, the ball would not have been rolling to begin with if it had not been pushed or thrown. Thus, Aquinas says that our practical experience tells us that any observable motion should be traceable back to the original mover. When the universe began, then, something had to be there to start all of the motion that we see today. Aquinas says that God is this "original mover."

While philosophers can mount several objections to St. Thomas Aquinas' argument, it nevertheless shows how important motion is in the universe. Thus, it is important for us to be able to study and understand motion. It is so important that an entire branch of science is devoted to the study of motion. The science of **mechanics** is a branch of physics, and it deals with analyzing and understanding objects in motion.

Now if you want to study the motion of an object, what's the first thing you need to know? You need to know its **position**. If the position of an object changes, we know that the object is in motion. That should seem like a rather obvious statement to you, but it really is not. Think about it. Suppose you placed a book on a picnic table and then stepped back three feet to observe it resting on the table. Is the book in motion? Your first answer might be "no," but that answer is only partially correct. Certainly as far as you are concerned, the book is not moving because it's just sitting there on the table. What if a person on the moon were able to use a very powerful telescope to observe the book? Would he or she conclude that the book is in motion? Yes! You see, even though the book is resting on the table, it is rotating along with the rest of the earth. You don't notice that motion, however, because you are rotating right along with the book. Thus, *relative to you*, the book is not moving. The person on the moon, however, is not rotating with the earth. As a result, he or she thinks that both you and the book are moving because *relative to him or her*, your position is changing.

What does this tell you about position? **Position must always be given *relative* to something else**. That "something else" is usually called a **reference point**.

<u>Reference point</u> - A point against which position is measured

In the case of the book I was discussing, you could say that its position *relative to you* was 3 feet in front of you. In that case, you are the reference point. As time went on, that position never changed, so you would conclude that the book was not moving. If the person on the moon were to mark the book's position relative to the moon, then that position would constantly change, indicating that *relative to the moon*, the book was moving. In that case, the moon was the reference point. The observer on the moon could, however, use the same reference point that you did. If the observer saw both you and the book, the observer could say that the book was three feet in front of you. If the observer continued to use you as the reference point, the observer would also conclude that the book was not moving because its position relative to you remained the same.

This little discussion illustrates one of the most important concepts in all of physics:

**All motion is relative**.

In other words, motion depends on the reference point that is used. In the case of the book, if your position is used as the reference point, the book is not in motion. If the moon's position is used as the reference point, the book is in motion. Thus, the motion of any object depends on the reference point that is used to describe that object's position.

---

**ON YOUR OWN**

9.1 Suppose you go to a department store that has two floors, and you find an escalator (a moving stairway) that allows you to travel to the second floor. Perhaps because you are a shady-looking character, three security guards are watching you. The first one is on the escalator with you. The second one is on the first floor near the escalator but not on the escalator. The third is on the other escalator that is moving down. Relative to which security guard(s) are you in motion? Relative to which security guard(s) are you not in motion?

---

### Speed:  How Quickly Motion Occurs

If an object is in motion, its position is changing. Over time, that will result in a certain distance which the object travels. If I take the distance an object travels and divide by the time it takes to travel that distance, I end up getting the object's **speed**. I can write that mathematically as:

$$\text{speed} = \frac{\text{distance}}{\text{time}} \tag{9.1}$$

Of course, you are already familiar with the concept of speed. After all, you know that the speed limit on most interstate highways is 65 miles per hour. This means that if a car is traveling the speed limit, it will travel 65 miles each hour it is on the road.

Notice, then, that speed needs to have units attached to it in order to really understand what it means. If I say that I want you to walk with a speed of 65, could you do it? Well, it all depends on the units, doesn't it? You certainly could walk with a speed of 65 feet per minute, right? In fact, you would have to walk really slowly to match that speed. No matter how fast you try to walk, however, there is no way you could walk with a speed of 65 miles per hour! Thus, the units attached to speed are very important.

In physics, this is true of *all* quantities that you measure or calculate. The units on the quantity are just as important as the quantity itself. For example, when I took high school physics, my teacher allowed us to do something I would *never* allow you to do. On the day before our first test, he said, "I will allow you to use a 3x5 card on the test. You can write anything you want on the card in order to help you with the test." Of course, he was far too easy on his students, but nevertheless, I was quite happy about it. I even raised my hand and said, "You mean we can use any 3x5 card we want?" He replied, "Yes." The next day, I brought a 3 foot by 5 foot card into class. It had notes scribbled *all over it*! In the end, he had to let me use it on the test because he had not mentioned the units!  Thus, units are very important when communicating physical quantities.  Any answer you give will be counted wrong unless you give the proper units!

Since units are so important in physics (and all sciences, really), you need to know how to deal with them in mathematics equations.  Study the following example problems to help you see how this is done.

---

**EXAMPLE 9.1**

**A car travels 78 miles down the highway.  It takes the car 1.2 hours to travel that far.  At what speed is the car traveling?**

Speed can be calculated using Equation (9.1).  All we need to know is the distance (78 miles) and the time (1.2 hours).  I can put those into the equation and come up with an answer:

$$\text{speed} = \frac{78 \text{ miles}}{1.2 \text{ hours}} = 65 \frac{\text{miles}}{\text{hour}}$$

Notice what I did here.  When I put the values for speed and time in the equation, I *kept their units with them*.  This is very important.

**When working with physical quantities in equations, keep the units with the numbers.**

Once I put the numbers in there, look at what I did.  Since "78 over 1.2" means "78 divided by 1.2," I divided 78 by 1.2 and got 65.  Look at what I then did with the units.  I left the units in the same way they appeared in the equation.  That's how I got $65 \frac{\text{miles}}{\text{hour}}$.  When we have units in a fraction like this, we usually use the term "per" to represent the line in the fraction.  That's why these units are called "miles per hour."

**What is the speed of the car from the previous problem in meters per second?  (1 mile = 1609 meters, 1 hour = 3600 seconds)**

In this problem, we are told to report the answer in metric units rather than English units.  How can we do that?  Well, way back in Module #1, you learned how to convert from unit to unit.  If we convert 78 miles to meters and 1 hour to seconds, we can then re-use Equation (9.1).  First, let's convert from miles to meters:

$$\frac{78 \cancel{\text{ miles}}}{1} \times \frac{1609 \text{ meters}}{1 \cancel{\text{ mile}}} = 125502 \text{ meters}$$

If you don't remember how to do this, go back and review Module #1. Now we need to convert the time from hours to seconds:

$$\frac{1.2 \; \text{hours}}{1} \times \frac{3600 \, \text{seconds}}{1 \; \text{hour}} = 4320 \, \text{seconds}$$

Now we can use *those* numbers in our speed equation:

$$\text{speed} = \frac{125502 \text{ meters}}{4320 \text{ seconds}} = 29.1 \; \frac{\text{meters}}{\text{second}}$$

If you do this calculation with a calculator (as you should), you will notice that the answer is 29.05138889. I rounded that to 29.1. When you take chemistry, you will learn about "significant figures," which will tell you when to round a number off. For this course, don't worry too much about where to round off a number. Your answers will be right even if you round off at a different place than I do. Now realize that 29.1 meters per second and 65 miles per hour *are both the same speed.* They simply express that speed in different units.

When a physical quantity involves units, you must carry the units along with the quantity in any equation that you use. That will allow you to determine the proper units for your answer. Try these "on your own" problems to make sure you understand what I am talking about.

**ON YOUR OWN**

9.2  What is the speed of an aircraft that travels 115 miles in 30 minutes? Put your answer in units of miles per hour.

9.3  When measuring the speed of a snail, the best unit to use is millimeters per minute. A snail takes all day (12 hours) to travel 5 meters. What is its speed in millimeters per minute?

Velocity: Speed and Direction

In everyday conversation, you probably use the terms "velocity" and "speed" interchangeably. When you want to sound smart, you probably say "velocity," otherwise, you probably say "speed." In physics, however, there is a big difference between speed and velocity. Velocity contains more information than does speed. Speed tells you how quickly an object moves, while velocity tells you how quickly *and in what direction* the object is moving. This might not sound like a big difference, but it really is. If an airplane pilot who is trying to land a plane tells the control tower that the plane is moving at 122 miles per hour, that's not enough for the control tower to tell the airplane where to land. The pilot must tell the control tower at what speed *and what direction* the plane is traveling. When the pilot does that, he or she is telling the control tower the plane's *velocity*.

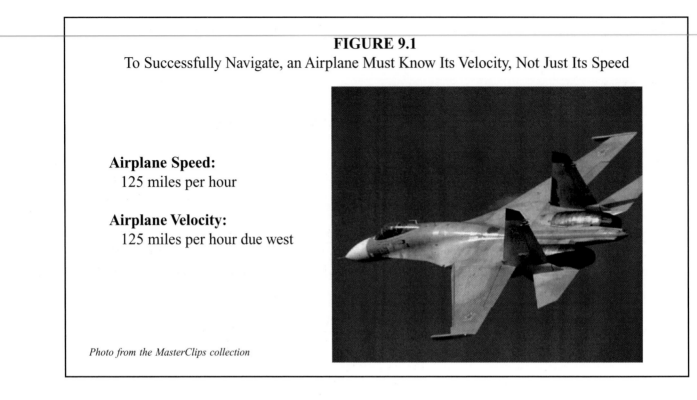

**FIGURE 9.1**
To Successfully Navigate, an Airplane Must Know Its Velocity, Not Just Its Speed

**Airplane Speed:**
125 miles per hour

**Airplane Velocity:**
125 miles per hour due west

*Photo from the MasterClips collection*

When a physical quantity carries information concerning direction, we call it a **vector quantity**. When the physical quantity does not carry information concerning direction, we call it a **scalar quantity**.

Vector quantity - A physical measurement that contains directional information

Scalar quantity - A physical measurement that does not contain directional information

Using this terminology, speed is a scalar quantity while velocity is a vector quantity. Why is the distinction between speed and velocity so important? Perform the following experiment to find out!

**EXPERIMENT 9.1**
The Importance of Direction

Supplies:

- Four eggs
- Two strips of reasonably strong cardboard (like the cardboard you find on the back of writing tablets)
- Many books
- A pair of scissors
- Lots of newspaper or paper towels
- Kitchen table

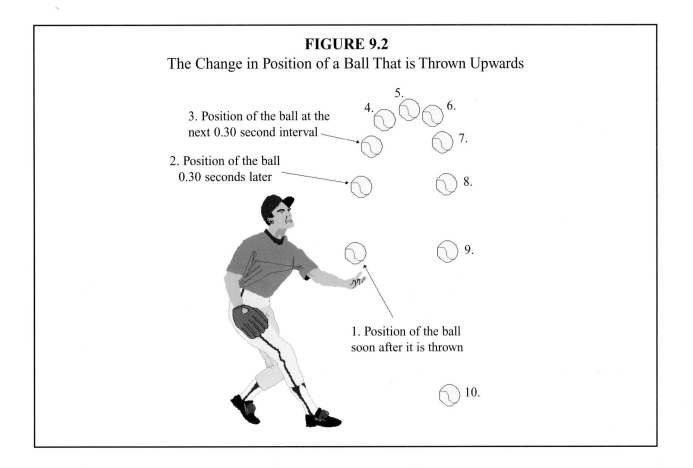

**FIGURE 9.2**
The Change in Position of a Ball That is Thrown Upwards

3. Position of the ball at the
next 0.30 second interval

2. Position of the ball
0.30 seconds later

1. Position of the ball
soon after it is thrown

4. 5. 6. 7. 8. 9. 10.

In this figure, I am not drawing multiple balls. Each image of the ball in the figure is a drawing of the same ball. It was thrown up in the air by the softball player, and I am showing you its position every 0.30 seconds. Thus, the image of the ball closest to the pitcher's hand represents where the ball would be shortly after the pitcher released it. The next image represents where that ball would be 0.30 seconds later. The next one is drawn at the position it would occupy in the next 0.30 seconds, and so on. Each ball image in the figure, then, represents the position of the ball in 0.30 second intervals.

Now look closely at the figure. The distance between the first image of the ball and the second image of the ball is fairly large. The distance between the second and third image is significantly smaller, however. The distance between the third and fourth images is even smaller, and the distance between the fourth and fifth is still smaller. Starting at the next image, however, the distance between images begins to grow again. How can this be explained?

These images each represent the position of the ball 0.30 seconds after the previous image. Since the ball's position changed over each time interval, we know that it was traveling with a certain velocity. Over the first 0.30 second time interval, the ball traveled up a certain distance. Over the next 0.30 second time interval, the ball traveled up, but not nearly as far. What does that tell us about the difference in the velocities between the two time intervals? In the first time interval a much larger distance was traveled than in the second time interval, despite the fact that each interval was 0.30 seconds. If the ball travels less distance in the second time interval, that tells us that the ball's velocity is lower in the second time interval than in the first. Using that same reasoning, all the way up to the fifth image of the ball, the ball's velocity decreased.

What happened after the fifth image of the ball? The distance between the images of the ball begins to increase. This tells is that during that time, the ball's velocity was increasing. Thus, the ball starts out with a certain velocity given to it by the softball player. That velocity decreases until it reaches the very top of its path, and then the velocity starts increasing again. What do we call this phenomenon? We call this phenomenon **acceleration**.

Acceleration - The time rate of change of an object's velocity

When an object is in motion and its velocity changes, we say that the object has experienced acceleration. Although the word definition of acceleration is important, we can also express the definition of acceleration mathematically:

$$\text{acceleration} = \frac{\text{final velocity} - \text{initial velocity}}{\text{time}} \tag{9.2}$$

Thus, the acceleration of an object can be calculated if you take the difference in its velocities over a certain time interval and divide by the number of seconds in that time interval.

Let's think for a moment about the units that will go along with acceleration. Remember, as my former high school physics teacher learned, the units on a physical quantity are just as important as the quantity itself. If we want to learn about acceleration, then, we need to learn about its units. The units on velocity are a distance unit divided by a time unit. Thus, units like meters/second, miles/hour, and kilometers/minute are all valid velocity units. When I take a unit like that and divide by time, what do I get? Well, let's look at a quick example:

---

**EXAMPLE 9.3**

**In Figure 9.2, the ball has a velocity of 2.0 feet per second downwards when it is at position #6 in the figure. By the time it reaches position #7, the ball has a velocity of 11.6 feet per second downwards. What is the ball's acceleration?**

To calculate acceleration, we use Equation (9.2). The initial velocity is 2.0 feet per second down and the final velocity is 11.6 feet per second down. As the figure indicates, the time interval is 0.30 seconds.

$$\text{acceleration} = \frac{\text{final velocity} - \text{initial velocity}}{\text{time}}$$

$$\text{acceleration} = \frac{11.6 \ \dfrac{\text{feet}}{\text{second}} - 2.0 \ \dfrac{\text{feet}}{\text{second}}}{0.30 \ \text{seconds}} = \frac{9.6 \ \dfrac{\text{feet}}{\text{second}}}{0.30 \ \text{seconds}} = 32 \ \dfrac{\dfrac{\text{feet}}{\text{second}}}{\text{second}}$$

What kind of unit is that? Well, we could say that it is "feet per second per second," but there is a better way to express it. Remember that a fraction merely represents a situation in which you divide the numerator by the denominator. Thus:

$$32 \ \frac{\dfrac{\text{feet}}{\text{second}}}{\text{second}} = 32 \ \frac{\text{feet}}{\text{second}} \div \text{second}$$

How do we divide by a fraction? We invert and multiply:

$$32 \ \frac{\text{feet}}{\text{second}} \div \text{second} = 32 \ \frac{\text{feet}}{\text{second}} \times \frac{1}{\text{second}} = 32 \ \frac{\text{feet}}{\text{second}^2}$$

Thus, the acceleration can be expressed as <u>32 feet per second$^2$ downwards</u>.

The units on acceleration, then, are a distance unit divided by a time unit squared. Thus, units like feet/second$^2$, meters/second$^2$, miles/hour$^2$, and kilometers/minute$^2$ are all valid acceleration units.

Now that you know the units which accompany acceleration, you need to know a few more specifics. Acceleration is a vector quantity. This means it contains directional information. How do you attach directional information to acceleration? Well, in order to determine the direction of acceleration, you need to know the direction of the velocity, and you need to know whether velocity is increasing or decreasing. Remember, acceleration is change in velocity. Velocity can change in one of three ways. If an object speeds up, the velocity obviously changes. When an object slows down, the velocity changes as well. Finally, if an object changes direction, the velocity changes. In all three of those cases, there is acceleration because there is a change in the velocity.

We can determine the direction of the acceleration if we examine how the velocity is changing. For example, suppose a car is heading west and begins to increase its speed. The car is accelerating, but in what direction? Well, since the westward velocity is getting larger, the change in velocity results in *more* westward movement. Thus, the acceleration must have a direction of west. Suppose that car were to then begin to slow down. What's the direction of the acceleration then? Well, if the westward velocity decreases, that means the acceleration is going *against* the velocity. Thus, the acceleration's direction is east. If an object is speeding up, then, its acceleration is in the same direction as its velocity. If it is slowing down, its acceleration is in the opposite direction as its velocity. See how that works in the following example problems.

## EXAMPLE 9.4

**A rock is dropped from a bridge into a river. It starts out with zero initial velocity and it hits the river 2 seconds later, traveling with a velocity of 19.6 meters per second downwards. What is the acceleration?**

The rock starts off with no velocity. Thus, its initial velocity is zero. Its final velocity is 19.6 meters per second, and the time is 2 seconds. We can now just plug those numbers into our equation:

$$\text{acceleration} = \frac{\text{final velocity} - \text{initial velocity}}{\text{time}}$$

$$\text{acceleration} = \frac{19.6 \frac{\text{meters}}{\text{second}} - 0 \frac{\text{meters}}{\text{second}}}{2 \text{ seconds}} = \frac{19.6 \frac{\text{meters}}{\text{second}}}{2 \text{ seconds}} = 9.8 \frac{\text{meters}}{\text{second}^2}$$

The rock sped up, because it started at zero and ended traveling 19.6 meters per second downwards. Thus, the acceleration must be in the same direction as the velocity. Therefore, the acceleration is 9.8 meters per second² downwards.

**A bicyclist is traveling down a road at 18 feet per second to the east. The cyclist sees an obstacle in the road ahead, so he hits the brakes. In 1.8 seconds, the cyclist has come to a complete halt. What is the cyclist's acceleration?**

To determine the acceleration, we need to know the initial velocity, the final velocity and the time. Well, before the brakes are slammed, the cyclist is traveling 18 feet per second east. That's the initial velocity. In 1.8 seconds (that's the time), the cyclist comes to a complete halt. What is the final velocity? If the cyclist is at a halt, the velocity is zero. Thus, the final velocity is zero. This makes the equation:

$$\text{acceleration} = \frac{\text{final velocity} - \text{initial velocity}}{\text{time}}$$

$$\text{acceleration} = \frac{0 \frac{\text{feet}}{\text{second}} - 18 \frac{\text{feet}}{\text{second}}}{1.8 \text{ seconds}} = \frac{-18 \frac{\text{feet}}{\text{second}}}{1.8 \text{ seconds}} = -10 \frac{\text{feet}}{\text{second}^2}$$

Now what does this mean? When we subtracted 18 from zero, we got -18. When we divided that number by 1.8, the negative sign stayed around. What does a negative acceleration mean? Well, it tells you about the direction of acceleration. The bicyclist slowed down. That means the acceleration is in the opposite direction as the velocity. That's what the negative means. It is reminding you that the cyclist slowed down, making the acceleration opposite of the velocity.

Since the velocity's direction is east, you know the acceleration is <u>10 feet per second$^2$ to the west</u>. Notice that I dropped the negative sign. Why? Well, the negative sign helped me determine the direction of the acceleration. Thus, I didn't really drop the negative, I just turned it into a direction. That's what you should do as well. If you come across a negative acceleration, you should use that negative to help you determine the direction, but only the direction should show up in your answer.

Before we leave this example, there is a point of terminology I want to make. Some people use the term "deceleration" to describe acceleration which slows the speed of an object. Although that is an accepted term in everyday English, it is not an acceptable term in physics. When we talk about acceleration which slows an object down, we do not say deceleration. Instead, we give the direction of the acceleration. That tells a physicist whether an object slows down or speeds up.

When solving physics problems, there is one thing for which you must always be on your guard. I want to use the subject of acceleration to show you what that is. Study the next example problem carefully.

---

**EXAMPLE 9.5**

**A sportscar travels from 0 to 60 miles per hour north in 6.1 seconds. What is its acceleration?**

At first glance this seems like an easy problem. We are given the initial velocity (0), the final velocity (60 miles per hour north), and the time (6.1 seconds). Thus, we just put it into the equation, right?

$$\text{acceleration} = \frac{\text{final velocity} - \text{initial velocity}}{\text{time}}$$

$$\text{acceleration} = \frac{60 \frac{\text{miles}}{\text{hour}} - 0 \frac{\text{miles}}{\text{hour}}}{6.1 \text{ seconds}} = \frac{60 \frac{\text{miles}}{\text{hour}}}{6.1 \text{ seconds}}$$

There is something terribly wrong with that equation. Can you see it? The numerator of the fraction has a unit of miles per hour. The denominator has the unit "seconds." *THAT IS NOT ALLOWED!* In order to do math on numbers with units, the units must agree with one another. You cannot have feet and miles in the same equation; you can't even have millimeters and centimeters in the same equation. Every unit for length must be the same, every unit for time must be the same, and so on. In this equation, we have hours and seconds (both units of time) in the same equation. We cannot have that. We must convert one of those two quantities. The 6.1 seconds is easiest to convert, so that's what we'll do. Since there are 3,600 seconds in an hour:

$$\frac{6.1 \text{ seconds}}{1} \times \frac{1 \text{ hour}}{3600 \text{ seconds}} = 0.00169 \text{ hours}$$

Now that we have all time units in agreement, we can really use the acceleration equation:

$$\text{acceleration} = \frac{\text{final velocity} - \text{initial velocity}}{\text{time}}$$

$$\text{acceleration} = \frac{60 \frac{\text{miles}}{\text{hour}} - 0 \frac{\text{miles}}{\text{hour}}}{0.00169 \text{ hours}} = \frac{60 \frac{\text{miles}}{\text{hour}}}{0.00169 \text{ hours}} = 35503 \frac{\text{miles}}{\text{hour}^2}$$

That's a big number! Since the car's speed increased, the acceleration and velocity have the same direction. The acceleration, then, is 35503 miles/hour² north.

When looking at a physics problem, then, you need to figure out the equation you are going to use. If you are looking for velocity or speed, you use Equation (9.1). If you are solving for acceleration, you use Equation (9.2). Then you determine where the values you are given fit into the equation. Finally, you need to make sure that all of the units agree with one another. If you end up with kilograms and grams in the same equation, for example, you cannot solve the equation until you have converted one of those mass units to the other. Make sure you can do all of this by solving the "on your own" problems below.

**ON YOUR OWN**

9.6 A child is sledding. He starts at the top of the hill with a velocity of zero, and 3 seconds later, he is speeding down the hill at 21 meters per second. What is the child's acceleration?

9.7 Once that same child reaches the bottom of the hill, the sled coasts over a long, flat section of snow. If the child's velocity when the sled starts coasting is 24 meters per second east, and the child coasts for 12 seconds before coming to a halt, what is the child's acceleration?

9.8 A good runner can keep up a pace of 0.15 miles per minute for quite some time. If a runner starts from rest and settles into a velocity of 0.15 miles per minute south after 3 seconds of running, what is the runner's acceleration?

The Acceleration Due to Gravity

In your everyday experience, you know that in order to get something moving, you must push it. In the next module, you will learn why this is the case. Before you do, however, let me remind you that there is one situation in which you do not need to push something to get it moving. When you drop something, you need not push it. It starts moving all by itself. Why? Gravity, of course. But what does gravity *do* in order to make a dropped object begin to move?

In order to make a dropped object begin to move, gravity gives that object some acceleration. In the next module, you'll learn how gravity does that. In this module, however, I want you to learn a few consequences of that fact.

Whenever any object is falling towards the earth without anything inhibiting its fall, we say that the object is in **free fall**.

Free fall - The state of an object that is falling towards the earth with nothing inhibiting its fall

In free fall, gravity accelerates an object. Without some force inhibiting the motion, the object will continue to speed up because it is under constant acceleration due to gravity. If you drop a rock from a tall cliff, it will continue to pick up speed until it hits the ground below. That's free fall.

You need to learn something about the acceleration that objects experience while they are in free fall. It is best illustrated by experiment.

---

**EXPERIMENT 9.2**
The Acceleration Due to Gravity is Independent of the Object Falling

Supplies:

- A large (at least 21 cm by 27 cm), heavy book
- A small (about 3 cm by 3 cm) piece of paper

Introduction - One of the properties of free fall is that all objects experience the same acceleration regardless of their physical makeup. That tends to go against your everyday experience. This experiment shows you that it is, indeed, true.

Procedure:

A. Hold the book in one hand and the paper in the other. Hold both of them out at arm's length, and make sure that they are at exactly the same height. Make sure that there are no obstructions beneath the two objects so that they can fall to the floor without running into something.
B. Now, release them both at precisely the same instant. Note what happens. Specifically, note which object (the book or the paper) hits the ground first. If they hit simultaneously, note that.
C. Next, repeat the experiment in a slightly different way. This time, place the piece of paper on top of the book and hold the book out at arm's length with both hands. Now release the book and paper. Note what happens this time.

---

What happened in this quick experiment? In the first part, the book hit the ground first. That is what you would expect from your everyday experience. After all, the book is heavier than the paper. Thus, it should fall faster than the paper, right? This leads most people to believe that gravity accelerates heavy things faster than it accelerates light things. After all, both the book and the paper were being accelerated by gravity as they fell. The book fell faster, so it must have experienced more acceleration, right?

If that's the case, how can we explain the second part of the experiment? In that situation, the piece of paper stayed on top of the book, falling just as fast as the book fell! Why did this happen? The paper was not stuck to the book; therefore, it did not *have* to stay on the book. If it were really experiencing a smaller acceleration due to gravity than the book, the book should have started traveling faster than the piece of paper, eventually pulling away from it. Instead, they both fell at exactly the same velocity. Why? They both fell at exactly the same velocity because they both experienced the same acceleration. Thus, the conclusion I just stated from the first part of the experiment is wrong. How, then, do we explain the first part of the experiment?

The explanation has to do with something we call **air resistance**. You see, when an object falls through the air, there are several gaseous molecules (like nitrogen and oxygen) and atoms (like argon) that are in the object's way. In order to fall, the object must shove the gaseous molecules and atoms out of its way. Well, the molecules and atoms resist this movement, and thus the object must force its way through them. A heavy object is much better at doing this than a light object. Therefore, heavy objects fall faster than light objects not because their acceleration due to gravity is larger, but because they are not as strongly affected by air resistance as light objects are.

The fact that light objects are affected by air resistance more than heavy objects is illustrated by the first part of the experiment. When you held the book and paper in each hand and dropped them, they were both subject to air resistance. Since the paper was much more affected by air resistance than the book, it fell more slowly, because it had a harder time shoving through the molecules and atoms in the air. When you placed the paper on top of the book in the second part of the experiment, however, the book shoved the molecules and atoms in the air out of the way. The paper, therefore, did not have to. As a result, it was not subject to air resistance. Under those circumstances, then, the paper and the book fell with the same velocity, demonstrating the fact that gravity accelerates all objects equally.

What we learn from the experiment, then, is that when we neglect air resistance, all objects falling near the surface of the earth accelerate equally. I will discuss air resistance in the next module, but a detailed understanding of that difficult subject is beyond the scope of this course. Therefore, when dealing with objects falling near the surface of the earth, we will always neglect air resistance. For most relatively heavy objects, this is a reasonable thing to do, because air resistance does not affect heavy objects very much.

In fact, any object that is affected greatly by air resistance cannot experience free fall when dropped near the surface of the earth. After all, remember the definition of free fall. It tells us that in order to really experience free fall, there can be no obstructions. Air resistance is an example of such an obstruction; thus, objects significantly affected by air resistance do not experience free fall when dropped near the surface of the earth. We will be neglecting air resistance, however. As far as we are concerned, then, when an object falls near the surface of the earth, we will say it is in free fall.

Well, now that we know all objects accelerate equally under the influence of gravity, we need to know *what* that acceleration is. Near the surface of the earth, the acceleration due to gravity is 9.8 meters per second$^2$. In English units, that turns out to be 32 feet per second$^2$. These are numbers that you must memorize.

**The acceleration due to gravity for any object is 9.8 meters/second$^2$ in metric units and 32 feet/second$^2$ in English units.**

Whenever you do problems involving free fall, you will use one of those values for acceleration. Which one will you use? Well, that depends on the problem. If the problem deals with metric units, you will use 9.8 meters per second squared. If the problem deals with English units, you will use 32 feet per second squared. You will see what I mean in a moment.

It turns out that because the acceleration an object experiences in free fall is constant, there is one neat thing we can do. We can actually determine how far an object falls given just the time it is in the air. In other words, if we time an object as it falls, we can use the acceleration due to gravity to determine the distance it fell. We can do this with the following equation:

$$\text{distance} = \frac{1}{2} \cdot (\text{acceleration}) \cdot (\text{time})^2 \tag{9.3}$$

You will learn where this equation comes from if you take high school physics. For right now, just accept the equation and study the following example to see how it is used.

---

**EXAMPLE 9.6**

**A person is standing on a bridge overlooking a river. If she drops a rock from the bridge, and it takes 1.2 seconds for it to hit the river, how many meters did the rock fall?**

We are trying to determine the distance over which the rock fell. For that, we use Equation (9.3). We know the time (1.2 seconds) and we know that the acceleration is due to gravity alone. Do we use 9.8 meters per second$^2$ or 32 feet per second$^2$? Well, the problem wants the answer in meters, so we had better use the acceleration that has meters in it:

$$\text{distance} = \frac{1}{2} \cdot (\text{acceleration}) \cdot (\text{time})^2$$

$$distance = \frac{1}{2} \cdot (9.8 \; \frac{meters}{second^2}) \cdot (1.2 \; seconds)^2$$

$$distance = \frac{1}{2} \cdot (9.8 \; \frac{meters}{\cancel{second}^2}) \cdot (1.44 \; \cancel{second}^2) = 7.056 \; meters$$

Notice what happened here. The acceleration has units of meters per second$^2$. We then multiplied that by time$^2$. Since time had units of seconds, when we squared it, the units became seconds$^2$. What happened then? When the acceleration unit was multiplied by the time unit, the result was that the second$^2$ unit canceled, leaving just the meters unit. Since distance is measured in meters, it is good that the equation worked out that way.

It turns out that this will always happen in physics and chemistry. When you use physical quantities in an equation, the units will always work out like they did here. That's the reason the units in an equation must agree with one another before you can solve the equation. If they do not, units that are supposed to cancel will not be able to and the answer will be nonsense. This answer is not nonsense, however. The rock fell 7.056 meters.

If you think about it, this little fact of physics can be incredibly useful. Perform the following experiment to see what I mean.

### EXPERIMENT 9.3
Measuring Height With a Stopwatch

Supplies:

- A stopwatch (must read hundredths of a second)
- A ball or rock (something heavy so that air resistance won't be a factor)
- A chair or small stepladder
- A tape measure (A meterstick or yardstick will work, if you do not have a tape measure.)

Introduction - Sometimes, it is hard to measure the height of something because you do not have a ruler large enough. In this experiment, you will see how to measure the height of something like that.

Procedure:

A. Stand on the chair or stepladder and hold your rock or ball so that it touches the ceiling of the room.

B. Hold the stopwatch in your other hand. Simultaneously drop the rock or ball and start your stopwatch. When the rock or ball hits the ground, stop the stopwatch.

C.  Read the time from the stopwatch and write it down.

D.  Perform steps (A-C) ten times, each time writing down the result. Most likely, the result will differ from one time to the next. That's okay. *Please realize that this is not busywork.* There is a very important reason you must do this ten times. I will explain that reason when you finish the experiment.

E.  Once you have done the experiment ten times, average the results by adding them all together and dividing by ten. Unless you live in a *very* tall house, the result you get should be less than 1 second.

F.  Use that time and Equation (9.3) to determine the distance over which the rock or ball fell. If the tape measure you have is marked off in feet, use 32 feet per second$^2$ for the acceleration. If it is marked off in meters, use 9.8 meters per second$^2$ as the acceleration.

G.  Now measure the height of the ceiling with your tape measure or ruler.

H.  Compare your two measurements. They should be within 15% of each other .

What did you learn in the experiment? Well, you should have learned that you do not need to have a ruler to measure the height of something. In your experiment, you used the time that it took for a rock or ball to fall from the ceiling as a way to measure the height of the ceiling. When you checked your result with the measurement you got from a tape measure, you should have seen that the measurements agree to within a few percent.

Why didn't they agree exactly? Well, remember back in Module #4 when I discussed experimental error? Experimental error is the reason that the measurements did not match exactly. First of all, there was experimental error when you measured the height of the ceiling with the tape measure. Why? Think about it. The tape measure had to be perfectly straight in order to read the true height of the ceiling. How could you be sure you were holding it perfectly straight? You couldn't. Thus, error was introduced. Also, I'm sure it was hard to determine exactly where to read the tape measure. Thus, another error was introduced there. My point is that the measurement you got from the ruler or measuring tape had some experimental error in it.

What about the measurement you got by dropping the rock? There was experimental error in that as well. After all, you tried as hard as you could to start the stopwatch and drop the rock or ball simultaneously, but there was no way to be sure that you did. You might have started the stopwatch an instant before you dropped the rock; you might have dropped the rock an instant before you started the stopwatch. There is almost no way to tell. Also, there was no way to tell that you stopped the stopwatch at the same instant that the rock or ball hit the ground.

In the end, then, there were errors in your measurement. That's the reason I had you do the experiment 10 times and average the result. If you look at your data, you will see that the times you measured varied quite a bit. They varied because of experimental error. By averaging 10 results, you lowered the effects of experimental error. After all, in some of the trials you probably started the stopwatch before you dropped the rock. In other trials, however, you probably started the stopwatch after you dropped the rock. By averaging your results together, you helped those two types of errors cancel each other out.

Averaging out several trials of the same experiment is a common way that scientists try to minimize the effects of experimental error. The process of averaging does not *eliminate* experimental error, but the more trials you do, the less effect the experimental error will have. Thus, if you did the experiment 50 times and averaged the result, it would have less experimental error than the result you had.

So, in the experiment, you had two numbers, each of which had experimental error. Which was better? In this case, your measurement with the tape measure was probably better than your measurement from dropping the rock or ball. Why? Well, the experimental error was probably lower in the case of the tape measure. After all, when you dropped the rock, the time it took for the rock to fall was pretty small. In then end, the experimental error associated with starting and stopping the stopwatch was probably very important. At the same time, although there were problems using the tape measure, they were not that severe.

What if you wanted to measure the height of your house, however? At that point, the rock or ball would take a lot longer to fall. Thus, the experimental error associated with stopping and starting the stopwatch would be lower. At the same time, it would be much harder to use the tape measure. At that point, then, dropping a rock would most likely give you a more accurate measurement than would measuring the height with a tape measure.

In the end, when a scientist makes a measurement, he or she needs to consider the experimental error involved. In one case, one technique might have the least amount of experimental error. In the case of your experiment, for example, the tape measure method of measuring height had the least experimental error, so that result is probably the correct one. In another case, another method might prove to have less experimental error. In the case of measuring the height of your house, for example, the rock-dropping method would probably give you the best answer. In the end, then, whenever a scientist does an experiment, he or she must be keenly aware of the potential experimental errors. If not, the experiment might very well be meaningless.

---

**ON YOUR OWN**

9.9 A ball is dropped from the roof of a house. If the ball takes 1.1 seconds to fall, how many feet tall is the house?

9.10 In order to measure the height of a skyscraper, a person stands on the roof and drops a ball. The instant that he drops the ball, he yells to an observer on the ground. The observer starts the stopwatch. When the observer sees the ball hit the ground, the observer stops the stopwatch. From the time elapsed, the observer calculates the height of the skyscraper. List all experimental errors that are associated with this experiment.

---

## STUDY GUIDE FOR MODULE #9

1. Define the following terms:

   a. Reference point
   b. Vector quantity
   c. Scalar quantity
   d. Acceleration
   e. Free fall

2. If an object's position does not change relative to a reference point, is it in motion relative to that reference point?

3. A glass of water sits on a counter. Is it in motion?

4. A child is floating in an inner tube on a still lake. His position does not change. He watches two girls jog along the shore of the lake. The girls are keeping perfect pace with each other. Neither is pulling ahead of nor falling behind the other.

   a. Relative to whom is the child in motion?
   b. Relative to whom is the first girl in motion?
   c. Relative to whom is the second girl not in motion?

5. What is the speed of a boat that travels 10 miles in 30 minutes? Please answer in miles per hour.

6. What is the speed of a runner who runs 6 kilometers in 45 minutes? Please answer in meters per second.

7. Label each quantity as a vector or scalar quantity. Also, identify it as speed, distance, velocity, acceleration, or none of these.

   a. 10 meters
   b. 1.2 meters/second$^2$ east
   c. 3.4 feet/hour and slowing

   d. 56 liters
   e. 2.2 miles/minute west
   f. 2.2 millimeters/year

8. A car and a truck are traveling north on a highway. The truck has a speed of 45 miles per hour and the car has a speed of 57 miles per hour. If the truck is ahead of the car, what is the relative velocity?

57 miles per hour north

45 miles per hour north

9. If an object travels for 15 minutes with a constant velocity of 12 miles per hour west, what is the acceleration?

10. A sportscar goes from a velocity zero to a velocity of 12 meters per second east in 2 seconds. What is the car's acceleration?

11. A train takes a long time to stop. That's what makes trains so dangerous to people who cross the tracks when one is near. If a train is traveling at 30 miles per hour south and takes 12 minutes to come to a stop, what is the train's acceleration?

12. A very picky physicist states that it is impossible for any object to experience free fall near the earth's surface. Why is the physicist technically correct?

13. Even though the physicist in question #12 is technically correct, why do we go ahead and assume that heavy objects are in free fall when they fall near the surface of the earth?

14. A long ,vertical glass tube contains a feather and a penny. All of the air is pumped out and the tube is inverted, causing the penny and the feather to fall. Which hits the bottom first, the feather or the penny?

15. What is the height of a building (in meters) if it takes a rock 4.1 seconds to drop from its roof?

16. A balloonist drops a rock from his balloon. It takes 7 seconds for the rock to fall to the ground. What is the balloonist's altitude in feet?

17. A scientist decides to measure acceleration by measuring the distance that a moving object travels in a set time interval. The scientist notices that in every thirty second interval, the object travels less distance than it did in the previous interval. Is the direction of the acceleration the same as or opposite to the velocity?

## MODULE #10: Newton's Laws

## Introduction

In the previous module, you learned a lot about analyzing motion. You now understand and can calculate both velocity and speed. You know about acceleration. You even know a little bit about free fall. This knowledge and those skills are very valuable in trying to understand the physical Creation around you. However, in all of what you have learned so far, you have not understood *why* objects in motion behave the way that they do. That's what I hope you will learn in this module.

The history of humankind's attempts to understand the physical nature of motion really begins with the ancient Greeks. In particular, the Greek philosopher **Aristotle** (384 - 322 B.C.) is considered the father of modern scientific thought. He spent a great deal of his life observing the things around him and trying to draw conclusions about the nature of the world. His teachings guided scientific inquiry for almost 2000 years.

During the time of the Renaissance, however, scientists began to notice many discrepancies between the theories of Aristotle and their observations of the world around them. Aristotle's teachings had become so ingrained in the minds of the scientific community, however, that most scientists were quite resistant to giving them up. It took many years of careful experiments by several Renaissance scientists to turn the tide and dispose of Aristotle's mistakes. Three scientists are considered pivotal characters in this accomplishment: **Copernicus, Galileo,** and **Newton**. In this module, I will concentrate on Newton. In a later module, I will discuss Copernicus and Galileo in more detail.

## Sir Isaac Newton

Sir Isaac Newton was born in England in 1642. From an early age, he was interested in learning about how the world worked, and he devoted his life to performing experiments designed to help him understand Creation. He is also credited with many, many discoveries. He laid down three laws of motion which will dominate this module. These three laws of motion formed the basis of modern physics and, of course, are still considered true today. He developed a theory that described gravity and its effects, and he did the famous prism experiment (you will study it in a later module) which showed that white light is composed of many colored rays. Finally, in order to help his scientific investigations, Newton developed a new kind of mathematics which we now call "calculus." Amazingly enough, these accomplishments were completed in less than 18 months! Because of these and other achievements, Sir Isaac Newton is considered the father of physics. Newton died in 1727, but not without leaving behind an incredible legacy.

Clearly, Sir Isaac Newton was a genius. Most physics books spend considerable time on this fact, but they do not tell the whole story. They typically leave out the fact that Newton was a serious Christian who spent as much time studying the Bible as he did studying science. *The Columbia History of the World* actually says, "At the end of his days he spent more time studying and writing about the prophecies in the book of Daniel than he did in charting the heavens." Isaac Newton believed that in studying science, he was actually learning about God. In fact, it was his strong belief in God that made him study science. After all, he reasoned, studying science was a way of learning about Creation, and learning about Creation was a way of learning about God.

Of course, Newton also realized that studying Creation cannot be the sole means of learning about God. That's why he spent so much time studying the Bible as well. Newton applied his strong mind to interpreting scripture and wrote many commentaries on passages in the Bible. He was especially drawn to the book of Daniel, as the quote from *The Columbia History of the World* indicates. Clearly Newton had a great sense of priorities. He recognized the importance of science, but he also realized that learning about God is even more important. Scientists today could learn an important lesson from this brilliant man.

## Newton's First Law of Motion

As I mentioned in the previous section, Newton laid down three laws of motion that are the basis of physics. His first law, often referred to as the **law of inertia** says the following:

Newton's First Law - The velocity of an object will not change unless the object is acted on by an outside force.

What does this law mean? Basically, it means that if an object is at rest, it will stay at rest until a force causes it to move. In the same way, it means that an object in motion will continue in motion at its current velocity until a force causes its velocity to change.

Now that might seem to be a pretty obvious statement to you, but in Newton's time, this statement flew in the face of all previous scientific thought. You see, Aristotle had taught that the natural state of an object is for the object to remain at rest. An object, therefore, would not move until it was forced to move. In addition, if an object was forced to move, it would stop as soon as possible after the force was removed.

How did Aristotle come up with that idea? Well, it tends to make sense given our everyday experience. After all, if I put a rock on a sidewalk, it will just sit there. It will continue to sit there until I force it to move by kicking it. Once I kick it, however, the rock will not continue to move indefinitely, will it? Of course not! It will skitter across the sidewalk for a little while and then eventually come to rest. Based on observations such as this, Aristotle believed that all objects "desire" to be at rest. Thus, if they are at rest, they will stay at rest until forced to do otherwise. If they are not at rest, they will come to rest as soon as possible after all forces on the object are removed.

Now the first thing you need to see is the difference between this idea and Newton's First Law of Motion. Both Aristotle and Newton agree that an object at rest will stay at rest until acted on by an outside force. They disagree, however, when it comes to an object in motion. Aristotle says that an object in motion will come to rest as soon as possible after all forces on the object are removed. It will do that because it "wants" to be at rest. Newton's First Law says quite the opposite. It says that once an object starts moving, it will *continue to move indefinitely* until it is acted on by an outside force. Newton's Laws indicate that there is no preferred state for an object. Objects neither "want" to be at rest nor do they "want" to stay in motion. Instead, they stay in whatever state they are placed until acted on by an outside force.

Based on your everyday experience, which sounds more logical, Newton's First Law or Aristotle's idea? Aristotle's idea does, of course! After all, in our everyday experience, things that are in motion tend to slow down and stop unless continually pushed along by an outside force. Thus, everyday experience lends a lot of support to Aristotle's position. Because of this, it took quite a bit of experimenting on the part of Newton to convince others that his law was correct. Try some experiments of your own.

---

## EXPERIMENT 10.1
### Two Inertia Experiments

Supplies:

- A coin
- A 3-inch by 5-inch index card (note that I listed the units)
- A small glass (like a juice glass)
- A raw egg
- A hard-boiled egg

Introduction - Newton's First Law of Motion goes against our everyday experience. Experiments such as these help you visualize *why* this law of motion is really true.

Procedure:

First Experiment:

A. Place the small glass on the table, open side up.
B. Place the index card on top of the glass so that it covers the opening. Center the index card so that the center of the card is over the center of the glass.
C. Place the coin on the center of the index card.
D. Now flick the card quickly with your fingers so that it moves forward, uncovering the glass. What happened to the coin?
E. Set up the experiment again. This time, instead of flicking the card, just grasp the card with your fingers and slowly pull it away from the glass. Keep the card level as you pull it away. What happened this time?

Second Experiment

A.  Place the hard-boiled egg on the table.  Now spin the egg and watch how it spins.  You should not try to spin the egg on one of its ends.  Instead, allow the egg to lay on the table on its side and then spin it in that position.
B.  Do the same thing with the raw egg.  Note the difference in the way the eggs spin, if any.
C.  Next, spin the hard-boiled egg, and once it is spinning, reach down and stop it.  The instant after you stop it, let it go again.  Note what happens.
D.  Do the same thing with the raw egg.  Note what happens in this case.

Let's start with the second experiment first.  You should have noticed a difference in the way that the eggs spun.  The raw egg has liquid inside, whereas the hard-boiled egg does not.  That's why they spin differently.  Now, what explains the results in steps (C) and (D)?  In step (C), once you stopped the egg, it should have stayed motionless after you let it go.  In step (D), however, as long as you let the egg go very soon after you stopped it, the egg should have begun spinning again.  Why is there a difference?  It stems from the same reason you initially saw a difference in the way that the eggs spin.

The raw egg is filled with liquid.  When you get the egg spinning, the liquid inside the egg spins as well.  When you stopped the egg and instantly let it go again, the egg stopped spinning, but the liquid inside it did not.  Thus, when you let go again, the spinning liquid forced the raw egg to start spinning again.  The hard-boiled egg, of course, did not exhibit this effect, because there is no liquid in the hard-boiled egg.  When you stopped the hard-boiled egg, everything stopped; thus, when you let go, there was no motion.

Think about how to interpret this using Newton's First Law of Motion.  Initially, the raw egg had no motion.  It therefore continued to stay at rest until it was acted on by the force of you spinning it.  Once in motion, it stayed in motion until you stopped it abruptly with your hands.  Although your hand applied enough force to stop the egg itself, it did not apply enough force to stop the liquid.  Thus, when you let go, the liquid was still in motion.  This motion applied a force to the egg, causing it to spin again.

What would happen if you stopped the raw egg and then held it for a few seconds.  When you let go, would it spin again?  Of course not!  If you hold onto the egg long enough, you will eventually apply enough force to stop both the egg *and* the liquid inside it.  At that point, both the egg and the liquid inside would be at rest and then remain at rest until acted on by an outside force.

Please realize that your experiment contradicts what Aristotle would predict.  He would predict that once you stopped the raw egg from spinning, it would remain motionless no matter how long you held it.  After all, once you stopped the egg, it would be back in its "natural" state of rest.  Once there, it would not want to change from its natural state.  Therefore, the egg and its contents would no longer move.  That's not what the experiment demonstrates, however.  The

Introduction - In this experiment, you will make a prediction about the outcome of an experiment.  If you really understand Newton's First Law, you will correctly predict the result.

Procedure:

A.  Use the scissors to cut a quarter of the pie pan away.  Examine the figure under step "B" to see what I mean.
B.  In this experiment, you are going to roll the marble into the pie pan as shown below.  The marble will roll around the pan, guided by the pan's walls.  When it hits the edge where the quarter was cut out, it will begin to roll on its own.

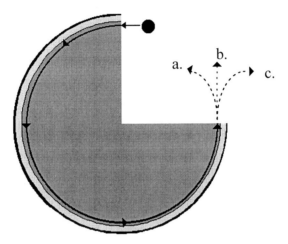

Before you actually do this, however, I want you to first predict where the ball will roll once it begins to roll on its own.  There are three possible choices.  Write down your prediction (a, b, or c).
C.  Now you should actually perform the experiment.  With one hand, hold the pie pan in place so that it doesn't move.  With the other hand, propel the marble straight into the pan, so that it rolls around the side of the pan as shown above.  Watch which way it ends up moving.  Note whether you were right or wrong.

Why did the ball end up moving the way it did?  Well, consider Newton's First Law of Motion.  When you rolled the ball into the pie pan, you gave it a certain velocity.  It would have continued to travel with that speed in that direction, but it ran into the wall of the pie pan.  The wall exerted a force on the ball, causing it to change direction.  As it began traveling in a new direction, the wall curved, exerting more force on it, causing it to continue to change direction.  This continued to happen, causing the marble to travel in a circle.  That all stopped the moment the wall ended.  At that point, there was no more force acting on the ball.  Thus, the ball continued moving without changing its velocity.  Looking at the drawing in the experiment, the ball was traveling straight up right before the wall ended.  Thus, once the wall ended, it would continue to travel straight up.  Thus, path "b" is the correct answer.

Most students choose path "a." They think that the ball will continue to travel in a circle. Remember, however, that the ball travels in a circle because the wall of the pie pan exerts a force on it, causing it to change direction. You started rolling the ball straight. Thus, it will continue to roll straight until it is acted on by an outside force. Once it hit the wall of the pie pan, it was acted on by an outside force, so it stopped moving straight and started moving in a circle. Once that force was removed, however, the ball no longer traveled in a circle, because the force causing it to travel in a circle was no longer acting on it. Thus, it started moving straight. That's the essence of Newton's First Law of Motion.

---

**ON YOUR OWN**

10.1 A cowboy is riding his horse at a fast gallop. Suddenly, the horse digs his feet in and stops. As a result, the cowboy falls off the horse. Will the cowboy fall forwards, backwards, to the left, or to the right?

10.2 A car is traveling down the road at 30 miles per hour. A truck, driven by a reckless driver, comes up from behind with a speed of 50 miles per hour. The truck slams into the back of the car. Will the car's passengers be flung forwards or backwards in their seats?

10.3 A bomber is dispatched to drop a bomb on a military base. The figure below illustrates three points at which the bomb could be dropped. At which point should it happen?

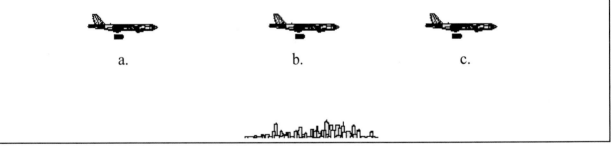

a.                              b.                              c.

---

Before I leave this section, I want to use Newton's First Law of Motion to explain a phenomenon that is probably very familiar to you. Have you ever spun yourself around really fast and then suddenly stopped? How did you feel when you stopped? You felt dizzy. It turns out that this is a consequence of how your body maintains its balance along with Newton's First Law. In order to maintain balance, you have certain canals in your ears. These canals, called **semicircular canals**, are full of tiny particles called "otoliths," or "ear sand." These particles rest on tiny hairs that sense their position. The position of the otoliths at any given time sends signals to your brain. These signals tell the brain what nerves it must activate to control whatever muscles that are necessary to keep your balance so that you don't just fall over.

Well, when you start spinning, the otoliths start spinning as well. That tells your brain you are spinning and allows it to control the muscles necessary to make sure that you don't fall down as you spin. When you stop suddenly, the otoliths have so much inertia that they continue to spin for a while, until the friction between the otoliths and the hairs of the semicircular canals can force them to stop.  While the otoliths are spinning, the hairs send messages to your brain telling it that you are still spinning.  This confuses the brain, because the eyes and muscles are sending it signals that you have stopped.  Dizziness is the result.  Once the otoliths in your semicircular canals stop spinning, however, the dizziness goes away.

## Friction

Friction is the reason that Newton's First Law of Motion goes against your everyday experience.  After all, when you roll a ball down a sidewalk, it does not continue to roll forever.  Instead, it rolls for a while and then stops.  Observations such as this forced Aristotle to conclude that all objects "want" to remain at rest and that an outside force must be used to cause and sustain motion.  It took the brilliance of Newton to show that the force of friction was an "invisible" force which caused objects to slow down and eventually come to a halt.  Without that frictional force, objects in motion would continue in motion indefinitely.

But what exactly is friction?  We know it exists.  We know it causes objects in motion to slow down and eventually come to a halt, but what *is* it?  Perform the following experiment to give you some idea of what friction is.

---

**EXPERIMENT 10.3**
Friction

Supplies:

- An unfinished board that is at least 2 feet long
- A block eraser
- An ice cube
- A small block of wood
- A relatively flat rock
- Sandpaper
- Books
- A ruler

Introduction - Friction is present any time there is motion.  In this experiment, you will learn what causes friction

Procedure:

A.  Place the board on the ground.
B.  Put the ice cube, block of wood, rock, and eraser all at one end of the board.
C.  Begin the experiment by lifting the board on the same side that you placed all of the objects.  Leave the other side of the board on the ground, making the board tilt.  Continue to tilt the board until the side you have lifted is high enough to stick a book under it.  At that point, stick the book under that end of the board and allow the board to rest there, as illustrated below:

D.  Note whether or not any of the items begin to slide down the board.  If so, measure the height of the book, and note which items began to slide at this height.

E.  Continue to increase the height of the stack one book at a time.  Each time, check for objects beginning to slide.  If an object begins to slide, note which object it was and the height of the books which caused it to slide.  Do this until all objects have begun sliding down the board.

F.  Now take the board and use your hand to note how rough or smooth its surface is.

G.  Next, use the sandpaper to sand down the board.  In the end, you want the board to be noticeably smoother than when you started.

H.  Repeat the experiment with the sanded side of the board facing up.

I.  Clean everything up and put it all away.

What happened in the experiment?  Well, if everything went okay, you should have noticed that some objects (like the ice cube) slid down the board sooner than other objects.  In addition, you should have seen that the height at which each object slid down the board decreased after the board had been sanded.  Why?  Well, as soon as you tilted the board, gravity began pulling down on the objects, trying to force them to slide down the board.  They did not move initially because of friction.  Despite the fact that gravity was pulling them down, friction was fighting gravity, holding them in place.  The higher you tilted the board, the stronger gravity was able to pull the objects down the board.  When the force of gravity's pull becomes stronger than friction, the object would begin to slide down the board.

Thus, by tilting the board and waiting for the objects to slide down, you were measuring the strength of the frictional force between the board and each object.  Objects which slid down the board when the board was tilted only a little (like the ice cube) had only a small frictional force holding them in place.  Objects that did not slide down the board until it was tilted very high had a large frictional force holding them in place.

What do the results tell you?  Concentrate for a moment on the difference between the experimental results before and after the board was sanded.  After the board was sanded, it was smoother.  Objects slid down this smoother board with less tilt than they did before the board was smoothed down.  What does that tell you?  It should tell you that friction depends (at least to some degree) on the smoothness of the surfaces which are touching each other.  The smoother the board, the lower the friction.

What is friction, then?  It is a force which exists whenever two surfaces are touching each other.  Where does it come from?  Well, the experiment gives you a clue.  The smoother the surface, the less the friction.  Thus, friction is caused by rough surfaces.  Wait a minute, though. The ice cube certainly wasn't very rough.  Nevertheless, there was still friction between it and the board.  Also, the rock was probably a lot rougher than the eraser, but most students will find that the rock slid down the board at a more gentle tilt than did the eraser.  How do we understand these results?  Examine the following figure:

**Figure 10.1**
Why Friction Exists

Suppose a box is sitting on the floor.  From experience, we know that if someone were to give the box a quick shove, it might slide across the floor a little, but it would eventually come to a halt.  Newton's First Law says that once the box is put in motion by the shove, it should stay in motion until acted on by an outside force.  Since the box stops sliding, we know that there must be an outside force.  I already explained that the outside force which stops the box is friction. The question is, why does friction exist?  Let's picture the box sitting on the floor:

Magnify this point
where the box and the
floor meet.

From our point of view, the surface of the box and the surface of the floor are both pretty smooth. However, if we were to magnify a very small portion of the box and the floor where the two surfaces meet, you would see a completely different picture:

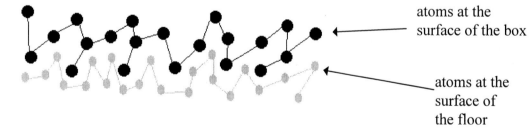

atoms at the
surface of the box

atoms at the
surface of
the floor

You see, on the atomic scale, there are no really smooth surfaces.  All surfaces have grooves and bumps in them.  The grooves and bumps on one surface catch in the grooves and bumps on the other surface.  Every time the grooves and bumps catch on each other, they push against each other, causing a force that fights against motion.

You should now see more clearly why friction exists.  It exists because on the atomic scale, there is no such thing as a smooth surface.  A surface might feel smooth to the touch, but it really is not smooth.  On the atomic scale, it is rough.  The bumps on one rough surface catch and rub against the grooves on another surface.  That's what causes friction.  Why, then, did the rough rock slide down the board before the "smoother" eraser?  Remember that friction exists where the surfaces touch each other. Even though the rock feels rough, at the places where it touches the board, it is smoother on the atomic scale than is the eraser. On the atomic scale, the eraser is *incredibly* rough. Thus, its bumps catch and rub against the grooves of the board, while the board's bumps catch and rub against the eraser's grooves, creating a lot of friction.

The experiment, combined with the explanation in the figure, leads us to a definition of friction:

Friction - A force resulting from the contact of two surfaces. This force opposes motion.

Since the jagged edges between two surfaces catch and rub, friction will always oppose motion. That's why Aristotle was fooled. It is impossible to have motion without surfaces rubbing together. As a result, once motion begins, friction opposes the motion and eventually causes it to stop. Aristotle observed the fact that objects in motion eventually halted, and since he did not know about friction, he insisted that this was because objects "wanted" to stay at rest. Now that we know about friction, we know that Aristotle's idea was wrong and Newton's First Law of Motion is right!

You should have been bothered by something I just said. I said that motion was impossible without surfaces rubbing together. You should have immediately thought, "What about free fall?" After all, in free fall, the object that is falling isn't rubbing up against any other surface is it? Yes, it is! It is rubbing up against the molecules and atoms in the air! Thus, objects in free fall experience friction as well. We already talked about that kind of friction. We called it **air resistance**. Air resistance is the friction experienced by objects traveling through the air. Because a moving object must rub up against and push away molecules and atoms in the air through which it travels, it experiences friction.

---

**ON YOUR OWN**

10.4 Suppose you were to repeat Experiment 10.3, this time using a metal sheet instead of a board. Would the objects slide down at a lower height, a higher height, or about the same height as before?

10.5 Suppose you were to drop an object from the top of a building and measure its speed the instant before it hits the ground. Suppose further that you did the experiment twice: once on a clear, sunny day and once during a thick fog. Would there be any difference in the speed of the object? If so, on which day would the object be traveling faster?

---

## Newton's Second Law of Motion

Newton's Second Law of Motion allows us to become more familiar with a term that we have been using quite a bit: **force**. Although we all have some idea of what "force" means, a physicist has a very specific meaning when he or she uses the term "force." That specific meaning comes from Newton's Second Law of Motion.

Newton's Second Law - When an object is acted on by an outside force, the strength of that force is equal to the mass of the object times the resulting acceleration.

In other words, if you push on an object, the amount that it accelerates depends on two things: the mass of the object and the magnitude of the force with which you push. Newton's Second Law is more often expressed with an equation rather than with words:

$$\text{Force} = (\text{mass}) \cdot (\text{acceleration}) \tag{10.1}$$

Notice that the equation says "the force is equal to the mass times the acceleration." This is identical to what the above definition says. Thus, the equation is equivalent to the definition.

What is force, then? Well, a force is essentially a push or a pull exerted on an object in an effort to change that object's acceleration. Equation (10.1) tells us that we can calculate force by multiplying mass and acceleration. Let's think about the units that result when we make this multiplication. In physics, we typically work with relatively large things, so mass is usually measured in kilograms. Acceleration, as you recall, has a distance unit over a time unit squared. In metric units, that's usually $m/\text{second}^2$. When we multiply these two quantities together, we get the unit $\frac{kg \cdot m}{\sec^2}$. This rather complicated unit is often referred to as the "Newton," in honor of Sir Isaac Newton. This is fitting. Since Newton is the most important scientist in all of physics, he deserves to have a unit that belongs in the most important equation in all of physics. This unit is something you'll have to remember:

**The Newton is the standard unit of force and is defined as a $\frac{kg \cdot m}{\sec^2}$**

Now, of course, any unit that has a mass unit multiplied by a distance unit divided by a time unit squared would be considered a force unit. Thus, $\frac{g \cdot km}{\min^2}$ would also be a valid force unit, we just don't use it that often. One force unit that you might see occasionally is the "dyne." It is used when you are dealing with smaller objects and forces, and is equivalent to a $\frac{g \cdot cm}{\sec^2}$. To give you an idea of how much force is associated with these units, if you were to hold a gallon of water in your hand, it would pull your hand down with a force of 40 Newtons. On the other hand, when a fly lands on your finger, it pushes your finger down with a force of approximately 1,000 dynes. Thus, whereas one Newton is a pretty significant force, one dyne is a very, very small amount of force.

The only thing left to learn about force is that it is a vector quantity. If you think about this, it should make sense. After all, if you push an object, the direction that it will begin to accelerate depends on the direction in which you push it. If you push left, the object will accelerate to the left. If you push right, the object will accelerate to the right. Thus, if acceleration is a vector quantity, force must be as well. In fact, any acceleration that occurs as a result of a force must be in the same direction as the force.

We now know about force. It is a vector quantity whose magnitude is usually measured in Newtons. When a force is applied to an object, that object will experience an acceleration in the same direction as the applied force. The magnitude of the acceleration depends on both the magnitude of the force and the mass of the object. Massive objects take a lot of force to achieve even a little acceleration. Objects that have little mass need only a little force to achieve a large acceleration. Now that we know what force is, we can use Equation (10.1) in some problems.

---

**EXAMPLE 10.1**

**A man's car (mass = 334 kilograms) has broken down and he is pushing it to a gas station. Ignoring friction, what force (in units of Newtons) must the man push with in order to make the car accelerate 0.10 meters per second squared to the east?**

This problem gives the mass of the car and the acceleration. It asks us to calculate force. Thus, we use Equation (10.1) to solve the problem.

$$F = (mass) \cdot (acceleration)$$

$$F = (334 \, kg) \cdot \left( 0.10 \, \frac{m}{sec^2} \right) = 33.4 \, \frac{kg \cdot m}{sec^2}$$

Since the final unit is the same as a Newton, we know that we used the correct units in the problem. Since the acceleration is always in the same direction as the force, we know that the man must push with a force of 33.4 Newtons to the east.

---

If you think about the answer to that last problem, you should be a bit confused. The answer says that the man must push his car with a force of 33.4 Newtons to the east. Now remember, if you hold a gallon of water in your hand, the force you feel pulling the gallon of water down is 40 Newtons. That's not a lot of force. Thus, this problem tells us that pushing a car is a bit easier than holding a gallon of water in our hands. That doesn't make much sense, does it?

Why doesn't the answer make any sense? There is a small phrase in the problem that answers this question. The problem says, "Ignoring friction." That destroys the reality of the problem, doesn't it? After all, friction exists in *all* motion. Thus, it exists in this problem as well. Ignoring friction causes the result of the problem to be rather unrealistic. To solve the problem realistically, then, we must take into account the effects of friction.

How do we do this?  Well, to take the effects of friction into account, you need to under-stand that when multiple forces are applied to an object, they add together to make a total force. That *total* force is the force mentioned in Equation (10.1).  Let's go back to the problem of a man pushing his car.  Since the man is pushing, he is obviously applying a force.  We all know that if he doesn't push hard enough, the car will not move.  Why?  Because there is friction between the surface of the tires and the surface of the road.  This friction opposes motion.  Thus the car will not move until the man applies *more* force than friction can apply.

What happens after the car starts moving, however?  Does friction go away?  Of course not!  Friction continues to fight against the motion.  Examine Figure 10.2 to see what I mean:

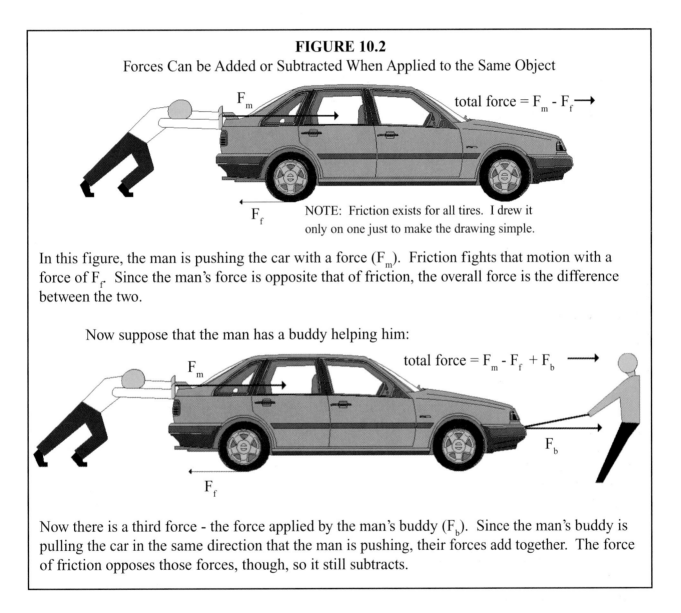

**FIGURE 10.2**
Forces Can be Added or Subtracted When Applied to the Same Object

$F_m$    total force = $F_m$ - $F_f$ ⟶

$F_f$    NOTE:  Friction exists for all tires.  I drew it only on one just to make the drawing simple.

In this figure, the man is pushing the car with a force ($F_m$).  Friction fights that motion with a force of $F_f$.  Since the man's force is opposite that of friction, the overall force is the difference between the two.

Now suppose that the man has a buddy helping him:

$F_m$    total force = $F_m$ - $F_f$ + $F_b$ ⟶

$F_b$

$F_f$

Now there is a third force - the force applied by the man's buddy ($F_b$).  Since the man's buddy is pulling the car in the same direction that the man is pushing, their forces add together.  The force of friction opposes those forces, though, so it still subtracts.

In the end, then, friction simply subtracts from the force being applied in an attempt to move the car.  If the man applies 300 Newtons of force to the car in an easterly direction and the frictional force is 290 Newtons, the total force will be 10 Newtons to the east. If the man's buddy helps by pulling with another 150 Newtons to the east, then the total force will be 160 Newtons to the east. Make sure you understand this by studying the example problem.

---

**EXAMPLE 10.2**

**In order to clear an area, a construction worker pushes on a large rock (mass = 300 kg) that is in the way. Once he gets the rock moving, it begins to accelerate at 0.12 meters/second² to the north. If the construction worker is able to apply 400 Newtons of force, what is the frictional force between the rock and the ground?**

This is a problem involving force, mass, and acceleration. We will therefore have to use Equation (10.1). We know the mass of the rock and its acceleration, so we can figure out the force:

$$\text{Force} = (\text{mass}) \cdot (\text{acceleration})$$

$$\text{Force} = (300 \text{ kg}) \cdot (0.12 \ \frac{\text{meters}}{\text{second}^2})$$

$$\text{Force} = 36 \text{ Newtons}$$

Now what is this force? It is the *total* force acting on the rock. This total force is made up of the force applied by the construction worker and the frictional force which opposes it. Thus, after the frictional force is subtracted from the force applied by the construction worker (400 Newtons), there are 36 Newtons of force pointed north. In the end, then, the frictional force must be 364 Newtons, because when you subtract 364 from 400, you get 36. Thus, because we know the total force (from the equation) and the force applied by the construction worker, we determined that the frictional force is <u>364 Newtons to the south</u>. How do I know that the frictional force is directed south? It is directed south because the motion is to the north, and friction *always* opposes motion.

---

Notice the reasoning I used to solve this problem. Since I was given the mass and the acceleration, I knew that I could calculate force using Equation (10.1). What allowed me to solve the problem was the fact that I knew *what* that force represented. Since I used the mass of the rock and the acceleration of the rock, the force I calculated was the *total force* acting on the rock. That total force was made up of 2 components: the force applied to the rock by the construction worker *and* the force being applied to the rock by friction.

Have you ever noticed that it is harder to get something moving than to keep it moving? For example, if you are trying to push a broken-down car, it is very hard to get the car moving. You have to push really hard. As soon as the car starts moving, however, you suddenly do not have to push as hard, and the car will continue to roll. Why is that? Well, physicists usually split friction up into two classes: **kinetic friction** and **static friction**.

Kinetic friction - The friction that exists between surfaces when at least one of those surfaces is
                   moving relative to the other

Static friction - The friction that exists between surfaces when neither surface is moving relative
                  to the other

It turns out that static friction is always greater than kinetic friction. Thus, before the broken-down car starts moving, you are fighting static friction. This is a large force, so you must, in turn, apply a large force so as to overcome it. Once the car gets moving, however, it is moving relative to the surface of the road. You are then fighting kinetic friction, which is a smaller force.

In the end, then, when something is stationary relative to the surface upon which it sits, the frictional force (static friction) is large, and the object is hard to move. Once the object begins moving relative to the surface, the frictional force (kinetic friction) is smaller. Thus, it is easier to keep moving. Of course, the most important question is, "*Why* is static friction greater than kinetic friction?"

Actually, if you think about why friction exists, the explanation is really pretty simple. Remember, friction exists because the surface of an object and the surface upon which it sits are both rough. They have bumps and grooves, as shown in the lower portion of Figure 10.1. When an object is at rest relative to the surface upon which it sits, the bumps of one surface tend to nestle deeply into the grooves of another. This causes the surfaces to grip one another rather tightly. The deeper the grooves and larger the bumps, the tighter the grip becomes. Once the object gets going, however, the bumps and grooves really don't have a chance to settle into each other because they move past each other before they have a chance to line up well. As a result, they do not interact as strongly, and they can't push against each other with as strong a force as they did when the object was just sitting there.

---

### EXAMPLE 10.3

**A postal worker needs to push a large box (mass = 100 kg) across the floor. The static frictional force between the box and the floor is 196 Newtons, while the kinetic frictional force is only 110 Newtons. How much force is necessary to get the box moving? If the box accelerates at 1.0 meters per second² to the west when the force is applied, how much force did the postal worker use?**

In order to get the box moving, the postal worker must apply more force than what static frictional force is capable of supplying. Thus, the postal worker must apply a little more than 196 Newtons of force to get the box moving. The second part of the problem asks us to calculate the actual force applied by the postal worker. Since we know the box's mass and acceleration, we can use Equation (10.1) to determine the force acting on the box.

$$\text{Force} = (\text{mass}) \cdot (\text{acceleration})$$

$$\text{Force} = (100 \text{ kg}) \cdot (1.0 \; \frac{\text{meters}}{\text{second}^2})$$

$$\text{Force} = 100 \text{ Newtons}$$

Now remember, this is the *total* force acting on the box. All forces acting on an object work together to give the object its acceleration. Since we used the box's acceleration, the force that results is the total of all forces acting on the box.

Thus, 100 Newtons is the *total* force acting on the box. What are the components of this force? Well, certainly the postal worker applies a force to the box, but so does friction. Since friction opposes motion, it subtracts from the postal worker's force. Which frictional force do we use? The box is moving, so we need to use the kinetic frictional force. So, the postal worker's force *minus* the frictional force equals 100 Newtons. The frictional force is 110 Newtons, so the postal worker applied a force of 210 Newtons to the west.

---

**ON YOUR OWN**

10.6 A toy car (mass = 15 kg) rolls across the floor with no person or engine pushing on it. If the car rolls north and experiences an acceleration of 1.1 meters per second$^2$ to the south, what is the kinetic frictional force between the car and the floor?

10.7 Suppose a child wanted to keep the car in problem 10.6 moving at a constant velocity. What force would the child need to apply in order to accomplish this feat?

10.8 A child takes her cat (mass = 5.0 kg) out for a "walk." The cat is, of course, resisting the child with a force of 35 Newtons. In addition, the static frictional force between the cat and the ground is 20 Newtons, while the kinetic frictional force is 12 Newtons. The child is determined to get the cat moving, so she pulls on the leash. What force is necessary to get the cat moving? If the child drags the cat with an acceleration of 2.0 meters per second$^2$ to the east, with what force is the child pulling?

---

Newton's Third Law of Motion

Well, I've discussed two of Newton's Laws of motion. The last one is the easiest of the three. It can be stated as follows:

<u>Newton's Third Law</u> - For every action, there is an equal and opposite reaction.

This is a saying you've probably heard before.  However, I need to make sure that you understand exactly what it means.  Perform the following experiment to find out.

---

**EXPERIMENT 10.4**
Newton's Third Law

<u>Supplies</u>:

* A plastic, 2-liter bottle (like the kind soda comes in)
* A stopper that fits the bottle  (It could be rubber or cork, but you cannot use the screw-on lid.  It has to be something that plugs up the opening of the bottle but can be pushed out by a pressure buildup inside the bottle.  Modeling clay can work as well.  You could also try a large wad of gum, as long as the gum has dried out and has the texture of firm rubber.)
* A cup of vinegar
* Two teaspoons of baking soda
* Aluminum foil
* Four pencils
* Eye protection such as safety goggles or safety glasses

<u>Introduction</u> - Newton's Third Law of Motion states that for every action there is an equal an opposite reaction.  You will observe this law at work and, as a result, understand its meaning. **You may want to do this experiment outside, because it is loud and messy!**

<u>Procedure</u>

A. Pour about a cup of vinegar into the 2-liter bottle.
B. Put the four pencils on the floor and then set the bottle on its side on top of the pencils.  Do this carefully so that none of the vinegar spills out.
C. Take the aluminum foil and make a long, thin trough.  The trough should be thin enough to fit inside the mouth of the bottle.
D. Once you have made the trough, fill it with two teaspoons of baking soda.
E. Gently push the trough into the bottle, so that it floats on top of the vinegar.  Try to spill as little baking soda as possible.
F. **Be careful to stay on the side of the bottle.  You should not be in front of or behind it!** Carefully use the stopper to plug up the mouth of the bottle.
G. **Staying to one side of the bottle**, roll the bottle to the side, allowing the baking soda to mix with the vinegar.  For best results, make sure the bottle stays on the pencils.
H. Stand away to one side of the bottle. **BE SURE TO STAY TO ONE SIDE OF THE BOTTLE. DO NOT GET IN FRONT OF OR BEHIND IT!** Note what happens.

---

What happened in the experiment?  When the baking soda mixed with the vinegar, a chemical reaction took place.  The sodium bicarbonate in the baking soda reacted with the acetic acid in the vinegar.  One of the products of that reaction is carbon dioxide gas.  As the carbon dioxide gas formed, it filled up the bottle. Eventually, so much gas was formed that the bottle became pressurized. This exerted an enormous force on the stopper. Eventually, that force was great enough to push the stopper right out of the bottle. What happened as a result? The bottle started moving in the opposite direction.

What you saw was Newton's Third Law in action. The gas exerted a force (an action) on the stopper. In response, the stopper exerted a force (a reaction) on the gas. Newton's Third Law states that these two forces are equal but opposite. Thus, the gas pushed the stopper one direction, and the stopper pushed the gas the other direction. As a result, the stopper flew off in one direction and the bottle (which contained the gas) flew off in the opposite direction.

The "action" in Newton's Third Law of Motion really refers to a force. Thus, Newton's Third Law says that every time a force is applied to an object, an equal but opposite force is applied by that object. In your experiment, the gas applied a force to the stopper. In response, the stopper applied an equal but opposite force on the gas.

One more example should help. Suppose you jump onto a trampoline. When you hit the trampoline, you exert a force on the trampoline. What does Newton's Third Law say will happen? The trampoline will exert an equal but opposite force on you. How can you tell that this is happening? Well, the trampoline's surface bends. This tells you that you are exerting a force on the trampoline. How do you know that the trampoline is exerting a force back? You start to slow down, stop, and then accelerate in a completely different direction. According to Newton's First Law of Motion, you could have never done that if a force had not acted on you. That force was the equal and opposite force described in Newton's Third Law. Thus, you exerted a force on the trampoline (causing the surface to bow), and the trampoline exerted a force right back on you (causing you to accelerate in a different direction).

It is very important to realize that the equal and opposite forces talked about in Newton's Third Law do not act on the *same* object. If that were the case, then there would never be any motion. After all, if equal and opposite forces act on the same object, they cancel each other out and the resulting force would be zero. Instead, the equal and opposite forces discussed in Newton's Third Law affect *different* objects. In the experiment, the gas exerted a force on the stopper. The equal and opposite force was exerted not on the stopper, but on the gas. Thus, the two forces acted on two completely different objects. Thus, both objects ended up moving. In the second example, you exerted a force on the trampoline, causing it to bend. The trampoline then exerted an equal and opposite force on you, causing you to accelerate up rather than down. Once again, the two forces worked on two *separate* objects. One force worked on the trampoline, the other on you. Both objects moved, since the forces did not cancel, because they acted on different objects.

Newton's Third Law of Motion explains a lot of things that happen to us. For example, have you ever fired a gun? When you fire a gun, it "kicks" back towards you. People who shoot guns for the first time are often surprised by this effect. In fact, there are many cases in which novices have broken a shoulder because they were firing a rifle and were not expecting the "kick." When it happened, the rifle hit their shoulder with enough force that it actually broke a bone! What causes the rifle's "kick?" Well, when you pull the trigger, you cause a chemical reaction to take place in the bullet. That reaction produces a lot of heat and gas. The gas is under pressure, so it exerts a force on the bullet, pushing the bullet out at an amazing speed. In response, the bullet pushes back against the gas in the rifle. That's what causes the "kick."

Newton's Third Law of motion also explains how rockets and missiles fly. When a rocket or missile is launched, its fuel begins burning. As the fuel burns, it produces hot gas in great volumes. The pressure caused by the gas being formed pushes against the gas already in the rocket. In response, the gas being pushed out pushes back, causing the rocket or missile to move in the opposite direction. This force is often called the **thrust** of the rocket. Thus, a rocket or missile flies because gases are constantly being shoved out of its bottom. The equal and opposite reaction in Newton's Third Law forces the rocket to move in the opposite direction.

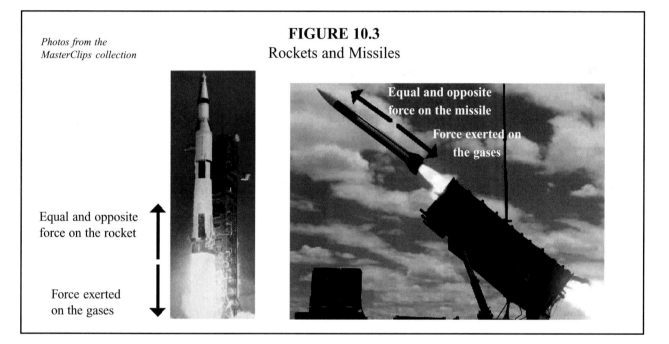

**FIGURE 10.3**
Rockets and Missiles

*Photos from the MasterClips collection*

Equal and opposite force on the rocket

Force exerted on the gases

Equal and opposite force on the missile

Force exerted on the gases

Make sure you really understand Newton's Third Law of Motion by answering the following "on your own" problems.

**ON YOUR OWN**

10.9 A tennis player hits a ball with her racquet. The ball was traveling towards the player but, once she hits it with the racquet, the ball begins traveling in the opposite direction. During the hit, the strings on the racquet bow. What evidence do you have that the racquet exerted a force on the ball? What applied the equal and opposite reaction as required by Newton's Third Law, and where was the force applied? What evidence do you have for this force?

10.10 An ice skater stands on the ice in his skates. He is holding a ball. Assuming that friction is so small it can be ignored, what will happen to the ice skater if he suddenly throws the ball hard to the west?

In this module, you learned about the laws that govern motion. Despite the fact that they were written in the early 1700's, they still guide physics as the main laws that govern how objects move! Notice that each law deals with force. Although we intuitively know what a force is, in the next module, you will learn about where forces come from.

# ANSWERS TO THE ON YOUR OWN PROBLEMS

10.1 <u>The cowboy will fall forwards off of the horse</u>. While the horse is galloping, the cowboy and the horse have the same velocity. When the horse suddenly stops, the only force that can stop the cowboy is the friction between him and the saddle. If the horse stops quickly enough, friction will not have time to do this. As a result, the cowboy continues to travel at the velocity he had, which is much faster than the horse's velocity once it stops. Thus, the cowboy falls forward, right over the horse.

This actually happened to the famous actor Christopher Reeve. He was in an equestrian (horse-riding) competition, and he was making his horse jump over some fences. The horse was running towards one fence at a quick pace and, for no apparent reason, stopped dead in its tracks. Mr. Reeve fell forward off of the horse and landed head-first on the fence. This caused a spinal cord injury which left him a quadriplegic.

10.2 Before the truck hits, the passengers in the car are traveling with the car at 30 miles per hour. When the truck comes up from behind and hits the car, it will push the car forward, accelerating the car. Thus, the car will begin traveling faster than 30 miles per hour. The passengers, however, are still traveling at 30 miles per hour, so they will be "<u>flung backwards</u>" in their seats until the backs of their seats apply enough force to accelerate them to the same velocity as the car.

10.3 The bomb should be dropped from <u>point a</u>. Remember, the bomb has been traveling with the plane. Thus, it has the same velocity as the plane. When it is dropped, it will continue to have that velocity. Since it takes time for the bomb to fall, if the bomb were dropped at point b, it would pass by the base, being carried on by its initial velocity. If the bomb is dropped at point a, however, the bomb will continue to approach the base as it falls. If the bomber times it right, the bomb will hit the military base by the time it reaches the ground.

10.4 Typically, metal is smoother than wood. Thus, you would expect less friction from the metal. As a result, it should take less force to get the objects moving. Thus, <u>the objects will fall at a lower height</u>.

10.5 Remember from your study of weather that fog is the result of water condensing on cloud condensation nuclei close to the ground. This makes the air thicker. Thus, the air resistance would be greater on a foggy day than on a clear, sunny day. Since air resistance is larger, the final velocity will be smaller on the foggy day. So, <u>yes, there would be a difference, and the object will travel faster on the clear, sunny day</u>.

10.6 Since the car is not being pushed, the only force acting on it is friction. Thus, the acceleration is due completely to friction. We have the mass and the acceleration, so we can calculate the force:

$$\text{Force} = (\text{mass}) \cdot (\text{acceleration})$$

$$\text{Force} = (15 \text{ kg}) \cdot (1.1 \ \frac{\text{meters}}{\text{second}^2})$$

$$\text{Force} = 16.5 \text{ Newtons}$$

Since the car is moving, this is the kinetic frictional force. Thus, the kinetic frictional force is 16.5 Newtons south.

10.7 The child wants to keep the car moving at a constant velocity. What does that tell us about acceleration? When the velocity is *constant*, there is *no change*. This means that acceleration (which is the *change in* velocity) must be zero. Thus, the child wants the car to have zero acceleration. How much force is that?

$$\text{Force} = (\text{mass}) \cdot (\text{acceleration})$$

$$\text{Force} = (15 \text{ kg}) \cdot (0 \ \frac{\text{meters}}{\text{second}^2})$$

$$\text{Force} = 0 \text{ Newtons}$$

The force on the car, then, must be zero. Does this mean the child must apply no force? NO! Remember, the force we get from Equation (10.1) is the *total* force. We know from the last problem that friction is applying a force of 16.5 Newtons against the motion. To get a total force of zero, then, the child must exert a 16.5 Newton force in the direction of the car's motion. This will counteract friction, allowing the car to move at a constant velocity.

10.8 To get the cat moving, the child must overcome all forces which resist motion. The cat is resisting motion at 35 Newtons. As long as the cat stands still, the static frictional force also resists motion at 20 Newtons. Thus, there is a total of 55 Newtons of force resisting motion. To get the cat moving, then, the child must exert more than 55 Newtons of force.

Since we know the mass and acceleration of the cat, we can calculate the force to which the cat is subjected:

$$\text{Force} = (\text{mass}) \cdot (\text{acceleration})$$

$$\text{Force} = (5.0 \text{ kg}) \cdot (2.0 \ \frac{\text{meters}}{\text{second}^2})$$

$$\text{Force} = 10 \text{ Newtons}$$

What is this force? It is the *total* force to which the cat is subjected. We know that the cat resists motion at 35 Newtons and, once the cat starts moving, friction resists the motion at 12 Newtons (the kinetic frictional force). Thus, there are 47 Newtons resisting motion. Motion, however is occurring, with a total force of 10 Newtons. Thus, there are 47 Newtons being applied to overcome friction, plus another 10 to make acceleration. The child, therefore, is exerting <u>57 Newtons</u> of force.

10.9 <u>We know that the racquet exerted a force on the ball because its velocity changed.</u> The ball had to slow down, stop, and then start moving in a new direction. This is a change in velocity, which means there was acceleration, which means there was a force. <u>The equal and opposite force demanded by Newton's Third Law of Motion was applied by the ball on the racquet. We know that the ball exerted a force on the racquet because the strings on the racquet bowed.</u>

10.10 If the ice skater throws the ball, he must exert a force on it. In compliance with Newton's Third Law of Motion, the ball will apply an equal and opposite force on the skater. Since there is no friction, that force will cause the skater to accelerate. Thus, <u>the skater will begin to move in the opposite direction as the ball</u>. You do not normally get shoved backwards when you throw a ball because the force does not overcome the friction between you and the ground. Thus, the ball does exert a force on you, but you don't notice it because friction resists the force.

# STUDY GUIDE FOR MODULE #10

1.  Define the following terms:

a.  Friction
b.  Kinetic friction
c.  Static friction

2.  State Newtons' three laws of motion.

3.  In space, there is almost no air, so there is virtually no friction.  If an astronaut throws a ball in space with an initial velocity of 3.0 meters per second to the west, what will the ball's velocity be in a year?

4.  A boy is running north with a beanbag in his hands.  He passes a tree, and at the moment he is beside the tree, he drops the beanbag.  Will the beanbag land next to the tree?  If not, will it be north or south of the tree?

5.  Suppose the situation in question #4 is now changed.  The boy is running, but now his friend stands beside the tree with the beanbag.  As the boy passes, he barely taps the beanbag, causing it to fall out of his friend's hands. Will the beanbag land next to the tree?  If not, will it be north or south of the tree?

6.  A busy shopper is driving down the road.  Many boxes lie piled on the back seat of the car, evidence of shopping activity.  Suddenly, the shopper must hit the brakes to avoid a collision.  Will the boxes be slammed farther back into the back seat or will they slam into the front seat where the driver can feel them?

7.  When roads get wet, they get slick.  Obviously, then, the friction between a car's tires and the road decreases when the road is wet.  Why?

8.  In order to get his broken-down car moving, a man must exert an enormous amount of force.  Once it is moving, however, the man need not exert nearly as much force to keep it moving.  Why?

9.  A child is pushing her toy across the room with a constant velocity to the east.  If the static friction between this toy and the floor is 15 Newtons while the kinetic friction is 10 Newtons, what force is the child exerting?

10.  A father is trying to teach his child to ice skate.  As the child stands still, the father pushes him forward with an acceleration of 2.0 meters per second$^2$ north.  If the child's mass is 20 kilograms, what is the force with which the father is pushing. (Since they are on ice, you can ignore friction.)

11. In order to move a 15-kilogram object, a force of more than 25 Newtons must be exerted. Once it is moving, however, a force of only 20 Newtons accelerates the object at 0.1 meters per second$^2$ to the west. What is the force of static friction between the object and the surface upon which it sits? What is the force of kinetic friction?

12. The static frictional force between a 500 kilogram box of bricks and the floor is 500 Newtons. The kinetic frictional force is only 220 Newtons. How many Newtons of force must the worker exert to get the box moving? What force must the worker exert to accelerate the box at 0.1 meters per second$^2$ to the south?

13. In order to shove a rock out of the way, a gardener gets it moving by exerting just slightly more than 100 Newtons of force. To keep it moving at a constant velocity eastward, however, the gardener needs only to exert a 45 Newtons force to the east. What are the static and kinetic frictional forces between the rock and the ground?

14. Two men are trying to push a 710-kg truck. The first exerts a force of 156 Newtons east and the second exerts a force of 220 Newtons east. The truck accelerates at 0.20 meters per second$^2$ to the east. What is the kinetic frictional force between the truck and the road?

15. A child pushes against a large doghouse, trying to move it. The doghouse remains stubbornly unmoved. What exerts the equal and opposite force which Newton's Third Law of Motion says *must* happen in response to the child's push? What is that force exerted on?

16. In a baseball game, a player catches a fast-moving ball. The ball stops in the player's hand. What evidence tells you that the player exerted a force on the ball? What exerts the equal and opposite force required by Newton's Third Law? What evidence does the player have for this force?

17. A man leans up against a wall with a force of 20 Newtons to the east. What is the force exerted by the wall on the man?

# MODULE #11: The Forces in Creation - Part 1

## Introduction

In the previous module I talked a lot about force. Indeed, the concept of force is integral to the physics of motion. What is force, however? It's easy to say that when you push on something, you exert a force. That's true, but there are many other ways that force is exerted in Creation. When you drop a ball, it accelerates downward. Since the ball accelerates, it must be experiencing a force - the force of gravity. But what is gravity? In this module, you will hopefully find out. Along the way, you will learn about the other forces that exist in Creation and how they are generated.

## The Four Fundamental Forces of Creation

Believe it or not, physicists think that there are only four different types of force in Creation: the **gravitational force**, the **electromagnetic force**, the **weak force**, and the **strong nuclear force**. These forces are called "fundamental" forces, because all forces in Creation can be traced back to one of them. I am going to discuss each of these forces in detail, but first, I want to give you a brief overview of them all.

The gravitational force is the easiest one to recognize. When you drop a ball, it accelerates towards the earth because the gravitational force attracts the ball to the earth. The moon orbits the earth because the moon and the earth are attracted to one another by the gravitational force which exists between them. In fact, any two object that have mass are attracted to one another via the gravitational force. Of all four forces in Creation, this is the weakest. In addition, it is always an attractive force.

The electromagnetic force is the force that exists between particles with electrical charge. Unlike the gravitational force, the electromagnetic force can be either attractive or repulsive, depending on the charge of the objects involved. Two positively-charged objects, for example, repel each other, as do two negatively-charged objects. A positively-charged object and a negatively-charged object, however, attract one another.

The weak force governs certain radioactive processes in atoms. It is, by far, the hardest of the four forces to comprehend. Physicists have used a variety of mathematical models and experimental results to show that the electromagnetic force and the weak force are, in fact, different facets of the same force. Thus, they combined the two names and called this force the **electroweak force**. In reality, then, there are only three fundamental forces in Creation. In this course, however, we will discuss the electromagnetic force and the weak force separately, as the mathematics required to understand how they are the same is rather intense!

The strong force is the force that holds the center of the atom (called the **nucleus**) together. In a later module, I will talk more about this force and the structure of the atom. For now, you just need to know that it is the strongest force in Creation. Although this force is strong, its range is very, very small. Because its range is so small, it applies only to atoms.

## The Gravitational Force

As I mentioned before, the gravitational force is the easiest of the three fundamental forces to recognize. This is mostly because we experience gravity every day. Although easy to recognize, the gravitational force is surprisingly hard to truly understand. Even today, scientists are not sure what *causes* the gravitational force. We have two major theories that try to explain what gravity is, but we really do not know which (if either) is correct. There are even those who say that *both* theories are correct! Needless to say, we still have a *lot* to learn about this force!

Even though we still have a lot to learn about gravity, we have come a long way in understanding this perplexing force. At one time, scientists did not even know that the gravitational force which causes a ball to fall to the earth is the same as the force that holds the planets in orbit around the sun. It took the brilliance of Sir Isaac Newton (surprise!) to show that gravity is a universal force, which applies to small things near the earth's surface as well as large things such as planets.

In fact, Newton developed an equation (which he called the **Universal Law of Gravity**) which allows physicists to calculate the strength of the gravitational force between two objects. Although that particular equation is beyond the scope of this course, it leads to three general principles which I want you to know:

1. **All objects with mass are attracted to one another by the gravitational force.**

2. **The gravitational force between two masses is directly proportional to the mass of each object.**

3. **The gravitational force between two masses is inversely proportional to the square of the distance between those two objects.**

What do these principles mean?

Well, the first principle tells us that all matter is attracted to all other matter. If you look around the room you are in, every object that you see is attracted to every other object that you see. In addition, they are all attracted to the earth. The earth is attracted to the sun, etc., etc. This is why Newton called his law the "universal" law of gravity. He called it universal because it applies to anything in the universe which has mass.

The second principle tells us that the strength of the gravitational force between two objects increases as the mass of either object increases. Suppose I have two objects, and I measure the gravitational attraction which exists between them. Then, suppose I replace one of those objects with an object whose mass is twice as big. The new gravitational attraction I measure will be twice as large as the one I had previously measured. If I then replaced the other object with one whose mass was twice as large, the gravitational attraction would get twice as large again. Compared to my first measurement, this gravitational attraction would be four times as large.  So whatever factor by which the mass of each object changes, the gravitational force changes by that same factor.

The final principle says that the gravitational force is "inversely proportional" to the square of the distance between the objects.  The term "inversely proportional" means that when the distance is big, the force is small.  Conversely, when the distance is small, the force is big.  This effect is so strong, however, that the gravitational force between two objects changes as the *square* of the distance between the objects.  In other words, suppose I took two objects and measured the gravitational force that exists between them.  Then, suppose I pulled the objects away from each other so that the distance between them doubled.  If I were to then measure the gravitational force between them, I would see that it decreased by a factor of 4 (which is two squared).  Thus, when the distance between two objects increases by a given factor, the gravitational force decreases by the square of that factor.  Alternatively, if the distance between two object decreases by some factor, the gravitational force increases by the square of that factor.

Let me put all of this together for you in a couple of example problems.

---

**EXAMPLE 11.1**

**The gravitational force between two objects separated by a distance of 3 centimeters is measured.  The objects are then brought closer together so that the distance between them is only 1 centimeter.  What is the gravitational attraction now compared to when it was first measured?**

When the objects are moved closer together, the distance between them *decreases* by a factor of 3.  Since Newton says that the gravitational force is inversely proportional to the square of the distance between the masses, we know is that the gravitational force *increased*. The distance between the objects was changed by a factor of 3 (from 3 cm to 1 cm).  The square of 3 is 9.  Thus, the gravitational force will now be 9 times larger than is was previously.

**The gravitational force between two objects separated by a distance of 5 centimeters is measured.  Both objects are then replaced.  The first object is replaced with one that has half of its mass, and the second object is replaced by one that has 8 times its mass.  What is the gravitational attraction now compared to when it was first measured?**

Newton says that the gravitational force between two objects is directly proportional to the mass of the objects.  Thus, when the first object is replaced with one with half of its mass, the gravitational force is cut in half as well.  When the second is replaced with an object that has 8 times more mass, the gravitational force is increased by a factor of 8.  In total, then, the gravitational force was first cut in half and then that value was increased by a factor of 8.  This leads to a gravitational force which is 4 times larger than the original force.

---

Make sure you really understand this by doing some "on your own" problems.

---

**ON YOUR OWN**

11.1  The gravitational force between two objects (mass$_1$ = 10 kg, mass$_2$ = 6 kg) is measured when the objects are 10 centimeters apart.  If the 10 kg mass is replaced with a 20 kg mass and the 6 kg mass is replaced with a 3 kg mass, how does the new gravitational attraction compare to the first one that was measured?

11.2  The gravitational force between two objects (mass$_1$ = 1 kg, mass$_2$ = 2 kg) is measured when the objects are 10 centimeters apart.  The objects are then replaced with two different ones (mass$_1$ = 4 kg, mass$_2$ = 1 kg) and the distance is decreased to 5 centimeters.  How does the new gravitational attraction compare to the first one that was measured?

---

There are a couple of things that you must keep in mind when you think about the gravitational force.  Remember, it is the weakest of all forces.  When you place two books on the table, they are attracted to one another by the gravitational force.  Why don't they just move towards each other?  Well, the gravitational force is so weak that it cannot even overcome the friction that exists between the books and the table.  As a result, the books stay stationary, not because they aren't attracted to one another, but because the attraction is so weak that it cannot overcome static friction.  To give you some idea of how weak the gravitational attraction is, think about the force it would take to hold a fly when it lands on your hand.  The force is so small that you don't really feel it.  Well, that force is approximately *1,500 times larger* than the gravitational attraction of two average textbooks placed 10 cm away from each other!

Now although the gravitational force between objects in our every day experience is so weak that it can be neglected, when the mass of an object is huge, the gravitational force can become considerable.  For example, when you drop a ball, the gravitational force that makes it fall comes from the attraction between the ball and the earth.  The mass of the ball is rather small, but the mass of the earth is *really* large.  Thus, the gravitational attraction between the ball and the earth is large because the mass of the earth is so large.  The gravitational force is a weak force, but it can become substantial when one of the objects involved has a really huge mass.

There is one more thing you need to realize about the gravitational force.  Think about the situation in which you are dropping a ball.  The ball falls because it is attracted to the earth by the gravitational force.  Thus, the earth applies a gravitational force to the ball, pulling it towards the earth.  What does Newton's Third Law of Motion say?  It says that whenever a force is applied, an equal and opposite force must be applied in reaction.  What is that equal and opposite force here?  Well, if the *earth* applies a gravitational force on the *ball*, the *ball* must apply an equal but opposite force on the *earth*!  Thus, the ball is attracted to the earth, but at the same time, the earth is attracted to the ball.

Wait a minute.  Because the earth applies a force on the ball, the ball moves towards the earth (it falls).  If the ball applies an equal but opposite force on the earth, what does the earth do?  *It moves towards the ball.*  In other words, when you drop a ball, it falls to the earth.  Because of Newton's Third Law of Motion, however, at the same time, *the earth rises towards the ball*! That statement seems rather crazy, but it is true. When an object falls towards the earth, the earth also rises towards the object.

How can we make any sense of this? When we drop a ball, we don't feel the earth accelerating towards the ball. Why? Well, think of Newton's Second Law of Motion. It says that the force applied to an object equals the object's mass times the resulting acceleration. The force that the ball applies to the earth is *equal* to the force that the earth applies to the ball. Since the ball's mass is rather small, the acceleration that results from the force applied by the earth is rather large. When the ball applies that same force to the earth, however, the resulting acceleration is really tiny, because the earth's mass is so huge. Thus, the only reason we don't feel the earth accelerating upwards to meet the ball is because Newton's Second Law of Motion says that the same force will accelerate objects of small mass much faster than objects of large mass. As a result, the acceleration of the earth is so tiny that it barely moves before the ball has fallen all the way to the ground.

The important point for you to draw from all of this is that any two objects exert equal gravitational forces on each other. When two objects rest on a table, for example, the first object exerts a certain amount of gravitational force on the second object. In compliance with Newton's Third Law of Motion, then, the second object applies an equal and opposite force on the first object. This means that the first object will pull the second object towards itself, while the second object will pull the first object towards itself. Thus, we often call the gravitational force a "mutual" force, because whatever gravitational force object number one exerts on object number two, an equal force will be exerted by object number two on object number one.

## Force and Circular Motion

Now that you know a bit about the gravitational force itself, you need to see how the gravitational force acts throughout God's Creation. You know, of course, that the gravitational force causes objects near the surface of the earth to fall. That is one way in which the gravitational force acts in Creation. I have already covered that extensively in Module #9, where I concentrated on the motion of free fall. Another way that the gravitational force acts is to hold the planets and their moons in an orderly arrangement which we call the "solar system." I will concentrate on that in the next section of the course.

Before you can learn about how the gravitational force works in our solar system, you must first learn about how objects move in circles. To learn about this important concept, perform the following experiment.

**EXPERIMENT 11.1**
Force and Circular Motion

Supplies:
- A mechanical pen
- A black marker
- Thin string or thread (preferably white)
- 5 metal washers, all the same size

- Stopwatch
- Something to cover your eyes, such as safety goggles or safety glasses
- Scissors

Introduction - Circular motion requires a special kind of force.  In this experiment, you will learn a few things about that force and its properties.

Procedure:

A.  Set up your experimental device by following these instructions:

1. Unscrew the bottom part of the casing from the pen.

2. Remove the insides from the pen and set everything aside except for the bottom part of the casing.

3.  Thread about a foot of string through the casing.  If you are having trouble getting the string all the way through, stick the string in the pointed side of the casing and suck on the other side with your mouth.  The suction will pull the string through.  Tie one washer on the end that is on the pointed side of the casing and tie two washers at the other end.

B.  Lay your device on the table and pull the string so that about 6 inches of string comes out the pointed side of the casing.  Next, use your marker to make a strong black mark all around the string, right where it comes out the *other side* of the casing.  The mark needs to be easy to see.

make mark here                                        six inches

C.  Now hold the device by grasping the pen.  Make sure that the pointed end of the pen points up.  Begin twirling the single washer on the end so that it moves in a circle.

D.  Get used to how this thing operates.  Notice that as you twirl the washer faster, the string pulls out the end, making the circle which the washer sweeps out longer.  If you slow the twirling down, the string goes the other way, making the circle smaller.

E.  Adjust the rate that you are twirling until the black mark that you made is visible right at the bottom of the pen casing.  This tells you that there are six inches of string extended from the pointed end of the casing. In other words, the radius of the circle swept out by the single washer is 6 inches.

F. Watch the washer as it moves in a circle. You are going to begin counting the number of full circles that the washer makes. This can be a little tricky, so get used to the motion of the washer, keeping the black mark just at the bottom of the casing.

G. When you are ready, start the stopwatch and time how long it takes for the washer to make 20 full circles. Do this five times and average the result.

H. Next, tie two more washers onto the end of the string that already has two washers on it. That way, there are now four washers on one end and one washer on the other.

I. Repeat steps (E-G), determining how long it takes the washer to make 20 full circles in this new configuration.

J. Finally, as the washer is still twirling around, cut the four washers off of the string with the scissors. **Make sure no one else is near when you do this. Also, make sure there are no breakables in the room!** Note what happens.

What happened in the experiment? Let's start with the last part of the experiment. When you cut the washers from the end of the string, the washer that was twirling around suddenly went flying off in a given direction. Why? Circular motion requires a special force, which physicists call **centripetal** (sen trip' uh tul) **force**.

Centripetal force - Force that is always directed perpendicular to the velocity of an object

The washers hanging on the end of the string were supplying that centripetal force. Gravity was pulling them towards the earth, which, in turn, caused the washers to pull on the string. Thus, the washers were pulling on the string with a force equal to the force with which gravity was pulling on them. When you cut the washers from the string, the washer that was traveling in a circle suddenly sped off, traveling in a straight line. It did so because the centripetal force which was causing it to turn in a circle was suddenly removed.

This should tell you something about circular motion. In general, an object tends to travel in a straight line. The only way you can change that is to apply a force. If that force happens to be perpendicular to the velocity of the object, the object will begin to curve. If the force *continues* to be directed perpendicular to the velocity of the object, then the object will move in a circle. Now think about it. When a force is applied, an acceleration must occur. Does that mean an object can never travel in a circle at a constant speed? Of course not! When an object moves in a circle at a constant speed, there is still an acceleration because the object's *direction* keeps changing. Since the direction keeps changing, that means the velocity (which includes direction) keeps changing as well. That's an acceleration. Not surprisingly, this acceleration is called **centripetal acceleration**.

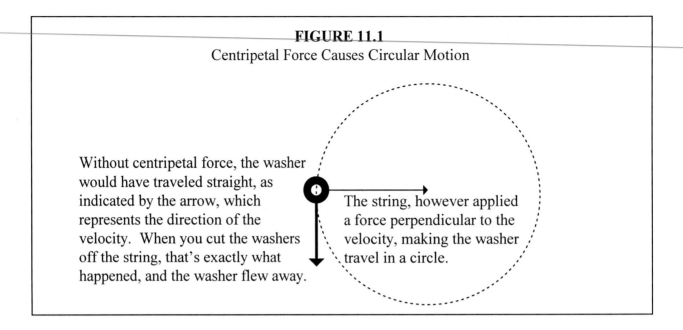

**FIGURE 11.1**

Centripetal Force Causes Circular Motion

Without centripetal force, the washer would have traveled straight, as indicated by the arrow, which represents the direction of the velocity.  When you cut the washers off the string, that's exactly what happened, and the washer flew away.

The string, however applied a force perpendicular to the velocity, making the washer travel in a circle.

In the end, then, circular motion requires centripetal force, which is a force that stays perpendicular to the direction of the velocity.  In order to stay perpendicular to the velocity, the force will always be directed towards the center of the circle.

What did you learn from the first part of the experiment?  Well, if things went well, you should have noted that it took *less* time for the washer to make 20 circles when there were four washers hanging on the other end of the string rather than just two.  This indicates that the washer traveled *faster* when there was more weight on the string.  More weight would be the same as more centripetal force.  Thus, the larger the centripetal force, the faster an object can travel in a circle.  Also, in order to adjust where the black mark was, you should have noticed that when the washer moved faster, more string was pulled out the end and thus the larger the circle of motion became.  Conversely, when the speed of the washer slowed down, the string fell through the pen casing, causing the size of the circle swept out by the washer to decrease.  This leads us to a few important points regarding centripetal force:

1. **Circular motion requires centripetal force.**

2. **The larger the centripetal force, the faster an object can travel in a circle.**

3. **The larger the centripetal force, the *smaller* the circle of motion.**

You need to remember these general principles of circular motion.

Before you leave this section, I need to dispel another myth.  Have you ever been riding in a car, and when the car took a sharp turn, you were thrown towards one side of the car?  Some people say that you were thrown to one side of the car because the circular motion of the car exerted a "centrifugal (sen trif' uh gul) force" on you.  That is not true.  No force is exerted on you at all.  Instead, you are simply experiencing Newton's First Law of Motion in action.

What do I mean?  Well, before the car takes the curve, both you and the car are traveling straight.  When the driver turns the steering wheel, the friction between the road and the tires exerts a force on the car.  That force is perpendicular to the velocity of the car, so the car experiences a *centripetal* force.  This causes the car to move in a circle.  You, on the other hand, have no force acting on you.  Thus, you continue to move straight.  As you move straight, you seem to be "flung" towards one side of the car.  When you hit the side of the car, another passenger, or the seat belt's restraint, then you also begin experiencing a centripetal force and you also begin traveling in a circle.  No force acts on you *until* you start traveling in a circle with the car.  Thus, there is no such thing as "centrifugal force."  It is a myth that has developed due to a lack of understanding in physics.  The supposed "force" that you feel is no force at all.  It is, instead, Newton's First Law of Motion at work.

---

**ON YOUR OWN**

11.3  Consider an object traveling in a circle as shown below:

If the arrow indicates the direction of the circular motion, draw an arrow representing the direction of the object's velocity at the instant it is shown above.

11.4  In the same drawing, draw another arrow indicating the centripetal force which the object experiences.

---

The Gravitational Force at Work in Our Solar System

As I already discussed in Module #7, the earth orbits the sun in an oval orbit which we call an "elliptical orbit."  That orbit and the axial tilt of the earth combine to produce the seasons of weather which we experience.  The figure I showed for the orbit of the earth (Figure 7.3) exaggerated the oval nature of the orbit just to make the illustration easier to understand.  In fact, the orbit of the earth around the sun is nearly circular.  Why?  Well, the earth is traveling with a speed of approximately 30,000 meters per second relative to the sun.  To put that in terms more familiar to you, that is about the same as a speed of  68,000 miles per hour!  The earth, therefore, is moving fast relative to the sun.

Remember what Newton's First Law of Motion says about objects in motion.  It says that they will stay in motion, with the same velocity, until acted on by an outside force.  Thus, the earth would move in a straight line with a speed of 30,000 meters per second unless acted on by an outside force.  We know that the earth, in fact, travels around the sun.  Therefore, there must be an outside force.  That force is the gravitational attraction between the earth and the sun.  This gravitational attraction applies a force perpendicular to the earth's velocity; it applies a centripetal force. As a result, the earth travels in an orbit that is very nearly circular.

There are, of course, other planets that orbit the sun as well. In each case, they are traveling with a certain speed relative to the sun and, in each case, the gravitational attraction between the planet and the sun results in a centripetal force. Thus, in each case, the planets orbit the sun in nearly circular orbits. That's why our solar system looks like it does.

---

**FIGURE 11.2**

The Solar System

*Illus. from The MasterClips collection*

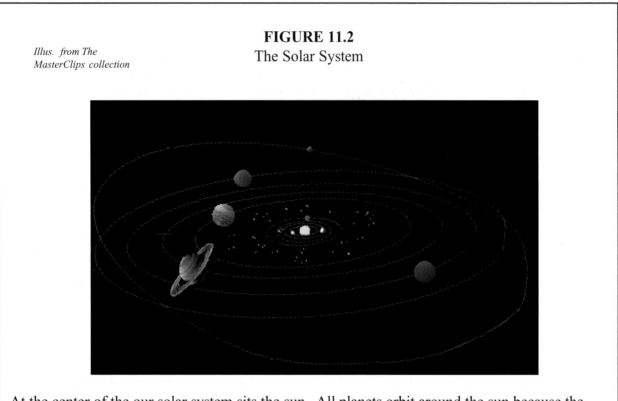

At the center of the our solar system sits the sun. All planets orbit around the sun because the gravitational attraction between each planet and the sun exerts a centripetal force. The closest planet to the sun is Mercury, and continuing out from there, you find Venus, Earth, and Mars. Between Mars and the next planet (Jupiter), you find the solar system's highest concentration of asteroids (discussed below). Beyond Jupiter, you find Saturn, Uranus, Neptune, and Pluto.

---

Notice that with the exception of Pluto's orbit, the orbits of all the other planets are nearly perfect circles. That's not quite the case, because all planets have slightly oval orbits. Nevertheless, to you and me, the orbits look pretty much circular. Although Figure 11.2 is nice because it shows you the solar system as a whole, the huge scale of the solar system makes it hard to see all of the planets. Thus, Figure 11.3 shows the solar system in a less precise manner, but one in which you can concentrate on each individual planet.

## FIGURE 11.3
### The Planets in the Solar System
(The relative sizes of the planets are reasonably drawn to scale)

*Illus. from The MasterClips collection*

sun

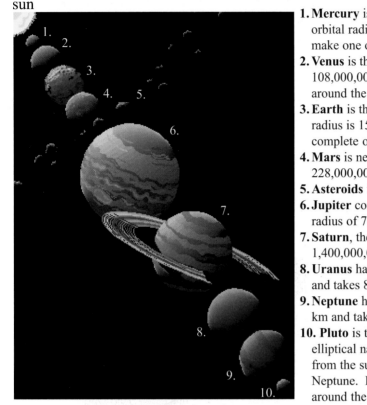

1. **Mercury** is the planet closest to the sun. Its average orbital radius is 58,500,000 km, and it takes 0.24 years to make one orbit around the sun.
2. **Venus** is the next planet out. Its average orbital radius is 108,000,000 km, and it takes 0.62 years to make one orbit around the sun.
3. **Earth** is the "third rock from the sun." Its average orbital radius is 150,000,000 km and it takes one year to make a complete orbit.
4. **Mars** is next, with an average orbital radius of 228,000,000 km, and an orbit time of 1.88 years.
5. **Asteroids** fill the gap between Mars and Jupiter.
6. **Jupiter** comes after the asteroids, with an average orbital radius of 780,000,000 km and an orbit time of 11.86 years.
7. **Saturn**, the next planet, has an average orbital radius of 1,400,000,000 km and an orbit time of 29.46 years.
8. **Uranus** has an average orbital radius of 2,900,000,000 km and takes 84.01 years to make one full orbit.
9. **Neptune** has an average orbital radius of 4,500,000,000 km and takes 164.79 years to make one full orbit.
10. **Pluto** is the farthest from the sun, although the highly elliptical nature of the orbit makes its average distance from the sun (4,400,000,000 km) just under that of Neptune. It takes Pluto 247.7 years to make a full orbit around the sun.

Since the sizes of the planets and their distances from the sun are so large, it is hard to get mental images of them. To visualize the relative sizes of the planets, try this. Suppose that the earth was the size of a ping-pong ball. Mercury would be the size of a small marble; Venus would also be about the size of a ping-pong ball; Mars would be a big marble (the kind you use to shoot small marbles); Jupiter would be about the size of a beach ball; Saturn would be the size of a basketball; Neptune and Uranus would each be softball-sized (with Neptune being just slightly smaller than Uranus); and Pluto would be the size of an apple seed. In this scenario, the sun would just barely fit in your bedroom.

To visualize the relative distances of the planets from the sun, imagine rolling out a roll of toilet paper. The toilet paper is divided into little squares. Suppose you rolled out enough toilet paper so that 90 little squares of it are lying on the floor, all stretched out. Assuming that the sun is at the end of the roll, Mercury would be at the perforation that marks the end of the first square; Venus would be at the second perforation; earth would be at the third; Mars would be at the fifth; Jupiter would be just beyond the fifteenth; Saturn would be at the 30th; Uranus would be just before the 60th; while Neptune and Pluto would each be near the 90th perforation, with Neptune just a bit closer to the sun than Pluto.

Typically, the planets of the solar system are placed into one of two groups: the **inner planets** (Mercury, Venus, earth, and Mars) and the **outer planets** (Jupiter, Saturn, Uranus, Neptune, and Pluto). The distinct break that you see in Figure 11.2 and the separation by the high concentration of asteroids seems to make this distinction a natural one. In addition, the inner planets are small and mostly composed of rock and iron. The outer planets, on the other hand, are much larger and consist mostly of helium, hydrogen, and ice.

These planets each exert a gravitational force on every object in the solar system, and as a result, most planets have objects that orbit around them. The earth, for example, is orbited by the moon. Typically, when an object orbits around a planet, we call that object a **satellite** of the planet. Although the earth has only one notable satellite, some planets have several. Mars, for example, has two small satellites: Phobos (diameter of 21 km) and Deimos (diameter of 12 km). Jupiter has 16 known satellites. The four biggest were discovered by Galileo (a scientist we will discuss later) and are consequently called the **Galilean satellites**. They are Io, Europa, Callisto, and Ganymede. Pluto has one satellite (Charon), but it is rather remarkable, being more than half the size of Pluto itself! Many consider Pluto and Charon to be a double-planet system, since they are so close in size.

Saturn, Uranus, Jupiter, and Neptune all have satellites as well, but they also have another interesting feature: **planetary rings**. We usually think of Saturn when we think of rings, because Saturn's rings are so pronounced. The rings of Saturn are actually composed of more than 100,000 individual rings, each surrounding the planet. Each ring is an aggregate of small bodies of rock, ice, and frozen gases. These bodies vary greatly in size from dust particles (0.0005 cm diameter) to boulders (10 m diameter), and they all orbit the planet. Although Saturn's rings are, by far, the most popularly-known, Uranus has at least nine rings encircling it. The first were discovered in 1977. Neptune has at least 5 rings, which were not discovered until 1989. Jupiter has at least two rings, the first of which was seen in 1979. These relatively recent dates of discovery explain why the presence of rings on these planets is not well-known.

In addition to the planets in the solar system, asteroids are shown in both figures. Asteroids are small, rocky bodies that orbit the sun under the same gravitational influence that governs the orbits of the planets. Although there are asteroids all over the solar system, the primary concentration of asteroids exists between Mars and Jupiter. They range in size. The largest known asteroid (Ceres) has a diameter of about 1000 km, and the smallest is merely a microscopic grain.

Let me ask you a question at this point. Of all the planets in the solar system, which receives the most insolation (energy from the sun)? Obviously, Mercury does, because it is closest to the sun. Thus, you would expect Mercury to be the hottest planet in the solar system, right? Wrong! Mercury is warm (it reaches about 810 $^o$F) during the day, but it is really cold (it reaches -290 $^o$F) at night. Venus is, in fact, the warmest planet in the solar system, with a relatively constant temperature of about 858 $^o$F.

If Venus is farther away from the sun than Mercury, how does it get hotter? Well, Mercury has a very thin atmosphere, whereas Venus has a very thick atmosphere. Its atmosphere is about 96 times as thick as earth's atmosphere. In addition, Venus' atmosphere is almost entirely made up of *carbon dioxide*. Remember what carbon dioxide is? It's a greenhouse gas. Thus, even though Venus receives significantly less insolation than Mercury, its strong greenhouse effect traps nearly all the energy it receives. This regulates the temperature (Venus has the most steady temperature of all the planets) and makes it quite warm. All planets farther from the sun than Venus have temperatures that decrease as their distance from the sun increases. The decrease is not steady, however, due to atmospheric considerations. Thus, while Jupiter is only slightly cooler than Mars, Saturn is *significantly* colder than Jupiter.

Now if you think about it, there are *a lot* of gravitational forces at play in the solar system. The sun is the most massive object around, so its gravitational force is, by far, the strongest. Thus, the bulk of the properties of the solar system are governed by the gravitational attraction that exists between the sun and every other object in the vicinity. Nevertheless, each planet and asteroid also attracts every other planet and asteroid, because the gravitational force is an attractive force that is present between all objects which have mass.

All of these gravitational forces work together to produce certain effects. For example, even though the orbit of a planet is mostly influenced by its gravitational attraction to the sun, the other planets' gravitational forces can cause small variations in its motion. These variations are called **perturbations** (pur tur bay' shuns) by physicists, and they can be mapped by careful study. Such studies led to the discovery of both Neptune and Pluto. In 1846, French scientist Urbain Jean Joseph Leverrier mapped the perturbations in Uranus' orbit and used them to calculate the position of a previously-undiscovered planet. With the help of those calculations, German astronomer Johann Gottfried Galle then found the planet Neptune. In 1905, a similar prediction was made by the American scientist Percival Lowell, and the result was the discovery of Pluto.

Perturbations which affect asteroids can cause even more dramatic effects. When an asteroid's orbit is perturbed enough, it can be thrown out of its standard orbit and towards a planet. Many asteroids are flung towards earth, for example. When they intersect earth's orbit, they are called **meteoroids**. When they actually hit earth's atmosphere, they experience an enormous amount of friction (due to air resistance), which causes them to heat up to high temperatures. This causes them to become white-hot, making brilliant streaks of light in the sky. At that point, they are called **meteors**. The intense heat usually breaks up the meteor, except for a few small pieces which fall to the ground and are called **meteorites**.

Although most meteors burn up when they interact with the earth's atmosphere, exceptionally large ones can survive, hitting the surface of the planet with great impact. Since the surface of earth is constantly eroding due to weather and wind, most evidence of such incidences is gone, except for a few very large craters. Other planets, however, bear the striking scars of meteor impacts, as shown in Figure 11.4.

**FIGURE 11.4**

Craters on Venus Caused by the Impact of Meteors

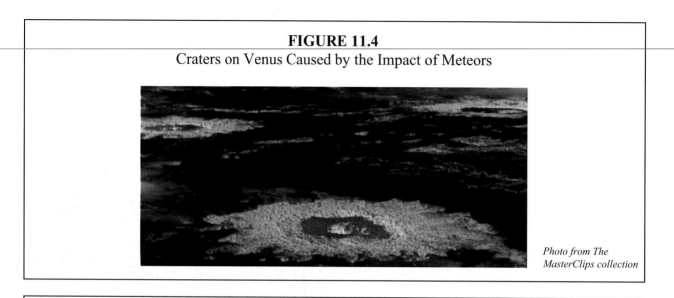

*Photo from The MasterClips collection*

---

**ON YOUR OWN**

11.5  Which receives more insolation, Mars or Saturn?

11.6  Saturn, Uranus, and Neptune have at least three things in common.  List them.

11.7  A scientist collects a rock that she says must have come from an asteroid.  What should the scientist call this rock?

---

Comets

In addition to planets and asteroids, gravity works on **comets** as well.  Comets are called "dirty snowballs" by some physicists.  They get that nickname because they are mostly composed of dust grains, chunks of dirt, and ice.  The "ice" that I refer to is not just frozen water, but also frozen carbon dioxide (which we call "dry ice"), frozen ammonia, and frozen methane (in its gaseous form, we call methane "natural gas").  Comets are typically less than 300 km in diameter.

Comets orbit the sun in very elliptical orbits that typically take them very close to the sun and then send them far from the sun (see Figure 11.5).  When they are far from the sun, comets are not detectable except by the most advanced telescopic devices.  However, when their elliptical orbit takes them close to the sun, something amazing happens.  Its proximity to the sun causes the "dirty snowball" to heat up.  This causes the ice on the surface of the comet to turn directly into a gas, forming a "fuzzy" atmosphere around it.  When a substance turns from solid to gas, we say it has **sublimed**.  At this point, the chunk of dust, dirt, and ice that makes up the solid part of the comet is called the **nucleus** of the comet, and the "fuzzy" atmosphere around the comet is called the **coma** (koh' muh).

Because the gases in the coma are heated by the comet's proximity to the sun, they begin to emit light, causing them to "glow."  The gases from the coma usually form a long, glowing

**tail**. Figure 11.5 shows a picture (left) and the orbit (right) of comet Kohoutek, which was visible in the night sky during the last quarter of 1973 and the early quarter of 1974.

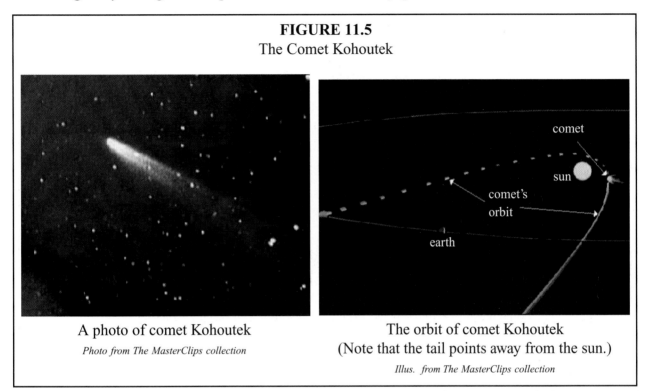

**FIGURE 11.5**
The Comet Kohoutek

A photo of comet Kohoutek
*Photo from The MasterClips collection*

The orbit of comet Kohoutek
(Note that the tail points away from the sun.)
*Illus. from The MasterClips collection*

In the photograph, you can see the coma (the bright spot at the front of the comet) and the tail. Note from the illustration of its orbit how close the comet comes to the sun. The enormous amount of insolation it receives at that proximity to the sun is what makes the coma and causes it to glow. Note also that the comet's tail points away from the sun. This is typical of most comets. You see, there are certain gases that are constantly being emitted from the surface of the sun. The gases are pushed away from the sun, causing a "wind," which physicists call the **solar wind**. This wind blows the gases of the coma away from the nucleus of the comet, giving the comet its tail. Although some comets are bright enough to be seen with the naked eye, most are not.

When a comet is far from the sun, it has neither coma nor tail. It is simply a "dirty snowball." When its elliptical orbit takes it near to the sun, however, the insolation from the sun forms the gaseous coma. The solar wind then pushes those gases away from the sun, forming the tail. Thus, when a comet is close to the sun, it is composed of a nucleus, a coma, and a tail. Once it passes away from the sun, the gases of the coma either blow away or freeze, and once again the comet is simply a "dirty snowball."

If you think about it, each time a comet makes its pass near the sun, it loses a significant amount of mass. After all, some of the ice that comprises it sublimes, and much of the dust and dirt blows off as well. Thus, with enough passes near the sun, a comet will simply disintegrate. Unlike planets, then, comets are transient objects in the solar system. Some could last for a long time because it takes them a long time to orbit around the sun. Nevertheless, they will only survive for a certain number of orbits.

The time that it takes for a comet to orbit the sun is used as a means of classification. The **short-period** comets are comets that take 3 - 9 years to make an orbit. Typically, a short-period comet's orbit takes it no farther than Jupiter before it turns around and heads back to the sun. Encke's comet has the shortest known orbital time, which is 3.3 years. The **long-period** comets typically have orbits that extend to the planet Neptune, and they can take quite a while (more than 9 years up to a few thousand years) to orbit the sun. The famous Halley's comet has an orbital period of 76 years, making it a long-period comet. If you were paying attention in 1997, you saw the Hale-Bopp comet, which has a calculated orbit time of more than 3,000 years. Finally, there are **very long-period** comets whose orbits carry them so far out to the edges of the solar system that they take more than 5,000 years to make one orbit. Physicists have identified some comets which they postulate will never make more than one trip around the sun because their orbits are so large!

If comets are transient objects in the solar system, where do they come from? Well, that's an interesting question. We know that some asteroids become comets when their orbit around the sun is perturbed significantly. Physicists think that only a few comets are formed in that way, however. Where do the rest come from? The answer to that question is a bit tricky. Remember, comets are only bright when they pass by the sun. Once they are far from the sun, they lose their coma and tail, and become small, dark chunks of dirt, dust, and ice. That makes them *very* hard to detect. Thus, their origins remain a bit of a mystery.

In 1950, Dutch astronomer Jan Oort proposed an hypothesis that comets come from a big shell of icy bodies which surrounds the solar system well beyond Pluto. This shell is now called the "**Oort cloud**" by astronomers. Although many textbooks talk about the Oort cloud as a fact, it remains only an hypothesis to explain where comets come from. Since even our best telescopes could not hope to see such small, dark bodies so far away, the Oort cloud exists only hypothetically.

The hypothesis of the Oort cloud was given some credence in 1992, however, when a 150-mile wide body was discovered just beyond Neptune. In 1951, astronomer Gerard Kuiper had suggested that if the Oort cloud exists, a smaller body of comet material should exist just beyond Neptune. Astronomers decided that this 150-mile wide body must be just that, so they named it the **Kuiper belt**. In 1992, the Hubble space telescope confirmed that the Kuiper belt was, indeed, real and was composed of comet material. The strong evidence produced has convinced most astronomers that short-period comets originate from this Kuiper belt. Most likely, a chance collision between two bodies in the Kuiper belt sends one of them hurtling towards the sun, and a comet is born.

Since short-term comets seem to come from the Kuiper belt, it is probably not all that unlikely that long-term comets and very long-term comets come from similar sources. Thus, the Oort cloud hypothesis is at least consistent with what we know. Unfortunately, confirmation of the Oort cloud may take quite some time. After all, it took a lot of effort and technology to determine that the Kuiper belt exists. It will, most likely, take an even longer time to be able to detect comet material that might be much, much farther away from us.

**ON YOUR OWN**

11.8  The diagram below maps out two orbits around the sun.  Which would most likely belong to a comet that would be relatively easy to see?  Can the other orbit still be that of a comet?

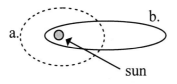

sun

## What Causes the Gravitational Force?

Notice that so far you have learned a lot about gravity and its effects, but you still do not know what causes it.  That's the situation physics was in until the last 80 years or so.  Up until then, physicists could calculate gravitational forces, determine what would happen as a result of gravitational forces, and predict the future positions of the planets, asteroids, and comets in the solar system.  Nevertheless, they had no idea what really causes the gravitational force.

That all changed in 1916 when Albert Einstein proposed his **General Theory of Relativity**.  This theory is a broad theory that attempts to explain an entire way of looking at physics.  The details are far, far beyond the scope of this course.  Nevertheless, one of the by-products of Einstein's General Theory of Relativity was the first explanation of what *causes* the gravitational force.  The best way to explain what Einstein's theory says is to start with an experiment.

**EXPERIMENT 11.2**
The "Bent Space" Theory of Gravity

Supplies:

- A soft seat cushion from a couch (A soft bed will work as well.)
- A bowling ball (A heavy rock will work as well.)
- A marble

Introduction - Einstein's General Theory of Relativity concludes that the gravitational "force" is not really a force at all.  It is actually a result of the fact that mass bends space.  This experiment will help illustrate such a strange concept.

Procedure:

A.  Lay the seat cushion on the floor.  If you are using a bed, just stand next to the bed.
B.  Find a spot on the cushion which is away from the center of the cushion but relatively flat.  Lie the marble on that point so that it stays there without rolling.
C.  Now lay the bowling ball at the very center of the cushion.  Note what happens to the marble.
D.  Next, take the bowling ball off of the cushion and smooth it out so that it is reasonably flat again.
E.  Roll the marble (slowly) straight across the cushion, but not near the center.  Note that it rolls reasonably straight.
F.  Put the bowling ball back in the center of the cushion and roll the marble along the same path that you rolled it before, with the same slow speed.  Note the path that the marble takes.

Einstein's General Theory of Relativity states that space is not always the way it appears to us.  Suppose, for example, that you did not know the world was round.  Would you think that it was?  Probably not.  After all, the earth looks pretty flat all around you.  Thus, you would probably think that the earth is flat.  We know that this is not the case, though.  Despite what it looks like from our vantage point, we know that the earth is round.  In the same way, Einstein postulated that although it does not appear to change at all, space actually bends in the presence of an object with mass.

In the first part of your experiment, the seat cushion represents space.  With nothing on the seat cushion, it stayed relatively flat.  However, when a massive object (the bowling ball) was placed there, the entire seat cushion bent.  The bend was greatest in the middle and least around the edges, but nevertheless, the entire seat cushion bent.  In response, the marble rolled towards the bowling ball.  This is Einstein's picture of gravity.  Space (the seat cushion) bends in the presence of mass (the bowling ball).  As a result, all objects (the marble) accelerate towards the mass.  This makes it look like a force is being applied to an object.

In the second part of your experiment, you watched the marble roll straight across the flat seat cushion.  When the bowling ball was once again placed on the seat cushion, the marble did not roll straight.  Instead, it rolled in a curved path.  According to Einstein, this is why planets orbit the sun.  In his theory, the planets are all actually moving in a straight line.  Because space is so strongly bent by the mass of the sun, however, that straight line is deformed until it becomes a circle.  Thus, as far as the planets are concerned, they are traveling in a straight line.  Space itself, however, causes that straight line to become a circle.

I know that this is a terribly complicated picture to put in your head.  That's why I tried to illustrate it to you with an experiment.  If you think of the marble as a planet, it rolled straight as long as space (the cushion) was flat.  As you soon as you bent space (the cushion) with a massive object (the bowling ball), however, the planet (the marble) then moved in a curved path.  If the object deforms space enough, that curved path becomes a circle.

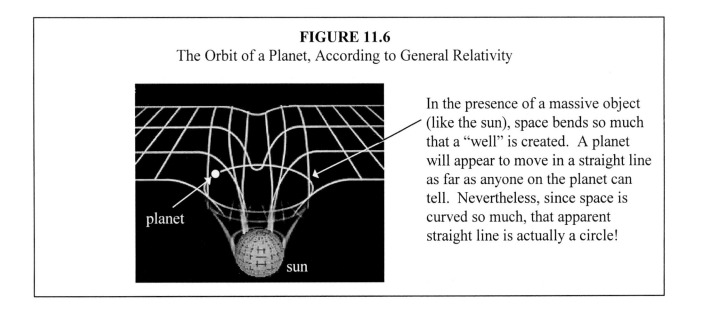

**FIGURE 11.6**
The Orbit of a Planet, According to General Relativity

In the presence of a massive object (like the sun), space bends so much that a "well" is created. A planet will appear to move in a straight line as far as anyone on the planet can tell. Nevertheless, since space is curved so much, that apparent straight line is actually a circle!

planet

sun

If Einstein is right, then, gravity is not really a force at all. It is, instead, a consequence of how mass bends space.

Is Einstein right? Well, we aren't really sure. The General Theory of Relativity has had success in explaining certain things about space that could not be explained before. Perhaps the biggest success of Einstein's theory is its ability to fully explain the way Mercury orbits around the sun. Although the details of this observation are beyond the scope of this course, I can tell you that using all we knew about gravity before Einstein's theory, Mercury's orbit around the sun could only be predicted with an accuracy of about 92%. Using the equations of general relativity, however, Mercury's orbit is explained exactly.

Einstein's General Theory of Relativity also predicts that light will bend when it comes close to a massive object, like a star. After all, light must stay in the confines of space. Thus, if space bends, light should bend as well. Since Newton's law of universal gravitation only predicts an attraction between masses, and since light has no mass, Newton would not predict an interaction between light and massive objects. Astronomers have observed that when light passes near a star, its path does bend. That's another piece of evidence supporting Einstein's theory. Because of these evidences, Einstein's Theory of General Relativity is considered a reliable theory. Nevertheless, it has not been tested nearly enough to become a law. Thus, its explanation of gravity still remains a theory. It is a good theory, but it is still a theory.

There is another attempt to explain what causes the gravitational force. If anything, it is even more difficult to comprehend, but once again, let's try an experiment.

## EXPERIMENT 11.3
### The Graviton Theory of Gravity

Supplies:

- Two balls (Baseball-sized balls are best, but any will do)
- Two people to help you
- A stopwatch or a watch with a second hand
- A large, open space

Introduction - Another theory regarding what causes gravitational force is the idea that massive objects exchange tiny particles called "gravitons." This experiment shows why that could create an attractive force.

Procedure:

A. Take one ball for yourself and hand the other to one of your helpers. The other helper needs to hold the stopwatch.
B. Stand about 1 foot away from the helper who has the ball.
C. Have the helper with the stopwatch start the stopwatch and, at the same time, yell "go." When he or she yells "go," throw the ball to your other helper, while he or she throws the ball to you. Then, right away, throw the balls back to one another so that you have the same balls that you originally had. This all needs to happen in less than a second.
D. Every second, your helper with the stopwatch should yell "go" again, and you need to exchange balls with your other helper and then exchange them back again, all within a second. Do this for 10 times or so.
E. Now both you and your helper with the ball should each take a giant step backwards, taking you farther apart from each other. Repeat the procedure, exchanging and re-exchanging balls every second for 10 times or so.
F. Repeat step (E) three or four times, continually stepping farther and farther away from your helper with the ball. If it gets too hard, you can stop.
G. Does the procedure become harder or easier as you move farther and farther away from each other?

The other theory of gravity says that two massive objects tend to exchange tiny particles called "**gravitons**." These gravitons must be exchanged within a very tiny time frame, so, just like in your experiment, the closer two massive objects are, the easier it is for them to exchange gravitons. Thus, in your experiment, you and your helper with the ball were representing massive objects. The balls were gravitons, and your helper with the stopwatch was making sure that you exchanged balls within a certain time frame. As you and your helper got farther and farther apart from one another, it got harder and harder to exchange balls within the time interval, didn't it?

Now, if you and your helper were forced to do this continually, what would you do?  You would move close to one another, to make it easier, right?  Well, if massive objects do exchange gravitons, and if they must be exchanged within a certain small time interval, massive objects would probably move closer to one another as well.  That, then, could be what causes the attractive gravitational force.  Massive objects are attracted to one another because they exchange gravitons.

There is evidence for Einstein's General Theory of Relativity.  Is there any evidence for the graviton theory?  Well, not exactly.  Gravitons have never been observed, and we have never witnessed massive objects exchanging particles.  Thus, there is no evidence as of yet for this theory.  Why would anyone believe it?  Well, the *other* forces in nature (the electromagnetic force, the weak force, and the strong force) all can be explained by the idea of particle exchange.  Thus, it is natural to think that the other force in Creation should be explained that way as well.

Wait a minute.  Did I just say that this strange theory of particle exchange explains the other forces in Creation?  I sure did!  Believe it or not, negatively-charged particles are attracted to positively-charged particles because they exchange small particles (called "photons") with one another.  I will tell you about that at length in an upcoming module.  In addition, the other two forces are explained in the same way.  Thus, even though there is no evidence at this point that gravity is caused by the exchange of gravitons, it seems like a likely explanation, since the other forces in Creation are explained in a similar way.

Indeed, all physicists agree that gravitons would be very, very hard to detect.  Thus, even if they do exist, we should not be surprised that we haven't see them yet.  Of course, most physicists admit that Einstein's explanation is better right now, since it at least has some evidence supporting it.  In fact, there are some that postulate both theories as true.  They assume that curved space *induces* the exchange of gravitons.  Thus, it is even possible that both theories are true.  At the same time, of course, it is possible that neither theory is true.  After all, even the data that backs up Einstein's theory is scant at best.

---

**ON YOUR OWN**

11.9  If Einstein's General Theory of Relativity is true, how many forces are there in Creation?

11.10  Suppose that a great physicist one day detected massive objects exchanging small particles with each other.  That would not be conclusive evidence for the graviton theory.  There is one other thing that must be shown to really provide conclusive evidence for the graviton theory.  What is it?

---

## A Brief History of Our View of the Solar System

In this module, you have learned a lot about gravity and how it works to make the solar system look like it does.  Believe it or not, however, all of this was known *before* human beings ventured into space.  Even Einstein's Theory of General Relativity was produced long before spaceflight was developed.  How in the world could scientists learn so much about the solar system without venturing out into it?  That is a very interesting story, and it is one worth recounting to you here.

The motions of the stars and moon in the night sky have always fascinated people.  Since the beginnings of recorded history, human beings have tried to understand them.  Indeed, most calendars (even ancient ones) were based on the appearance of the moon in the sky.  As time went on, people realized that if they could *predict* the motions of the stars, moon, and sun, keeping track of dates and times would be relatively easy.

The ancient Greeks were probably the first to develop a systematic view of the motion of the stars and the moon.  Although many other cultures developed intricate calendars and the like, the ancient Greeks were the first to develop a systematic theory based on observations of the night sky.  In the second century AD, the Greek astronomers Hipparchus and Ptolemy mapped the motion of 1000 stars and thought of them as a fixed backdrop.  They placed them on the surface of a sphere, called the "celestial sphere," and then said that the earth was at the very center of the sphere.  The moon and the planets, then, moved about in the sphere on circular orbits that were arranged within the sphere in a very complex way.

This was the start of what is called the **geocentric** view of our solar system.  In a geocentric system, the earth is placed at the center of the solar system.  Although there were several problems with this geocentric view of things, the ancient Greeks were able to use this system to predict the motion of the moon and other planets better than anyone else had ever done.  Thus, although it was far from perfect, the success of the theory made it popular among scientists.

Minor adjustments and commentaries were made on the geocentric theory, but it remained intact essentially from the second century AD until the sixteenth century AD.  By that time, too much data had been piled up that was inconsistent with the theory.  Things began to change in 1543 when a Polish scientist named Nicolaus Copernicus wrote a book called *On the Revolution of Heavenly Bodies*.  In that book, he examined the geocentric theory in light of the known data and found it sorely lacking.  He showed that a great deal more of the data could be explained if you viewed the solar system as a series of concentric circles, with the sun at rest in the very center.  This was the beginnings of what physicists call the **heliocentric** view of the solar system, where the earth was taken out of the center and replaced with the sun.

Copernicus was raised and educated in the Roman Catholic church.  At that time, the Roman Catholic church adhered strictly to the geocentric view of the solar system.  After all, since God created man, he must be the most important aspect of Creation.  Therefore, his dwelling place (the earth), must be at the center of everything.  The Roman Catholic church also pointed to a scripture in the Old Testament (Joshua 10:12-13) in which Joshua commands the sun to stand still and, through the power of the Lord, it did.  The Roman Catholic church argued that Joshua would not have to command the sun to stand still if it was at rest in center of the solar system!

Copernicus' work was put on the Roman Catholic church's list of banned books, and little attention was paid to it again until 1609 when the Italian physicist Galileo Galilei made a crude telescope and pointed it skyward. He was able to use that telescope to notice the phases of Venus, which could only be explained with Copernicus' theory. He also discovered the four major moons of Jupiter, as well as the rings of Saturn. This lent more evidence for the heliocentric view because it showed that there were many bodies (the moons and rings of other planets) which did not orbit around the earth. If they were not constrained to orbit around the earth, why should the other planets be so constrained?

When Galileo, a well-respected scientist, tried to publish a work showing all of the evidence in favor of the Copernican system, the Roman Catholic church put him on trial. They were firmly in support of the geocentric view, and they would not allow even a great scientist such as Galileo to say otherwise. Because Galileo was deeply committed to his church and did not want to be excommunicated, he publicly recanted his belief in the Copernican system. As a result, the Roman Catholic church was lenient on him, and his punishment was house arrest for the remainder of his life. Even though he publicly recanted his belief in the heliocentric system, he still collected data that supported it during his house arrest.

At about the same time (1580 - 1597), a Danish astronomer named Tycho Brahe and his German assistant, Johannes Kepler, began compiling a huge amount of data on the motion of the planets. As a result of the data, Kepler devised a series of rules which the planets always followed. They became known as "Kepler's Laws." Even though these laws did nothing to explain *why* the planets moved as they did, they clearly indicated that the motion of the planets was guided by an overriding principle.

That principle was laid out by Sir Isaac Newton. When he formulated his universal law of gravitation, he showed that the heliocentric view was the best way in which to understand the solar system. By that time, so much evidence had been accumulated that the Roman Catholic church had to back off of its desire to cling to the geocentric theory, and the heliocentric theory quickly dominated the scientific community.

After Newton's time, astronomy really took off. The telescope became one of the most widely-used instruments in physics. New stars were charted, the surfaces of planets were studied, and accurate predictions were made regarding the motion of the planets. After a while, physicists even developed a means of measuring the distance to a planet using a telescope. As technology increased, our ability to gather more data increased. Today, we can study the chemical composition of stars, comets, and other objects in space. We can do all of that and more without even venturing into space!

Notice what happened in this story. From the second century AD to the sixteenth century AD (1400 years), not much progress was made in the field of astronomy. That's because the scientists of the time were working with a flawed theory. No matter how much they tried, they could not get the geocentric view of the solar system consistent with the data. Nevertheless, they just kept trying. Rather than throwing out the bad theory and coming up with a new one, they just kept trying to make the old one work.

Through the efforts of Copernicus, Galileo, Kepler, Brahe, and Newton, however, a new theory slowly took over. Once it really took hold, incredible advances were made in only a few centuries. This story should teach all scientists a valuable lesson: don't cling to theories simply because they have been well-established in the scientific community. If you can't get the data to agree with the theory, find a better one! That's what will advance science.

In my opinion, scientists are doing the same thing today with the theory of evolution. Just like the geocentric theory, the theory of evolution has become well-established in the scientific community. As a result, it has a lot of support. Nevertheless, nearly all data that relates to the origin of life on the planet squarely contradicts the theory of evolution. If scientists want to really advance the science of biology, they need to throw evolution away and work in a better theoretical framework. A creationist framework is much more in agreement with the data, so that's a good place to start!

Before I end this module, I do want to comment on the scripture reference mentioned above (Joshua 10:12-13). Although the Roman Catholic church interpreted that verse as evidence for the geocentric theory, it is not. The verse reads as follows:

"Then spake Joshua to the Lord in the day when the Lord delivered up the Amorites before the children of Israel, and he said in the sight of Israel, Sun, stand thou still upon Gibeon; and thou, Moon, in the valley of Ajalon. And the sun stood still, and the moon stayed, until the people had avenged themselves upon their enemies. Is not this written in the book of Jasher? So the sun stood still in the midst of heaven, and hasted not to go down about a whole day."

Does this scripture verse indicate that the sun moves around the earth? Of course not! It indicates that Joshua, the people of Israel, and the writer of the book of Jasher thought that it did! Note that the first reference to the sun standing still is a quote from Joshua. The second reference is the observation of the people, and the last is a reference to another book. In each case, then, this verse is simply telling us what happened from the people's perspective.

You see, the Bible is the single most accurate historical document of its time (See *Evidence that Demands a Verdict* by Josh McDowell or *Reasonable Faith: The Scientific Case for Christianity* by Dr. Jay L. Wile.). As a historical document, it must quote its subjects accurately. That's all that's happening here. The Bible is doing its normal, accurate reporting of what happened. Thus, it tells you what happened from the perspective of those who made or watched it happen.

## ANSWERS TO THE ON YOUR OWN PROBLEMS

11.1 When the masses are changed, the distance between them is not changed. Thus, we don't have to worry about that. When the 10 kg mass is replaced by a 20 kg mass, the gravitational attraction will increase by a factor of 2, because the mass is increased by a factor of 2. When the 6 kg mass is replaced with the 3 kg mass, the gravitational attraction is reduced by a factor of 2, because the mass was reduced by a factor of 2. In the end, the gravitational attraction increased by a factor of 2 and then decreased by a factor of 2. The result, then, is that <u>the gravitational force stayed the same</u>.

11.2 When the 1 kg mass is replaced by the 4 kg mass, the gravitational attraction increases by a factor of 4. When the 2 kg mass is replaced with the 1 kg mass, the gravitational force decreases by a factor of 2. Finally, when the masses are moved from 10 cm to 5 cm, the distance goes down by a factor of 2. This means that the gravitational attraction increased by a factor of $2^2$, or 4. Thus, the gravitational force increased by a factor of 4, decreased by a factor of 2, and increased by a factor of 4. Thus, the gravitational force went up by a factor of 4 x 1/2 x 4. This is an <u>increase by a factor of 8</u>.

11.3 The velocity of an object traveling in a circle is always straight. The centripetal force is what keeps it moving in a circle. Thus:

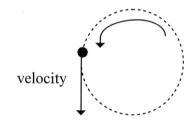

11.4 The centripetal force that keeps an object moving in a circle is always pointed towards the center of the circle:

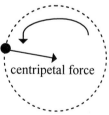

11.5 The insolation that a planet receives is dependent solely on its proximity to the sun. The closer to the sun, the more insolation a planet receives. Thus, <u>Mars receives more insolation than does Saturn</u>.

11.6 There are many things that these planets have in common. <u>They are all outer planets, they have similar compositions, they all have rings, they all have satellites, and they are all quite cold</u>. Any three of these would work.

11.7  If the rock came from an asteroid, the asteroid must have first become a meteoroid and then burnt up in the atmosphere to become a meteor.  Finally, the remnants which fell to the ground are known as meteorites.  Thus, she should call it a <u>meteorite</u>.

11.8  The most easily observed comet will be the one that gets bright.  In order for a comet to get bright, it must come close to the sun.  Thus, <u>orbit (b) is the orbit of the easily observed comet.</u> <u>Orbit (a) can still be the orbit of a comet</u>, however.  A comet is a comet whether or not it ever develops a coma and tail.  A comet is simply a "dirty snowball" in space.

11.9  If Einstein's Theory of General Relativity is true, then the gravitational force is not really a force.  Instead, it is just a consequence of what mass does to space.  As a result, there would only be <u>3 fundamental</u> forces.  An answer of 2 is acceptable, if you think of the electroweak force as one force.

11.10   In order for the graviton theory to be true, the exchange of particles must be done within a certain time frame.  If this is not the case, there is no impetus for the masses to move close together.  Thus, <u>it needs to be shown that the exchange of particles is restricted to a certain time frame</u>.

## STUDY GUIDE FOR MODULE #11

1. Name the four fundamental forces in Creation. Which two forces are really different aspects of the same force?

2. Which is the weakest of the fundamental forces? Which is the strongest?

3. Name the three principles of Newton's Universal Law of Gravitation.

4. The gravitational force between two objects ($mass_1$ = 10 kg, $mass_2$ = 6 kg) is measured when the objects are 10 centimeters apart. If the 10 kg mass is replaced with a 20 kg mass and the 6 kg mass is replaced with a 12 kg mass, how does the new gravitational attraction compare to the first one that was measured?

5. The gravitational force between two objects ($mass_1$ = 10 kg, $mass_2$ = 6 kg) is measured when the objects are 10 centimeters apart. If the distance between them is increased to 40 centimeters, how does the new gravitational attraction compare to the first one that was measured?

6. The gravitational force between two objects ($mass_1$ = 1 kg, $mass_2$ = 2 kg) is measured when the objects are 12 centimeters apart. If the 1 kg mass is replaced with a 5 kg mass, the 2 kg mass is replaced with a 4 kg mass, and the distance between the objects is reduced to 4 centimeters, how does the new gravitational attraction compare to the first one that was measured?

7. If the moon orbits the earth because the earth exerts a gravitational force on the moon, what is the equal and opposite force required by Newton's Third Law of Motion?

8. What kind of force is necessary for circular motion? Give the definition of that force.

9. What are the three principles of circular motion?

10. A child is twirling a toy airplane on a string:

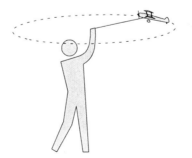

a. If the child increases the speed of the plane, will the string need to exert more or less force on the plane?

b. If the child keeps twirling at the same rate but allows more string out, making the circle bigger, will the string need to exert more or less force?

11. What is "centrifugal force?"

12. In the following diagram, the ball is traveling from point "A" to point "B." Draw the velocity of the ball and the force it experiences if it is traveling at constant speed.

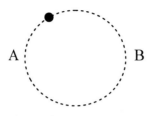

A          B

13. List the inner planets and the outer planets.

14. List the planets of the solar system from the closest to the sun to the farthest from the sun.

15. List the planets that have rings.

16. Where are most of the asteroids in the solar system?

17. What causes an asteroid to become a meteor?

18. What are the three parts of a comet? Which of those parts is always present in a comet?

19. During what part of a comet's orbit are all three parts present?

20. Are comets' orbits circular or elliptical?

21. Where do physicists think that short-period comets come from?

22. What causes gravity, according to Einstein's Theory of General Relativity?

23. What causes gravity, according to the graviton theory?

# MODULE #12: The Forces in Creation - Part 2

## Introduction

I want to continue my discussion of the four fundamental forces in nature by turning next to the electromagnetic force. I am sure that you are at least somewhat familiar with this force. It is the force that makes electricity flow in an electrical circuit, holds electrons in an atom, and makes lightning. What you might be surprised to find out is that this very force also attracts the north pole of a magnet to the south pole of a magnet. This causes the compass needle to point north, refrigerator magnets to stick to the refrigerator, and electrical motors to turn.

At one time, physicists thought that the force which governs electricity was completely different than that which governed magnetism. After all, electricity and magnetism seem so different, how could they both be governed by the same source? It took the genius of a Scottish physicist named James Clerk Maxwell to demonstrate that both electricity and magnetism were, in fact, different facets of the same force. When Maxwell demonstrated this fact, enormous advances were made in the study of electrical and magnetic phenomena in physics. As a result, many people refer to Maxwell as the founder of modern physics. He is generally ranked with Albert Einstein and Isaac Newton as one of the three most important figures in the history of science. Because of his importance, a brief biography is in order.

## James Clerk Maxwell

Born in a remote region of Scotland in 1831, Maxwell was home-educated until being accepted to Edinburgh University at the age of 16. The University offered him admission when a group of scientists there read a paper on geometric curves which he had written at age 14. They were so impressed with it that they immediately accepted him as a student. When he came to the university, all of the professors were amazed at his ability to design experiments which explained anything that interested him. He quickly outgrew the experimental facilities at Edinburgh University and transferred to Cambridge University in England to continue his studies.

After graduating from Cambridge, he took a teaching post at King's College and there met **Michael Faraday**, the inventor of the electrical generator and the electrical transformer. Although great with experiments, Faraday lacked the physical and mathematical insight of Maxwell. Together, they made a great team. Maxwell put Faraday's theories on a firm mathematical foundation, and as a result, real advances were made in the study of electricity and magnetism.

When he was 42, he published a book entitled *Treatise on Electricity and Magnetism.* In it, he used forty mathematical equations to show that electricity and magnetism were, indeed, governed by exactly the same force. As with most revolutionary works, it was not accepted right away. The later experiments of Heinrich Rudolph Hertz lent so much weight to Maxwell's work that it eventually became the guiding force of electromagnetic study. With time, Maxwell's forty equations have been reduced to only 4, but they still bear the name "Maxwell's Equations."

With 2 to 4 years of post-calculus mathematics, you can *begin* to understand Maxwell's Equations.

James Clerk Maxwell was known for many other things. He developed the kinetic theory of gases which allows chemists and physicists to explain the behavior of a gas under almost any set of conditions. That theory was later expanded to apply to all matter. It is now called the "kinetic theory of matter," and I touched on it in Module #3 when I explained the concept of temperature. In addition, Maxwell was the first to explain how we see in color, and he also developed the field of thermodynamics, which you will learn about in chemistry.

Clearly, Maxwell is a genius of the caliber of Newton. He was also just as devoted a Christian as was Newton. This really shouldn't surprise you. Many philosophers (Pierre Duhem and Stanley Jaki, for example) credit Christianity with the birth of the scientific method, so it is not surprising that most of the founders of modern science had a strong Christian faith. Maxwell's devotion to Christianity was demonstrated in the extemporaneous prayers he would say. One example is, "Teach us to study the works of Thy hands, that we may subdue the earth to our use and strengthen our reason for Thy service." As was the case with Newton, Maxwell studied science as a means of serving Christ. Today more than ever, science needs people like James Clerk Maxwell!

## The Electromagnetic Force

As I said before, everyone has some experience with the electromagnetic force. Nevertheless, to make sure that we all "start on the same page," I want to go over the basics. The best way to start is by having you perform an experiment.

---

**EXPERIMENT 12.1**
Electrical Attraction and Repulsion

Supplies:

- Two balloons  (Round balloons work best, but any kind will do.)
- Thread
- Cellophane tape

Introduction - This experiment teaches you when electrically-charged objects attract one another and when they repel one another. It will also tell you something about the properties of the electromagnetic force.

Procedure:

A. Blow up the balloons and tie them off so that they each stay inflated.

---

B. Tie some thread to one of the balloons and attach the other end of the thread to the ceiling with some tape, so that the balloon hangs from the thread. Make the length of the thread such that the balloon hangs at about the same height as your chest.
C. Take the balloon that is hanging by the thread and rub it in your hair a little. This will cause the balloon to pick up some electrical charge. Now back away from the balloon and allow it to hang there.
D. Take the other balloon and rub it in your hair just a little. Now, hold this balloon in both of your hands and slowly bring it close to the balloon that is hanging from the thread. What happens?
E. Vigorously rub the balloon that is in your hands in your hair. Once again, bring it close to the balloon that is hanging on the thread. Note the difference in the way that the balloon on the string behaves as compared to what it did in step (D).
F. Next, take a piece of tape that is at least 15 cm long and tape it to the top of a table. Leave a little part of it unfastened, so that you can remove it in a moment.
G. Quickly rip the tape off of the table and grasp it at both ends. Hold the tape near the balloon, with the sticky side facing the balloon. What happens?

Why did the hanging balloon behave the way that it did in the experiment? Well, when you rub a balloon in your hair, it picks up some stray electrons that are in your hair. This causes the balloon to pick up an overall negative charge. Since you rubbed both the hanging balloon and the balloon in your hand in your hair, both of them developed a negative charge. When you brought one close to the other, they began to repel each other, because charges that have the same sign repel each other. The repulsion was greater the closer the balloons got together. Also, when you rubbed the balloon in your hand more vigorously in your hair, it picked up more negative charge, which also increased the repulsion. This brings me to the first rule of electrical charge:

### Like charges repel one another.

Two positively-charged objects will repel each other, as will two negatively-charged objects. The first object will exert a repulsive force on the second, and in compliance with Newton's Third Law, the second will exert an equal and opposite force on the first.

When you stuck the tape onto the table and then ripped it off, you were actually causing the tape to lose negative charges. This is because the tape leaves electrons behind in the sticky residue left on the table. Since the tape lost negative charges, it became positively-charged. When you held that up to the balloon, the balloon was attracted to it because negatively-charged matter attracts positively-charged matter. This brings me to the second rule of electrical charge:

### Opposite charges attract one another.

When a negatively-charged particle is in proximity to a positively-charged particle, a mutual attractive force will develop. The first will exert a force on the second and, in compliance with Newton's Third Law, the second will exert an equal and opposite force on the first.

The experiment also demonstrated the way that the force between electrically-charged particles varies with various conditions. For example, the more vigorously you rubbed the balloon on your hair, the more charge it collected and, as a result, the stronger it repelled the other balloon. Thus, the larger the electrical charge, the stronger the force. Also, the closer you brought the balloons together, the stronger the repulsion became. That's because the force between electrical charges increases the closer the charges are to one another.

In fact, just like there were three principles regarding gravitational force, there are three principles regarding the force that exists between electrical charges. They are:

1. **All electrical charges attract or repel one another, depending on whether they have opposite charges or similar charges.**

2. **The force between charged objects is directly proportional to the amount of electrical charge on each object.**

3. **The force between charged objects is inversely proportional to the square of the distance between the two objects.**

Does this look familiar at all? It should. After all, if you replaced "electrical charge" with "mass," you would essentially have Newton's Universal Law of Gravitation! Indeed, the force between electrically-charged particles behaves identically to the gravitational force.

That's another reason why many physicists believe in the graviton theory of gravity. After all, they say, it would be an incredible coincidence if the gravitational force behaved just like the electromagnetic force unless they were both caused by essentially the same thing. Since the electromagnetic force is produced by the exchange of particles (see below), then the gravitational force must be produced by the exchange of particles as well. Otherwise, it would not behave just like the electromagnetic force.

Scientists who are Christians, however, have no problem with the fact that there are many "coincidences" in Creation. Since one Creator designed and put into place all of the laws that govern the universe, it should not be surprising that they are similar. Thus, although there is some "tidiness" to believing in the graviton theory, there is no real reason to. If Einstein's Theory of General Relativity is right (as I think it is), there is no need to believe in the graviton theory. After all, God could have designed space so that it curves just right in the presence of mass so that, as a result, the gravitational force and electromagnetic force behave essentially the same.

Since you have already dealt with example problems related to the gravitational force, I will not do any example problems on how to predict the change in the electrical force when the charge or the distance between objects changes. Nevertheless, as the "on your own" problems demonstrate, you need to know how to do them. They are, however, exactly like the gravitation problems that you did, so you should be all set.

**ON YOUR OWN**

12.1  For the diagrams below, use a solid arrow to point out the direction of the force exerted on object #2 by object #1.  In addition, draw a dashed arrow to indicate the direction of the force exerted on object #1 by object #2.

a.

b.

12.2  Two charged particles are placed 16 centimeters from each other and the resulting force is measured.  The charge on object #1 is then halved and the charge on object #2 is reduced by a factor of four.  The distance between the objects is also reduced to 4 centimeters.  How does the new force compare to the old force?

## Photons and the Electromagnetic Force

As I said in the previous module, the electromagnetic force is actually produced through the exchange of particles.  Believe it or not, the particles exchanged are actually small bits of light, called **photons**.

Photons - Small "packages" of light that act just like small particles

In the previous module, you learned how the exchange of particles can generate an attractive force.  Opposite charges are attracted to each other through the exchange of photons, much like you were attracted to your helper in Experiment 11.3 through the exchange of balls.  How does the exchange of particles lead to a repulsive force?  That's a bit too hard to explain here.  You will just have to believe that like charges repel one another because of the exchange of photons. If you go on to study physics in college, you will eventually learn enough physics and mathematics to see why.  For now, you just have to trust me!

Part of the reason this is hard for you to believe is that you have no evidence for it.  After all, when you did the experiment, you didn't see the balloons glowing, did you?  You didn't see light going between the tape and the balloon.  How in the world, then, can I say that the force between electrically-charged objects is governed by the exchange of photons?  The answer to this question lies in a discussion of the nature of light.  I don't want to have that discussion now, however, because I want to stay focused on the phenomena associated with electricity and magnetism.  For now, then, I will just tell you that the vast majority of light in Creation is invisible to you and me.  As a result, it is rare for us to actually see the photons being exchanged by charged particles.  Although it is rare, it nevertheless happens in certain situations.  In fact, all of the light that you actually do see originates in the exchange between two charged particles.

How can I say that?  Well, let's start simple.  When you ignite a candle, you see light coming from it, right?  You see light because a chemical reaction has generated heat.  That heat has moved around some electrons in the atoms of wick, the candle, and the surrounding air. When those electrons move in certain specific ways, they no longer need to exchange as many photons with the positively-charged particles to which they are attracted. Thus, there are "extra" photons left over. Some of those photons just happen to be the photons that your eyes detect as the pleasant, yellow light of the flame. Thus, the light from the flame of a candle is really comprised of photons that were once exchanged by charged particles but are now no longer needed for that task.

The lights that light your home also send out photons that were once exchanged by charged particles. In much the same way as a candle produces light, a standard light bulb produces light by first producing heat. The heat comes from an electrical current which heats up the filament in the light bulb. This causes electrons in the filament and in the gas that is inside the light bulb to move around. When those electrons move in certain ways, they no longer need to exchange as many photons with their positively-charged partners as they used to. As a result, the "extra" photons are ejected, and they hit your eyes as white light.

If you are still having problems believing that photons are exchanged between charged particles, then there is one more thing you need to remember. The idea that the electromagnetic force is governed by the exchange of particles explains the three principles of the electrical force between charged particles. The more charge a particle has, the more photons it can exchange. This tells you why the electrical force between charged particles is directly proportional to the charge of the particle.

The exchange of particles also explains why the electrical force between charged objects is inversely proportional to the square of the distance between the objects. Suppose you wanted to throw a ball at a person but had a blindfold on and therefore could not see that person. If you just randomly threw the ball at the person, your chance of hitting him or her goes down as the distance between you and the person increases. After all, the farther away the person is, the harder it is to hit him or her, even when you *can* see. It turns out that when you randomly throw a ball at a person, the chance of you hitting him or her *is inversely proportional to the square of the distance between you*. Thus, the ability for charged particles to exchange photons also is inversely proportional to the square of the distance between them. As a result, the electrical force is inversely proportional to the square of the distance between them.

In addition to such arguments, physicists can actually use mathematics to essentially prove that charged particles exchange photons. Thus, the idea that the electromagnetic force is governed by the exchange of photons is a rather solid fact in modern physics.

---

### ON YOUR OWN

12.3 A black object is heated until it glows with a nice, orange-yellow glow. If the black object has no net electrical charge, where does the light come from?

## How Objects Become Electrically Charged

In Module #3, I told you that atoms are composed of positively-charged protons, negatively-charged electrons and neutral neutrons. In an atom, there are as many protons (positive charges) as there are electrons (negative charges). As a result, atoms are electrically neutral. When an atom loses electrons, however, it ends up having more positive charges than negative charges and thus has a net positive charge. It is then called a positive ion. When an atom picks up extra electrons, it ends up with more negative charges than positive ones. This gives it an overall negative charge, making it a negative ion.

How do atoms gain or lose electrons? Well, one way is through chemical reactions. Unfortunately, that means of gaining or losing electrons is a bit complex. You will learn about it when you reach chemistry. There are, however, two other ways that atoms can gain or lose electrons. I will cover them here. The best way to start is to do an experiment.

---

### EXPERIMENT 12.2
Making and Using an Electroscope

Supplies:

- A glass
- A plastic lid that fits over the glass  (It can be larger than the mouth of the glass, but it cannot be smaller. The top of a margarine tub or something similar works quite well.)
- A paper clip
- 2 5-cm x 1.5-cm strips of aluminum foil (the thinner the foil the better)
- A balloon
- A pair of pliers

Introduction - In this experiment, you will discover two ways in which objects become charged.

A. Take the paper clip and use your hands and the pliers to twist it into a shape that looks something like this:

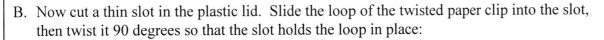

B. Now cut a thin slot in the plastic lid. Slide the loop of the twisted paper clip into the slot, then twist it 90 degrees so that the slot holds the loop in place:

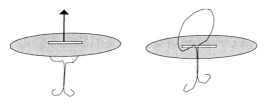

---

C. Next, hang the two strips of foil on the two hooks so that they look like this:

D. Finally, place the lid on top of the glass, so that the foil strips hang on the inside of the glass.

You have just made an **electroscope**. An electroscope can be used to detect as well as store electrical charge. You will use it for these purposes in this experiment.

E. Inflate the balloon and tie it off so that it stays inflated. Next, rub the balloon in your hair to charge it. Now, slowly bring the balloon close to the paper clip without actually touching the paper clip. This is what should happen:

F. The foil strips should move away from each other as the balloon draws nearer. Making sure not to touch the balloon to the paper clip at any time, move the balloon away from the electroscope. The foils should relax again. If you bring the balloon close again, the foils will move away from each other again.

G. Now repeat the experiment, this time actually allowing the balloon to touch the paper clip. When you pull the balloon away, the foils should not relax completely. Instead, they should stay pulled apart from each other, at least a little. Try this a couple of times to see if you can get the foils to stay pulled apart from each other after you remove the balloon. If it is very humid, this won't work well.

H. For the last part of the experiment, touch the paper clip with your finger. This should make the foils fall back to their original position.

I. Next, bring the balloon close to the paper clip, but do not allow it to touch the paper clip. When you see the foils move away from each other, hold the balloon where it is and touch the paper clip with a finger from your other hand. Keep the finger resting on the paper clip. As soon as you touch the paper clip, the foils should relax. Then, *at the same instant*, pull both the balloon and your finger away. The foils should move away from each other again. This doesn't always work the first time, because timing is essential. If it doesn't work the first time, try it a few more times. It should eventually work. Once again, a high humidity will hurt the effectiveness of the experiment.

Now you need to know what happened in the experiment. The foil and the paper clip, like all forms of matter, have both positive and negative charges in them. The number of positive charges and negative charges, however, are equal; thus, the foil and paper clip have no overall charge. The balloon, because it picked up some stray electrons when you rubbed it in your hair, had more negative charges than positive ones, so it had an overall negative charge. When you brought it in close proximity to the paper clip, the negative charge of the balloon repelled the negatively-charged electrons in the paper clip and the foil. Since they were repelled, they traveled away from the balloon, which caused the ends of the foil to be rich with electrons. At the same time, the positive charges in the foils were attracted to the negative charges in the balloon. Thus, they left the foil and traveled towards the balloon. This made the foils poor in positive charges. In the end, then, the foils developed an overall negative charge, and the paper clip developed an overall positive charge, as shown below.

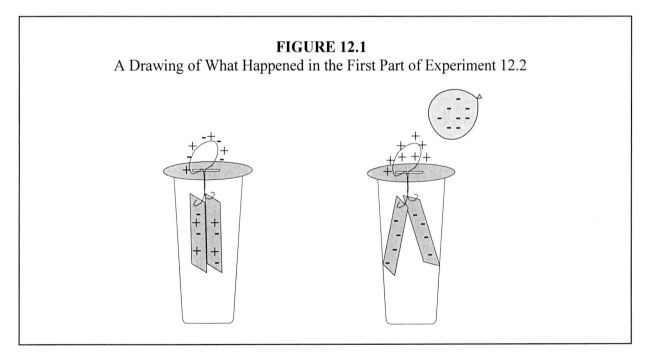

**FIGURE 12.1**
A Drawing of What Happened in the First Part of Experiment 12.2

The excess of negative charges in the foils caused each foil to become negatively charged. This made the foils repel each other, and that's why they pulled apart from each other.

If you did not touch the balloon to the paper clip, as soon as you pulled the balloon away, the foils should have relaxed back to their normal position. That's because once the negatively-charged balloon moved away, the electrons crammed together in the foil were able to travel back to their normal position, and the positive charges crammed together in the paper clip traveled back to their normal positions. This made everything neutral again. When that happened, the foils hung down normally again.

What happened in the next part of the experiment? When you touched the balloon to the foils, the foils moved apart again and, after you removed the balloon, they stayed apart. This is because when you actually touched the balloon to the paper clip, some of the balloon's extra electrons were able to flow into the paper clip and into the foils. This gave the system a bunch of extra electrons. When you pulled the balloon away, those extra electrons stayed. This caused a permanent negative charge to develop on the foils. Since the foils stayed negatively charged, they stayed away from each other. You ended up getting rid of the charge by touching the paper clip with your finger. When you did that, the extra electrons flowed into your body. This got rid of the negative charge on the foils, and the foils relaxed.

When you charge something up by touching an electrically charged object to it and allowing the charge to flow between the electrically charged object and the object that you are charging, physicists say that you are **charging by conduction**.

Charging by conduction - Charging an object by allowing it to come into contact with an object which already has an electrical charge

In other words, by allowing electrons to be conducted between the object you are charging and the object that already has a charge, you are charging by conduction.

Although you might think that this is the only way to charge an object, it is not. In the last part of the experiment, you also ended up charging the foils. In that case, when the balloon was moved near the paper clip, the electrons in the paper clip and foil moved away, concentrating negative charge in the foils, causing the foils to repel each other. When you touched your finger to the paper clip, however, the electrons could travel farther away from the balloon by traveling through your finger and into your body. Thus, you actually removed some of the electrons from the foil and paper clip. When you moved your finger and the balloon away at the same instant, the paper clip and foil were left with fewer electrons than they should have had, because some of those electrons ended up in your hand. This gave the foils and the paper clip an overall positive charge. Since the foils were both positively charged, they repelled each other, and they moved away from each other again, as pictured in Figure 12.2:

**FIGURE 12.2**
Charging By Induction

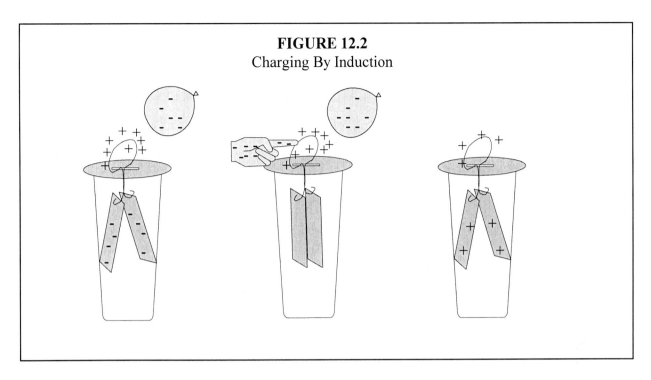

When you performed the experiment in this way, you induced the negative charges to leave the foil by giving them an escape route: your hand. This caused the foils to become positively charged when you took your hand and the balloon away. This, as you might imagine, is called **charging by induction**.

Charging by induction - Charging an object by forcing some of the charges to leave the object

Notice the practical effect of charging by induction. When you charge in this way, the resulting charge is the opposite of the charge you used.

In the experiment, when you charged by conduction, you gave the foils some of the extra charge that was on the balloon. This caused the foils to become negatively charged, which was the same charge as the balloon. When you charged by induction, you forced negative charges out of the foils, causing the foils to become positively charged, which was opposite of the charge on the balloon. Thus, charging by induction gives the object a charge opposite of the charge that you are using. When charging by conduction, the object you are charging gets the same charge as the charge you are using.

**ON YOUR OWN**

12.4 If you want to give an object a positive charge but the only source of charge you have is negative, would you charge the object by conduction or induction?

Electrical Circuits

One of the most useful aspects of the force that exists between charged-particles is that you can use it to make electrical circuits. In an electrical circuit, charges flow through a wire. The energy that those charges have can be used by electrical devices, and the result is something useful. For example, when a light bulb is hooked up to an electrical circuit, the light bulb glows. In order to understand how this works, you need to understand two things: how the charges begin moving in the first place, and how the energy of the moving charges is used by the light bulb. We'll start with the former concept and end with the latter.

In order to get electrical charges moving, you need something that generates the electromagnetic force. One device that does this is a battery. A battery is a device that stores electrical charge. The description of how a battery does this is a bit too difficult to explain here. Suffice it to say that one side of the battery contains chemicals which want to lose electrons while the other side contains chemicals which want to gain electrons. As a result, one side of the battery is a source of electrons, so it is considered negative. The other is the place where the electrons want to go, so it is considered positive. When those two sides are hooked together by a metal, the electrons will flow through the metal from the negative side of the battery to the positive side.

As you no doubt already know, a battery is rated by its voltage. Most cylindrical batteries are rated at 1.5 Volts, while the small, square batteries with electrical posts at the top are typically 9 Volts. What does this voltage mean? It tells you how much of an electromagnetic force the battery uses to push on the electrons. The higher the voltage, the larger the battery's electromagnetic force. The larger the electromagnetic force, the harder the electrons are "pushed" through the metal.

Now remember why we want the electrons to travel from one end of the battery to the other. We want to use their energy. Thus, the more voltage the battery has, the more energy the electrons have, and the more we can do with them. If you think about it, however, the voltage of a battery is not the only factor that determines how much gets done in an electrical circuit. Not only does the energy of each electron influence what gets done in an electrical circuit, but so does the *number* of electrons that travel through the circuit. After all, when ten electrons travel through an electrical circuit, ten times more work will get done than when only one electron travels through the circuit. Thus, not only the voltage of the battery, but also the amount of charged particles flowing through the circuit will determine what the circuit can do.

The number of electrons that flow through a circuit in a given amount of time is called the **electrical current**.

Electrical current - The amount of charge that travels through an electrical circuit each second

Electrical current is usually measured in Amps. When I look at an electrical circuit, then, I need to know both the current (Amps) and the voltage (Volts) of the circuit. They each work together to tell me how much an electrical circuit can do. For example, if you are playing with an electrical toy that works on a 9-Volt transistor radio battery and accidentally touched a bare wire while the toy is running, you might get shocked, but you won't die. That's because both the voltage and the current running through the toy's electrical circuit is low. On the other hand, if you were unfortunate enough to touch the bare wire of a fan that is plugged into a wall socket and running, you would almost certainly die, because the voltage and current running through that circuit are quite high.

It is important to realize that *only one* of these two quantities needs to be large for an electrical circuit to pack a good punch. The voltage in your car's battery is really only 12-15 Volts. That's not much more than the 9 Volt battery that runs an electrical toy. There are several hundred Amps of current that flow through the circuit when the car is running, however. That's about a million times more current than what's flowing through the circuit of an electrical toy! Thus, even though the voltage of a car's electrical circuit is low, the current is high, and the circuit can therefore provide a lot of energy. As a result, touching an exposed battery cable in a car that is running can be *very* dangerous!

That should make perfect sense. After all, the voltage simply tells you the energy that each electron has. Thus, if the energy per electron is really large, just a few electrons can pack a lot of energy. As a result, a circuit with low current but high voltage can be deadly. In the same way, if the voltage is low, the circuit could still have a lot of energy by just having an enormous number of electrons flowing through it. In that case, voltage would be low but current would be high. The combination would still be deadly.

Now that you know about voltage and charge, it is time to learn about electrical circuits. Suppose I take a metal wire and connect it to each side of a battery. The result might look something like this:

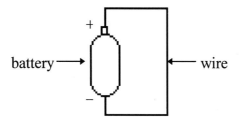

This is a very basic electrical circuit. Electrons will flow through the wire from the negative side of the battery to the positive side. In order to reduce the time it takes to draw circuits, physicists have developed symbols to represent the major components of an electrical circuit. A battery is symbolized with two parallel lines, one longer than the other. The positive side of the battery is usually represented by the longer line. In the end, then, the simple circuit above can be drawn as follows:

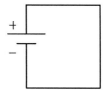

Since the longer line of the battery is supposed to represent the positive side, there is really no need to label the sides of the battery as positive and negative as I have in the drawing above. Thus, in all future circuit drawings, I will not. I just put them in this drawing to emphasize that the longer line represents the positive side of the battery whereas the smaller line represents the negative side.

The first thing you need to be able to do when you look at a circuit like this is determine how the current flows. Unfortunately, Benjamin Franklin caused no end of confusion over this very point. Although he is best remembered for his political endeavors as one of America's founding fathers, Franklin was actually one of the most respected scientists in his time. His theories and experiments regarding electricity were known and admired the world over. Many of his ideas laid the groundwork for our modern theories of electricity.

You see, batteries were invented long before anyone really understood what electricity was. As a result, scientists tried to study batteries and the electricity they produced to better understand what electricity was. In Ben Franklin's studies, he theorized that batteries had a positive and a negative side, and that electricity was comprised of particles which flowed from one side of a battery to the other. These ideas were readily accepted and highly regarded by scientists around the world.

Now, although Franklin's concept of positive and negative sides of a battery helped revolutionize the way scientists studied electricity, it has also caused a bit of confusion. You see, Franklin thought that the positive side of a battery had too many of these mysterious particles and the negative side had too few. Thus, he said that electricity must flow from the positive side of the battery to the negative side. Since his ideas were highly regarded, this idea was accepted the world over. Scientists from everywhere began drawing electrical circuits assuming that the electricity flowed from the positive side of the battery to the negative side.

As is usually the case with technological inventions, people began finding uses for electricity long before science figured out what electricity really was. Thus, engineers began designing electrical circuits, and they, too, drew the circuits assuming that electricity flowed from the positive side of the battery to the negative side. As time went on, however, science slowly showed the error of this assumption. The electron was discovered, and it was determined that electricity is actually the flow of these electrons. Thus, in reality, electricity flows from the negative side of the battery (where there are too many electrons) to the positive side of the battery (where there are too few electrons).

This conclusion, however, contradicted thousands of circuit drawings that had been made over the years. Engineers had always drawn current as flowing from the positive side of the battery to the negative side. They didn't want to stop doing it just because science had shown that the reverse was true. As a result, people just kept on drawing electrical current as starting from the positive side of the battery and flowing to the negative side, even though they knew it was wrong. This came to be known as **conventional current**, and it is still the way circuits are drawn today.

<u>Conventional current</u> - Current that flows from the positive side of the battery to the negative side.  This is the way current is drawn in circuit diagrams, even though it is wrong.

     The point to this long, drawn out discussion is that Ben Franklin's inaccurate assumption regarding how current flows forces us, when we draw electrical circuits, to draw current as flowing from the positive side of the battery to the negative side.  Even though we know that this is not what happens physically, we do it so as not to break with tradition.  Thus, in our original circuit diagram, the current can be pictured as follows:

In this diagram, the dotted line shows the path of the current in the wire.  Of course, even though the dashed line is not drawn right on top of the lines representing the wire, it is still understood that the current is actually flowing in the wire, not where the dashed line is drawn.

---

**ON YOUR OWN**

12.5  For the following circuit diagram, draw the current flow with a dashed line.  Then draw the actual flow of electrons with a solid line.

---

<u>Resistance</u>

     Now that we know how to get electrons flowing through an electrical circuit, the next logical step is to figure out how we can use the energy in those electrons to do something useful.  The best way to start is with a simple experiment.

**EXPERIMENT 12.3**
Current and Resistance

Supplies:

- A 1.5 Volt battery (Any AA, A, C, or D-cell battery will work. Do not use any battery other than one of those, though, because a **higher voltage will make the experiment dangerous**.)
- Aluminum foil

Introduction - In order to get something useful out of an electrical circuit, we must use the energy of the electrons flowing through the circuit. In this experiment, you will learn one way this is accomplished.

Procedure:

A. Make a small strip of aluminum foil that is about 1.3 times the length of the battery and only about 1 cm wide.
B. Lay the foil across the battery and, using your thumb an forefinger, pinch the foil so that it makes contact with both ends of the battery (see drawing below).

C. Hold the foil there for a few moments. Do you feel anything? Hold the foil for a while until you do.

The heat you felt comes from the electrons moving in the foil. As soon as you touched the aluminum to both ends of the battery, electrons flowed through the aluminum from the negative side of the battery to the positive side. The electrons accelerated under the electromagnetic force of the battery and, as a result, started moving quickly. As the electrons sped down the foil, they inevitably bumped into the atoms that make up the foil. These collisions caused heat, which you felt in your hands. Please realize that you could touch the aluminum foil because I knew that both the voltage *and* the current would be too low to cause you harm. **DO NOT DO THIS IN ANY OTHER SITUATION!!!!!!!** Since you do not know enough about electricity, you will not know what is safe and what is not. Playing with electricity is deadly. Don't do *anything* around electricity unless someone experienced tells you to!!!!

In electricity, we say that the collisions which made the heat you felt in the experiment *resist* the flow of electrons. Each metal resists electron flow differently, so we say that each metal has its own **resistance**.

<u>Resistance</u> - A measure of how much a metal impedes the flow of electrons

It turns out that the type of metal is not the only thing that determines resistance. The resistance of a wide piece of metal, for example, is lower than the resistance of a thin piece of the same metal. This is because the wider piece of metal allows electrons to spread apart from each other, reducing the concentration of electrons, and therefore reducing the probability of collisions between the electrons and the atoms in the metal. Also, as you might expect, the longer the metal, the larger the resistance, because the further electrons must travel, the more likely collisions between electrons and atoms in the metal become.

With the knowledge of current, electrical circuits, and resistance you have under your belt, you can finally begin to understand how the simplest electrical devices work. For example, consider an electrical heater. This could be a space heater used to warm up a room, a coil on an electrical stove, or even the wires on the inside of a toaster. When such a device is turned on, the heater begins to glow, emitting a large amount of heat. This works because the material used to make the heater has a certain amount of electrical resistance. Since there is resistance, the electrons that travel through the material experience collisions. These collisions make heat and light. The light causes the heater to glow, and the heat energy warms the room, cooks the food, or browns the bread.

One way we get electrons to do something useful in an electrical circuit, then, is to use a metal's resistance to convert the energy of the electrons speeding through the circuit into heat and light. The type of metal used to do this will influence the effect that you get. For example, most metals will resist the flow of electrons in such a way as to produce mostly heat and only a small amount of light. Those metals are used in heaters, stoves, and toasters. Other metals tend to produce more light than heat. Those metals are typically used in light bulbs.

It is important that you really see what's going on in an electrical circuit. Most people think that electrical devices "use up" electrons. Thus, you plug your appliance in, and it "eats up" the electricity that it pulls from the electrical socket. That's not what happens. The same number of electrons flow out of a toaster as the number which flowed into it. What the toaster does use up, however, is energy. The electrons lose energy in their collisions with the atoms of the metal, and that energy is then turned into heat and light.

---

**ON YOUR OWN**

12.6 A physicist measures the speed of electrons running through an electrical circuit. If the physicist measures the electrons right before they go into a toaster and right after they leave the toaster, will the measurements be different? If so, which will be the lower measurement?

## Switches and Circuits

With the tools you have learned so far, you can look at a simple circuit and determine in which direction the current flows. So let me ask you a question. In what direction does the current flow in this circuit?

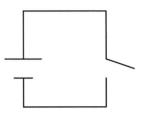

The answer is, no current flows in this circuit. Why? Remember, in order to have electricity, electrons must travel from one place to another. In the case of a circuit, they flow from one end of the battery to the other. The reason that they do this is because there is metal linking the two sides of the battery together. In the circuit drawn above, however, the metal does not link the two sides of the battery because there is a break in the wire. Thus, there is no current. Physicists call circuits such as the one drawn above **open circuits**.

Open circuit - A circuit that does not have a complete connection between the two sides of the battery. As a result, current does not flow.

Suppose I took the diagonally-pointing piece of wire and pushed it down so that its end touched the end of the other wire. Then what would happen? As soon as the two ends touched, there would be a completed connection between one end of the battery and the other. Thus, electrons would start to flow, and there would be current.

This is the way a switch works. When the switch is open, no current can flow and the device you are using does not work. When you flip the switch, however, a connection is made and electrons begin to flow, allowing the device you are powering to operate. This is illustrated in Figure 15.1, where a light is off and then turned on by a switch.

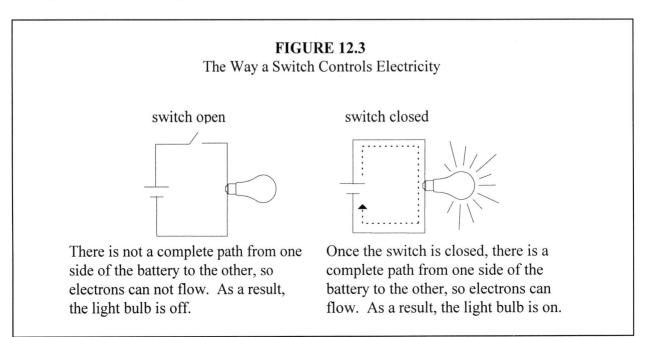

**FIGURE 12.3**
The Way a Switch Controls Electricity

switch open

switch closed

There is not a complete path from one side of the battery to the other, so electrons can not flow. As a result, the light bulb is off.

Once the switch is closed, there is a complete path from one side of the battery to the other, so electrons can flow. As a result, the light bulb is on.

You should now see that when you flip a light switch, you are changing the circuit which powers the light. If the light is off, the circuit is open. By flipping the switch, you are actually connecting the two sides of the power source together and electrons can therefore flow. That turns on the light. If you flip the switch again, you are breaking that connection, and the electron flow stops, turning the light off. That's how a switch works.

Series and Parallel Circuits

The idea that a break in an electrical circuit can stop the electron flow and thus stop the electrical device or devices in the circuit from working is, most of the time, quite useful. However, sometimes it's a real problem. Consider, for example the following circuit:

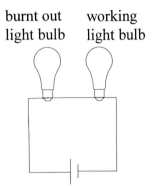

burnt out          working
light bulb        light bulb

In this circuit, *neither* of the light bulbs will light. Why? Well, a light bulb lights up because electrons flow through the filament of the bulb. The filament has a certain amount of resistance, which heats up the filament so much that it glows with a bright light. Now, the reason a light bulb burns out is that, eventually, the filament breaks due to wear and tear. When the filament breaks, the electrical connection from one side of the light bulb to the other is broken. Since the light bulb is a part of the circuit, this breaks the electrical connection of the entire circuit. Thus, a burnt-out light bulb is the same as an open switch! So, even though the second light bulb is okay, it will not light because electrons cannot flow through it.

When lights (or any electrical devices) are hooked up in this way, we say that they are hooked up in "series." All devices on such a circuit, called a **series circuit**, will cease to function when any one of the devices ceases to function. This, of course, is an undesirable situation. Luckily, such a situation can be avoided. For example, consider this circuit:

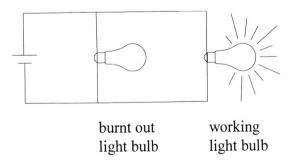

burnt out                working
light bulb              light bulb

In this case, the working light bulb still lights. Why? Well, look at the situation. Since the burnt out light bulb is like an open switch, current cannot flow through it. But, as you look at the drawing, you can see that electrons can still flow from one side of the battery to the other. They do not have to go through the burnt out light bulb. They can take the longer route, through the working light bulb, to get to the other end of the battery, as shown below:

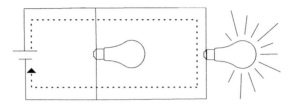

This allows the working light bulb to light up, even though the other light bulb is burnt out. When devices are hooked up in this manner, we say that they are hooked up in "parallel." A **parallel circuit**, then, allows the devices to work independently of each other. If one stops working, the others can still work, because current can still flow through them.

---

**ON YOUR OWN**

12.7 When strings of Christmas tree lights were first produced, they were hard to use year after year, because once a single light bulb on the string burned out, none of the lights would light up. Nowadays, if one light bulb on a string of lights burns out, the others stay lit. What is the difference between the way strings of Christmas tree lights used to be made and the way they are made now?

---

Magnetism

This module is supposed to be about the electromagnetic force, but I have spent the majority of it discussing electrical charge and electricity. What about magnetism? Well, as James Clerk Maxwell demonstrated, the force that is involved in magnetism is really the same as the force involved in electricity. Thus, a study of one is, in fact a study of the other. Nevertheless, I need to discuss a few basics about magnets before you finish this module. First, I want you to remember an experiment you did a while ago.

In Module #6, I discussed the earth's magnetic field. In order to demonstrate what caused earth's magnetic field, I had you wind a strip of aluminum around a nail and then run electricity through it. In the end, it made a magnet. The experiment demonstrated that the flow of charged particles (electrons, in this case) can create a magnetic force. Well, it turns out that *all magnetic force results from the flow of charged particles*! That might come as a bit of a surprise to you. After all, you know that there are such things as permanent magnets. These magnets have no electricity hooked up to them, but nevertheless, they are magnetic. How is their magnetic force generated by the flow of charged particles?

You first have to remember that all matter is composed of charged particles. All atoms contain positively-charged protons and negatively-charge electrons. As you will learn in the next module, the electrons in an atom are in constant motion. Thus, there is a continuous flow of electrons in all matter. Why isn't all matter magnetic, then? In your experiment, you created a magnetic force when electrons all flowed in one general direction. In order for a material to be magnetic, then, its atoms have to line up in a certain way so that the electrons in the material all have the same general motion. The atoms of most materials are not aligned in this way, so the electrons in the material have random motion. However, certain materials under certain conditions can have their atoms arranged so that the electrons have the same general motion. When that happens, the result is a magnet.

Your refrigerator magnets, then, are simply made of a material whose atoms are arranged in a particular way. The motion of the electrons within those atoms mimics the flow of electrons in an electrical circuit. Thus, magnetism is, in fact, a result of electrical flow. That's what Maxwell's equations proved and experiments such as Experiment 6.2 demonstrate.

Under what conditions can a material align its atoms in order to make a magnet? Some materials simply cannot. The nature of their atoms makes such alignment impossible. Other materials, such as iron, however, can be made into a magnet at any time. If you re-do Experiment 6.2, but this time allow the electricity to flow for a long, long, time, the nail will continue to be a magnet even after the electricity is turned off. You see, the magnetic field of the electrical current actually causes iron atoms to slowly align. If exposed to a strong enough magnetic field for long enough, iron will actually become a permanent magnet.

In the same way, most materials will not even respond to a magnet. For example, you can't stick your refrigerator magnets to one of the walls in your house, can you? Of course not. The reason is that the atoms which make up the material in your house's walls are simply impossible to align. Thus, they can never simulate the concerted flow of electrons. As a result, they cannot participate in a magnetic interaction.

### Permanent Magnets

Since you have some familiarity with permanent magnets, I want to spend a little time on them. If you've played with them at all, you'll recognize that there are two sides to a magnet. In physics, we call them the **north pole** and **south pole** of a magnet. In many ways, the poles in a magnet are much like charges. For example, if you point the north pole of a magnet toward the south pole of another magnet, the two poles will attract each other. If, however, you point the north pole of a magnet to the north pole of another one, they will repel each other. Thus, as I'm sure you're already aware, opposite poles attract one another and like poles repel one another, just like charges.

**Like magnetic poles repel one another, while opposite magnetic poles attract one another.**

You can never find just one pole of a magnet hanging around.  Whenever you have a magnet, you will always have a north pole and a south pole.  Thus, magnets are called "**dipoles**" because magnetic poles always come in pairs: one north and one south.  Now I say this as a fact, but we are not 100% sure that it is a fact.  There are scientists out there looking for a magnetic pole isolated by itself.  Scientists call this the search for a magnetic **monopole**.  If such a thing were ever found, it would radically alter our understanding of magnetism, so that's why some scientists look for it.  I am doubtful, however, that they will ever find one.

So, as far as we know, magnets always come with two poles.  The image I will use to represent a magnet, then, is a long bar.  The bar will be split down the middle.  One half will be called the "south pole" of the magnet and the other will be the "north pole."

Although magnets come in all shapes and sizes, this will be my representation of a magnet.  In physics terms, we usually call this a "bar magnet."

You might think to yourself, "What if I take a magnet and split it right down the middle?  Wouldn't I have the north pole of the magnet in one hand and the south pole in the other?  Couldn't I then take those poles and separate them far away from each other, thereby making two magnetic monopoles?  Well, that's a good idea, but it just doesn't work.  Look at Figure 12.4 to see why.

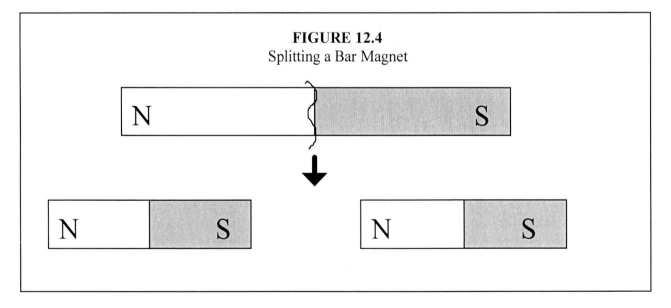

**FIGURE 12.4**
Splitting a Bar Magnet

As soon as you split a bar magnet, half of the north pole will turn into a south pole and half of the south pole will turn into a north pole.  Why does this happen?  Remember that permanent magnets exist because their atoms are aligned in a certain way.  When the material is cut and the pieces are pulled away from each other, the interactions between the atoms are altered.  As a result, the alignment is altered as well.  The alignment is altered so as to turn part of the north pole into a south pole and part of the south pole into a north pole.  The result, then, is two smaller magnets, each of which has a north and a south pole.

Let's concentrate on one individual pole for a moment.  Remember, the magnetic nature of the pole is caused by the alignment of the atoms in the material.  It turns out that not all of the atoms in a material need to line up in order to make a magnet.  In fact, only a small fraction of the atoms in a material need to line up to get some magnetic effect.  As more atoms line up, you have more electrons simulating the flow of electricity, and the result is a stronger magnet.  Thus, the strength of a magnet depends on what percentage of the atoms in the material are aligned.  The larger the percentage, the stronger the pole of a magnet.

Do you want to guess how the magnetic force between poles varies with the strength of the poles?  Not surprisingly, the magnetic force is directly proportional to the strength of each pole involved.  Also not surprisingly, the strength of the magnetic force is inversely proportional to the square of the distance between the poles.  This is expected, of course, because electricity and magnetism are really just different aspects of the same force.  Thus, the force between the poles of a magnet behaves the same as the force between charges.

The force between the poles of a magnet is sometimes illustrated with **magnetic field lines**.  These are shown in Figure 12.5.

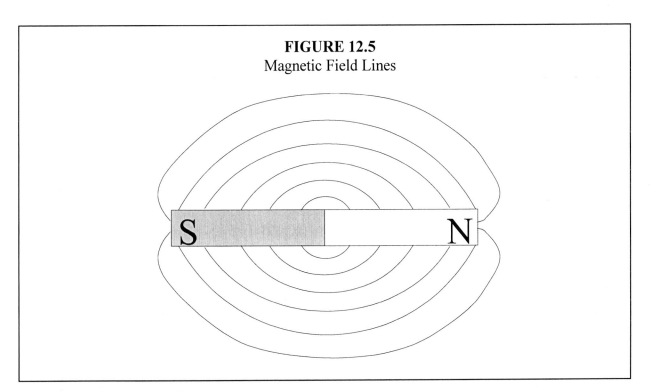

**FIGURE 12.5**
Magnetic Field Lines

These lines indicate the direction that the magnetic force pushes at any point near the magnet.  If you take a magnet and cover it with paper and then sprinkle iron filings on the paper, they will line up right along the lines drawn in the figure, because that's how the magnetic force pushes magnetic materials. Their significance is important, but the details are too complex to discuss here. If you take physics in high school, you will learn all about magnetic field lines then.

---

## ON YOUR OWN

12.8 Suppose you have two wires lying side-by-side. In one wire, the current flows one way, and in the other wire, the current flows the opposite way. Could you wrap those wires around a nail and make a magnet?

12.9 A scientist studies the relative strength of two magnets. The first one has 12% of its atoms aligned. The scientist places the north pole of that magnet a certain distance from the south pole of a standard magnet and then measures the attractive force. He then takes the north pole of the second magnet he is studying and places it the same distance away from the south pole of the same standard magnet. The attractive force is 4 times as strong as the first one he measured. What percentage of the second magnet's atoms are aligned?

12.10 Just like magnetic field lines, scientists also use electrical field lines to illustrate the force that exists between electrical charges. From what you learned about magnets, draw the electrical field lines for the following situation:

positive charge                     negative charge

---

# ANSWERS TO THE ON YOUR OWN PROBLEMS

12.1  Like charges repel one another.  Thus, in part (a), each object will exert a force pushing the other object directly away.  Opposite charges attract one another.  Thus, in part (b), each object will exert a force pulling the other directly towards itself.

12.2  The electromagnetic force is directly proportional to the charge of each object.  Thus, when one object's charge is halved, the electromagnetic force is halved.  When the charge of the other object is dropped by a factor of four, the electromagnetic force is reduced by an additional factor of four.  The electromagnetic force is inversely proportional to the square of the distance between the charges.  Thus, when the distance is decreased by a factor of four, the force increases by a factor of four squared, or 16.  The total change, then, is $\frac{1}{2} \times \frac{1}{4} \times 16 = 2$.  This means that the new force is <u>twice as strong as the old force</u>.

12.3  Light comes from the interaction of charged particles.  Even though the black object has no *net* electrical charge, it is still comprised of protons and electrons, which are each charged.  Thus, <u>the light comes from the interactions between protons and electrons in the object</u>.

12.4  <u>You would charge by induction</u>.  Induction always gives you the charge opposite to that which you are using.

12.5  We draw current flow from the positive to the negative, even though that is incorrect.  The positive side of the battery is the longer edge of the battery.  Thus, conventional current flows from the positive side to the negative side.  Since electrons are negative, however, the actual flow is from negative to positive:

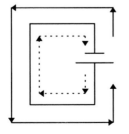

12.6  The toaster uses the energy of the electrons.  Thus, they have less energy after they leave the toaster.  This reduces their speed.  <u>The speed will be lower for the electrons that leave the toaster</u>.

12.7 Since modern Christmas tree lights can continue to work even after a few bulbs are burnt out, <u>modern Christmas tree lights are wired in parallel</u>. Since the old ones would cease to work when one burnt out, <u>the old Christmas tree lights were wired in series</u>.

12.8 <u>You could not make a magnet that way</u>. Think about it. The one wire will certainly cause a magnetic field, as will the other. However, since the currents are opposite of each other, the magnetic forces generated will be opposite as well. Thus, they will cancel each other out, resulting in no net magnetic force.

12.9 The magnetic force is directly proportional to how many atoms are aligned. If the force is 4 times greater, then there are four times as many atoms aligned. Thus, <u>the second magnet has 48% of its atoms aligned</u>.

12.10 Remember, the electrical and magnetic forces are really different aspects of the same force. Thus, their properties are the same. Notice that the only real difference between this picture and Figure 12.5 is that we have a positive and negative charge instead of a north and south pole. Since the forces are really the same, however, the resulting field lines should be the same.

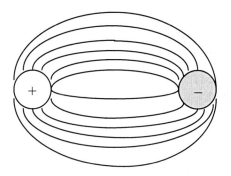

**STUDY GUIDE FOR MODULE #12**

1. Define the following terms:

a. Photons
b. Charging by conduction
c. Charging by induction
d. Electrical current
e. Conventional current
f. Resistance
g. Open circuit

2. For the following situations, draw the force exerted by the solid object with a solid arrow. Draw the force exerted by the dashed object with a dashed arrow:

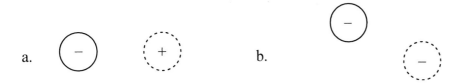

a.                                    b.

3. The force between the south pole of a magnet and the north pole of another magnet is measured. If the distance between the poles is increased by a factor of 3, how does the new force compare to the old one? Is the force attractive or repulsive?

4. Two charged particles are placed 10 centimeters from each other and the resulting force is measured. The charge on object #1 is then doubled and the charge on object #2 is left the same. The distance between the objects is also reduced to 5 centimeters. How does the new force compare to the old force?

5. What causes the electromagnetic force?

6. Given your answer to question #5, why don't charged particles glow?

7. If you were to use a positively-charged rod to charge an object by induction, what charge will the object get?

8. If you were to use a positively-charged rod to charge an object by conduction, what charge will the object get?

9. An electrical circuit uses a large voltage but a small current. Is the energy of each electron high or low? Are there many electrons flowing through the circuit, or are there few? Is the circuit dangerous?

10. Under what conditions is an electrical circuit reasonably safe?

11. Draw the conventional current flow in the following circuit.

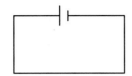

12. What is wrong with conventional current?

13. You have two wires. One is long and the other is short. Which has more resistance?

14. You have two wires. One is thin, and the other is very thick. When the same current is run through each wire, which will get hotter?

15. In which circuit will the light bulb glow?

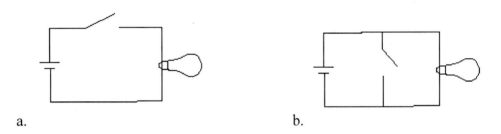

a.                                          b.

16. Three lights are in a room. When one burns out, they all go out. When the burnt-out one is replaced with a good light, the other two lights work again. Are the lights wired in a parallel circuit or a series circuit?

17. If it takes a flow of charged particles to make a magnet, where is the charged particle flow in a permanent magnet?

18. Is it possible to have a permanent magnet with only a north pole?

19. Is it possible to make a magnet from something that is not a magnet?

20. If a material does not respond to a magnet, what can you conclude about the atoms in that material?

## MODULE #13: The Forces in Creation - Part 3

### Introduction

In the two previous modules, you learned about the gravitational force and the electromagnetic force. Now it's time to learn about the two "other" forces in Creation, the weak force and the strong nuclear force. I put "other" in quotes to emphasize that although we often think about the weak force as a separate force, scientists now know that the weak force is simply another manifestation of the electromagnetic force. Thus, many scientists call the electromagnetic force and the weak force together the "electroweak force." The processes governed by the weak force are so different than those governed by the electromagnetic force, however, that it is better for us to think of the weak force as an entirely different force.

You will notice that there are not any experiments in this module. Although this is unfortunate, it cannot be avoided. In this module, I will be discussing atoms and portions of atoms. As a result, everything I want to cover in this module is too small to see, even with the most powerful microscope. Thus, you can only do experiments concerning the concepts in this module if you have some very sophisticated equipment! Despite the lack of experiments, there are many interesting things in this module, so please read it carefully and try to understand it.

### The Structure of the Atom

In Module #1 I talked a bit about atoms. I want to extend that discussion now, adding a little more detail about what an atom looks like. Now remember, we can't really see atoms. However, we can do experiments on them and see how they react. Based on the results of those experiments, we can develop theories about what an atom looks like. As long as the theories are in agreement with the experimental data, then the theories can be assumed to be accurate. Thus, what we know about the structure of an atom comes from indirect observation, not direct observation. Nevertheless, the theories we have developed are consistent with so much of the data related to atoms, we assume that the theories are pretty accurate.

The first thing that these theories tell us is that the atom is made up of three smaller particles: **protons**, **neutrons**, and **electrons**. These three particles all have different properties. First of all, the electron is a tiny particle. It has a mass of approximately 0.00000000000000000000000000091 grams. Now that's small! (Remember, the mass of a fly is about 1 gram.) It also has a negative electrical charge. In fact, the motion of electrons through a wire is what we call "electricity." When you flip a light switch to turn on a light, for example, electrons travel through the wire to the light. The energy that the electrons have in their motion is converted to light energy and, as a result, the light glows.

Protons are thousands of times larger than electrons. The mass of a proton, for example, is approximately 0.0000000000000000000000017 grams. That's *a lot* heavier than an electron, but it's still pretty small! Like electrons, protons have electrical charge as well. Unlike electrons, however, the electrical charge of protons is positive. Since we know that opposite charges attract one another, we can conclude that protons and electrons are attracted to one another. This will become important in a moment.

The last particle, the neutron, is slightly (0.2 %) heavier than the proton. There are two other important differences between the proton and the neutron. First, the neutron has no electrical charge. It is considered electrically neutral, which is where it got the name "neutron." The other interesting difference between the proton and the neutron is that, by itself, the neutron is not a stable particle. A neutron that is not a part of an atom will eventually "fall apart" into a proton, an electron, and a smaller particle called a "neutrino." Once a neutron becomes part of an atom, however, it will stay a neutron for as long as it stays in the atom.

These three particles have a very specific arrangement in the atom. The Bohr model of the atom tells us that they are arranged as illustrated in Figure 13.1.

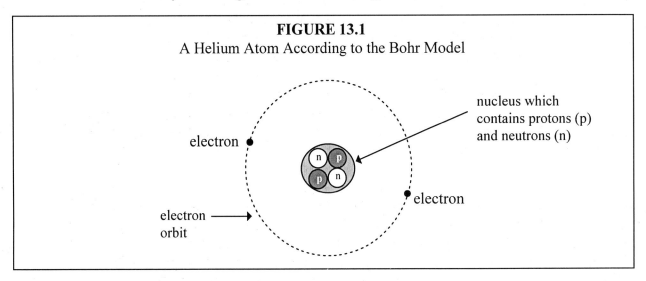

**FIGURE 13.1**

A Helium Atom According to the Bohr Model

In the Bohr model, the neutrons and protons are packed together tightly in the center of the atom, which is called the **nucleus**.

Nucleus - The center of an atom, containing the protons and neutrons

The term "nucleus" is used in many ways. In biology, the nucleus of a cell is the part of the cell that contains the DNA. Thus, although I have defined nucleus here as the center of the atom, please realize that you will see that term again used in other ways.

The electrons are not in the nucleus. Instead, they orbit around the nucleus in circles, much like the planets orbit around the sun. Why do the electrons orbit around the nucleus? They are attracted to the positive charge of the protons in the nucleus. Therefore, the electrical attraction between the protons and the electrons provides the centripetal force necessary to allow for circular motion. Thus, just like the gravitational attraction between the planets and the sun allows the planets to orbit the sun in circle, the electrical attraction between the electrons and protons allows the electrons to travel around the nucleus in a circle.

Since we are talking about a nitrogen atom here, we know it has 7 protons because all isotopes of nitrogen have 7 protons. Since all atoms have the same number of electrons and protons, <u>this atom has 7 electrons</u>. With 7 protons and 8 neutrons in the nucleus, the mass number is 15 (7 + 8), so we call this atom <u>nitrogen-15</u>.

**Which of the following atoms is an isotope of nitrogen-15?  What is its name?**

**a. an atom with 5 protons, 5 electrons, and 10 neutrons**
**b. an atom with 8 protons, 8 electrons, and 7 neutrons**
**c. an atom with 8 protons, 8 electrons, and 8 neutrons**
**d. an atom with 7 protons, 7 electrons, and 7 neutrons**

Two atoms are isotopes if they have the same number of protons but different numbers of neutrons. As we determined earlier, there are 7 protons, 7 electrons, and 8 neutrons in nitrogen-15. Thus, any isotope of nitrogen-15 will also have to have 7 protons. It must have something other than 8 neutrons as well. Thus, <u>the atom in choice (d) is an isotope of nitrogen-15. Its name is nitrogen-14</u>, because its mass number is 7+7=14.

---

**ON YOUR OWN**

13.1  The element sodium is made up of all atoms with 11 protons. How many protons, electrons, and neutrons are in a sodium-23 atom?

13.2  All atoms with 8 protons are oxygen atoms. If a particular oxygen atom has 8 neutrons, what is its name and how many electrons does it have?

13.3  Of the following atoms, two are isotopes. Which ones are they?

a. An atom with 16 protons, 16 electrons, and 17 neutrons
b. An atom with 17 protons, 17 electrons, and 16 neutrons
c. An atom with 16 protons, 16 electrons, and 18 neutrons
d. An atom with 18 protons, 18 electrons, and 17 neutrons

---

The Periodic Chart of the Elements

Since the number of electrons in an atom is responsible for determining the vast majority of an atom's properties, and since the number of electrons is the same as the number of protons, it is convenient to think about the atoms in Creation in terms of what elements they belong to. Remember, an element is a collection of atoms that all have the same number of protons. This means that atoms which belong to the same element have essentially the same properties. As a result, it makes sense to group atoms together in terms of how many protons they have. Chemists have created a very organized way to do this. It is called the **Periodic Chart of the Elements**.

# PERIODIC CHART OF THE ELEMENTS

| 1A | 2A | 3B | 4B | 5B | 6B | 7B | 8B | 8B | 8B | 1B | 2B | 3A | 4A | 5A | 6A | 7A | 8A |
|---|---|---|---|---|---|---|---|---|---|---|---|---|---|---|---|---|---|
| 1 **H** 1.01 | | | | | | | | | | | | | | | | | 2 **He** 4.0 |
| 3 **Li** 6.94 | 4 **Be** 9.01 | | | | | | | | | | | 5 **B** 10.8 | 6 **C** 12.0 | 7 **N** 14.0 | 8 **O** 16.0 | 9 **F** 19.0 | 10 **Ne** 20.2 |
| 11 **Na** 23.0 | 12 **Mg** 24.3 | | | | | | | | | | | 13 **Al** 27.0 | 14 **Si** 28.1 | 15 **P** 31.0 | 16 **S** 32.1 | 17 **Cl** 35.5 | 18 **Ar** 39.9 |
| 19 **K** 39.1 | 20 **Ca** 40.1 | 21 **Sc** 45.0 | 22 **Ti** 47.9 | 23 **V** 50.9 | 24 **Cr** 52.0 | 25 **Mn** 54.9 | 26 **Fe** 55.8 | 27 **Co** 58.9 | 28 **Ni** 58.7 | 29 **Cu** 63.5 | 30 **Zn** 65.4 | 31 **Ga** 69.7 | 32 **Ge** 72.6 | 33 **As** 74.9 | 34 **Se** 79.0 | 35 **Br** 79.9 | 36 **Kr** 83.8 |
| 37 **Rb** 85.5 | 38 **Sr** 87.6 | 39 **Y** 88.9 | 40 **Zr** 91.2 | 41 **Nb** 92.9 | 42 **Mo** 95.9 | 43 **Tc** (98) | 44 **Ru** 101.1 | 45 **Rh** 102.9 | 46 **Pd** 106.4 | 47 **Ag** 107.9 | 48 **Cd** 112.4 | 49 **In** 114.8 | 50 **Sn** 118.7 | 51 **Sb** 121.8 | 52 **Te** 127.6 | 53 **I** 126.9 | 54 **Xe** 131.3 |
| 55 **Cs** 132.9 | 56 **Ba** 137.3 | 57 **La** 138.9 | 72 **Hf** 178.5 | 73 **Ta** 180.9 | 74 **W** 183.9 | 75 **Re** 186.2 | 76 **Os** 190.2 | 77 **Ir** 192.2 | 78 **Pt** 195.1 | 79 **Au** 197.0 | 80 **Hg** 200.6 | 81 **Tl** 204.4 | 82 **Pb** 207.2 | 83 **Bi** 209.0 | 84 **Po** (209) | 85 **At** (210) | 86 **Rn** (222) |
| 87 **Fr** (223) | 88 **Ra** 226.0 | 89 **Ac** (227) | 104 (261) | 105 (262) | 106 (266) | 107 (264) | 108 (269) | 109 (268) | | | | | | | | | |

| 58 **Ce** 140.1 | 59 **Pr** 140.9 | 60 **Nd** 144.2 | 61 **Pm** (145) | 62 **Sm** 150.4 | 63 **Eu** 152.0 | 64 **Gd** 157.3 | 65 **Tb** 158.9 | 66 **Dy** 162.5 | 67 **Ho** 164.9 | 68 **Er** 167.3 | 69 **Tm** 168.9 | 70 **Yb** 173.0 | 71 **Lu** 175.0 |
|---|---|---|---|---|---|---|---|---|---|---|---|---|---|
| 90 **Th** 232.0 | 91 **Pa** 231.0 | 92 **U** 238.0 | 93 **Np** (237) | 94 **Pu** (244) | 95 **Am** (243) | 96 **Cm** (247) | 97 **Bk** (247) | 98 **Cf** (251) | 99 **Es** (252) | 100 **Fm** (257) | 101 **Md** (258) | 102 **No** (259) | 103 **Lr** (262) |

Each box in the periodic chart (which I often just call "the chart") represents an element. The first box, for example, represents the simplest element in Creation, hydrogen. Like helium, hydrogen is a gas that is lighter than air. Unlike helium, however, hydrogen is explosive when exposed to oxygen and a spark or flame. If you look at the box, you will see that it has an "H" in it. This is the chemical symbol for hydrogen. The number above the "H" is the atomic number of hydrogen. Remember, the atomic number tells you how many protons an atom has. This tells us, then, that the element hydrogen is comprised of all atoms which have 1 proton in their nuclei.

It turns out that there are three isotopes of hydrogen. Hydrogen-1 has one proton, one electron, and no neutrons. This is considered the simplest atom in Creation. Hydrogen-2 (sometimes called "deuterium") has one proton, one electron, and one neutron. Hydrogen-3 (sometimes called "tritium") is also an isotope of hydrogen. All of these atoms have 1 proton, but they have different numbers of neutrons. Thus, we say that hydrogen has 3 isotopes: hydrogen-1, hydrogen-2, and hydrogen-3. Chemists tend to abbreviate things whenever possible. As a result, you can also refer to these isotopes as $^1$H, $^2$H, and $^3$H. In this abbreviation scheme, we use the chemical symbol to tell us what element the atom belongs to, and then we put the mass number as a superscript before the symbol.

If you look to the far right of the chart, you will see that the next box is labeled with "He" and has an atomic number of 2. This is the box that represents helium. As you already know, helium has two protons, and that's why its atomic number is 2. As you look at other boxes on the chart, you will see that they all contain either one-letter or two-letter chemical symbols. Additionally, if there is only one letter in the chemical symbol, it is capitalized. If there are two letters in the symbol, the first is capitalized but the second is not.

In general, the chemical symbol for an element consists of the first one or two letters of the atom's name. Sulfur (atomic number 16), for example, is given the chemical symbol "S," while neon (atomic number 10) is represented by the symbol "Ne." That's not too bad. Although an element is usually given a chemical symbol that consists of the first one or two letters in its name, we do not always use the *English* name of the element. For example, iron (atomic number 26) is given the chemical symbol "Fe." Why? Well, the Latin name for iron is *ferrum*. Likewise, the element potassium (atomic number 19) is given the chemical symbol "K" from its Latin name *kalium*. Thus, the chemical symbol for an element is the first one or two letters from the English or Latin name of the element.

What about the number that appears underneath the chemical symbol for each element? That's the mass of the element. The units of this mass measurement are called "atomic mass units" or "amu," and they represent a very tiny amount of mass. You will learn more about that when you take chemistry. One thing you must understand about this mass is that is an *average mass*. Remember, each element is actually a collection of atoms, each of which is an isotope of that element. The element carbon (chemical symbol "C"), for example, is really a collection of $^{12}$C, $^{13}$C, and $^{14}$C atoms. Each of these atoms have different masses, because they each have different numbers of neutrons in their nucleus. Thus, the mass listed for carbon (12.0 amu) in the chart is actually an average of the masses of $^{12}$C, $^{13}$C, and $^{14}$C. Once again, you will learn more about this when you take chemistry.

Looking at the chart as a whole for a moment, you will notice that the boxes are arranged in a very strange fashion. The boxes are not put in a square or rectangular grid. Instead, they are put in columns and rows that have different sizes. Some columns are taller than others, and some rows are shorter than others. In addition, there are two rows of boxes at the bottom of the chart that seem to have been pulled out of the middle. Why such a strange arrangement? Well, it turns out that this arrangement actually allows a chemist to look at the chart and quickly discern many of the properties of each element, just by finding where that element's box appears in the chart. Unfortunately, you need to study the chart in a lot more detail before you can do that! When you take chemistry, you will learn much more about what the chart actually tells us.

Even though you do not know a lot about the chart, you can already use it to learn a great deal about what an atom looks like according to the Bohr model. For example, by looking at the chart, a chemist can tell you that the Bohr model of a $^{12}$C atom is as follows:

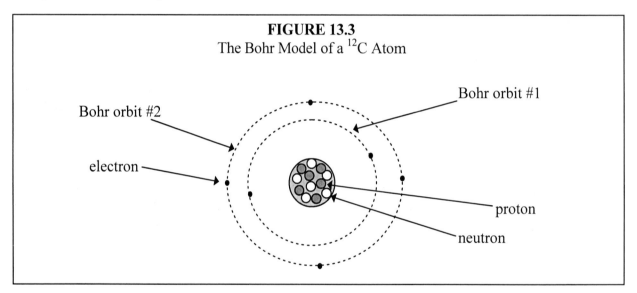

**FIGURE 13.3**
The Bohr Model of a $^{12}$C Atom

How did I get that picture? Well, first I looked at the chart and saw that the element symbolized by "C" has an atomic number of 6. That told me there are 6 protons and 6 electrons in a $^{12}$C atom. Since the mass number is 12, that tells me that there are also 6 neutrons, because the number of neutrons and protons must add up to the mass number. As a result, I put 6 protons and 6 neutrons in the nucleus. Then, I put the 6 electrons orbiting around the nucleus.

How did I know to use more than one orbit in the picture? Well, it turns out that you can't just stuff as many electrons as you want into a single orbit. After a while, the orbit gets "too full" of electrons. Thus, in the Bohr model of the atom, there are several orbits that the electrons can occupy. These orbits are referred to in many different ways. I like to refer to them as **Bohr orbits**, and give them numbers. As illustrated in the figure, the orbit closest to the nucleus is the first Bohr orbit, and the next one is the second Bohr orbit. If this atom needed more orbits, there would be a third Bohr orbit, a fourth Bohr orbit, etc. Some chemists refer to these orbits as **energy levels** because the energy of the electrons increases the larger the orbit is. Finally, some chemists call the **electron shells** because each orbit of electrons is a "shell" that covers up the nucleus.

Because the orbits increase in size the further they are away from the nucleus, each subsequent Bohr orbit can contain more electrons. The first few Bohr orbits and their electron capacities are listed in Table 13.1.

**TABLE 13.1**

| Bohr Orbit | Electron Capacity |
| --- | --- |
| 1 | 2 |
| 2 | 8 |
| 3 | 18 |
| 4 | 32 |
| 5 | 50 |

When you build up an atom, then, you put as many electrons as you can in the first orbit, then continue with the second orbit and continue to add more orbits until you have put in all of the electrons that exist for that atom.

---

**EXAMPLE 13.2**

**Draw what the Bohr model says an aluminum-27 ($^{27}$Al) atom would look like.**

The element Al has an atomic number of 13. That means there are 13 electrons and 13 protons. Since the mass number is 27, that tells us there are 14 neutrons. Thus, we put 13 protons and 14 neutrons in the nucleus. Since there are 13 electrons, we will use 2 electrons to fill up the first Bohr orbit, 8 to fill up the second, and we will still have 3 more to put in the third.

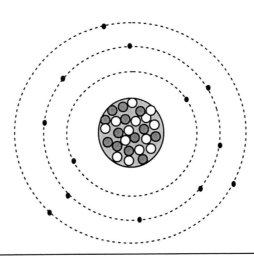

**ON YOUR OWN**

(Use the Periodic Chart to answer these questions.)

13.4  Draw a picture of a $^{19}$F atom, according to the Bohr model.

13.5  If you were to draw a picture of any isotope of cesium (Cs), what would be the largest Bohr orbit you would use and how many electrons would be in it?

Before you leave this section, I must once again point out to you that although the Bohr model gives us a good idea of what an atom looks like, we know that it is not correct.  Thus, the pictures of atoms that you draw based on the Bohr model are reasonable approximations of what an atom looks like, but they are *not* really correct.  Currently, the quantum-mechanical model is what most chemists consider to be an accurate representation of what an atom looks like.  You will learn a little bit about that model when you take chemistry.

The Strong Nuclear Force

Ever since you first saw Figure 13.1, something should have started to bother you.  Over and over again, as I drew pictures of atoms, I continually lumped the protons and neutrons together in the nucleus of the atom.  Remember, the nucleus is very small (a marble in a major-league baseball stadium), therefore, the protons and neutrons are crammed in to a very tight space.  This results in a bunch of protons *very* close to one another.  That should bother you.  After all, protons are positively charged.  What happens when two objects with the same charge are put near each other?  They *repel* each other!  Remember, like charges repel, and opposite charges attract.  The attraction between the protons and electrons keeps the electrons orbiting the nucleus.  What about the repulsion between the protons, however?  Why do they stay tightly-packed within the nucleus when they obviously repel one another?

This question puzzled scientists for quite a long time.  Experiments done in the laboratory indicated that, just as you would predict, protons repel each other when put in close proximity to one another.  Nevertheless, other experiments conclusively showed that as a part of an atom, protons exist tightly-packed with one another in the nucleus.  Thus, scientists suggested that there must be a short-range, attractive force called the **strong nuclear force** which attracts protons and neutrons to one another.  They assumed that this force acted over such a short range that it was only important when protons were extremely close to one another, as is the case with the nucleus.  Thus, under "normal" conditions, protons are so far apart from each other that the only force they experience is the electromagnetic force, which causes them to repel one another.  When placed in a nucleus, however, the protons are so close to one another that the strong nuclear force has a chance to operate.  Scientists assumed that the strong nuclear force was so strong that it overcame the repulsive electromagnetic force, holding the protons together in the nucleus.

It is important for you to realize that scientists had *no idea* what caused the strong nuclear force.  Indeed, the strong nuclear force stayed shrouded in mystery for quite some time.  Nevertheless, scientists concluded that the strong nuclear force *must* exist, or the nucleus would never hold together.  They also concluded that the strong nuclear force *must* be attractive because it would have to overcome the repulsive electromagnetic force that exists between protons.  Finally, they concluded that it *must* act over a very short range, or we would be able to see it work in situations other than a nucleus.  Thus, although scientists had *no idea* what caused the strong nuclear force, observations of atoms allowed them to conclude a lot of things about the *nature* of this force.

Things began to change in 1935 when Hideki (hi dee' kee) Yukawa (you kah' wah) proposed that the strong nuclear force occurs as a result of the fact that protons and neutrons can exchange tiny particles with one another.  In his initial theory, Yukawa called these tiny particles **pions** and actually made a rough prediction of what their mass should be.  In 1947, these pions were discovered by experiment, and their mass was, indeed, roughly what Yukawa predicted.  Yukawa's explanation of the strong nuclear force revolutionized our understanding of the nucleus, and as a result, he was awarded the Nobel prize in physics.

Now remember  from Module #12 that the electromagnetic force is understood to result from the exchange of photons between charged particles.  Thus, the strong nuclear force is similar to the electromagnetic force in the sense that they are both governed by the exchange of particles.  However, the particles are different, and that causes a difference in the nature of the two forces.  First of all, photons can exist for a very long time. Pions, on the other hand, cannot.  Pions are part of a vast class of particles that physicists call "short-lived particles."  As a result, although pions do exist, they only exist for a very short time.  Therefore, when two protons exchange a pion, they must do so *very* quickly because the pion cannot exist for very long.

This probably sounds strange to you.  After all, you have heard that matter cannot be created or destroyed.  Why, then, are pions short-lived particles?  The fact is that pions are made from the mass of a proton or neutron.  Thus, if two protons decide to exchange a pion, one proton must "give up" a little bit of its mass and make the pion.  That pion can then be given to another proton.  That proton will return the favor, creating a pion from its own mass and sending it to the first proton.  The same thing can happen between two neutrons, or between a neutron and a proton.  Because pions can only live for a short time, however, the protons and neutrons must stay very close to one another.  Thus, the strong nuclear force can only operate over very small distances.

Once again, this might sound very strange, but many, many experiments back up this theory of the strong nuclear force.  A nucleus is actually a very active place!  Protons and neutrons are packed closely together, and they are constantly making, giving up, and receiving pions!  The pions are exchanged among the protons and neutrons in the nucleus rapidly because they cannot exist for a very long time.  Thus, you can picture the nucleus as a scene of wild activity, with all of the constituents of the nucleus madly making and exchanging pions with each other.

The strong nuclear force is a great example of how science works these days.  Long before pions were discovered, scientists had figured out a great deal about the strong nuclear force.  They had already concluded that it *must* exist, otherwise the nucleus would explode due to the repulsive electromagnetic force between protons.  They had also concluded that it *must* be a force which operates over a very short range because it seems to exist only within the confines of the nucleus.

When the pion was finally discovered, scientists then understood *why* the strong nuclear force exists and *why* it operates over a short range. It exists as a result of the exchange of pions, and it is short-range because the pions exist for but an instant. Thus, protons and/or neutrons can only exchange pions when they are extremely close to one another. In the end, then, scientists had used observations to determine that a mysterious force exists, they developed a theory as to what might cause that force, and they then went looking for experimental evidence to back up the theory. This is very typical of how scientific research is done today.

---

### ON YOUR OWN

13.6 Suppose a new force is discovered, and scientists determine that it is governed by the exchange of a particle known as the "wileon." If the lifetime of a wileon is greater than that of a pion but shorter than that of a photon, what is the range of this new force relative to the range of the strong nuclear force and the electromagnetic force?

---

### Radioactivity

I mentioned in the introduction that I want to talk about the weak force in this module. Once again, let me remind you that the weak force is really just another aspect of the electromagnetic force; therefore, many physicists say that there are only three forces in Creation: the gravitational force, the strong nuclear force, and the electroweak force. I don't really want to spend much time discussing the weak force because there is really no difference between it and the electromagnetic force. However, I do want to discuss the process which the weak force governs: **radioactivity**. In fact, the weak force governs only a portion of radioactive processes, but I want to talk about radioactivity in general.

There is an enormous amount of misunderstanding when it comes to radioactivity, so I want to pay extra attention to this subject. Hopefully, I can dispel some of the myths that most people believe about this complicated subject. Radioactivity is a result of atoms which we call **radioactive isotopes**.

Radioactive isotope - An atom whose nucleus is not stable

When an atom has a nucleus that is not stable, the nucleus must decay in order to become stable. This process is called **radioactive decay**, and it can take on several different forms.

One way that an unstable nucleus can decay is through **beta decay**.

Beta decay - The process by which a neutron turns into a proton by emission of an electron

In beta decay, a nucleus actually changes one of its neutrons into a proton. It does so by making the neutron emit an electron. If you think about it, this process makes some sense. After all, a neutron is electrically neutral. If a neutron were to somehow emit an electron, it would be getting rid of a negative charge. If it starts out neutral and "spits out" a negative charge, what would be left? A positive charge! Thus, when a neutron spits out an electron, the result is that the neutron turns into a proton!

Consider, for example, the uranium isotope $^{239}$U. Based on the chart, you know that uranium has 92 protons and 92 electrons. The mass number indicates that there must therefore be 147 neutrons in the nucleus of a $^{239}$U isotope. It turns out that the nucleus of this atom is unstable. It has too many neutrons. To fix this problem, a neutron changes into a proton by emitting an electron. What is the result of this process? If a neutron turns into a proton, the nucleus will no longer have 92 protons. Instead, as soon as the neutron turns into a proton, the result will be a nucleus with 93 protons. After all, there were 92 protons, and then a neutron changed into a proton. This means that, in the end, there will be 93 protons.

Once the nucleus of this atom has 93 protons, the atom is no longer an isotope of uranium. Instead, the chart tells us that all atoms with 93 protons are called neptunium (Np) atoms. Thus, when $^{239}$U goes through beta decay, the result is that it turns into $^{239}$Np. When beta decay occurs, the nucleus actually changes so that the atom is now a completely different element! In order to do this, a neutron in the nucleus emits an electron. In the terminology of nuclear physics, we call $^{239}$U the **radioactive isotope** and the $^{239}$Np that results from the beta decay the **daughter product**. Since the electron produced comes from beta decay, we call it a **beta particle**. Nevertheless, it is just an electron. In other words, the radioactive isotope $^{239}$U emits a beta particle so as to decay into the daughter product $^{239}$Np.

If all of this is a bit confusing to you, don't worry. In a little while, I will give you a few examples that will hopefully clear everything up. For right now, however, I want to talk about other forms of radioactivity. The next form of radioactive decay is called **alpha decay**. Once again, this kind of radioactive decay starts with a radioactive isotope. Instead of emitting a beta particle in order to become stable, however, some radioactive isotopes emit an **alpha particle** instead. An alpha particle is a small nucleus that contains 2 protons and 2 neutrons. That should sound familiar to you. An alpha particle is actually the nucleus of a helium atom! Thus, when alpha decay occurs, a nucleus actually "spits out" two protons and two neutrons in the form of a helium nucleus!

Like beta decay, this process will turn the radioactive isotope into a completely different element. For example, an isotope of polonium, $^{214}$Po, has such an unstable nucleus that it actually ejects 2 protons and 2 neutrons from the nucleus. The chart tells us that polonium has 84 protons. If it ejects 2 of them, the result is only 82 protons. Thus, the polonium turns into lead (Pb). What's the mass number of this lead daughter product? Well, the nucleus spits out 2 protons and 2 neutrons. Since the mass number is the sum of the protons and neutrons in the nucleus, this tells us that the mass number loses 4. So the daughter product is $^{210}$Pb.

The last form of radioactivity I want to discuss is **gamma decay**. In gamma decay, a radioactive isotope becomes stable by emitting a **gamma ray**. This is probably the easiest form of radioactive decay to understand because a gamma ray is actually just a high energy photon. When a radioactive isotope goes through gamma decay, the isotope doesn't change its identity at all. For example, $^{229}$Th is a radioactive isotope that goes through gamma decay. When this isotope decays, it starts out with 90 protons and 139 neutrons in its nucleus, and it ends up with the same number of protons and neutrons. The only thing that the gamma ray does is take energy away from the nucleus. Thus, gamma rays are emitted by radioactive isotopes that have too much energy in their nucleus. The gamma ray takes that energy away, but the radioactive isotope does not change in any other way.

As I said a moment ago, this might all be quite confusing to you. However, if you study the following examples, I think you will finally understand what I've been discussing here.

---

**EXAMPLE 13.3**

$^{14}$C **is a radioactive isotope that goes through beta decay. What is the daughter product of this decay?**

According to the chart, carbon has an atomic number of 6. This tells us that a $^{14}$C atom has 6 protons and 8 neutrons in its nucleus. When a radioactive isotope undergoes beta decay, one of its neutrons turns into a proton. Thus, it will end up with one more proton and one less neutron. The daughter product (the nucleus that results from the beta decay), then, will have 7 protons and 7 neutrons. According to the chart, all atoms with 7 protons are symbolized with an "N." The mass number of this nitrogen atom will be 7+7=14. The daughter product is $\underline{^{14}N}$.

$^{232}$Th **is a radioactive isotope that goes through alpha decay. What is the resulting daughter product?**

According to the chart, thorium (Th) atoms have 90 protons. Thus, this particular atom has 90 protons and 142 neutrons in it. When it goes through alpha decay, it actually spits out 2 protons and 2 neutrons in the form of a helium-4 nucleus. The result will be only 88 protons and 140 neutrons in the daughter product. The chart tells us that Ra is the symbol for all atoms with 88 protons. The mass number of the resulting nucleus will be 88+140 = 228. Thus, the daughter product is $\underline{^{228}Ra}$.

If a $^{22}$Na **atom undergoes gamma decay, what nucleus will be produced?**

Gamma decay simply takes energy away from the nucleus in the form of light. It does not change the identity of the nucleus. So the daughter product is still $\underline{^{22}Na}$.

---

**ON YOUR OWN**

13.7  What is the daughter product that results from the beta decay of $^{90}$Sr?

13.8  What is the product of the alpha decay of $^{241}$Am?

## The Dangers of Radioactivity

Now that you know what radioactivity does (takes an atom with an unstable nucleus and turns it into an atom with a stable nucleus), you might be interested in knowing why everyone is so afraid of radioactivity. Well, part of the fear is based totally on ignorance, and part of the fear is based on fact. Radioactivity *can be* dangerous, but it is *not always* dangerous. That's a good thing, too, because we are *constantly* being exposed to radioactivity. If you have brick or mortar in the walls of your home, they are radioactive. By standing near them, you are exposed to beta particles. You are exposed to gamma rays when you are outside in the sun. If you have a smoke detector in your house, you are exposed to alpha particles because the main detection component of a smoke detector goes through alpha decay. In fact, you are exposed to beta particles each time you get close to someone because people themselves are radioactive! It's a good thing, then, that radioactivity is not always dangerous.

The first thing you have to understand is why radioactivity can be dangerous. Radioactivity does not act like a poison. A poison is dangerous because it chemically reacts with your body, causing chemical processes to occur in your body which should not occur. This upsets your body's chemistry, causing sickness or even death. Some poisons actually build up in your body. As you take them in small doses, they do not cause you any problems. However, as they continue to build up in your body, they eventually start causing chemical reactions that shouldn't happen in your body, and that's when you are in trouble.

Unlike poisons, radioactivity is not dangerous because it can upset your body's chemistry. It also cannot build up in your body. Instead, radioactivity affects your body much like a tiny machine gun. You see, the danger in radiation comes from the particles that are emitted during the radioactive decay. Depending on the isotope involved, radioactive decay involves a nucleus "spitting out" something. In alpha decay, the nucleus spits out an alpha particle (composed of 2 protons and 2 neutrons). In beta decay, it spits out a beta particle (which is just an electron). In gamma decay, the nucleus spits out high energy light. There is nothing chemically poisonous about these things. They are dangerous, however. They are dangerous because they have a lot of energy.

When produced as a result of radioactive decay, alpha particles, beta particles, and gamma rays have *a lot* of energy. As a result, they begin speeding away from the nucleus that emitted them. If you happen to be unfortunate enough to be in the way of the emitted particle, it might collide with one of the smallest constituents of your body, a cell. Every living organism is made up of tiny living units called cells. That's what the emitted particle hits. The vast majority of the time, when an alpha, beta, or gamma particle collides with a cell, it results in the cell's death. Every now and again, however, the cell will not die. If the particle hits the cell just right, it might mutate the cell's DNA rather than kill the cell.

Do you see why I say that radioactivity acts like a tiny machine gun? When you have a sample of radioactive material, each atom in that sample can "shoot" one "bullet" (an alpha particle, a beta particle, or a gamma ray). Since there are trillions and trillions of atoms in even a small sample of matter, that means that a sample of radioactive isotopes can shoot off trillions and trillions of these "bullets." If you happen to be in the path of these "bullets," each "bullet" that hits you will most likely kill an individual cell. Thus, a radioactive sample is like a tiny machine gun that kills you one cell at a time. Every now and again, however, rather than killing a cell, the particle will cause a mutation in the cell's DNA.

Sounds dangerous, doesn't it? Well, it *can* be dangerous, but *not necessarily*. You see, your body *expects* cells to die. God therefore designed your body to reproduce cells. This helps you grow and mature, and it also replaces cells that die. When you scratch an itch, for example, you actually kill as many as several hundred cells. This is no problem, as your body quickly replaces them. Thus, as long as your cells do not die faster than they can be replaced by your body, there is no real problem.

When your cells are being destroyed by the little "bullets" that are being "shot" from a sample of radioactive isotopes, then, there is no problem as long as the "bullets" are not killing your cells faster than your body can replace them. If you are exposed to too much radiation too quickly, then your cells will be killed faster than your body can replace them, leading to radiation burns, organ damage, and the like.

What about the chance for mutating a cell's DNA? Isn't that bad? Well, yes, but once again, it depends on the amount of mutation that is going on. Everyone's body has a few mutant cells. Most of them simply die off. The bad thing about mutation is that a mutant cell can result in cancer or some other sickness. This happens only rarely, however, so a few mutant cells in your body is not a bad thing. Everyone has them. The problem only occurs when you have too many mutant cells. Thus, as long as you are not exposed to too much radiation, the danger is minimal.

In the end, then, the important thing to remember about the danger of radioactivity is that it depends on the level of radioactivity to which you are exposed. A small amount of radioactivity is reasonably safe; a large amount is not. How much radioactivity exposure is too much? Well, scientists have examined that issue and have come up with certain limits to the amount of radiation exposure that a person should have. As a result, they limit the number of X-rays (a source of gamma rays) a person can have in a year, and they limit the amount of exposure that people who work with radioactive isotopes can have.

Remember when I said that brick and mortar are radioactive, as well as smoke detectors and other people? The amount of radioactivity you are exposed to from these sources is hundreds of times lower than what scientists consider to be a safe level of radiation exposure. Thus, even though you are exposed to radioactivity from these sources, the cellular mutation and cellular death that results from them is so low that they are still quite safe.

Even if you are in a position in which you are exposed to large amounts of radioactivity, there are ways you can protect yourself. For example, it is possible to stop the little "bullets" before they ever reach your body. For example, alpha particles are extremely weak in terms of how much matter they can travel through. If you put a piece of paper between you and the radioactive source emitting the alpha particles, the vast majority of those alpha particles will stop in the paper.  As a result, they will never hit you.  Beta particles can travel through obstacles a bit better.  It typically takes a thin sheet of metal to stop most of the beta particles coming from a radioactive isotope that emits them.  Finally, gamma rays are the strongest type of radiation, requiring several inches of lead to stop them.

Thus, one way you can protect yourself is to block the radiation before it hits you.  This method is called "shielding."  The other way you can protect yourself from an intensely radioactive source is to simply move away from it.  The farther you move away, the fewer "bullets" can hit you.  Of course, most people will never be exposed to a large amount of radiation in their lifetime, so they will never be faced with such a situation.

---

**ON YOUR OWN**

13.9 People who regularly work with large samples of radioactive isotopes sometimes wear special suits that are lined with a thin layer of lead or other heavy material.  What kinds of radiation are these people protected from when wearing such a suit?

---

## The Rate of Radioactive Decay

Remember, most radioactive isotopes shoot only one "bullet," and then they are done.  After all, the reason an isotope is radioactive in the first place is that its nucleus is unstable.  Once it goes through whatever radioactive decay it goes through, the result is usually a stable nucleus.  Once the nucleus is stable, there is no more need for radioactive decay, so the isotope is no longer radioactive.  For example, when $^{14}C$ beta decays into $^{14}N$, the nitrogen atom is stable and, therefore, no longer radioactive.  Thus, once a $^{14}C$ atom emits a single beta particle, it is no longer radioactive; therefore, it emits no more beta particles.

Although there are some radioactive isotopes that must emit several particles before becoming stable, the general rule is that one radioactive isotope emits one particle and then stops.  However, even a small sample of radioactive isotope has trillions and trillions of atoms in it.  Thus, even if each isotope emits only one "bullet," a small sample can emit trillions and trillions of "bullets."  Nevertheless, at some point, nearly all of the isotopes will have gone through the radioactive decay process.  At that point, there will be essentially no radioactive isotopes left in the sample, and the result will be that the sample will no longer be radioactive.

If I have a sample of a radioactive isotope, how long will it take before all of the atoms in the sample have gone through the decay process and the sample is no longer radioactive?  Well, it depends on the isotope.  For example, consider the case of $^{214}Po$.  I mentioned this radioactive isotope when I first discussed alpha decay.  This isotope emits an alpha particle and, as a result, turns into the stable atom $^{210}Pb$.  If I have a sample of $^{214}Po$, it will go through alpha decay so quickly that in about *one thousandth* of a second, all of the $^{214}Po$ atoms will have emitted an alpha particle and the result will be a sample of lead that is no longer radioactive.  Thus, $^{214}Po$ goes through radioactive decay rather quickly.  On the other hand,  $^{14}C$ beta decays into $^{14}N$

rather slowly. If I have a sample of $^{14}$C, it will take more than 50,000 *years* for the vast majority of atoms to undergo beta decay. Thus, a sample of $^{14}$C stays radioactive for a long, long time!

Is there any way to predict how long it will take for a radioactive isotope to decay into something that is no longer radioactive? Not really. However, the rate is easily measured. As a result, nuclear physicists have cataloged the rate of decay for thousands of radioactive isotopes. This rate is typically listed in terms of something called the **half-life** of the isotope.

Half-life - The time it takes for half of the original sample of a radioactive isotope to decay

For example, the half-life of $^{14}$C is 5,730 years. This means that if I have 100 grams of $^{14}$C, in 5,730 years, there will only be 50 grams of it left. The other half of the sample will have gone through beta decay and turned into $^{14}$N. What would happen in the next 5,730 years? Would I have 0 grams left? No. In the next 5,730 years, half of the *remaining* $^{14}$C would decay, leaving only 25 grams of $^{14}$C.

Each time the half-life of a radioactive isotope passes, half of *what was there at the beginning of the half-life* decays away. Thus, after 1 half-life, 100 grams of radioactive isotope will turn into 50 grams of radioactive isotope. After 2 half-lives, half of *that* will decay, leaving only 25 grams of radioactive isotope. After the next half-life, half of *that* will decay, and there will only be 12.5 grams of radioactive isotope left. In other words, the amount of radioactive isotope keeps getting divided by 2 after each half-life. Study the following example to make sure you understand what I mean.

---

**EXAMPLE 13.4**

$^{55}$Cr is used in scientific research. It is a radioactive isotope with a half-life of 2 hours. If a scientist starts with 1000 grams of $^{55}$Cr, how many grams of $^{55}$Cr will be left in 8 hours?

Since the half-life of the radioactive isotope is 2 hours, every 2 hours, the amount of radioactive isotope remaining will be cut in half. After 2 hours, then, the amount of isotope will decrease to 500 grams. After another 2 hours, the amount will decrease to 250 grams. In the next 2 hours, the amount will decrease to 125 grams, and in the next 2 hours, the amount will decrease to 62.5 grams. That completes the 8-hour time period. Thus, after 8 hours, there will be 62.5 grams of $^{55}$Cr left. This tells us that the rest of the sample (937.5 grams) went through the decay process in 8 hours, turning into a sample of stable atoms.

---

Something should be bothering you at this point. Earlier in this very section I mentioned that after a certain period of time, a radioactive sample will cease to be radioactive because nearly all of its atoms will undergo the radioactive decay process and become stable. However, the previous discussion of half-life indicates that a sample of radioactivity never completely decays away. After all, if the amount of radioactive isotope is simply cut in half after every half-life, the amount will never drop to zero. Thus a radioactive sample will never get rid of all of its radioactivity.

While that is technically true, the fact is that from a practical standpoint, the amount of radioactive isotope in a sample drops off so quickly after a few half-lives that eventually there is very little radioactive isotope left. At that point, for all practical purposes, the amount of radioactive isotope can be assumed to be zero. Consider the example problem for a moment. The scientist started out with 1000 grams of $^{55}Cr$. After a mere 20 hours (10 half-lives), there would be only 0.9766 grams of $^{55}Cr$ remaining! Thus, after only 10 half-lives, the amount of radioactive isotope decreases by more than a factor of one thousand! So, even though a sample of isotope never really goes away completely, at some point, the amount of radioactive isotope left is so small that it can be ignored.

If we keep a radioactive isotope around long enough, then, it will cease to be radioactive. Of course, each radioactive isotope has its own half-life. Some half-lives are short (like those of $^{214}Po$ and $^{55}Cr$), while others are quite long. As I already mentioned, the half-life of $^{14}C$ is 5,730 years! That's pretty long. There are half-lives even longer than that, however. The half-life of $^{238}U$ is 4,500,000,000 years! Thus, just because a radioactive sample *eventually* loses its radioactivity, it can sometimes take a *very* long time for this to happen!

---

**ON YOUR OWN**

13.10  The half-life of $^{131}I$ is 8 days. If you start with a 40 gram sample of $^{131}I$, how much will be left in 24 days?

---

## Radioactive Dating

The fact that radioactive isotopes decay at a measurable rate allows scientists to use radioactive decay as a means of dating objects whose age we do not know. This is known as **radioactive dating**. Although radioactive dating can be accurate under certain circumstances, it is important to note that it has some serious weaknesses as well. As a result, radioactive dating techniques must be viewed rather critically. Despite the fact that some scientists will try to convince you that radioactive dating is an accurate means of determining the age of an object, the scientific facts tell quite a different story.

The best way of examining the strengths and weaknesses of radioactive dating is to examine one of the radioactive dating methods in detail. Since $^{14}C$ is probably the best known radioactive dating technique, I will discuss that one. As I have already mentioned, $^{14}C$ decays by beta decay with a half-life of 5,730 years. It turns out that all living organisms contain a certain amount of $^{14}C$, making all living organisms somewhat radioactive.

Interestingly enough, living organisms continually exchange $^{14}C$ with their surroundings. Human beings, for example, exhale carbon dioxide, some of which contains $^{14}C$. In addition, human beings eat other organisms (plant and animals), which contain $^{14}C$ as well. Finally, as you learned way back in Module #2, part of the air that we inhale is made up of carbon dioxide, some of which contains $^{14}C$. Thus, organisms are continually exchanging $^{14}C$ with their environment. The practical result of all of this exchange is that, at any time when an organism is alive, it contains the same amount of $^{14}C$ as does the atmosphere around the organism.

This changes when the organism dies, however. At that point, the $^{14}C$ exchange ceases. Thus, the organism cannot replenish its supply of $^{14}C$, and the amount of $^{14}C$ in the organism begins to decrease. Every 5,730 years, half of the $^{14}C$ in the organism will decay away. In general, then, organisms that have been dead a long time tend to have less $^{14}C$ in them as compared to those that have been dead for only a short time.

Now if you think about it, this fact can be used to measure the length of time that an organism has been dead. After all, if we know how much $^{14}C$ was in an organism when it died, and if we measure the amount of $^{14}C$ in it now, the difference will be the amount of $^{14}C$ that has decayed away. Since we know how quickly $^{14}C$ decays, this can tell us how long the organism has been dead. Pretty simple, right?

Well, it *would* be simple, *if* we knew how much $^{14}C$ was in the organism when it died. The problem is , how do we figure that out? After all, no one was around to measure the amount of $^{14}C$ in the organism when it died; thus, we must make an *assumption* about how much $^{14}C$ would have been measured if someone had been there to measure it. As I have said before, there is nothing wrong with making assumptions in science. The trick is that we have to know our assumptions are accurate.

In the case of $^{14}C$ dating, scientists assume that, on average, the amount of $^{14}C$ in the atmosphere has never really changed that much. They assume that the amount of $^{14}C$ in the atmosphere today is essentially the same as it was 100 years ago, 1,000 years ago, etc. Thus, when the age of a dead organism is being measured with $^{14}C$ dating, we assume that the amount of $^{14}C$ it had when it died was the same as the amount of $^{14}C$ that is in the atmosphere now. That gives us a value for how much $^{14}C$ was initially in the dead organism. We can measure the amount of $^{14}C$ that is in the organism now and then determine how long the organism has been dead.

Notice, however, that the age we get from this process is completely dependent on the assumption that we made about how much $^{14}C$ was in the organism when it died. If that assumption is good, the age we calculate will be accurate. If that assumption is bad, the age we calculate will not be accurate. So the question becomes, "Is the assumption accurate?" In short, the answer is "no."

Through a process involving tree rings, there is a way we can measure the amount of $^{14}C$ in the atmosphere in years past. When a tree is cut down, the rings in the tree's trunk can be counted to determine how old the tree is. Each ring represents a year in the life of the tree. We know which ring corresponds to which year by simply counting the rings from the outside of the trunk to the inside.  Well, it turns out that through a rather complicated process, we can actually measure the amount of $^{14}$C in a tree ring and use it to determine how much $^{14}$C was in the atmosphere during the year in which the tree ring was grown.  As a result, scientists have determined the amount of $^{14}$C in the atmosphere throughout a portion of the earth's past.

Scientists have studied the $^{14}$C content in tree rings that are as many as 3,000 years old. From these measurements, scientists have determined the amount of $^{14}$C in the atmosphere over the past 3,000 years.  What they have seen is that the amount of $^{14}$C has varied by as much as 70% over that time period.  The variation is correlated to certain events that occur on the surface of the sun.  As a result, *we know* that the amount of $^{14}$C in the atmosphere has not stayed constant.  Instead, it has varied greatly.  Thus, *we know* that the initial assumption of $^{14}$C dating is wrong.  Thus, one must take most $^{14}$C dates with a grain of salt.  After all, we know that the assumption used in making those dates is wrong.  Consequently, we cannot put too much trust in the results!

Notice that I said we must take "most" $^{14}$C dates with a grain of salt.  Why "most?"  Why not "all?"  It turns out that since we can determine the amount of $^{14}$C in the atmosphere during the past using tree rings, we can actually use that data to help us make our initial assumption.  As a result, the assumption becomes much more accurate.  The problem is, however, that we don't have $^{14}$C measurements for tree rings that are older than 3,000 years.  Thus, we can only make an accurate assumption for organisms that have died within the last 3,000 years.  As long as the organism died in that time range, we can use tree ring data to help us make an accurate assumption of how much $^{14}$C was in the organism when it died.  For organisms that have died longer than 3,000 years ago, we have no tree ring data, so we have no way to make an accurate assumption.  As a result, we cannot really believe the $^{14}$C date.

In the end, then, the $^{14}$C dating method can be believed for organisms that have been dead for 3,000 years or less.  Thus, it is a great tool for archaeology.  If an archaeologist finds a manuscript or a piece of cloth (both cloth and paper are made from dead plants), the archaeologist can use $^{14}$C dating to determine its age.  As long as the result is about 3,000 years or younger, the date can be believed.  If the date turns out to be older than 3,000 years, it is most likely wrong.

So you should see that radioactive dating involves a pretty important assumption.  If the assumption is good, the date obtained from radioactive dating is good.  If the assumption is bad, the result obtained from radioactive dating will be bad.  Now there are a lot of other radioactive dating techniques besides $^{14}$C dating.  Unfortunately, they all suffer from a similar malady.  In every radioactive dating technique, we must make assumptions about how much of a certain substance was in the object originally.  Such assumptions are quite hard to make accurately.

The difficulty of making these assumptions can be seen in the fact that radioactive dates have been demonstrated to be wrong in many, many instances.  John Woodmorappe, in his book *Studies in Flood Geology*, has compiled more than 350 radioactive dates that conflict with one another or with other generally accepted dates.  These erroneous dates demonstrate that the assumptions used in radioactive dating cannot be trusted. As a result, the dates that one gets from radioactive dating cannot be trusted, either.

Unfortunately, many in the scientific community are unwilling to admit to the inadequacies of radioactive dating because many scientists like its *results*. Because certain radioactive decay schemes have long, long half-lives, the dates that one calculates from these methods can be breathtakingly large. For example, there are rocks on the planet that radioactive dating techniques indicate are more than 4 *billion* years old. It turns out that many scientists *want* the earth to be that old because they believe in the discredited hypothesis of evolution. This hypothesis *requires* a very old earth, and radioactive dating techniques provide dates that indicate the earth is very old. As a result, they turn a blind eye to the inadequacies of radioactive dating because it gives them an answer that they want! Hopefully, as time goes on, this unfortunate situation will change!

## ANSWERS TO THE ON YOUR OWN PROBLEMS

13.1  Since all sodium atoms have 11 protons, this one has <u>11 protons</u>. This tells us that it also has <u>11 electrons</u>. Since the mass number is 23, we know that the sum of protons and neutrons in the nucleus must equal 23. The only way this can happen is if sodium-23 has <u>12 neutrons</u>.

13.2  Since all oxygen atoms have 8 protons, this oxygen atom also has 8 protons. This tells us that it has <u>8 electrons</u>. The name of an atom is its element name (oxygen) followed by the mass number. The mass number is the sum of protons and neutrons in the nucleus. Since there are 8 protons and 8 neutrons, the mass number is 16. This means the name is <u>oxygen-16</u>.

13.3  Isotopes have the same number of protons in their nuclei, but different numbers of neutrons. Only (a) and (c) have the same number of protons. They each have 16. In addition, they have different numbers of neutrons. The atom in (a) has 17 neutrons and the atom in (c) has 18 neutrons. Thus, since they have equal numbers of protons but different number of neutrons, <u>(a) and (c) are isotopes of one another</u>.

13.4  The element symbolized by "F" (fluorine) has an atomic number of 9 according to the chart. This means all atoms symbolized by "F" have 9 protons. This means they also have 9 electrons. Since only 2 electrons fit in the first Bohr orbit, we will need to use the second Bohr orbit. That will hold an additional 8 electrons, which is one more than we need. Since the mass number is 19, this tells us that the sum of protons and neutrons in the nucleus is 19. Thus, the atom must have 10 neutrons.

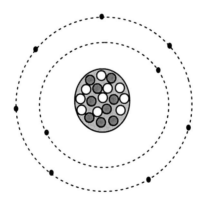

13.5  According to the chart, Cs has an atomic number of 55. This means there are 55 protons and 55 electrons in the atom. The first Bohr orbit will hold 2. The next one will hold 8. That gives us a place to put 10 electrons so far. The third Bohr orbit holds 18. Now we have room for 28 electrons. There are still 27 to go, however. That's okay, though, because the fourth Bohr orbit holds 32. Thus, there is plenty of room for the extra 27 electrons. <u>The largest orbit will be the fourth Bohr orbit, and there will be 27 electrons in it</u>.

13.6  Since the wileon lives longer than the pion, the particles which exchange wileons can be farther apart than those that exchange pions. This means the force has a longer range than the strong nuclear force. Since the wileon does not live as long as a photon, however, the range is not as great as the electromagnetic force. Thus, ~~the range of this force is larger than the strong~~ ~~nuclear force but less than the electromagnetic force.~~

13.7  According to the chart, the element Sr has an atomic number of 38. This means all Sr atoms have 38 protons. Since the mass number is 90, there must be 52 neutrons in the nucleus. In beta decay, a neutron turns into a proton. Thus, the daughter product will have one less neutron and one more proton than $^{90}$Sr. This means it will have 39 protons and 51 neutrons. According to the chart, atoms with 39 protons are symbolized by "Y." The mass number is the sum of protons and neutrons, so it is still 90. Therefore, the daughter product is $\underline{^{90}Y}$.

13.8  According to the chart, the element Am has 95 protons. Since the mass number is 241, this means that there are 146 neutrons in the nucleus. In alpha decay, the nucleus loses 2 protons and 2 neutrons. So the daughter product will have only 93 protons and 144 neutrons. According to the chart, an element with 93 protons is symbolized by "Np." The mass number of this daughter product is $93 + 144 = 237$. Thus, the daughter product is $\underline{^{237}Np}$.

13.9  Since alpha particles can be stopped by a sheet of paper, a thin sheet of metal will definitely stop them. Also, it takes a thin sheet of metal to stop beta particles, so the protective suit will stop them as well. Gamma rays take several inches of lead to stop, however, so the suit provides no protection against them. Thus, the suit protects against alpha and beta particles.

13.10  After 8 days have passed, the 40 gram sample will be cut in half, leaving only 20 grams. After another 8 days, that 20 gram sample will be cut in half to 10 grams. After another 8 days, that 10 gram sample will be cut in half to 5 grams. That's a total of 24 days. Thus, there will be 5 grams left after 24 days.

**STUDY GUIDE FOR MODULE #13**

(Use the Periodic Chart to answer these questions.  You will be able to use it on the test.)

1.  Define the following terms:

      a.  Nucleus
      b.  Atomic number
      c.  Mass number
      d.  Isotopes
      e.  Element
      f.  Radioactive isotope

2.  Order the three constituent parts of the atom in terms of their size, from smallest to largest.

3.  What force keeps the protons and neutrons in the nucleus?  What causes this force?

4.  What force keeps the electrons orbiting around the nucleus?

5.  What is an atom mostly made of?

6.  An atom has an atomic number of 34.  How many protons and electrons does it have?  What is its symbol?

7.  List the number of protons, electrons and neutrons for each of the following atoms:

      a. Neon-20 (neon's chemical symbol is "Ne")
      b. $^{56}$Fe
      c.  $^{139}$La
      d.  $^{24}$Mg

8.  Two atoms are isotopes of one another.  The first has 18 protons and 20 neutrons.  The second has 22 neutrons.  How many protons does the second atom have?

9.  Which of the following atoms are isotopes?

$$^{112}Cd, \; ^{112}Sn, \; ^{120}Xe, \; ^{124}Sn, \; ^{40}Ar, \; ^{120}Sn$$

10.  Draw what the Bohr model says an $^{16}$O atom would look like.

11. Draw what the Bohr model says a $^{25}$Mg atom would look like.

12.  What is the largest Bohr orbit in a uranium atom (the symbol for uranium is "U") and how many electrons are in it?

13.  Why is the strong nuclear force such a short-range force?

14. Determine the daughter products produced in the beta decay of the two radioactive isotopes shown below.

a. $^{98}$Tc          b. $^{125}$I

15. Determine the daughter products produced in the alpha decay of the two radioactive isotopes shown below.

a. $^{212}$Bi              b. $^{224}$Ra

16. A radioactive isotope goes through radioactive decay but the isotope's number of protons and neutrons does not change. What kind of radioactive decay occurred?

17. The half-life of the radioactive decay of $^{226}$Ra is 1600 years. If a sample of $^{226}$Ra originally had a mass of 10 grams, how many grams of $^{226}$Ra would be left after 3200 years?

18. The half-life of the man-made isotope $^{11}$C is 20 minutes. If a scientist makes 1 gram of $^{11}$C, how much will be left in one hour?

19. Why is radioactive dating unreliable in most situations?

20. List the three types of radioactive particles in the order of their ability to travel through matter. Start with the particle that cannot pass through much matter before stopping, and end with the one that can pass through the most matter before stopping.

# MODULE #14: Waves and Sound

## Introduction

Have you ever seen the ocean? I have. It's an amazing sight! Water stretches out as far as the eye can see, and waves crash against the shore on a regular basis. Consider the seashore pictured below:

**FIGURE 14.1**
Two Views of a Seashore

The view from the seashore                    The view from above

Notice the waves in the figure. Although they are easiest to see from the vantage point of the seashore, you can also see them from above, long before they hit the shore. There is a lot of energy in those waves. It turns out that a great deal of the energy in Creation is in the form of waves, and that's what we are going to learn about in this chapter.

Although waves like those pictured in Figure 14.1 are the ones with which you are most familiar, the waves that you see in the ocean or other large bodies of water are just one example of the waves that exist in God's Creation. In fact, water waves are not even the most prevalent kind of waves in Creation. **Electromagnetic waves**, some of which we call "light," are much more common than water waves. Waves in the air, which we call sound, are also quite common. As you study this module, you will learn how sound can be described in terms of waves. In the next module, you will learn the same thing about light. Before you can learn that, however, you need to know a few things about waves in general.

## Waves

Think for a moment about the waves with which you are already familiar: the waves that you find on water. From a sideways view, a wave might look something like what you see in Figure 14.2.

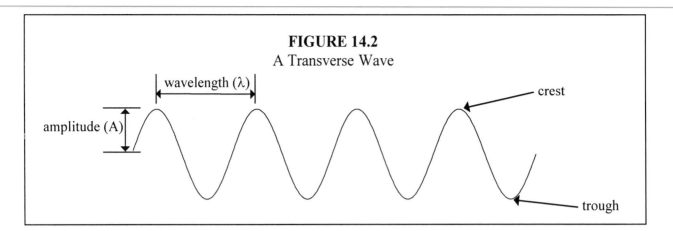

**FIGURE 14.2**
A Transverse Wave

wavelength (λ)

crest

amplitude (A)

trough

In a wave, you have both **crests** (the highest point on the wave) and **troughs** (the lowest point on the wave). The distance between the crests (or the distance between the troughs) is called the **wavelength (λ)** of the wave, while the height of the wave is the called the **amplitude (A)**. One characteristic of a wave that cannot really be drawn is **frequency**. The frequency of a wave indicates how many waves hit a certain point every second.

Suppose you were wading in the ocean at a beach. The amplitude of the waves would basically tell you how high the waves are. People riding surfboards would be happy if the waves had a large amplitude, because that would mean that the waves were high. People wanting a leisurely swim in the ocean would be more happy with small amplitude waves. The wavelength indicates how far apart the wave crests are. Frequency, on the other hand, indicates how many waves will hit you each second if you simply stand there and do not move.

It should make sense to you that frequency and wavelength are related in some way. After all, if the wave crests are far apart, not very many of them will hit you in a second. If the wave crests are close together, then several of them can hit you each second. Thus, when wavelength is large, frequency is small, and when wavelength is small, frequency is large. In other words, wavelength and frequency are inversely proportional to one another. When one gets large, the other becomes small.

I can be even more precise than that. Frequency and wavelength can be related to one another through the speed of the wave:

$$f = \frac{v}{\lambda}$$  (14.1)

In this equation, "f" represents the frequency of the wave, and "v" stands for the wave's speed. Although the symbol used for speed in Equation (14.1) is "v," it does *not* stand for the velocity of the wave. Remember, velocity includes direction, and the frequency and wavelength do not depend on the direction in which the wave is traveling. The funny-looking symbol, "λ," is the lower-case Greek letter "lambda," and it represents the wavelength.

First of all, we should examine the units of this equation.  Speed is measured in m/sec, while wavelength, since it is a distance, is measured in meters.  If I divide m/sec by m, what do I get?  I get 1/sec.  That's the unit for frequency.  This unit is often called **Hertz** (abbreviated as "Hz"), in honor of the German physicist Heinrich Rudolph Hertz.  Hertz discovered radio waves, which I will discuss in the next module.

In a moment, I'll use Equation (14.1) to analyze some waves, but first, I need to make a distinction between two different types of waves.  The wave pictured in Figure 14.2 is called a **transverse wave**.

Transverse wave - A wave whose propagation is perpendicular to its oscillation

That's a mouthful, isn't it?  Actually, this definition is rather simple once you get past the twenty dollar words.  The propagation of a wave is the direction of travel.  For example, the waves on an ocean travel towards the shore.  That's the direction of the wave's propagation.  The oscillation (ah suh lay' shun) of a wave refers to its up and down motion.  Once again, the waves cause the ocean to heave vertically up and down.  So, the waves move (propagate) horizontally (towards the shore), but they cause the ocean to heave (oscillate) vertically.  In this case, the propagation is perpendicular to the oscillation.  That's the kind of wave pictured in Figure 14.2.  The waves oscillate vertically and propagate horizontally.

There is another type of wave, however.  Some of the waves that we see in Creation are **longitudinal waves**.

Longitudinal wave - A wave whose propagation is parallel to its oscillation

The best way to think about a longitudinal wave is to pull out a slinky and stretch it out on the floor.  Hold one end of the slinky still, and then start moving the other end back and forth.  What will it look like?  It will look something like Figure 14.3.

**FIGURE 14.3**
A Longitudinal Wave

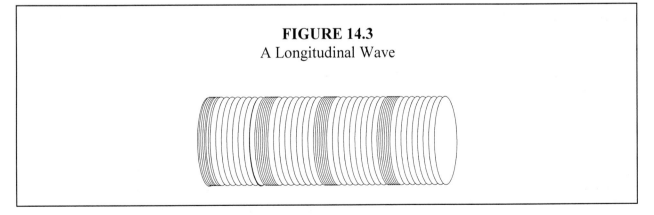

In this kind of wave, the wave propagates through the slinky, but the slinky also oscillates back and forth.  Thus, both the propagation and the oscillation of the wave are horizontal.

Although these two wave types are fundamentally different, Equation (14.1) applies equally to both. Since that is the case, let's use the equation to analyze a wave.

---

**EXAMPLE 14.1**

**What is the frequency of a wave that travels at a speed of 3 meters per second and has a wavelength of 0.5 meters?**

Remember, even though we use the symbol "v" in Equation (14.1), it means speed. Since we are given the speed and the wavelength, and since the units are consistent (both distance units are meters), we can just plug the numbers into the equation and get the answer:

$$f = \frac{v}{\lambda}$$

$$f = \frac{3\ \frac{\cancel{m}}{\sec}}{0.5\ \cancel{m}} = 6\ \frac{1}{\sec}$$

Physicists typically like to write "Hz" instead of "1/sec," so the answer is <u>6 Hz</u>. What does this answer mean? Well, it means that if you stand in the midst of this wave, 6 crests will hit you every second.

---

**ON YOUR OWN**

14.1 A longitudinal wave is suddenly stretched so that its wavelength is increased. If the speed of the wave does not change, what will happen to the wave's frequency?

14.2 Suppose you are wading on a beach which is experiencing waves that move with a speed of 0.5 meters per second and have a wavelength of 0.25 meters. If you stood still, how many waves would hit you every second?

---

Sound Waves

As I said in the introduction, sound is actually a kind of wave. It is important that you understand what I mean by that. Once again, think about the waves that you see in water. Why do you see those waves? You see them because water heaves up and down. The crests and troughs that result from such motion in the water produces visible waves. In physics terms, we say that water is the **medium** through which the waves in the ocean travel. We say that because water is the "stuff" that the wave causes to oscillate (move up and down).

All waves must have a medium through which to travel.  In other words, they all must have something which they cause to oscillate.  What is the medium through which sound waves travel?  Perform experiment 14.1 to find out.

---

### EXPERIMENT 14.1
The Medium Through Which Sound Waves Travel

Supplies:
- Plastic wrap
- Scissors
- Tape
- Candle (It needs to either be in a candle holder or be able to stand up securely on its own.)
- Match
- Plastic 1-liter or 2-liter bottle (the kind soda comes in)
- Large pot
- Wooden spoon
- Large bowl
- Rice

Introduction - All waves must travel through some kind of medium.  These two experiments demonstrate what the medium is for sound waves.

Procedure for Experiment #1:

A.  Cut away the base of the plastic bottle, so that there is a big hole at the bottom.
B.  Use the plastic wrap to cover the hole that was created when you cut away the bottle's base.  You want to do this in such a way as to stretch the plastic wrap nice and tight, like you are making a drum.  To do this, use the tape to secure the plastic wrap on one side of the bottle and then stretch the plastic wrap over the hole tightly.  This will deform the bottle.  That's okay.  Once you have stretched the plastic, secure it on the other side.  Continue to do this several times, using tape to hold the plastic wrap so that it is stretched tightly across the hole.
C.  You should now have a makeshift drum on at the bottom of the bottle.  If you flick it with your finger, you should hear a dull thump.  Hold the bottle so that the opening from which you drink is pointed towards your ear.  Flick the plastic wrap again and hear the sound as it comes through the bottle.
D.  Now light the candle.  Hold the bottle so that the opening from which you drink is pointed right at the flame.  Try to hold the opening as close to the flame as you can without melting it or catching it on fire!  See the illustration on the next page.

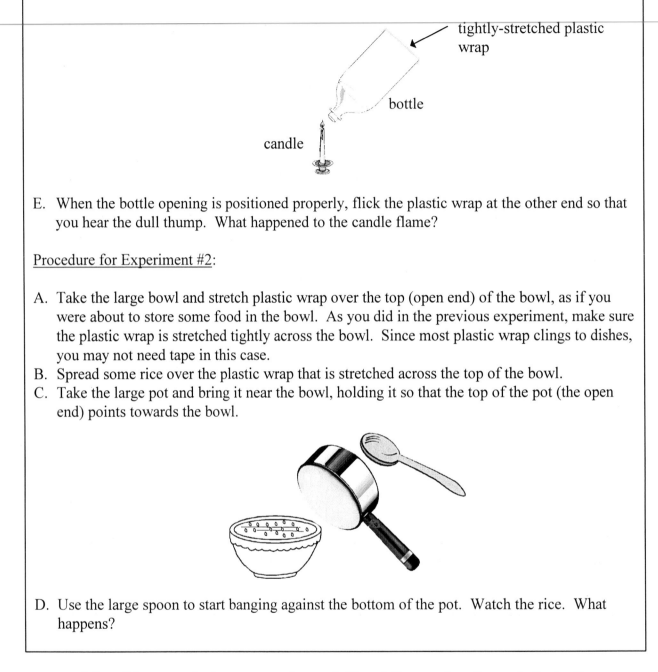

tightly-stretched plastic wrap

bottle

candle

E.  When the bottle opening is positioned properly, flick the plastic wrap at the other end so that you hear the dull thump.  What happened to the candle flame?

Procedure for Experiment #2:

A.  Take the large bowl and stretch plastic wrap over the top (open end) of the bowl, as if you were about to store some food in the bowl.  As you did in the previous experiment, make sure the plastic wrap is stretched tightly across the bowl.  Since most plastic wrap clings to dishes, you may not need tape in this case.
B.  Spread some rice over the plastic wrap that is stretched across the top of the bowl.
C.  Take the large pot and bring it near the bowl, holding it so that the top of the pot (the open end) points towards the bowl.

D.  Use the large spoon to start banging against the bottom of the pot.  Watch the rice.  What happens?

What did you see in the two experiments?  Hopefully, you "saw" sound.  In the first experiment, the sound that traveled through the bottle once you flicked the plastic wrap actually blew out the candle.  Why?  The medium through which sound travels is air!  Sound, therefore, causes air to oscillate when it travels.  As a result, the sound that came out of the bottle caused the air to oscillate enough so that the candle's flame actually blew out.  In the second experiment, the sound that you made when you hit the pan with the spoon caused the air to oscillate.  When that oscillating air hit the tightly-stretched plastic wrap, it caused the plastic wrap to start vibrating.  You saw the vibration because the rice grains on the plastic wrap began to bounce up and down.

The bowl in the second experiment is actually a pretty good illustration of the sound-sensing mechanism in your ears.  Each of your ears has a thin layer of tissue (called the "tympanic membrane") that is tightly stretched across the ear canal.  This structure is also called the "ear drum."  When the waves in air caused by sound enter your ear, they cause the tympanic membrane to start vibrating.  Those vibrations are then transmitted to your brain, and your brain interprets them as sound.

Think for a moment about the results of the first experiment and then answer this question:  Is sound a transverse or longitudinal wave?  Which do you think?  You know which way the sound traveled in the first experiment.  It traveled from one end of the bottle to the other, and then straight to the candle.  Do you think the air was oscillating parallel or perpendicular to the velocity of the wave?  Since the candle blew out, the air was most likely oscillating parallel to the motion.  Had the air been oscillating perpendicular to the motion, the flame might have flickered, but it probably would not have gone out.  The experiment, therefore, gives us this important fact to remember:

**Sound is a longitudinal wave that travels through air**.

In other words, sound causes the air itself to oscillate, and it oscillates parallel to the motion of the wave.  Without air (or some other medium), there can be no sound because there would be nothing for the wave to oscillate.

## The Speed of Sound

Now that you know a little bit about the nature of sound, I want you to understand how the properties of a sound wave affect the way you hear that sound.  Equation (14.1) and Figure 14.2 tell us there are basically four characteristics that describe a wave: speed, wavelength, frequency, and amplitude.  Perform the following experiment to learn about the first characteristic of sound waves: their speed.

**EXPERIMENT 14.2**
The Speed of Sound

Supplies:
- Two medium-sized rocks
- A person to help you
- A stopwatch
- A 250-meter stretch of sidewalk, pavement, gravel road, or lawn that is relatively straight
- A tape measure, meterstick, or yardstick

Introduction - Sound waves travel through air with a certain speed.  This experiment will allow you to estimate that speed.

Procedure:

A. Have your helper hold the meterstick and stand right next to you.
B. Walk 10 paces down the sidewalk. Try to make each step cover the same distance as the previous ones.
C. When you are done, have your helper measure the distance between where you started and where you ended up 10 paces later.
D. Repeat steps (B) and (C) twice more.
E. Average the three distances, then divide that average by 10. The result is the average distance in one pace.
F. Give your helper the two rocks and keep the stopwatch for yourself. Start at one end of the sidewalk and, once again, have your helper stand right next to you.
G. Walk the same kind of paces that you walked before until you have counted off enough paces to equal 250 meters. This tells you that you and your helper are roughly 250 meters apart.
H. Have your friend bang the two rocks together. He should hold the rocks so that it is easy for you to see when they hit each other. Notice that you hear the sound of them hitting each other a moment after you see them touch. That's because you are using light to see the rocks. Light travels so quickly that, at these kinds of distances, you can assume you see the rocks touch at the very instance they actually do touch. Sound, however travels much more slowly than light. As a result, you do not hear them bang together until after you actually see them bang together.
I. Now that you have seen the effect, it is time to measure how long it takes for the sound to travel from your helper to you. Once again, have your helper bang the rocks together. This time, however, start the stopwatch the moment you SEE the rocks touch each other, and stop the watch the moment you HEAR the bang. The stopwatch should indicate that less than a second has passed. Do this 10 times and average the result.
J. If you take 250 meters and divide it by the average of the times you measured, the result will be the speed of sound.

What speed did you get in the experiment? The answer may not be very accurate. After all, the distance you measured was not very precise. Also, there is a lot of experimental error involved in starting and stopping a stopwatch over such a short time interval. Even though you tried to average out that error by making the measurement 10 times and averaging the result, you can't get rid of the error. Nevertheless, you might have come close to the correct answer.

What is the correct answer? Well, it depends on the temperature. The speed of sound in air is given by the following equation:

$$v = (331.5 + 0.60 \cdot T) \ \frac{m}{sec} \tag{14.2}$$

In this equation, "v" stands for the speed of sound, while "T" stands for the temperature. In order for this equation to work, the temperature used must be in units of Celsius. To determine the correct measurement for Experiment 14.2, then, you would need to know the outside temperature in degrees Celsius. Then you could plug the temperature into the equation (the way I do it in the example below) and determine what the correct answer should be.

---

### EXAMPLE 14.2

**If the temperature is 68 °F (20 °C), what is the speed of sound?**

In order for Equation (14.2) to work, the temperature must be in Celsius. That's what's given in parentheses:

$$v = (331.5 + 0.60 \cdot 20) \ \frac{m}{sec}$$

$$v = 343.5 \ \frac{m}{sec}$$

Notice that I did not put the units for "T" into the equation. I am supposed to do that with *most* equations. With this equation, however, it is *set up* assuming that the temperature will be in Celsius. As a result, there is no need to include the unit in the equation, because the units have been worked out already. This is one of the *few* equations in which you need not carry the units through. You must remember, however, that the equation *requires* the temperature to be in Celsius. The answer, then, is 343.5 m/sec.

---

In your experiment, you probably should have gotten an answer between 290 and 400 m/sec. The experiment you performed was not all that accurate, however, so do not be concerned about the actual answer you got. One of the more important things to draw from the experiment is the experience of seeing the *cause* of a sound before hearing the *sound itself.*

The technique you used in Experiment 14.2 can also be used when watching a thunderstorm. If you've ever watched lightning before, you probably have experienced seeing a flash of lightning and a few moments later hearing the thunderclap. Remember from our discussion of lightning back in Module #8 that thunder and lightning are actually formed at the same time. When the return stroke of charge from the ground leaps to the cumulonimbus cloud in the storm, the air is heated very quickly. That causes the air to expand quickly. This causes a wave which, when it hits your ear, gets translated in the "boom" of thunder.

If lightning and thunder are created at the same time, the delay that you experience between seeing a lightning flash and hearing the thunder is due to the time it takes sound to travel to your ears. Remember, light travels very quickly. The speed of light is so great that the time it takes for light to travel even several miles is simply too small to measure. Thus, as far as we are concerned, we can assume that we see a lightning bolt essentially the same instant that it is formed.  Sound travels much more slowly, however.  As a result, we often do not hear the sound of the lightning being formed until much later.  Study the following example to see what I mean.

---

**EXAMPLE 14.3**

**A physicist is watching a thunderstorm.  She sees a flash of lightning and then hears a thunderclap 1 second later.  If the air temperature is a cool 15° C,  how far away from the physicist was the lightning formed?**

Because light travels so quickly, we can assume that the lightning was formed at the instant in which the physicist sees it.  The time delay that the physicist observes, then, is simply the time it took for the sound to travel from the point at which the lightning was created to the physicist. First, we need to know the speed of sound.  This can be determined by Equation (14.2):

$$v = (331.5 + 0.60 \cdot T) \; \frac{m}{sec}$$

$$v = (331.5 + 0.60 \cdot 15) \frac{m}{sec} = 340.5 \; \frac{m}{sec}$$

Now that we know the speed, we can determine the distance that the sound traveled.  Remember from Module #9 that speed is defined by Equation (9.1):

$$speed = \frac{distance}{time} \tag{9.1}$$

We can use algebra to re-arrange this equation:

$$distance = (speed) \times (time) \tag{14.3}$$

If you don't know algebra yet, don't worry.  Just treat this as a new equation: Equation (14.3).  This is an equation with which, given the speed and time, we can calculate the distance.  That's what we have in this problem.  We know the speed of sound, and we know the time it took for the sound to travel to the physicist.  Thus, we can calculate the distance it traveled:

$$distance = (speed) \times (time)$$

$$distance = (340.5 \; \frac{m}{sec}) \times (1 \; sec) = 340.5 \, m$$

The lightning, therefore, was formed <u>340.5 m</u> from the position of the physicist.

Although the way I solved the example is the most accurate way to determine how far away a lightning strike is, there is an easy method that gives relatively good results as well. As you learned in Module #8, thunderstorms usually are the result of cold fronts moving in under warm fronts. Thunderstorms, therefore, usually result in cooler temperatures. A "good guess" for the temperature in a thunderstorm is about 16 $^\circ$C. At that temperature, sound travels at about 341 meters per second. Well, 341 meters is about 1/5 of a mile. In other words, during a thunderstorm, you can estimate the speed of sound to be 1/5 of a mile per second. As a result, for every second of delay between the lightning strike and the thunder, the lightning strike was about 1/5 of a mile away. If you count 2 seconds between a lightning flash and the resulting thunder, the lightning struck about 2/5 of a mile away. Although I will *not* allow you to use this rule of thumb to answer problems, you can use it when you are watching lightning strikes!

---

**ON YOUR OWN**

14.3  What is the speed of sound in air when the temperature is 28 $^\circ$C?

14.4  During a thunderstorm, the temperature is 18 $^\circ$C. If you see a lightning flash and hear the thunder 1.5 seconds later, how far away did the lightning actually strike?

---

The Speed of Sound in Other Substances

Although we usually think of sound traveling through air, it is important to realize that sound can travel through any substance in which it can oscillate in order to make waves. When we hear a sound, it is usually the result of waves traveling through the air. That's not always the case, however. Do you remember Experiment 6.1? In that experiment, you listened to sound that traveled through a string. You did that experiment to illustrate the fact that the way in which sound waves travel through a substance can be used to determine the properties of that substance. In that module, I discussed how scientists have learned a great deal about the interior structure of the earth just by observing how waves travel through the earth.

Since Experiment 6.1 demonstrated to you that sound travels differently in different substances, it shouldn't surprise you that the speed of sound varies from substance to substance. Table 14.1 lists a few substances and the approximate speed of sound in each.

**TABLE 14.1**
The Speed of Sound in Certain Substances

| Substance | Speed of Sound | Substance | Speed of Sound |
|---|---|---|---|
| Air (25 $^\circ$C) | 346  m/sec | Steel | 5029  m/sec |
| Alcohol | 1186 m/sec | Aluminum | 5093  m/sec |
| Freshwater | 1435  m/sec | Iron | 5128  m/sec |
| Wood (oak) | 3848  m/sec | Glass | 5503  m/sec |

Do you notice a trend in the data?  Air is a gas, while alcohol and freshwater are liquids.  The rest of the substances in the table are solids.  Notice that the speed of sound in the liquids is about 3 times the speed of sound in air.  In addition, the speed of sound in the solids is somewhere between 2 and 5 times higher than the speed of sound in the liquids.  Thus, sound travels faster in liquids than it does in gases, and it travels faster in solids than it does in liquids.

What's the main difference between solids, liquids, and gases?  In Module #3, you learned that the main difference between the three phases of matter is the energy of motion of the molecules or atoms that make up a substance.  When the molecules or atoms do not move much, they are close together and the result is a solid.  When the molecules or atoms move a lot, they are far apart and the result is a gas.  Liquids are somewhere in between.  In general, then, sound tends to travel faster in substances whose atoms or molecules are closer together.  There are exceptions to this general rule, but those exceptions are due to the properties of the individual substance involved.

If you think about it, this should make sense.  After all, sound is a wave.  It must cause the medium through which it moves to oscillate.  If the atoms or molecules of a medium are close to one another, they can transmit this wave very effectively.  If they are far apart, it is harder for them to transmit the wave.  Thus, molecules or atoms that are close to one another can transmit a sound wave faster than can molecules which are far apart from each other.

If an object travels in a medium faster than the speed of sound, we say that the object is traveling at **supersonic** speeds.

Supersonic speed - Any speed that is faster than the speed of sound in the substance of interest

Some jets routinely travel through the air faster than sound can.  The Concorde jet, for example, travels across the Atlantic ocean at 2250 km/hour (625 m/sec).  In aviation, they often measure a jet's speed in terms of the speed of sound.  This speed unit is known as the **Mach** (mahk).  When a jet travels at the speed of sound in air, it is said to be traveling at Mach 1.  If a jet is traveling at 1.5 times the speed of sound, it is said to be traveling at Mach 1.5.  The Concorde's top speed, for example, is Mach 2.2, which means that it can travel 2.2 times faster than the speed of sound.  The NASA space shuttle exceeds Mach 10 after dropping out of orbit and when it is coming in for a landing!

An interesting phenomenon known as a **sonic boom** is generated when an object travels through air faster than the speed of sound.

Sonic boom - The sound produced as a result of aircraft traveling at or above Mach 1

This phenomenon is illustrated in Figure 14.4.

**FIGURE 14.4**
A Jet Forming A Sonic Boom

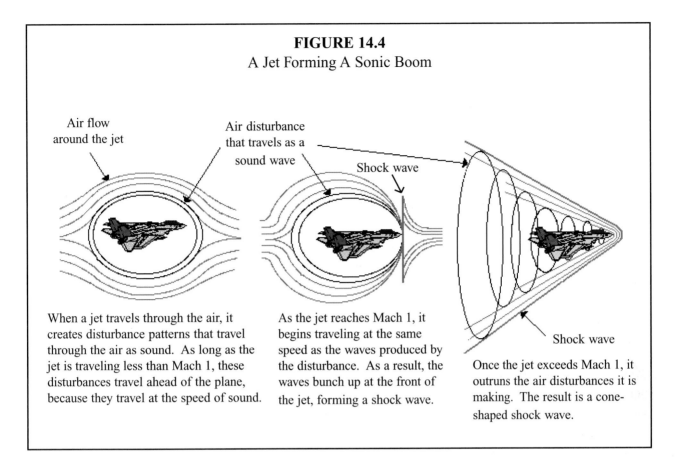

Air flow
around the jet

Air disturbance
that travels as a
sound wave

Shock wave

Shock wave

When a jet travels through the air, it creates disturbance patterns that travel through the air as sound. As long as the jet is traveling less than Mach 1, these disturbances travel ahead of the plane, because they travel at the speed of sound.

As the jet reaches Mach 1, it begins traveling at the same speed as the waves produced by the disturbance. As a result, the waves bunch up at the front of the jet, forming a shock wave.

Once the jet exceeds Mach 1, it outruns the air disturbances it is making. The result is a cone-shaped shock wave.

The physics behind a sonic boom is actually pretty simple. As a jet travels, it disturbs the air through which it passes. This creates waves in the air much like dropping a stone in water creates waves in the water. Waves in the air are sound waves. Thus, the waves created by the disturbance travel at the speed of sound. As long as the jet travels slower than the sound waves it produces (in other words, less than Mach 1), the sound waves travel ahead of the jet and everything is fine. When the jet reaches Mach 1, however, it moves right along with the sound waves it produces. This causes the crests of the waves to "pile up," making a huge wave called a shock wave. Like a thunderclap, this wave of air creates a very loud boom - a sonic boom. When the jet exceeds Mach 1, it actually outruns the sound waves it produces. This causes the waves to pile up at the edge of a cone. When that cone reaches your ears, you hear the sonic boom.

Sonic booms can be destructive to human ears, but they can also be destructive to buildings, etc. After all, remember that sound is a wave of air. When the huge wave associated with a sonic boom hits a building, it can shake the building rather dramatically. As a result, jets usually travel at or above Mach 1 only in areas of little or no population. The Concorde, for example, does not reach speeds of Mach 1 or higher until it is over the Atlantic Ocean.

**ON YOUR OWN**

14.5  Remember from Module #9 that the outer core of the earth is liquid but the inner core is solid.  If a geophysicist is studying how sound waves travel through the core, would he expect the sound waves to travel faster in the inner core or the outer core?

14.6  A jet is traveling at Mach 1.8 when the temperature of the surrounding air is 0 °C.  What is its speed in m/sec?

## Sound Wavelength and Frequency

You now know a lot about the speed of sound, so it is time to move on to the other characteristics of a wave.  In this section, I want to concentrate on how the wavelength and frequency of a sound wave affect what we hear as sound.  As you learned already, wavelength and frequency are inversely proportional to each other.  When wavelength is large, frequency is small, and vice-versa.  Thus, we often think of wavelength and frequency together.  Perform the following experiment to see how the wavelength of a sound wave affects how you hear the sound.

**EXPERIMENT 14.3**
Wavelength and Sound

Supplies:

- Water
- Glass or plastic bottle (A glass bottle is best, and 2-liter is the ideal size.  It must have a narrow neck.  A jar will not work.)

Introduction - The wavelength of sound waves has a dramatic effect on how we hear the sound.  This experiment demonstrates the effect.

Procedure:

A. Empty the bottle and rinse it out with water.
B. Hold the bottle up to your mouth so that the top edge of the bottle opening just touches your bottom lip.
C. Pursing your lips, blow across the top of the bottle.  It may take some practice, but you will eventually produce a sound that sounds like it is coming from a horn.  Blow a few times to get an idea of what that sound sounds like.
D. Fill the bottle 3/4 full of water and repeat steps (B) and (C).  Blow a few times to get a good idea of what the sound sounds like.  Write in your laboratory notebook how this sound differed from the first one that you made.

## The Volume of Sound

So far, I have discussed the speed, wavelength, and frequency of sound. It is now time to discuss the last aspect of a wave and see how it affects sound. In Figure 14.2, I noted that all waves have amplitude. How does the amplitude of a sound wave affect the sound you hear? Once again, this is best demonstrated by experiment.

---

### EXPERIMENT 14.5
The Amplitude of a Sound Wave

Supplies:

- If you have access to a stringed instrument such as a violin, guitar, cello, or banjo, that's all you need for this experiment. If you do not have access to such an instrument, you will need a rubber band and a plastic tub like the kind that margarine or whipped cream comes in.

Introduction - The amplitude of a wave tells you how big the wave is. For sound waves, the amplitude has a very easy to detect effect on the nature of the sound produced.

Procedure:

A. If you do not have a stringed instrument, make a simple one by stretching the rubber band all of the way around the plastic tub. Do this so that the rubber band stretches tightly across the open end of the tub as well as the bottom end of the tub. If you already have an instrument, skip to the next step.
B. Hold the instrument so that you can watch the strings (or rubber band) when you pluck them.
C. Pluck a string only slightly. Watch how the string vibrates and listen to the sound it produces.
D. Using the same string each time, pluck the string harder and harder. Do not pluck the string so hard that it will break, however! Each time you pluck harder, listen to how the sound changes and observe how the string vibrates.

---

What did you see and hear in the experiment? When you plucked the string only slightly, the string vibrated only slightly and the sound produced was not very loud. As you plucked the string harder, however, the string vibrated a lot more. In addition, the sound was louder. You should not have noticed any change in pitch between when the string was plucked hard or soft. You should only have noticed a change in volume. What does this tell you? When the string vibrates more vigorously, it pushes air farther than when it vibrates only slightly. Thus, the sound waves produced by a vigorously vibrating string have a larger amplitude than the sound waves produced by a string that vibrates only slightly. This tells us:

**The amplitude of a sound wave governs how loud the sound is.**

Large-amplitude sound waves are loud, small-amplitude sound waves are relatively quiet.

Remember when I discussed sonic booms earlier? A sonic boom is loud because when the sound waves produced by a supersonic jet begin to bunch up, their amplitudes add together. As a result, the amplitude of the sound wave that comes from a supersonic jet is huge. The same can be said for a thunderclap. The reason a thunderclap is so loud stems from the fact that the heat produced in a lightning strike is so large that the amplitude of the wave produced is large.

When you turn the volume up on your television, radio, or stereo, you are simply causing the device to produce sound waves of larger and larger amplitude. The larger the amplitude of the sound waves, the louder the sound is. Extremely loud sounds can damage your hearing because of the amplitude of the waves. Remember, your ear detects sound waves with the tympanic membrane. This is a tightly-stretched sheet of tissue in your ear. When sound waves hit your ear, the tympanic membrane begins to vibrate. The membrane will vibrate with the same frequency as the wave that hits it. Also, the larger the amplitude of the wave, the more violently the tympanic membrane will vibrate. If the membrane vibrates too violently, it can tear or even break completely. The result is severely damaged hearing or total deafness!

Now although it is possible to harm or destroy your hearing, your ears have a remarkable range when it comes to the loudness that they can withstand. They have a remarkable range because the tympanic membrane does not respond linearly with increasing sound wave amplitude. What I mean is that when the amplitude of a sound wave doubles, the violence with which the tympanic membrane vibrates does not double. It is specially designed to dampen the amplitude of the sound waves that touch it. As a result, a sound wave with ten times more amplitude does not sound ten times louder.

The excellent design of the human ear required scientists to develop a special scale to measure the loudness of a sound. We call this scale the **bel** scale, and it is named in honor of Alexander Graham Bell, the inventor of the telephone. The bel scale measures the **intensity** of a sound wave, which is essentially the amplitude squared. Thus, intensity is really just another way of expressing wave amplitude. In the bel scale, an increase in one bel corresponds to a tenfold increase in sound wave intensity. The threshold of human hearing is defined as 0 bels, and physical damage occurs in the ear when sounds reach the level of 13 bels.

You have probably never heard of bels before, but you have probably heard of **decibels**. The prefix "deci" means one tenth. Thus, a decibel is simply one tenth of a bel. Since the bel is a relatively large unit for sound, physicists tend to talk about decibels rather than bels. That's what I will do from now on. In terms of decibels, then, the threshold of human hearing is 0 decibels, and physical damage to the ears is caused when sound reaches a loudness of 130 decibels. Table 14.2 lists some common sounds and their loudness in decibels.

**TABLE 14.2**
The Loudness of Some Common Sounds

| Sound | Decibels | Sound | Decibels |
|---|---|---|---|
| Soft Whisper | 20 | Gasoline-Powered Mower | 95 |
| Normal Conversation | 40 | Typical Rock Concert | 115 |
| Busy Traffic | 70 | Physical Pain To Ears | 120 |
| Pneumatic Drill | 80 | Physical Damage to Ears | 130 |

Now remember, an increase of 1 bel (10 decibels) results in a sound wave intensity increase of a factor of ten. Thus, the sound waves that come from a soft whisper have 100 times (10 x 10) the intensity of the sound waves at the threshold of human hearing.

If you think about that for a moment, you should get a really good appreciation for how well our ears are designed! Since the threshold of human hearing is 0 decibels, and since physical damage occurs at 130 decibels, that tells us the human ear has a range of 13 bels. Each increase of one bel (10 decibels) is a factor of ten increase in the intensity of the sound waves. Thus, the human ear can detect sound waves as much as 10,000,000,000,000 times its threshold before it begins to be damaged. That is an *incredible* range! Human science cannot come up with any piece of equipment that can detect such a huge range of sounds! We can certainly come up with equipment that detects sound waves of lower intensity than human ears can detect, but those pieces of equipment will be destroyed by sound waves that we wouldn't even consider loud!

So no piece of human technology can match the human ear in terms of the range of sounds it is able to hear. Isn't that amazing? What does that tell you about the human ear? It tells you that there is no way such a marvelous wave detector could exist by chance! The range of sounds over which the human ear can hear is just one of the millions of examples that tell us this world and the life that inhabits it were *created*.

---

**EXAMPLE 14.4**

**The sound from a typical vacuum cleaner is about 60 decibels, while the sound of a rifle a meter away is about 140 decibels. How many times larger is the intensity of the waves coming from the rifle as compared to those coming from the vacuum cleaner?**

Remember, the bel scale is set up so that every increase in 1 bel is the same as a tenfold increase in the intensity of the sound wave. The first thing we have to do, then, is convert decibels back into bels. That's easy:

$$\frac{60 \text{ decibels}}{1} \times \frac{1 \text{ bel}}{10 \text{ decibels}} = 6 \text{ bels}$$

$$\frac{140 \ \cancel{\text{decibels}}}{1} \times \frac{1 \ \text{bel}}{10 \ \cancel{\text{decibels}}} = 14 \ \text{bels}$$

The rifle, then, is 8 bels louder than the vacuum cleaner. Since each bel unit represents a 10-fold increase in sound wave intensity, the total increase is calculated by taking 10 and multiplying it by itself 8 times. This means the intensity of the rifle's sound waves is 10 x 10 x 10 x 10 x 10 x 10 x 10 x 10 = <u>100,000,000 times larger</u> than the intensity of the vacuum cleaner sound waves.

---

**ON YOUR OWN**

14.10  The sound from a typical power saw has a loudness of 110 decibels.  How many times larger is the intensity of the sound waves from a power saw as compared to those of normal conversation (40 decibels)?

---

<u>Uses of Sound Waves</u>

Sound waves are useful to us in ways other than hearing.  Remember, we can't hear ultrasonic or infrasonic sound waves, but they are sound waves nevertheless.  Because of the way sound waves travel, we can use them to "see" things we otherwise cannot see.  As you already have learned, we can use sound waves to understand what the inside of the earth looks like, even though we have never seen it.  Typically, the sound waves used for this purpose are infrasonic, so they have frequencies lower than 20 Hz.

When sound waves encounter an obstacle, a portion of the wave travels through the obstacle, but another portion is reflected backwards.  The fraction of the wave reflected depends on the type of obstacle encountered.  One way you can experience the phenomenon of reflected waves is to stand at the edge of a canyon and yell.  You will hear an echo that results from the sound waves you produced reflecting off of the canyon walls and coming back to your ears again.

It turns out that whenever you talk in your house, a portion of the sound waves that you form is reflected off the walls and back into your ears.  You do not hear an echo, however.  Why?  Well, the walls in your home are simply too close.  Since sound travels relatively quickly, it hits the walls and bounces back to your ears so fast that your brain cannot tell the sound wave leaving your mouth from the one reflected off of the walls.  If you go to a canyon, however, the sound waves bounce back to your ears from a much greater distance.  As a result, your brain can distinguish between the original wave and the reflected one.

In general, a sonic wave must take about 0.1 seconds to reflect off of an obstacle and travel back to your ears for your brain to perceive it as an echo.  Based on the average speed of sound in air, then, you need to be about 34 meters away from an obstacle in order for you to hear an echo as a result of sound waves bouncing off of the obstacle.  That's why you only hear echoes in settings like canyons or long, empty hallways.

One application that uses reflected sound waves is the ultrasonic ruler. This device is a small box that emits ultrasonic waves. The circuitry in the device measures the temperature of the air and determines the speed of the waves. When the waves hit a wall or other obstruction, part of the wave is transmitted through the obstruction, and part of the wave is reflected back. That part which is reflected back is detected by the ultrasonic ruler, and the time it took to travel to the obstruction and back is measured by the circuitry. The ultrasonic ruler then uses the speed of the sound waves and the time it measured to calculate the distance from the device to the obstruction. Thus, a person simply holds the device and points it to a wall, and the device determines the distance to that wall with a precision of better than 0.5 cm.

A more popular application of ultrasonic waves is their use as a medical imaging tool. When a sound wave hits an obstruction, part of the wave is reflected, and part is transmitted. The reflected and transmitted waves are the same frequency, but they each have lower amplitudes than the original wave. If ultrasonic waves are directed at a human body, a portion of the waves get transmitted into the body. As those waves travel through the body, they will continue to travel until they hit another obstruction. At that point, a portion of the waves will be reflected, and a portion will be transmitted. If wave sensors are tuned to detect that portion of the waves that were transmitted through the body but reflected back by the first obstruction encountered in the body, the detectors can use the same principles that the ultrasonic ruler uses to determine the distance to the obstruction within the body.

If several such waves are directed across a large area in the human body, this procedure can determine the general shape of the obstruction within the body. The most popular application of this is used for pregnant mothers. Using this technique, the ultrasonic imager can produce the general shape of a fetus in the mother's body. An example of such an image is shown in Figure 14.6.

**FIGURE 14.6**
An Ultrasonic Image of a Human Fetus

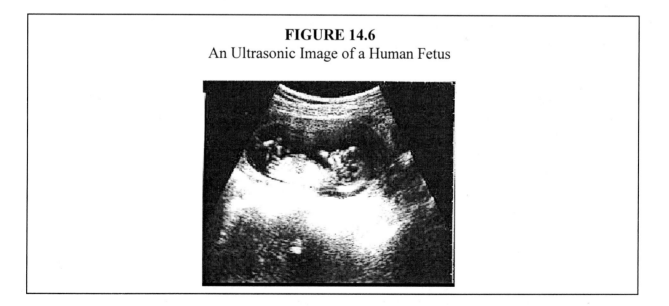

Another well-known application of this same basic technique is **sonar**. In sonar, ultrasonic waves are emitted, and sensors detect the reflected portions of those waves. The sensors end up creating an image of any obstruction in their path, much like the image shown in Figure 14.6. Although sonar is best known as the way a submarine tracks ships and other submarines, the most efficient sonar known to humankind exists in the bat.

Since bats tend to feed at night, they need to be able to "see" things in the dark. The way they do it is through a sonar system that produces images like that of the sonar in a submarine. The difference between a submarine's sonar and a bat's sonar, however, is that the bat's sonar provides significantly more information than a submarine's sonar. First of all, rather than just emitting one or a few frequencies of ultrasonic waves, bat sonar produces a wide range of ultrasonic frequencies. Because materials react differently to different frequencies of sound waves, this allows the bat to use the amplitude of the reflected waves to determine the nature of the obstacle that the ultrasonic waves reflected from. A bat's sonar is so precise in this regard that it can distinguish an insect from a stick or leaf by simply analyzing the amplitudes of the reflected sound waves for each frequency!

In addition, the bat can process the information given by its sonar system much more quickly than the fastest computer man can create. This allows it to identify obstacles and insects so quickly that it can fly around without running into anything and still detect, target, and eat up to five insects each second! All of this is done in a sonar system that has a mass of less than 1 gram! This makes the bat's sonar system millions of times more efficient than the best sonar human science can produce, and at the same time, it gives the bat a *lot* more information!

Although the bat's sonar system is the most efficient known to humankind, it is not the only natural sonar system. Porpoises use sonar to navigate as well because eyesight is limited underwater. Such technological marvels that sprinkle nature scream loudly and clearly that nature is not the result of chance, it is the result of design!

## ANSWERS TO THE ON YOUR OWN PROBLEMS

14.1  Wavelength and frequency are inversely proportional to one another.  Thus, if wavelength is increased, <u>frequency is decreased</u>.

14.2  When the question asks how many waves will hit you every second, it is asking for the frequency of the waves.  We have speed (0.5 m/sec) and wavelength (0.25 m), so we just need to use Equation (14.1):

$$f = \frac{v}{\lambda}$$

$$f = \frac{0.5 \ \frac{\cancel{m}}{sec}}{0.25 \ \cancel{m}} = 2 \ \frac{1}{sec}$$

This tells us that <u>2 waves will hit you every second</u>.

14.3  This is a simple application of Equation 14.2.  The temperature is already in degrees Celsius, so we are ready:

$$v = (331.5 + 0.60 \cdot T) \ \frac{m}{sec}$$

$$v = (331.5 + 0.60 \cdot 28) \frac{m}{sec} = \underline{348.3 \ \frac{m}{sec}}$$

14.4  To determine how far away the lightning struck, we will assume that the light from the lightning bolt reaches the physicist's eyes pretty much instantaneously.  Thus, the time delay between seeing the lightning and hearing the thunder tells us the distance.  First, however, we need to determine how quickly the sound travels:

$$v = (331.5 + 0.60 \cdot T) \ \frac{m}{sec}$$

$$v = (331.5 + 0.60 \cdot 18) \frac{m}{sec} = 342.3 \ \frac{m}{sec}$$

Now that we know the speed of sound in this thunderstorm, we can determine the distance the sound traveled:

$$distance = (speed) \times (time)$$

$$distance = (342.3 \ \frac{m}{\cancel{sec}}) \times (1.5 \ \cancel{sec}) = \underline{513.45 \, m}$$

14.5  Sound waves travel faster in solids than they do in liquids.  Thus, the sound waves will travel faster in the inner core than the outer core.

14.6  To determine the speed of the jet, we first have to determine the speed of sound.  After all, Mach 1.8 means 1.8 times the speed of sound.  Thus, we need to know the speed of sound in order to determine the speed of the jet.

$$v = (331.5 + 0.60 \cdot T)\ \frac{m}{sec}$$

$$v = (331.5 + 0.60 \cdot 0)\ \frac{m}{sec} = 331.5\ \frac{m}{sec}$$

Since sound travels at 331.5 m/sec, Mach 1.8 is 1.8 x (331.5 m/sec) = 596.7 m/sec.

14.7  A high pitch means a high frequency.  Waves with high frequency have short wavelengths.  Thus, the shorter the wind instrument, the higher the pitch.  Therefore, the piccolo produces the notes with the highest pitches.

14.8  Ultrasonic waves have *higher (larger) frequencies* than sonic waves.  This means they have smaller wavelengths.

14.9  As you run towards the car, you will encounter the crests of the waves faster than if you were standing still.  This means that the waves will seem to have a higher frequency when you run towards the car.  Thus, the horn's pitch will sound higher than its true pitch.  There is another way to think about this question.  Remember from Module #9 that velocity is relative.  Whether you approach the car or the car approaches you, you are both approaching each other.  Thus, the physics is the same either way.

14.10  The bel scale states that every bel unit corresponds to a factor of ten in the intensity of the sound waves.  Thus, we need to determine how many bel units the sound of a power saw is, as compared to the sound of normal conversation:

$$\frac{40\ \text{decibels}}{1} \times \frac{1\ \text{bel}}{10\ \text{decibels}} = 4\ \text{bels}$$

$$\frac{110\ \text{decibels}}{1} \times \frac{1\ \text{bel}}{10\ \text{decibels}} = 11\ \text{bels}$$

Since the power saw is 7 bels louder than normal conversation, the increase in sound wave intensity is 7 factors of ten higher.  Thus, the power saw has sound waves with intensities that are 10 x 10 x 10 x 10 x 10 x 10 x 10 = 10,000,000 times larger than the intensities of sound waves from normal conversation.

**STUDY GUIDE FOR MODULE #14**

1. Define the following terms:

a. Transverse wave
b. Longitudinal wave
c. Supersonic speed
d. Sonic boom
e. Pitch

2. In designing a car's horn, the engineers test the sound of the horn and decide that its pitch is too low. To adjust the horn, should the engineers change the electronics so as to produce sound waves with longer or shorter wavelengths?

3. A sound wave is traveling through air with a temperature of 30 °C. What is the speed of the sound wave?

4. If the sound wave in problem #3 has a wavelength of 0.5 meters, what is its frequency?

5. A sound wave has a speed of 345 m/sec and a wavelength of 500 meters. Is this wave infrasonic, sonic, or ultrasonic?

6. A physicist takes an alarm clock and puts it in an airtight chamber. When the chamber is sealed but still full of air, the physicist is able to hear the alarm despite the fact that he is outside of the chamber. If the physicist then uses a vacuum pump to evacuate essentially all of the air out of the chamber, will the physicist still be able to hear the alarm? Why or why not?

7. Are sound waves transverse waves or longitudinal waves?

8. You are watching the lightning from a thunderstorm. You suddenly see a flash of lightning, and 2.3 seconds later you hear the thunder. How far away from you did the lightning strike? (The temperature at the time is 13 °C).

9. Sound waves are traveling through the air and suddenly run into a wall. As the sound waves travel through the wall, do they travel faster, slower, or at the same speed as when they were traveling in the air?

10. In the situation described above, what happens to the amplitude of the wave? Is the amplitude of the wave smaller, larger, or the same as the amplitude before the wave hit the wall?

11. A jet aircraft is traveling at Mach 2.5 through air at 1 °C. What is the jet's speed in m/sec?

12. A jet travels through air at 464.1 m/sec. If the air has a temperature of 0 °C, at what Mach is the jet flying?

13. Why do jets travel at speeds of Mach 1 or higher only in sparsely-populated regions?

14. A guitar player is plucking on a string. If he takes his finger and pinches the string to the neck of the guitar so as to shorten the length of the string, will the pitch of the sound emitted increase, decrease, or stay the same?

15. You hear two musical notes. They both have the same pitch, but the first is louder than the second. If you compared the sound waves of each sound, what aspect(s) of the wave (wavelength, frequency, speed, and amplitude) would be the same? What aspect(s) would be different?

16. The horn on your neighbor's car is stuck, so it is constantly blaring. You watch your neighbor get into the car and drive away from you, heading towards the nearest place for automobile service. If you listen to the pitch of the horn from the time the neighbor gets into the car until the car goes out of sight, what will happen to the pitch of the horn?

17. You are riding your bicycle towards a stationary police car whose siren is blaring. Will the pitch of the siren sound lower, higher, or the same as it will sound when you actually stop your bicycle? (Assume the actual pitch of the siren stays constant.)

18. You are standing near an interstate highway trying to talk on a pay phone. You have raised your voice because of the noise, so the loudness of your voice is about 80 decibels. The sound of the traffic on the highway is about 100 decibels. How many times larger is the intensity of the traffic's sound waves as compared to those of your voice?

19. An amplifier can magnify the intensity of sound waves by a factor of 1,000. If a 30 decibel sound is fed into the amplifier, how many decibels will come out?

# Module #15: Light

## Introduction

In this module, you are going to study about light. This is obviously an important subject to study. Light is such a fundamental part of Creation that it is one of the first things mentioned in the Bible:

> In the beginning God created the heaven and the earth. And the earth was without
> form, and void; and darkness was upon the face of the deep. And the Spirit of
> God moved upon the face of the waters. And God said, Let there be light; and
> there was light. And God saw the light, that it was good... (Gen 1:1-4a)

Without light, life could not exist. The most common waves in Creation are light waves, so anyone who wants to learn about science needs to know a lot about the nature of light.

## The Dual Nature of Light

While sound is, in general, quite easy to understand, light is not. The first serious scientific investigations of light were done by none other than Sir Isaac Newton. In 1704, Newton published a book called *Optiks* in which he reported the conclusions of his research. In this book, Newton concluded that a beam of light behaved the same as a stream of particles which all moved in the same direction. This came to be known as the **particle theory** of light. According to this theory, light comes in little packets. We cannot see the individual packets of light, because they are simply too small to distinguish. Thus, just like a stream of water is really composed of individual water molecules, a beam of light is really composed of individual light particles.

The Dutch physicist Christian Huygens, who lived at the same time as Newton, disagreed with Newton's conclusions. He considered light to be a wave. He published his own work in which he could explain all of Newton's experiments assuming that light was a wave and not a particle. This was called the **wave theory** of light, and it was largely ignored at the time. In a few years, however, scientists began to do experiments that indicated light does, indeed, behave as a wave. As a result, by the early 1800's, most scientists believed in the wave theory of light.

Although most scientists were convinced of the fact that light was a wave, there was one fundamentally nagging question that scientists could not understand: what is the medium of a light wave? Remember, sound travels through air because it causes oscillations in the air. It travels through solids by causing oscillations in the atoms or molecules that make up the solid. What, however, do light waves oscillate? Scientists knew that light does not cause air to oscillate because light can travel through a vacuum. With nothing to oscillate, waves cannot travel. In the absence of air, then, sound does not exist. Thus, if you put an alarm clock in a vacuum, you will hear no sound coming from it. However, light travels through a vacuum with ease. What, then, does a light wave oscillate?

It took the brilliance of James Clerk Maxwell to answer this question. Hopefully, his answer will finally help you understand why electricity and magnetism are, in fact, one in the same thing. The experiments and conclusions of James Clerk Maxwell have led to the following generally accepted view of a light wave:

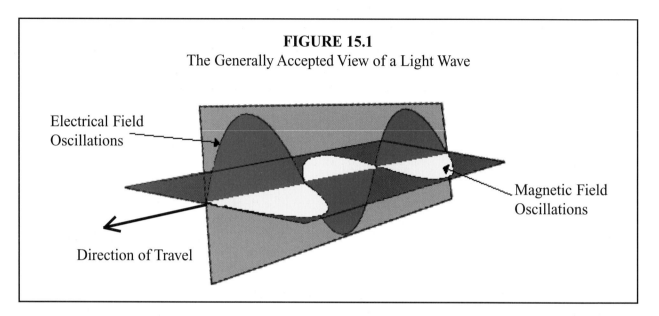

**FIGURE 15.1**
The Generally Accepted View of a Light Wave

Electrical Field
Oscillations

Magnetic Field
Oscillations

Direction of Travel

In this figure, you can see that a light wave is actually made up of two perpendicular waves. The first is an oscillating electrical field, and the second is an oscillating magnetic field. Both the magnetic field and the electrical field oscillate perpendicular to each other, as well as perpendicular to the direction the light travels.

Now do you see why electricity and magnetism are really the same thing? Both electricity and magnetism work together to produce light! A beam of light is actually a transverse wave in an electrical field and a transverse wave in a magnetic field. In order to make light, you must have both waves, and they must be perpendicular to one another. So wherever there is a magnetic field, there must be an accompanying electrical field. One cannot exist without the other. As a result, they are really different aspects of the same thing!

Notice that Maxwell's view of light allows us to understand why light can travel through a vacuum. The "stuff" that light causes to heave up and down is composed of an electrical field and a magnetic field. Thus, whether or not there are atoms or molecules around will not affect the ability of light to travel. The wave is simply composed of electrical and magnetic energy that oscillates back and forth. As a result, light waves are typically referred to as **electromagnetic waves**.

Electromagnetic wave - A transverse wave composed of an oscillating electrical field and a
magnetic field that oscillates perpendicular to the electrical field

Because light is a wave, Equation (14.1) applies just as well to light as it does to sound.

There should be something bothering you at this point. When I discussed the electromagnetic force, I said that it is governed by the exchange of small *particles* of light called photons. If scientists think of light as a wave, how can I say that particles of light exist? The answer to that question is that scientists today believe light has a **dual nature**. Light definitely has wave-like characteristics; thus, it can be thought of as a wave. However, light also has certain particle-like characteristics that *cannot* be explained if light is *only* a wave.

Because light has some properties that indicate it is a wave and other properties that indicate it is a particle, scientists have come up with the **quantum-mechanical theory of light**. In this theory, light is basically viewed as tiny packets of waves. Thus, unlike the wave we normally think of, light waves are not continuous. They are broken up in little packets, each of which is called a photon. Because of this dual nature, light can act as either a stream of photons (and be thought of as a particle) or a bunch of electromagnetic waves (and be thought of as a wave). Although this is a very confusing view of light, it is the best that scientists can do for right now.

To sum this all up, then, light is composed of little packets of waves. Each individual packet can be thought of as a particle, called a photon. At the same time, however, since each packet is composed of electromagnetic waves, light can also be thought of as a wave. Thus, light will sometimes behave as if it is a particle, and at other times it will behave as if it is a wave. Since the waves within a photon are electromagnetic, there is no need for atoms or molecules in order for light to travel. As a result, light can travel through any region of space, regardless of what occupies that portion of space.

How quickly do these wave packets travel? Well, in a vacuum, they move at a stunning 300,000,000 meters per second (about 670,000,000 miles per hour)! Sound travels through air at about 340 meters per second (about 760 miles per hour). Obviously, then, light travels *a lot* faster than does sound. Also, whereas the speed of sound is dependent on the temperature, the speed of light is not.

Although the speed of light does not depend on temperature, it does depend on *the substance* through which the light passes, just as the speed of sound depends on the substance through which sound passes. Unlike sound, however, the speed of light *decreases* the closer the atoms and molecules of the substance are. Examine Table 15.1 to see what I mean:

## TABLE 14.1
The Speed of Light in Certain Substances

| Substance | Speed of Light | Substance | Speed of Light |
|---|---|---|---|
| Air (25 °C) | 300,000,000 m/sec | Plastic | 189,000,000 m/sec |
| Alcohol | 225,000,000 m/sec | Crown Glass | 185,000,000 m/sec |
| Freshwater | 220,000,000 m/sec | Flint Glass | 175,000,000 m/sec |
| Acrylic | 200,000,000 m/sec | Diamond | 125,000,000 m/sec |

Notice that the speed of light in air is essentially the same as the speed of light in a vacuum. In liquids (alcohol and freshwater), light travels more slowly. In solids (acrylic, plastic, glass, and diamond), light travels even more slowly.

Do you remember Einstein's Theory of General Relativity? You learned a little bit about it when you learned about gravity. Well, Albert Einstein also developed a theory that is now known as the Special Theory of Relativity. One of the fundamental assumptions of this theory is that the speed of light in any substance represents the *maximum speed* that can ever be attained in that substance. For example, since the speed of light in air is 300,000,000 meters per second, the Special Theory of Relativity states that *nothing* can travel in air faster than 300,000,000 meters per second. In essence, then, the Special Theory of Relativity says that the speed of light is the ultimate speed limit because nothing can travel faster than light.

The details of this incredible theory are beyond the scope of this course, but it is important for you to realize that its fundamental assumption does, indeed, seem to be true. Many experiments confirm the predictions of special relativity, and no data contradicting the theory can be found. Therefore, most scientists consider it to be a valid scientific theory. As a result, the general view of science is that no matter how much energy you expend, you can never travel faster than the speed that light travels in the same substance.

---

**ON YOUR OWN**

15.1 Which of the pictures below is the best illustration of the quantum-mechanical theory of light?

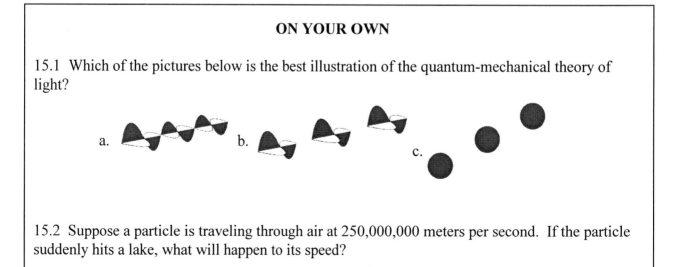

15.2 Suppose a particle is traveling through air at 250,000,000 meters per second. If the particle suddenly hits a lake, what will happen to its speed?

Wavelength and Frequency of Light

The frequency (and therefore the wavelength) of sound waves determines the pitch of the sound that you hear. What does the frequency (and therefore the wavelength) of light waves determine about the light? Perform the following experiment to find out.

---

**EXPERIMENT 15.1**
Seeing Different Wavelengths of Light

Supplies:

- A flat pan, like the kind you use to bake a cake
- A medium-size mirror (4-inch by 6-inch is a good size)
- A sunny window (A flashlight will work, but it will not be as dramatic.)
- A plain white sheet of paper
- Water

Introduction - In this experiment, you will see what the wavelength of light waves determines about the property of light. NOTE: This experiment is difficult to perform near noon.

Procedure:

A. Fill the pan with water. The water level should be high enough so that a significant portion of the mirror can be submerged.
B. Place the pan of water in direct sunlight from the window.
C. Immerse at least portion of the mirror in the water and tilt it so that it reflects the light up and back towards the window.
D. Use one hand to hold the plain white paper above the pan of water, between the pan and the window. Use the other hand to hold the mirror that is in the water so that it stays tilted.
E. Play with the tilt of the mirror and the position of the white sheet, trying to reflect sunlight with the mirror and land it on the white sheet of paper.

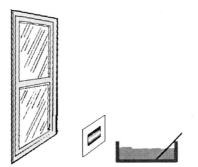

F. If you play with the position of the paper and the tilt of the mirror enough, you should eventually see a rainbow, as shown in the figure above. This may take a little work.

What did you see in the experiment? When light travels through different substances, it tends to bend. I will discuss this in much greater detail later on in this module. The amount that the light bends depends, in part, on the wavelength of the light. Thus, when the sunlight hit the water, it bent. Certain wavelengths bent farther than others. The mirror then reflected the light and it traveled back out of the water. When that happened, the light bent again. Once again, the amount that the light bent depended on the wavelength. That was enough to partially separate one wavelength of light from another. As a result, the reflected light was split into different wavelengths. This appeared to you as a rainbow.

The wavelength of light, then, determines the light's *color*. Figure 15.2 illustrates this point.

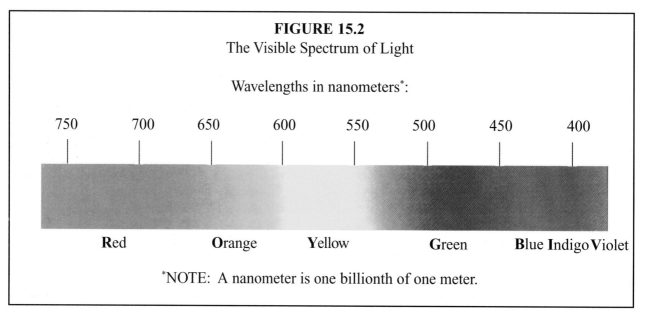

**FIGURE 15.2**
The Visible Spectrum of Light

Wavelengths in nanometers*:

750     700     650     600     550     500     450     400

Red            Orange      Yellow          Green       Blue Indigo Violet

*NOTE: A nanometer is one billionth of one meter.

What we see as white light is really light that is made up of many colors. If we separate the wavelengths, we get different colors. The longest wavelengths of light that we see are made up of various shades of red, while the shortest wavelengths of light that we see are made up of various shades of violet. The other colors (orange, yellow, green, blue, and indigo) have wavelengths in between.

Although you needn't memorize the wavelengths that each color corresponds to, you *do* need to memorize the *relative* size of the wavelengths in question. What I mean by this is that you need to know that red light has the largest wavelengths, orange light has smaller wavelengths, and so on. This is easy to do if you think about the colors as a single name. If you start with the color that corresponds to the largest wavelength (red) and you put the first letter of each color together, you come up with a man's name: ROY G. BIV. So if you think of ROY G. BIV every time you think of the colors of visible light, you will always know that red light has the longest wavelength, violet light has the smallest, and you will also know the order of all colors in between.

I am going to talk about color more in the last section of this module. For right now, however, I need to point out something very important. Just like there are plenty of sound waves that we cannot hear, there are plenty of light waves that we cannot see. The light which we see with our eyes we call the **visible spectrum** of light. This light is actually only a small part of the light that comes to us from the sun. It turns out that our planet is bathed with light of many, many different wavelengths and frequencies. Our eyes only perceive a small fraction of the total amount of this light. Figure 15.3 is a more complete representation of all light in Creation, which we call the **electromagnetic spectrum**.

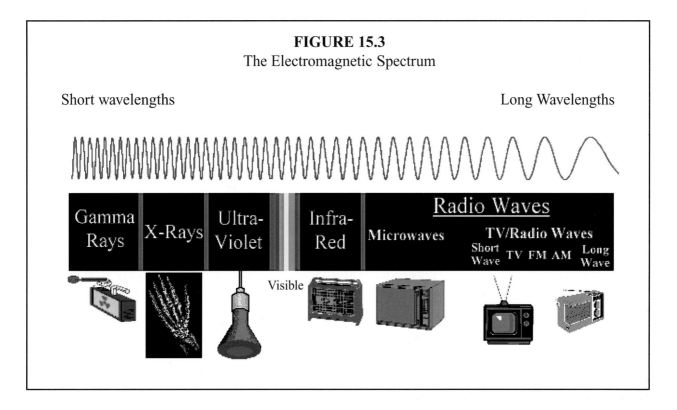

**FIGURE 15.3**
The Electromagnetic Spectrum

Since visible light is what we are used to, we usually look at the other parts of the electromagnetic spectrum in terms of where they fall relative to visible light. Light waves with wavelengths smaller than visible light are called **ultraviolet light**, **X-rays**, and **gamma rays**. Ultraviolet light has enough energy to kill any living tissue that it strikes. Medical professionals often use ultraviolet lamps (such as the one shown in the figure) to sterilize things. If you put something under an ultraviolet lamp, the ultraviolet light will kill any germs (bacteria, etc.) it strikes. As you learned in Modules #2 and #3, the ozone layer protects life on earth from the ultraviolet light that comes from the sun. X-rays, used in medicine so that doctors can see your internal structures without operating, have wavelengths even smaller than ultraviolet light. Finally, gamma rays, a form of radiation that you learned about in Module #13, have the shortest wavelengths.

Ultraviolet light has enough energy to kill living tissue on contact. It turns out that the shorter the wavelength, the more energy a wave has. Thus, X-rays have even more energy than do ultraviolet rays. In other words, X-rays have *more than enough energy to kill living tissue on contact*. Despite this fact, doctors shine X-rays right on a sick person in order to be able to make a diagnosis. This kills several cells in the patient's body. Why does a doctor take someone who is already sick and then shine X-rays on the person so that several of the patient's cells are killed? The answer to that is a quick risk/benefit analysis.

When you are given an X-ray, some of your cells do die. The cells also run the risk of being mutated. That sounds bad, but if you remember my discussion of radioactivity from Module #13, it's really not all that bad, as long as it happens in small doses. As long as a person doesn't get *too many* X-rays, the risks are not great. The benefits of an X-ray are large. It allows the doctor to make a good diagnosis of the patient's internal structures without operating. In this case, then, as long as the patient does not have too many X-rays, the benefits far outweigh the risks. For the technician who performs X-rays all day long at the hospital, however, there is great risk. If that person were exposed to X-rays each time a patient got an X-ray, far too many of his or her cells would die or mutate. In addition, there are no benefits to this exposure, as the technician is not being diagnosed for anything. As a result, the technician giving the patient an X-ray stands behind a shield to avoid the X-rays.

Light with wavelengths just larger than visible light is called **infrared light**. When a hot object gives off heat, most of the energy is in the form of infrared light. A space heater, for example, gives off a lot of heat. You can see the wires of the space heater glow red, but that is only a small portion of the energy it is emitting. Most of the energy that the space heater emits is in the form of infrared light, which you cannot see. If you remember the greenhouse effect discussion in Module #2, the earth gives up most of its energy in the form of infrared light. That's the light that greenhouse gases absorb to keep the atmosphere warm.

Light with wavelengths larger than infrared light makes up the portion of the electromagnetic spectrum called **radio waves**. It might surprise you that the radio and television signals you capture with an antenna are really just another form of light. You can't see this light, of course, but without it, you would never hear a radio program! The shortest-wavelength radio waves are not used for radio or television, however. They are the microwaves that you use to heat food quickly. Believe it or not, when you turn on your microwave oven, you are simply exposing your food to long wavelength light.

How does long wavelength light heat up your food quickly? Well, it turns out that the particular wavelengths of light used in microwave ovens are absorbed by water molecules in your food. When the light is absorbed, these molecules begin to spin due to the energy of the light that they absorb. When they start spinning, these molecules are subject to an enormous amount of friction from the other molecules in the food, and that friction generates heat. *That's* the heat which heats up your food. A microwave oven heats things quickly compared to a conventional oven because, in a conventional oven, the heat must travel into the food that is being cooked. As a result, the food must get hot on the outside before it can get hot on the inside. In a microwave oven, the microwaves are causing *all* of the water molecules *throughout* the food to spin. Thus, the food is exposed to heat all over right away. That makes the food cook a LOT more quickly.

Light of wavelengths longer than microwaves is used to transmit radio and television signals. When you tune a radio or change the channel on a television, you are telling the electronics in the device to look for a particular frequency (thus, a particular wavelength) of light.

Any light of that frequency which strikes the antenna is then picked up by the electronic circuitry in the device.  The information in that signal is decoded, and the result is the radio or TV program you wanted to hear.  Short-wave radio signals have smaller wavelengths than TV signals.  FM radio signals have longer wavelengths than either of those, but they have shorter wavelengths than AM radio signals.  Long-wave radio signals have the longest wavelengths of them all.

---

**ON YOUR OWN**

15.3  Without looking at Figure 15.2 or Figure 15.3, order the following colors in terms of *increasing* frequency:  yellow, indigo, red, green

15.4  If radio signals are really made up of light, why doesn't a radio station's antenna glow when it transmits its signals?

---

## Reflection

When you were studying sound waves in the previous module, I told you that when sound waves encounter an obstacle, a portion of the sound waves bounce off the obstacle and start traveling in another direction.  That's how we hear echoes.  Another portion of the sound waves begins traveling through the obstacle.  Well, under the right conditions, the same thing happens to light waves.  When light (or sound) waves bounce off of an obstacle, we call it **reflection**. Perform the following experiment to learn more about reflection.

---

**EXPERIMENT 15.2**
The Law of Reflection

Supplies:

* A flat mirror.  The mirror can be very small, but it needs to be flat.  You can always tell if a mirror is flat by looking at your reflection in it.  If the image you see in the mirror is neither magnified nor reduced, the mirror is flat.
* A white sheet of paper
* A pen
* A protractor
* A flashlight
* A sheet of black construction paper or thin cardboard
* Tape

Introduction - When light or sound waves reflect off an obstacle, the law of reflection allows us to determine where the reflected waves will go.  This experiment helps you determine that law.

Procedure:

A.  Take the construction paper and cut it into a circle that fits the face of the flashlight.  Make it so that if the circle were taped to the face of the flashlight, little or no light would escape.

B.  At the edge of the circle, cut a small slot, so that it looks like this:

C.  Now tape the circle to the face of the flashlight so that the only light which escapes comes through the slot.

D.  Lay the white piece of paper on a rectangular table or desktop so that its edge is even with the straight edge of the table.  Tape the paper down so that it does not move from this position.

E.  Use the protractor the way you learned in math class to make a line which is perpendicular to the edge of the table and is centered on the paper.  In the end, your setup should look like this:

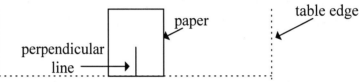

F.  Take the mirror and push it up against the edge of the table so that the line you drew is centered on the mirror and perpendicular to it.

G.  Turn on the flashlight and turn out the lights.

H.  Hold your flashlight so that the slot is on the bottom of the face, touching the paper.  Play with the way you are holding the flashlight until  the light coming from the slot causes a beam on the paper which hits the mirror at the same point that the line touches the mirror.  You should then see the beam reflect off of the mirror back onto the paper:

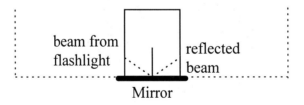

Mirror

I.  Use your pen to carefully trace the path of the beam as it travels from the flashlight and reflects off of the mirror.

J.  Turn on the lights.  Use your protractor to measure the angle of the line representing the path of the incoming beam relative to the perpendicular line that you originally drew.

K.  Measure the angle of the line representing the reflected beam relative to the same perpendicular line.

L.  Do steps (G) through (H) twice more, changing the positioning of the flashlight so that the angle which the incoming beam makes with the perpendicular line is different each time.  In each case, compare the angle made by the incoming beam to that of the outgoing beam.  What do you see?

Within experimental error, the angles you measured in each trial of the experiment should have equaled each other.  I will call the angle that the light ray from the flashlight made with the perpendicular line the **angle of incidence**.  The angle that the reflected light ray made with the perpendicular line is called the **angle of reflection**.  With that terminology, I can say your experiment should have indicated that the angle of reflection equals the angle of incidence.  That's the **Law of Reflection**.

<u>The Law of Reflection</u> - The angle of reflection equals the angle of incidence

Believe it or not, this simple law is responsible for how mirrors work.

To understand why, you first need to understand why we see things in the first place.  As you look at the words on this page, light reflects off of the page and up towards your eye.  The pattern of reflected light is read by your eye and is converted to electrical impulses that are sent to your brain.  I will discuss this process a bit more in a later section of this module.  Your brain then converts these electrical impulses into an image.  That's how you see.  That's also why you cannot see things without the aid of light.  Your eyes cannot send anything to your brain unless light reflects off of the thing that you are observing and then enters your eyes.  Only then can a message be sent to your brain so that it can form an image.

With this in mind, consider a woman looking at herself in a mirror.  Why does she see her foot, for example?  Well, light reflects off of her foot, hits the mirror, reflects off of the mirror, and enters her eyes:

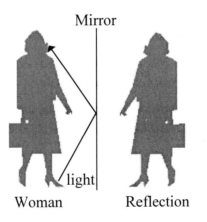

The thing to realize about this is that the woman's brain has always been conditioned to think that light travels in a straight line.  As a result, her brain extends the light backwards (as illustrated by the dotted line in the picture below).

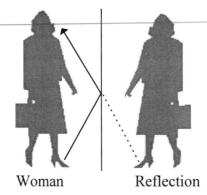

Woman                Reflection

This makes the woman's brain think that the image of her foot is actually inside the mirror because it thinks that the light hitting her eyes is coming from the start of the dotted line.

That's how images are formed in a mirror. The light that reflects off of a mirror is detected by an eye, and the brain which receives the eye's electrical impulses extends the light backwards to form an image inside the mirror. The image is, of course, fake. It is simply a result of the fact that the brain expects light to always travel in a straight line.

**ON YOUR OWN**

15.5  Draw the path of the light ray in the diagram below to show where the light eventually hits the screen:

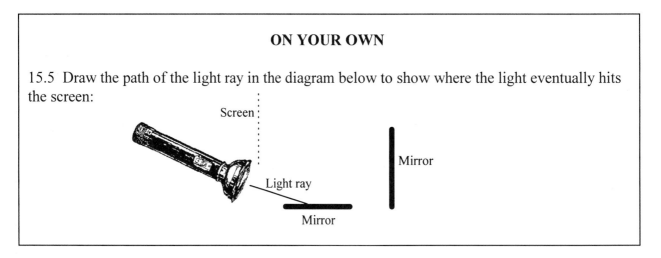

Screen

Light ray

Mirror

Mirror

## Refraction

As I mentioned before, when light or sound waves encounter an obstacle, reflection is not the only thing that can happen. In addition to bouncing off of an obstacle, light and sound waves can begin to travel through the obstacle, provided certain conditions are met. When this happens, we say that the light or sound waves have been **refracted**. Perform the following experiment to understand what happens in the process of refraction.

**EXPERIMENT 15.3**
Refraction of Light

<u>Supplies:</u>

- A square or rectangular glass or clear plastic pan  (If you have a flat bottle, it will work as well.  It just needs to be something with clear, flat sides that can hold water.)
- Water
- Milk
- A spoon
- A flashlight with the same cover you used in Experiment 15.2
- A sheet of plain white paper
- A pen
- A protractor
- A ruler

<u>Introduction</u> - When light encounters a transparent obstacle, some of the light will pass through the obstacle.  This experiment will show you how that happens.

<u>Procedure:</u>

A.  Take the plain white sheet of paper and draw a line longways down the middle of the paper.
B.  Use your protractor to draw another line perpendicular to the line you just drew.  This line should be about 3 inches from one of the edges of the paper and it should span the entire width of the paper.
C.  Use your protractor and ruler to draw a third line that starts at the edge of the paper nearest the line you just drew and travels through the intersection of the lines you drew in steps (A) and (B).  This new line should make a 45 degree angle with each of the other lines.  In the end, your paper should look something like this:

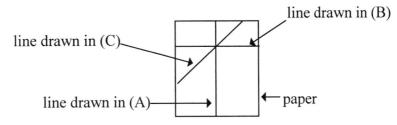

D.  Fill the pan halfway full of water and add 1/2 teaspoon of milk to the water.  Stir it up so that the water is a little cloudy.  This will allow you to see the beam of light as it travels through the water.

E.  Set the pan on the paper so that one of its flat edges is sitting right on the line that you drew in Step (B).

F.  Fix up your flashlight again so that it is just like what you used in Experiment 15.2.

G.  Lay the flashlight on the table with its slot down and then turn off the lights.

H.  Position the flashlight so that the light beam shines on the paper and follows the line you drew in Step (C) from the time it leaves the flashlight until it hits the pan.
I.  Look down into the water from directly above the pan.  You should see that when the beam hits the pan, two things happen.  First, part of the beam is reflected off of the pan.  The other part of the beam is refracted into the water.
J.  Look at the refracted beam relative to the line you drew in Step (C).  Does the light beam follow that line?
K.  Follow the light beam until it hits another one of the pan's sides.  What happens there?

What did you see in the experiment?  First of all, you should have seen that when the light beam hit the pan, part of it was reflected and part of it was refracted.  This is what happens most of the time when a wave hits a transparent obstacle.  Part of the wave will be reflected and part of it will be refracted.  There are certain circumstances where this does not happen, but they are rare.  Had you measured the angle of the reflected ray, you would have determined, as you did in the previous experiment, that the angle of reflection equals the angle of incidence.

Have you ever looked through a window and seen your own reflection?  The reason that you can look through the window into the outside world is because the window is transparent and light can pass through it.  That's why you can see the lights of a house through its windows.  However, not all of the light from the house makes it through the window.  When a wave encounters an obstacle, a portion of the wave is always reflected.  The reflection you see in a window is a result of the portion of light waves that are reflected off of the glass instead of refracted through it.

What did you notice about the refracted ray in the experiment?  The fact that the water was cloudy allowed you to see the ray as it traveled through the water.  You should have noticed that the light beam that came from the flashlight did not follow the line that you had aimed it along once it entered the water.  Instead, the light beam followed a path that was somewhere between the line you had aimed it along and the line that was perpendicular to the edge of the pan.  In other words, when the light ray entered the water, it was bent *towards* the line that was perpendicular to the surface that the light ray hit.  What happened when the light ray hit another side of the pan?  You should have once again seen that part of the light was reflected back into the water, and part of the light refracted back out into the air.

The fact that light rays bend when they are refracted is a general rule of physics.  In fact, the rule is even a bit more detailed than that.  In general, we can say that if you draw a line perpendicular to the surface that the light ray strikes, refracted light will bend towards that perpendicular line if light travels slower in the new substance than in the old substance.  If, on the other hand, light travels faster in the new substance than in the old substance, the light ray will bend away from the perpendicular line.

**When light refracts into a substance in which it must slow down, the light ray will bend towards a line that is perpendicular to the surface that it strikes.**

**When light refracts into a substance in which it can speed up, the light ray will bend away from a line that is perpendicular to the surface that it strikes.**

These two general rules can be summed up by Figure 15.4.

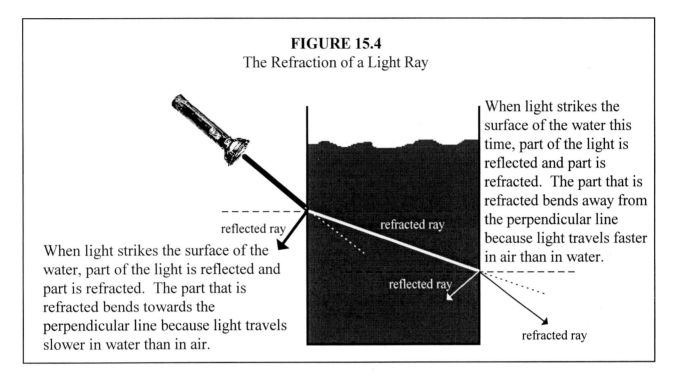

**FIGURE 15.4**
The Refraction of a Light Ray

reflected ray

refracted ray

When light strikes the surface of the water this time, part of the light is reflected and part is refracted. The part that is refracted bends away from the perpendicular line because light travels faster in air than in water.

When light strikes the surface of the water, part of the light is reflected and part is refracted. The part that is refracted bends towards the perpendicular line because light travels slower in water than in air.

reflected ray

refracted ray

The refraction of light through different substances is responsible for all sorts of optical illusions. Have you ever been traveling along a road on a hot summer day and noticed what appears to be a puddle of water in the middle of the road in front of you? When you got nearer to where you saw the puddle, it vanished. That "puddle of water" is an optical illusion that is the result of the refraction of light rays. When a road gets hot, a layer of hot air rests right above the road. When light from the sky encounters this layer of hot air, a portion of the light refracts. Rather than striking the road, it is bent into your eyes. Thus, you see a fuzzy image of the sky. Since the sky is blue, you think you are seeing a puddle of water. Instead, you are simply seeing light that comes from the sky and is refracted through the warm air to your eye. This kind of optical illusion is often called a mirage. People traveling in hot deserts see them regularly.

Perform the following quick experiment to see another typical optical illusion that is the result of light refraction.

---

### EXPERIMENT 15.4
#### The "Magical" Quarter

Supplies:

- A quarter
- A bowl that is reasonably deep and not transparent
- Water
- A pitcher or very large glass to hold the water

Introduction - Light that travels from one substance to another is bent according to the relative speed of light in each substance. This experiment demonstrates a common illusion that results from that effect.

Procedure:

A. Place the quarter in the bowl.
B. Sit in a chair and position yourself so that you can see the quarter in the bowl.
C. Now slowly scoot your chair back until you can no longer see the quarter, despite the fact that you are looking into the bowl.
D. Once you are at the point where you can no longer see the quarter, do not move your head. Slowly begin to fill the bowl with water from the pitcher. Continue to look at the bowl but do not move your head. Eventually, you should see the quarter re-appear.

---

Why did the quarter re-appear? The reason that you see the quarter is that light is reflected off of the quarter and hits your eyes. When you moved backward so that you could no longer see the quarter, light was still reflecting off of it. Because of the way you positioned your head, the light rays that reflected off of the quarter ran into the side of the bowl before they reached your eyes. Since the bowl was not transparent, the light could not travel through it. Many other light rays were reflecting off of the quarter and leaving the bowl, but those light rays were traveling so steeply that they ended up traveling above your eyes. As a result, no light rays from the quarter hit your eyes, so you did not see the quarter.

When you filled the bowl with water, the light rays were refracted as they left the water. Since light travels faster in air than in water, the light rays were bent away from a line perpendicular to the surface of the water. Thus, light rays were bent *towards* you. As a result, some of the light rays that traveled above your eyes when there was no water in the bowl were suddenly bent into your eyes by refraction, and you saw the quarter again. Figure 15.5 illustrates this effect:

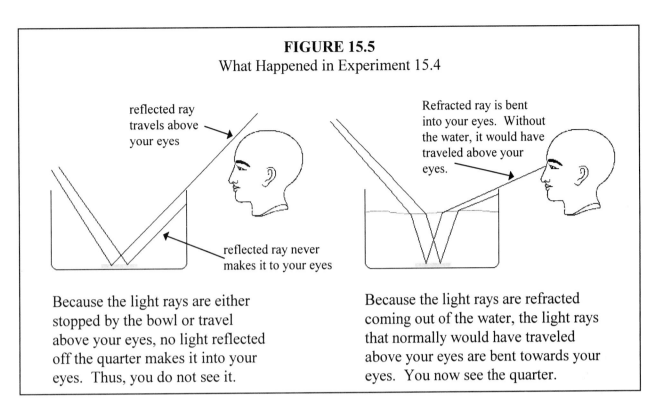

**FIGURE 15.5**
What Happened in Experiment 15.4

reflected ray travels above your eyes

reflected ray never makes it to your eyes

Refracted ray is bent into your eyes. Without the water, it would have traveled above your eyes.

Because the light rays are either stopped by the bowl or travel above your eyes, no light reflected off the quarter makes it into your eyes. Thus, you do not see it.

Because the light rays are refracted coming out of the water, the light rays that normally would have traveled above your eyes are bent towards your eyes. You now see the quarter.

Because of this effect, objects under water appear to be at a different place than they really are.

**ON YOUR OWN**

15.6 The following is a diagram of how a light ray travels from substance A through substance B:

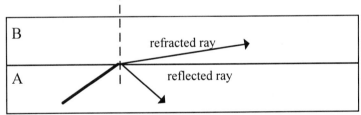

Does light travel faster in substance A or substance B?

15.7 A man is spear fishing. He looks into the water and sees a fish in front of him. When he aims his spear, should he aim it at the fish, in front of the fish, or behind the fish?

Before I leave this section, I need to point out two things. First, when light encounters an obstacle, refraction does not always occur. Depending on the substance, there are certain angles of incidence that lead only to reflection, not refraction. Although this situation is rare, it can be useful. **Fiberoptic** cables, for example, transport light over great distances because when light enters the cable, it cannot escape. When it hits the sides of the cable, there is little or no refraction; there is only reflection.  As a result, even a tiny amount of light can travel a great distance down such a cable.  When you take physics, you will learn more about this phenomenon.

The second thing I want to point out is that refraction depends, in part, on the wavelength of the light involved.  That's why you were able to separate light into its different colors in Experiment 15.1.  That's also why we see rainbows.  When there are many water droplets in the air, and when the sun shines on those water droplets, the refraction of light through those water droplets forms the beautiful arc of a rainbow.

**FIGURE 15.6**
Making a Rainbow

When white light hits a water droplet suspended in the air, some reflects and some refracts into the water droplet.  Since the amount of refraction depends partially on the wavelength of the light involved, this separates the white light into its colors.  As the refracted light travels through the water droplet, it eventually encounters the other side of the water droplet.  A portion of the light is refracted out of the water droplet, but a portion is reflected.  The light that is reflected travels to the other side of the water droplet, where once again, a portion is reflected and a portion is refracted.  That portion which is refracted has its wavelengths separated even more, because the amount of refraction depends in part on the wavelength of light.  With this second refraction, the light has been separated enough for us to distinguish the colors.

You need to notice a couple of things from the figure.  First of all, notice where the light enters the droplet of water and where it leaves.  This should tell you something.  In order to see a rainbow, there must be water droplets in the air, and the sun must be shining on them from *behind you*.  Since the light must be refracted, reflected, and refracted again to make the color separation noticeable, the only way you will see a rainbow is when you are positioned so that the light shines on the water droplet and the color-separated light leaves the water droplet on the same side.  This will only happen when the sun shines on the water droplets from behind you.  Not only does the sun have to be behind you, it needs to be at a certain angle.  After all, in order to see the rainbow, you must see light that refracts, reflects, and then refracts again.  That can only happen when the light shines on the water droplet at certain angles.  This is why you do not see a rainbow after every rain shower.  It depends on how high the sun is in the sky and where that position is relative to your position.

Second, you need to realize that you do not see all of the colors of the rainbow from one water droplet.  Of all the rays drawn on the left-hand side of the figure, only one reaches your eyes.  There are, however, many water droplets in the air.  Thus, you see the different colors from different water droplets.  Now look at the left-hand side of the figure again.  Which light is bent the lowest when it leaves the water droplet?  The red light is bent the lowest.  What water droplets will you see the red light from, then?  If the red light is bent low, then in order to reach your eye, the red light will have to come from the *highest* water droplets in the sky.  Since the violet light is bent the least, you will see that light coming from the lowest water droplets in the sky.  Now look at the right-hand side of the figure.  A rainbow will always appear with the red light on the top and the violet light on the bottom, because you will see the red light coming from the highest water droplets and the violet light coming from the lowest water droplets.

## Lenses

The fact that light rays tend to bend when they travel through transparent objects can be quite useful.  For example, consider a light ray traveling through the following object, which is made of glass:

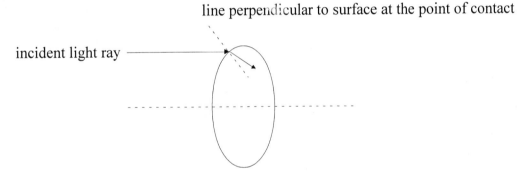

When the ray strikes the transparent object, it will be refracted.  This means that the light will bend towards a line which is perpendicular to the surface at the point of contact.  This situation is pictured above.

Now, the light ray will travel through the glass, along the path indicated above.  At some point, however, the light ray will reach the edge of the glass object and exit.  At that point, however, the substance through which the light is traveling will change.  Thus, the light will be refracted again.  Since light travels faster in air than it does in glass, the refracted light ray is bent away from the perpendicular. This will result in the following picture:

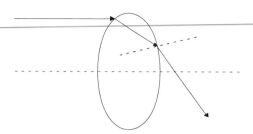

If you were to do this for several light rays that travel horizontally towards the object, you would get the following picture:

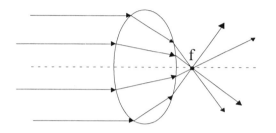

It turns out that a transparent object shaped like the one above will always focus horizontally-traveling light rays through a single point, called (of course) the focal point.  We call such an object a **converging lens**, because it makes all horizontal light rays converge to a single point.  You need to realize that I drew the object above very wide so that I could easily illustrate how the light ray refracts twice as it travels through the lens.  Generally, converging lenses are much thinner than that drawn in the diagrams above.

If I change the situation a little bit, I get a completely different result.  Suppose I made a glass object that is shaped as follows:

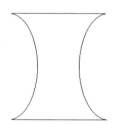

When light rays hit this object, refraction causes a completely different situation than what I got with the converging lens:

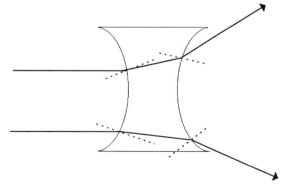

This kind of lens, called a **diverging lens**, bends light rays outwards, causing them to diverge away from one another. Once again, please realize that real diverging lenses are much thinner than what I have pictured here. Converging lenses and diverging lenses each have their applications. You will learn more about them when you take physics. Notice the difference between converging and diverging lenses. Lenses work because of their curvature. If the curvature changes, the way the lens works changes.

---

**ON YOUR OWN**

15.8 Consider the two lenses pictured below. Which one focuses light rays closest to the lens?

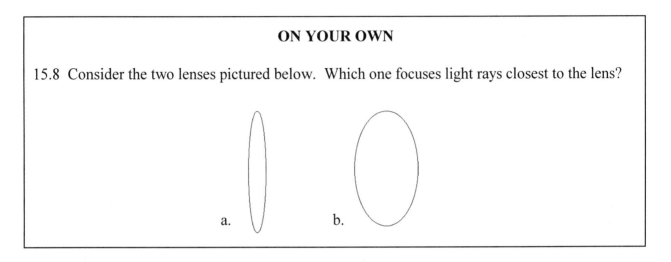

a.                    b.

---

The Human Eye

The most elegant application of a converging lens in all of God's creation can be seen in the human eye. Now, there are many, many marvelous facets of the eye, but I just want to concentrate on one: the way it handles light. As I have said before, the reason that we see things is that light reflects off of objects and enters our eyes. Our eyes then detect the light and send signals to the brain which forms an image in our mind. I want to study how the eye detects light. First, Figure 15.7 shows a simplified drawing of the human eye:

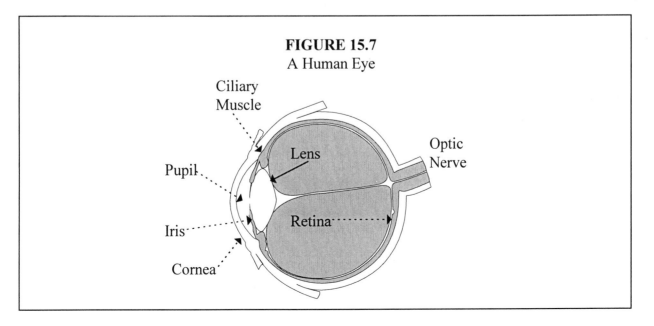

**FIGURE 15.7**
A Human Eye

In simple terms, the eye contains several different optical elements that all work together. The eye is covered by a thin, transparent substance called the cornea. It protects the eye from abrasions and the like. The iris is a cover that can open up wide or close down to just a small hole. This regulates how much light gets into the eye. The opening left by the iris is called the pupil. When you are in the presence of bright light, the iris closes down to allow only a small amount of light into the eye. This makes your pupil small. When there is little light, the iris opens wide, allowing a larger percentage of the light in. This makes your pupil look large. Once light enters the pupil, it is focused by a converging lens. The light is focused on the retina, which is made up of light-sensitive cells called **rods** and **cones**. When these cells feel light hitting them, they send electrical messages down the optical nerve to the brain, which decodes the messages and forms them into mental images.

Now, here's the really neat thing about the way the eye handles light. Have you ever watched a photographer focus his or her camera? The focus works by moving a converging lens back and forth inside a tube. As the converging lens moves, the point at which the light rays converge moves. A photographer moves the lens of his or her camera back and forth until the light rays converge so as to put the image right on the film of the camera. If the object moves in relation to the lens, the image will form someplace else. As a result, the lens must be moved again, in order to get the light rays to converge in the right place.

Just as a camera must focus images on its film in order to take a picture, your eye must focus images on its retina in order for you to see the image. The retina has light-sensitive cells that receive light and send signals to the brain based on the nature of that light. This allows your brain to form the image that you see. If you are to see an image, then, it must be focused on your eye's retina.  How does your eye focus the light to your retina?

Believe it or not, the eye *can actually change the shape of the lens* in order to keep the image in the same place, regardless of where the object is! This is accomplished with the ciliary muscle. It squeezes or expands the lens, which changes the lens's focal point. Thus, when an object moves in relation to the eye, the ciliary muscle changes the focal point of the lens to compensate, keeping the image focused on the retina! This is an amazing feat of physics. To give you some idea of just how amazing this is, think about modern-day cameras. Within the last few years, technology has given us sophisticated cameras. Some are sophisticated enough to have autofocus. The camera can automatically adjust the position of the lens so that the image stays in focus on the film. Even the most sophisticated camera on earth, however, is still 10,000 times slower in its autofocus capability as compared to the eye, and the image's focus is still 50 times less resolved!

Part of the reason for this is the difference between the way a camera focuses and the way your eye focuses. Remember, a camera focuses by moving the lens. The eye, on the other hand, changes the very shape of the lens in order to change how the light rays focus. Moving a lens in order to change where the light converges is not nearly as fast or as accurate as changing the shape of the lens. Unfortunately, cameras cannot use the faster, more accurate technique because *human science cannot make a lens like that which you find in the eye*! Thus, even the best that today's science has to offer cannot come close to mimicking the marvelous design of the eye.

Even Charles Darwin admitted that the eye is such a sophisticated work of engineering that the very idea of an eye forming by chance is preposterous. In his book, *The Origin of Species*, Darwin himself said:

> To suppose that the eye, with all its inimitable contrivances for adjusting the focus
> to different distances, for admitting different amounts of light, and for the correction
> of spherical and chromatic aberration, could have been formed by natural selection,
> seems, I freely confess, absurd in the highest degree. (*The Origin of Species*,
> Penguin Classics, London, 1985, p.217)

The way that the eye handles light is only one of many incredible feats that it can perform. Nevertheless, that alone was enough to convince Darwin that the formation of such an organ is beyond the reach of chance. Clearly, the eye was designed. It was designed by God.

Even the best of designs, however, can be ruined. Sometimes, due to flaws in genetics or due to overuse under the wrong types of circumstances, an eye can develop nearsightedness or farsightedness. These conditions develop when the eye's lens cannot be adjusted enough to keep the image from moving when the object moves. For example, if you are nearsighted, your eye can use its ciliary muscle to change the lens enough to keep the image of objects close to you focused on the retina. However, as the object moves farther and farther away, the lens cannot change its focal point enough to keep the image there. As a result, the image gets blurry because the light is focused *in front of* the retina, *not on* the retina. To compensate for this, corrective lenses are put in front of the eye. Because light is being refracted too strongly and thus focuses in front of the retina, diverging lenses are used. A diverging lens, as shown on page 392, refracts light rays away from one another. This compensates for the fact that the eye's converging lens refracts light too strongly, and the result is an image that is focused on the retina.

Pretty much the same scenario happens when a person is farsighted. In this case, the eye's lens can adjust to objects far away, but not to objects close to it. As a result, corrective lenses are made to refract the light rays entering the eye. In this case, however, converging lenses are used. As you might imagine, since nearsightedness is caused by the eye's lens refracting light too strongly, farsightedness is caused by the eye's lens refracting light too weakly. As a result, a converging lens must be used to correct farsightedness, as it helps refract the light in the right direction before the light hits the eye. This makes up for the fact that the eye's lens cannot refract light strongly enough on its own.

## How We Perceive Color

Another remarkable aspect of the eye is how it perceives color. To get an idea of how this marvelous process works, perform the following experiment.

---

**EXPERIMENT 15.5**
How the Eye Detects Color

Supplies:

* Two plain white sheets of paper (there cannot be lines on them)
* A bright red marker (A crayon will also work, but a marker is better.)

Introduction - Our eyes are marvelously designed to perceive color. In this experiment, you will use an optical illusion to learn how the eye does this.

Procedure:

A. Take one of the sheets of paper and make a thick cross on it with the red marker. The cross should be about 6 inches long, and the two legs which make it up should be about 3/4 of an inch thick. Color the entire cross so that you have a large, solid bright red cross in the middle of a white sheet of paper.
B. Take the clean sheet of white paper and put it underneath the sheet with the cross on it. Make sure the cross faces you so that you can see it.
C. Stare at the cross for a full 60 seconds. You can blink if you need to, but do not take your eyes off of the cross.
D. After a full 60 seconds of staring at the cross, quickly pull the top sheet of paper out of the way so that you can only see the clean sheet of paper on the bottom.
E. Note what happened in your lab notebook. There is about a 10% chance that you will see nothing. Most people, however, will see something rather dramatic.

---

What happened in the experiment? Most people will have seen a blue-green cross appear for a few seconds on the blank sheet of paper. After a few moments, it should have vanished, however. This optical illusion will not work for some people, especially if they have a tendency towards color blindness. Now let's discuss *why* this illusion occurred.

In order to see light, the retina of each eye is equipped with cells called rods and cones. The cone cells are sensitive to color, while the rod cells are not. The cone cells transmit electrical signals to the brain whenever they are hit by certain frequencies of light. The brain receives the electrical transmissions and uses them to form an image in your mind. It turns out that some cone cells are sensitive only to low-frequency visible light (red light) while others are sensitive to medium-frequency visible light (green light) while still others are sensitive to the higher frequency lights (blue light). When colored light hits these cells, they will only send signals to the brain if the light that they are sensitive to is hitting them. Thus, if a mixture of blue and yellow light hits your eyes, the medium and high- frequency cone cells transmit signals to your brain, but the low frequency cone cells do not. This is how your brain knows to construct an image in your mind which contains yellow and blue.

In the experiment, while you were looking at the red cross, all of your low- frequency cone cells were sending signals to the brain, but your other cone cells weren't doing anything. It turns out that cone cells get tired pretty quickly, and when they have sent the same signal to the brain for a period of several seconds, they eventually just shut off. The brain, sensing that no more signals are coming from the cone cells, assumes that they have shut off simply because they are tired, and it holds the same image in your mind until new signals come along. Thus, as you were staring at the cross, your low- frequency cone cells eventually shut off. Since no more signals were coming from the low- frequency cone cells, and since no signals had come from the medium and high- frequency cone cells, the brain was receiving no more signals. It therefore assumed you were still looking at the cross and continued to hold the image in your mind.

When you yanked the top sheet away, white light began to hit your eyes where only red light had hit them before. Since white light contains all frequencies, your medium and high-frequency cone cells began to receive light and transmit signals to your brain. Your low-frequency cone cells, however, were still shut off, so they didn't send any signals, even though they should have. The brain started receiving new signals, but only from the high and medium-frequency cone cells. So it constructed an image of green (medium frequency) and blue (high frequency) light. Eventually, however, your low- frequency cone cells realized that they had to start transmitting again, and, once they did, the brain realized that the eyes were seeing all energies of light and thus formed a white image in your mind.

Therefore, the way we perceive color is based on the frequency of the light that hits our eyes. Isn't it marvelous how well designed the eye is to handle such a complex operation? That should tell you something about how marvelous its Designer is!

## Adding and Subtracting Colors

Remember, despite the fact that your eye can discern more than 16 million different colors, it needs only three types of cone cells to do so. With cone cells that are sensitive to only three basic colors (red, green, and blue), your mind can construct a myriad of colors. Why? Well, these three colors are called **additive primary colors** because they can be added together in different proportions to produce virtually any color. Examine the next figure to see what I mean.

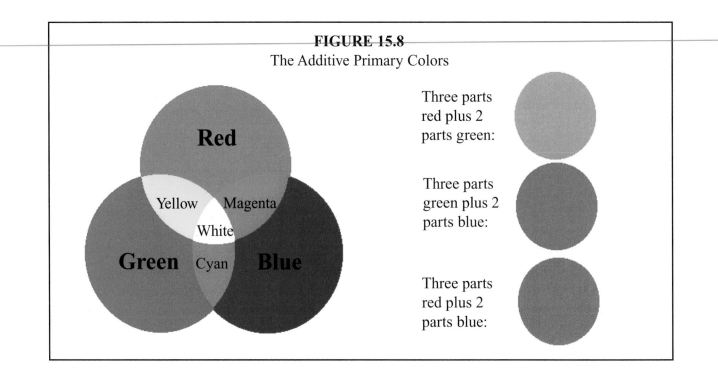

**FIGURE 15.8**
The Additive Primary Colors

        On the left-hand side of the figure, you see what happens when the three additive primary colors are added together. Equal parts of red and green, for example, make yellow. Equal parts of blue and green make the color cyan, and equal parts of blue and red make the color magenta. Finally, equal amounts of all three colors results in white. If we vary the amounts of the primary colors, the colors change. The right side of the picture, for example, shows you a few of the colors you can get when you add primary colors in unequal amounts. This is how a color television or a computer screen makes colors. These screens produce only the three additive primary colors. By adding those three colors in varying amounts, they can produce up to 16.7 million different colors!

        Although all of this makes sense, have you ever tried actually mixing red and green paints or food colorings? If you have, the result was NOT yellow, was it? It was probably mostly black. If red light and green light add to make yellow light, why don't red paint and green paint add to make yellow paint? The reason is that paints and dyes produce color in a *completely different* way than do color television sets and computer monitors. Remember, computer monitors and color televisions shine light in your eyes. That's why you can see these devices even when the lights are not on in the room. If you were to paint a picture and turn off the lights, however, you would no longer see the picture. That's because the picture does not shine light in your eyes. Instead, white light from sun or from a light bulb reflects off of the picture and hits your eyes. Thus, while televisions and computer monitors *generate* light which shines in your eyes, paints and dyes *reflect* light into your eyes. This makes a dramatic difference in how colors are generated.

        A red paint, for example, is red because when light strikes it, the chemical in the paint absorbs all wavelengths of light except those which correspond to the color red. White light hits the paint, but the only light we see reflected off of the paint is red light. Thus, we see the color as red. Green paint, on the other hand, absorbs all visible wavelengths except those that correspond to the color green.  Thus, when white light hits green paint, only green light wavelengths reflect off it.  As a result, we see the color as green because only green light reaches our eyes.

What happens, then, when you mix green paint and red paint?  Well, the red paint absorbs all colors of light except red, and the green paint absorbs all colors except green.  Between the two paints, then, *all visible wavelengths are absorbed*.  As a result, virtually no light gets reflected, and the apparent color is black, which is the absence of light.

Is there a way of mixing paints and dyes in order to come up with different colors?  Of course.  After all, there are color pictures in this course.  These colors are the results of color mixing as well.  We do not use red, green, and blue, however.  When mixing colors for dyes, inks, and paints, we mix the **subtractive primary colors** cyan, magenta, and yellow.  These colors mix so as not to absorb all wavelengths of light.  Cyan, for example, absorbs all visible wavelengths except those that correspond to blue and green.  Yellow, on the other hand, absorbs all visible wavelengths except those that correspond to red and green.  When yellow and cyan mix, then, all visible wavelengths are absorbed except green.  Thus, a mixture of yellow and cyan produces green.

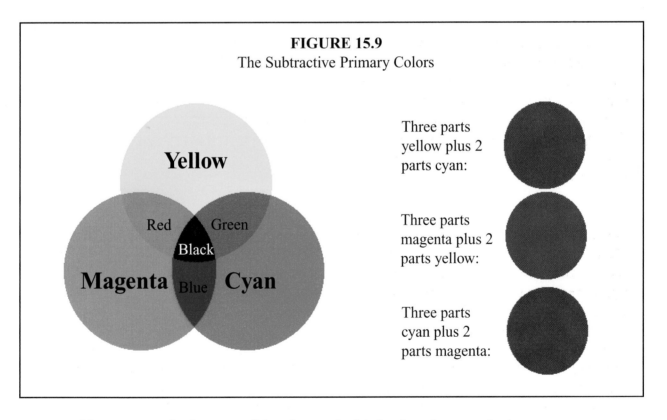

**FIGURE 15.9**
The Subtractive Primary Colors

If you were to look at any of the pictures in this book under a good microscope, you would actually see dots of cyan, magenta, yellow, and black.  When this book was printed, only those four inks were used.  Depending on how those inks were placed on the paper, however, different colors of light get reflected off of the page, resulting in all of the colors that you see in the book.

**ON YOUR OWN**

15.9  Suppose you have two flashlights.  You cover the first with green cellophane and shine it on a mirror.  When you look at the mirror, you see a green spot of light.  If you were to then take the second flashlight, cover it with red cellophane, and shine it on the same part of the mirror that the green spot is still shining, what color would you see?

15.10  Suppose you took a red shirt and put it in a dark room.  Then, suppose you took a flashlight and covered it with green cellophane as described above.  If you were to go into the dark room and shine the green cellophane-covered flashlight on the red shirt, what color would you see?

**ANSWERS TO THE ON YOUR OWN PROBLEMS**

15.1  Remember, the quantum-mechanical view theory, which is the currently accepted theory on the nature of light, states that light is made up of little packets of waves.  Thus, (b) is the best illustration of the current view of light.  The picture in (a) would be true if light were a pure wave, and the picture in (c) would be true if light were pure particles.

15.2  According to Table 15.1, light has a speed of 220,000,000 m/sec in water.  Nothing can travel faster than light in a given substance.  Thus, when the particle hits the lake, it must slow down so that it does not travel faster than the speed of light, in accordance with Einstein's theory of special relativity.

15.3 You can remember the relative wavelengths of light with the acronym ROY G. BIV.  Red has the longest wavelength, and violet has the shortest.  With that knowledge then, we can say that red has the longest wavelength, then yellow is next, followed by green.  Indigo has the smallest wavelength.  However, the question asked about frequency.  The longer the wavelength, the shorter the frequency.  Thus, in terms of *increasing* frequency it is, red, yellow, green, indigo.

15.4  A radio station's antenna does not glow because the light it emits is not visible.  Radio waves have wavelengths longer than visible light.

15.5  Each time the light is reflected, the angle it makes with the perpendicular must be the same before and after reflection.

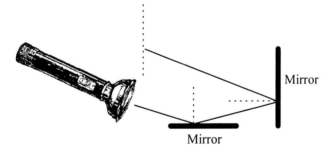

15.6  The refracted light ray bends away from the perpendicular when traveling from substance A to substance B.  When light travels into a substance in which it moves slower, the light bends towards the perpendicular. When light travels into a substance in which it moves faster, the light bends away from the perpendicular.  Thus, light travels faster in substance B than in substance A.

15.7  Consider the following diagram:

Because light rays will be refracted away from the perpendicular when they leave the water, the light will bend. The man's eyes will assume that the light has been traveling straight, however (remember the reflection discussion). Thus, his eye will extend the light backwards, making the fish appear farther back than the fish truly is. This is what happened in your experiment. When you added water to the bowl, the quarter appeared. It looked like it was farther away from you than it was in reality. Thus, the man must aim in front of the fish he sees.

15.8  Remember, lenses work because of their curvature. The more curvature they have, the more they will do their job. Thus, lens (b) will focus the light rays closest.

15.9  The mirror reflects all wavelengths that hit it. When the green hits it, it will reflect green. When the red hits it, it will reflect red. When both hit it, it will reflect both. When your eyes see both colors, your brain will add them to make yellow.

15.10  The red shirt is red because when light strikes it, it absorbs all wavelengths except red. The red is the only wavelength reflected from the shirt. Thus, when the green light shines on it, all of the green light will be absorbed. Nothing will be reflected back. Thus, the shirt will look black. In fact, it won't even look like a shirt. Without any light reflecting back from it, you will not even see the shirt!

## STUDY GUIDE FOR MODULE #15

1.  Define the following terms:

    a.   Electromagnetic wave
    b.   The Law of Reflection

2.  Explain the wave theory of light, the particle theory of light, and the quantum-mechanical theory of light.

3.  Sound waves cause air to oscillate.  What do light waves oscillate?

4.  What does Einstein's Special Theory of Relativity say about the speed of light?

5.  Light is traveling through water and suddenly breaks the surface and travels through air.  Did light's speed increase, decrease, or stay the same once it left the water?

6.  Order the following colors in terms of increasing wavelength:  orange, violet, yellow, green.

7.  Order the colors in problem #6 in terms of increasing frequency.

8.  Do radio waves have higher or lower frequencies than visible light?  What about X-rays?

9.  Infrared light is given off by any object that is losing heat.  The human body is almost always losing heat to the environment.  Why, then, don't human bodies glow at night, since they are emitting light?

10.  Light hits a mirror, making an angle of 15 degrees relative to a line drawn perpendicular to the mirror's surface.  What angle does the reflected light make with the same line?

11.  In the following diagram, will the man see his foot, despite the fact that the mirror does not reach the ground?

Mirror

12.  When light travels from one substance to another, what two things can happen to the direction of the light ray's travel?

13. In a physics experiment, a light ray is examined as it travels from air into glass. If the angle that the light ray makes with a line perpendicular to the glass surface is measured, will the refracted ray bend toward or away from that line?

14. When you look at objects underwater from above the water, they appear to be at a different position than the position they are truly at. Why?

15. In order for you to see a rainbow, what three conditions must be met?

16. What is the difference between a converging lens and a diverging lens?

17. Which of the following lenses is a converging lens? Which is a diverging lens?

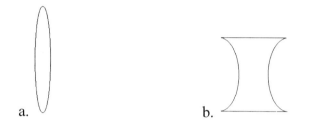

a.                                    b.

18. What is special about the way the eye focuses light as compared to the way a camera focuses light?

19. Suppose the cone cells on your retina that sense red light no longer work. If you look at a white piece of paper, what color would it appear to be? If you looked at a red piece of paper, what color would it appear to be?

20. A shirt is dyed so that it looks violet. What colors of light does the dye absorb?

21. A cyan dye is made of a mixture of substances which absorb all light colors except blue and green. If you took a cyan piece of paper and placed it in a dark room and shined red light on it, what would you see? What would you see if you shined green light on it?

# Module #16: An Introduction to Astrophysics

## Introduction

In the last module, you learned about light. In this module, then, it only seems natural to talk about the sources of light that exist in Creation as well as the general properties of their environment. In other words, in this module, I will cover stars and the universe. Now, of course, there is no way I can give a complete description of *either* of these interesting topics in just one module. Nevertheless, in this module, I will lay a foundation that will allow you to understand a little bit about that universe which surrounds you. Hopefully, this foundation will give you a reason to go out and learn more on your own.

## The Sun

The best place to begin a discussion of astrophysics is with the main source of light for our solar system: the sun. The first thing that you need to understand about the sun is that it is just one of billions and billions of light sources that exist throughout the universe: stars. When you look up into the night sky, you see countless points of light. Most of these points of light are stars. The sun that lights our planet is just one of those stars. It is the closest star to us; nevertheless, it is just a star.

Understanding how the sun works, then, will aid us in understanding the stars in general. First of all, the sun is huge. It is not the largest star in the universe, but it is really big by conventional standards. The sun is essentially spherical (a ball), with a diameter of roughly 864,950 miles. That's big! It is certainly the biggest thing in our solar system. This big ball can be split into four distinct regions, as illustrated in Figure 16.1.

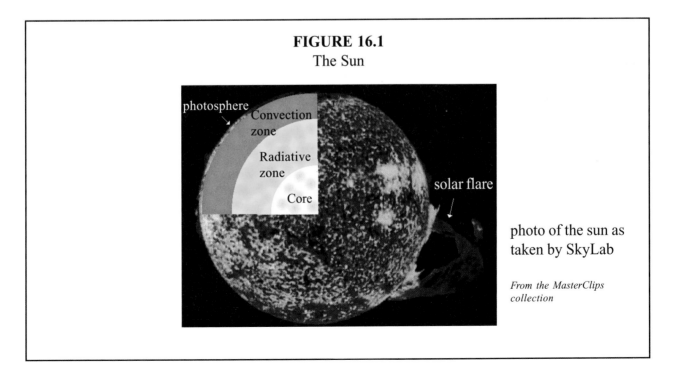

**FIGURE 16.1**
The Sun

photosphere
Convection zone
Radiative zone
Core
solar flare

photo of the sun as taken by SkyLab

*From the MasterClips collection*

These four regions of the sun (the core, the radiative zone, the convection zone, and the photosphere) all have different properties. The most interesting part of the sun is its core, so that's where I'll start.

To understand the nature of the sun's core, you must first understand that the sun is composed entirely of gases. Thus, the sun is not solid like the earth. It is a big ball of gas. The vast majority (90 %) of the gas that makes up the sun is hydrogen. Most of the rest is helium, and there are traces of many other gases as well. Nevertheless, you can think of the sun mostly as a big ball of glowing hydrogen gas.

Despite the fact that we think of hydrogen gas as something that's pretty light, when you get a *lot* of hydrogen gas together, it can be pretty massive. The sun's mass is roughly 2 million, trillion, trillion tons! This mass produces a powerful gravitational field which holds the hydrogen gas in the sun and, at the same time, holds the planets in orbit around the sun. The gravitational field of the sun is so powerful that in the **core** of the sun, the pressure that the hydrogen atoms experience is enormous.

This pressure is so enormous that the hydrogen atoms in the sun's core cannot exist in their normal form. Remember, hydrogen atoms have a proton and either 0, 1, or 2 neutrons in the nucleus, depending on the isotope involved. Each of these isotopes, however, has a single electron orbiting the nucleus. In the core of the sun, however, the hydrogen atoms cannot retain their electrons. The enormous pressure in the core creates so much heat that the electrons in the hydrogen atoms escape the attractive force the nucleus exerts on them. As a result, these hydrogen atoms are simply hydrogen nuclei. They are, in essence, "naked" atoms, having been stripped of their electrons.

These naked hydrogen atoms are constantly colliding with one another. These collisions happen frequently and with much violence. When two $^2$H (sometimes called "deuterium") nuclei collide in just the right way, something incredible can happen. The two nuclei can fuse together. The result is a $^3$He nucleus and a free neutron. This process, called **nuclear fusion**, is illustrated below:

**FIGURE 16.2**
Nuclear Fusion

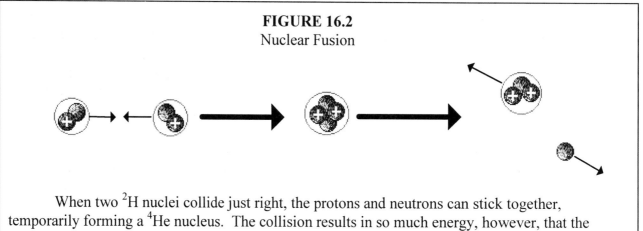

When two $^2$H nuclei collide just right, the protons and neutrons can stick together, temporarily forming a $^4$He nucleus. The collision results in so much energy, however, that the nucleus is unstable. To stabilize the nucleus, a neutron escapes. The result is a free neutron and a $^3$He nucleus.

Nuclear fusion results in the release of an enormous amount of energy. Why? Well, if you carefully measure the mass of the two $^2$H nuclei, you will find that together, they have just slightly more mass than the $^3$He nucleus and the neutron that results after fusion. What does that mean? Remember what an object's mass tells us. It tells us how much matter exists in an object. Thus, if the mass of the two $^2$H nuclei is greater than the mass of the $^3$He nucleus and neutron that are produced by nuclear fusion, there is obviously more matter in the two $^2$H nuclei. This tells us that, in the process of nuclear fusion, *matter is lost*.

Think about that for a moment. There is more matter *before* nuclear fusion than there is *after*. What happened? Where did the matter go? Well, do you remember Einstein's Special Theory of Relativity that I mentioned in the previous module? This theory assumes that nothing can travel faster than the speed of light. One of the consequences of this assumption is that matter is really just another form of energy. The reasons for this are far too complicated to explain here. Most scientists don't even understand them. Nevertheless, there is an enormous amount of evidence to support this idea, so most scientists believe it.

In fact, there is even an equation that relates mass and energy. It is a rather famous equation. You have probably seen it.

$$E = mc^2 \qquad\qquad (16.1)$$

In this equation, "E" is energy, "m" represents mass, and "c" is the speed of light. In other words, if you take mass and multiply it by the speed of light squared, you know how much energy that mass corresponds to.

Equation (16.1) tells us that the matter which is lost in the process of nuclear fusion is transformed into energy. Since the speed of light is so large, even a tiny amount of mass can be transformed into an enormous amount of energy. For every ounce of matter that is lost as a result of nuclear fusion, enough energy is made to run a 100 Watt light bulb for 750,000 years! That's pretty amazing, especially in light of the fact that at the core of the sun, 5 million tons of matter is being lost every second! Obviously, then, the nuclear fusion that takes place at the core of the sun produces *a lot* of energy.

What happens to this energy? Some of it heats up the core, maintaining its temperature of 27,000,000 °F. Most of it, however, is converted to light. The photons produced make their way out of the core, into the next layer of the sun, the **radiative zone**. In the radiative zone, the gases are still tightly-packed, but they are not pressurized enough to cause nuclear fusion to occur. Nevertheless, because the atoms are so tightly packed, photons keep colliding with them. As a result, it takes a long time for a photon to travel through the radiative zone.

Once out of the radiative zone, the photons are typically absorbed by gases in the **convection zone**. In this region of the sun, the gases are not as tightly packed as they are in the radiative zone. When these gases absorb the photons that come out of the radiative zone, the energy of the photons heats up the gases. As a result, the gases begin to rise. Much like air bubbles that rise through a pot of boiling water, these hot gases rise through the convection zone until they reach the surface, which we called the **photosphere**.

The photosphere is the only part of the sun that we actually see. When gases in the convection zone reach the photosphere, they transfer their extra energy to the gases in the photosphere. This causes the gases from the convection zone to cool down a bit. When they cool down, they sink back to the bottom of the convection zone, where they pick up more photons and start the process all over again.

The gases in the photosphere take the energy from the gases in the convection zone and rise to the top of the photosphere. There, the energy is released in the form of light. This light has all of the wavelengths of the electromagnetic spectrum; thus, the sun is continually producing radio waves, visible light, ultraviolet light, X-rays, and gamma rays. If you look at the picture in Figure 16.1, you will notice that the photosphere looks spotty. Each of those bright spots is the result of a pocket of gas that has risen to the top of the photosphere to emit its light.

There is one more thing in Figure 16.1 that deserves discussion. Notice on the lower, right-hand side of the sun there is a great protruding structure. It is called a **solar flare**. Although scientists still are not sure exactly *how* these solar flares happen, they know it has something to do with the sun's magnetic field. The sun has a very strong magnetic field which stores an enormous amount of energy. Periodically, this energy is released. The result is a solar flare. These flares release a large amount of high-energy particles, some of which reach earth. Many times, satellite communications and other electromagnetic phenomena are disturbed due to these high-energy particles.

---

### ON YOUR OWN

16.1  As I mentioned already, the sun is 90 % hydrogen and the rest is mostly helium. As time goes on, will that composition change? If so, will the amount of hydrogen increase or decrease? What about helium?

16.2  Which of the four regions of the sun has the lowest temperature?

---

Before I leave this section, it is important that I point out to you that the vast majority of the knowledge we have about the sun comes from indirect observation. As a result, we may have a few of these "facts" wrong. For example, although we know that the sun does get a good share of the energy it emits from nuclear fusion, we are not sure that nuclear fusion is the sole source of power for the sun. Physicists have been studying the particles that are emitted by the sun, and there is at least some evidence that nuclear fusion does not account for all of the energy that the sun emits. For right now, however, there is no other process we know of that can power the sun, so we assume that nuclear fusion is the sole source of power. That may change as we study the sun more and more. In the same way, many of the "facts" that I have told you so far (and many of the "facts" that I tell you in the rest of this module) may change as the result of more scientific research.

## Nuclear Energy

Since I talked about energy from nuclear fusion in the previous section, it is worthwhile to spend a few moments discussing the nuclear energy that we are trying to use here on earth. The sun is powered by nuclear fusion. That's not the kind of nuclear power we use here on earth. On earth, we use **nuclear fission** to produce some of the energy that we use. What's the difference between nuclear fusion and nuclear fission? Let's start with the definitions.

Nuclear fusion - The process by which two or more small nuclei fuse to make a bigger nucleus

Nuclear fission - The process by which a large nucleus is split into two smaller nuclei

Notice the difference between the two. In nuclear fusion, nuclei are joining together. In the sun, for example, two hydrogen nuclei fuse to make a larger, helium nucleus. In nuclear fission, a large nucleus is split into two smaller nuclei.

An example of the nuclear fission process is shown in the figure below.

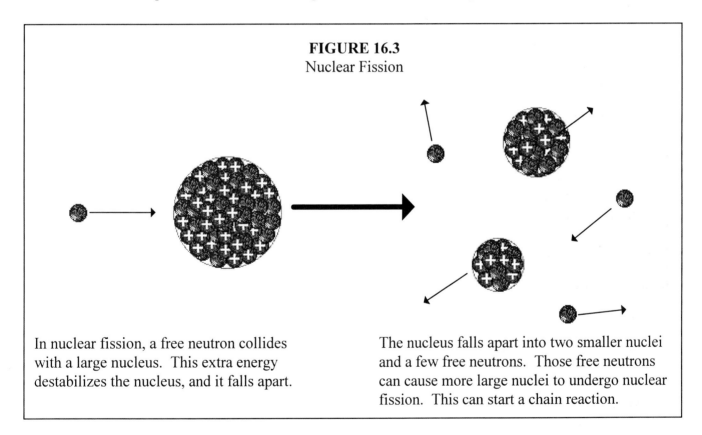

**FIGURE 16.3**
Nuclear Fission

In nuclear fission, a free neutron collides with a large nucleus. This extra energy destabilizes the nucleus, and it falls apart.

The nucleus falls apart into two smaller nuclei and a few free neutrons. Those free neutrons can cause more large nuclei to undergo nuclear fission. This can start a chain reaction.

If you were to carefully measure the mass of the neutron and the large nucleus before the nuclear fission took place, and if you were to measure the mass of both nuclei and all of the neutrons produced at the end of the process, you would find out that, just as in the case of nuclear fusion, some mass is missing. That mass gets converted to energy, in the form of heat and light.

Although there are examples of nuclear fission that do not happen as illustrated in Figure 16.3, the process illustrated there is an example of what happens in nuclear bombs and nuclear power plants. Notice that the process requires two things to get it started: a large nucleus (typically $^{235}$U or $^{239}$Pu) and a free neutron. Notice also what this process produces: two smaller nuclei and a few free neutrons. Thus, the process *produces* one of the things that it *needs to get started*: a free neutron.

What does this mean? Well, if you have a bunch of $^{235}$U "lying around" somewhere, when a free neutron happens to come along and strike one of the nuclei, nuclear fission will happen. That process will generate a few more free neutrons, which *can each start another fission process*. This can continue so that every single fission process goes out and starts several more fission processes. Thus, the number of fission processes starts growing rapidly. This is called a **chain reaction**.

If a chain reaction starts in the presence of enough $^{235}$U, the number of fission processes can grow so rapidly that energy is created at an enormous rate. The rate becomes so enormous that, eventually, the energy is produced too quickly and the result is a huge explosion. This is the basis of the atomic bomb. In an atomic bomb, enough $^{235}$U (or $^{239}$Pu) is put in the warhead so that once the chain reaction starts, an explosion is inevitable. The important issue, however, is that *enough* of the large nucleus ($^{235}$U or $^{239}$Pu) is present for the chain reaction to occur. This is called a **critical mass**.

Critical mass - The amount of isotope necessary to cause a chain reaction

If you have a critical mass of $^{235}$U, for example, then you can make a bomb. If you do not have a critical mass, you cannot make a bomb.

Without a critical mass of the large nucleus, the nuclear fission will never lead to a chain reaction, so it will never cause a nuclear explosion. However, it will still produce a *lot* of heat. That heat can be harnessed by an electrical generator and can then be used to make electricity. That's the basis of a nuclear power plant. Nuclear fission is run without a critical mass of the large nucleus. As a result, the fission will never lead to a nuclear explosion, but it can be used to make electricity.

The wonderful thing about using nuclear fission to make electricity is that the fuel for nuclear power is reasonably cheap and will last a long, long time. The downside is that nuclear fission can be quite dangerous. Now it is important to realize that the danger of nuclear fission is *not* that a nuclear power plant can create a nuclear explosion. That's physically impossible! In order to make a nuclear explosion, you must have a critical mass of the large nucleus you are using. Since nuclear power plants *do not* have a critical mass of the large nucleus, they *cannot* explode.

Even though nuclear power plants cannot explode, other nasty things can happen. In a normally operating nuclear power plant, the rate at which the fission processes occur is heavily controlled. If the control operations fail, then the reaction starts producing too much energy. This will not lead to an explosion, but it can produce so much heat that everything in the vicinity, including the reactor itself, will begin to melt. When this happens, it is called a **meltdown**, and the results can be devastating.

This is what happened at the Chernobyl nuclear power plant in the Soviet Union. This particular nuclear power plant did not have many safety protocols and, when the primary cooling system which helps control the rate of the nuclear reaction failed, there was nothing that could keep the reaction from running out of control. As a result, the reactor began to melt. This caused widespread fire throughout the plant, and resulted in the release of an enormous amount of radioactive isotopes. More than 30 people were killed as a result of the fires and structural damage in the power plant itself, and thousands were exposed to high levels of radiation. To this day, no one can live near where the plant was because the radioactive contamination is so high.

Nuclear power in the form of nuclear fission, then, can be quite dangerous. You have to understand, however, that *all* forms of power production are dangerous. Since 1900, for example, more than 100,000 people have been killed in American coal mines due to mining accidents and black lung, a malady that is caused by exposure to too much coal dust. Coal is used primarily for the production of energy. Studies indicate that nuclear power is responsible for less death and fewer health maladies than any other form of power production that we have today.

Nuclear power in the form of fission also has another serious drawback: the byproducts are radioactive. We have no safe way of disposing this radioactive waste. This can eventually lead to serious environmental problems. Of course, other forms of energy production also lead to serious environmental problems. Coal-burning power plants, for example, dump pollution into the air. The *amount* of pollution they dump into the atmosphere has been reduced considerably (remember the discussion in Module #2). Nevertheless, they still emit pollutants. They are, in fact, the principal contributors to the acid rain problem.

Although nuclear power in the form of nuclear fission can be dangerous and polluting, it is not clear that it is any more dangerous and polluting than other forms of energy production. There are those who think it is, in fact, one of the safest and cleanest forms of energy production. In France, for example, the scientific community is so convinced that nuclear power is (overall) the safest form of power production that more than 90% of the country runs on electricity produced by nuclear power plants.

In order to make energy production safer, better for the environment, and longer-lasting, scientists are trying to use nuclear fusion instead of nuclear fission to produce electricity. Nuclear fusion has no harmful by-products. Remember, when nuclear fusion occurs in the sun, the products are helium and a free neutron. Helium is not radioactive, and has no toxic chemical properties either. Thus, using nuclear fusion to produce electricity would completely eliminate the radioactivity problem caused by nuclear fission. It is also much safer than nuclear fission. Experiments indicate that nuclear fusion is much easier to halt, allowing for the nuclear fusion process to be stopped quickly. This would avert any meltdown possibilities. Finally, the fuel for nuclear fusion ($^2$H) is virtually unlimited and very inexpensive. Nuclear power from nuclear fusion, then, would be safe, cheap, and almost limitless.

Why don't we use nuclear fusion to make electricity, then? The answer is that from a *technological* viewpoint, we have not mastered the process yet. We *know* that nuclear fusion can be used to make energy. After all, it powers the sun. However, nuclear fusion can happen in the sun because of the intense heat and pressure in the sun's core. In order to get nuclear fusion to work, we have to essentially re-create that environment here on earth. That's a tough job! Right now, nuclear physicists can, indeed, cause nuclear fusion to occur in a variety of different ways. However, in each way used so far, there is an enormous amount of energy wasted in order to create the conditions necessary for the nuclear fusion. As a result, the total energy produced is rather small. In other words, right now we have to put an enormous amount of energy into a nuclear fusion reaction, and we don't get much more than that amount of energy back. As a result, nuclear fusion is not an economically viable process for the large-scale production of energy.

In the end, then, we know that there are some drawbacks to nuclear fission. Some consider those drawbacks to be quite serious; others consider them to be about the same or even a little less than what other forms of power production have. If scientists are ever able to overcome the technological problems associated with nuclear fusion, the result would be a much safer, cleaner, and cheaper form of power production. Whether that will ever happen, however, remains to be seen.

---

**ON YOUR OWN**

16.3 In a nuclear physics experiment, two $^7$Li atoms collide to form $^{12}$C and two neutrons. Is this nuclear fission or nuclear fusion?

16.4 Suppose nuclear physicists discovered a fission process that always produced two smaller nuclei and *only one* neutron. Would this eliminate the danger of meltdown in a nuclear power plant? Why or why not?

---

## Classifying The Stars in the Universe

The principle tool that scientists use to study the universe is the telescope. Since the telescope collects light, the only structures that can be studied with telescopes are those structures that emit or reflect light. With telescopes, then, scientists have been able to study the planets in our solar system (because they reflect light from the sun) and the stars outside the solar system (because they emit their own light). As a result, the most well-studied structures in the universe are stars.

When scientists study things, they typically like to classify them. Next year, you should start an in-depth study of biology in which you will learn the classification scheme that biologists use to classify all of the living organisms on the planet. Scientists like to classify the things that they study because classification is a way of taking a large amount of data and ordering it into a manageable system. Thus, when scientists began seriously studying the stars, they searched for ways in which the stars could be classified.

One thing that astronomers noticed early on was that different stars have different colors. When observing our sun, for example, astronomers noted that it appears white. You may think it appears yellow, but that's because you usually see it drawn as a yellow orb in the sky. When observing the sun directly, however, you will notice that the light which it emits is white. Not all stars emit white light, however. There are stars that predominately emit red/orange light, stars that predominately emit yellow light, and so on.

As astronomers began studying this phenomenon, they began theorizing as to why different stars produced different colors of light. As time went on, evidence began to accumulate that a star's color is actually related to its temperature. It seems that blue stars are the hottest stars in the universe. White stars (like our sun) are a bit cooler than blue stars; yellow stars are cooler yet; and red/orange stars are the coolest of all. The better our technology grew, the better we began to be at determining the temperature of a star. Nowadays, astronomers look at individual wavelengths of light in a process called spectroscopy (speck tros' cuh pea). You will learn more about spectroscopy when you take chemistry. The brightness of certain specific wavelengths of light emitted by a star allows astronomers to measure the approximate temperature of the star.

When an astronomer does such an analysis of a star, he or she places it into one of seven classes. Each class is designated by a letter, called the **spectral letter** of the star. The star's temperature determines which spectral letter is assigned to the star, according to the following table.

### TABLE 16.1
Spectral Letters and Star Temperatures

| Temperature ($^o$F) | Spectral Letter |
| --- | --- |
| Less than 5,500 | M |
| 5,500-8,000 | K |
| 8,001 - 10,300 | G |
| 10,301 - 12,500 | F |
| 12,501 - 17,000 | A |
| 17,001 - 37,000 | B |
| more than 37,000 | O |

The temperature of the sun (not the core temperature), for example, is 10,000 $^o$F. This makes it a type G star.

By itself, the classification of stars into spectral groups is not all that useful; however, if you combine this information with one other piece of information, you get a pretty interesting result. Not only do stars vary by color, they also vary by brightness as well. This is easy to see. If you look up into the night sky, you will find that some stars are bright and others are dim. Why is that?

There are two factors that affect how bright a star is in the night sky. The first is simply how intense the light it emits is. Obviously, the more intense the light that a star emits, the brighter it is. The other factor, however, is the star's distance from us. The farther a star is from the earth, the dimmer it appears. When astronomers observe a star, then, they have to factor in the distance in order to really determine how bright the star is. In a later section of this module, I will tell you how we measure the distance from us to the stars. For right now, however just assume that we can.

When an astronomer observes the brightness of a star and then corrects for the distance from the earth to the star, the result is called the **magnitude** of the star.

Star magnitude - The brightness of a star on a scale of -8 to +17. The *smaller* the number, the *brighter* the star.

The magnitude of the sun, for example, is +5, while the magnitude of the star Sirius is +2, and the magnitude of the star Rigel is -7. This means that Rigel is the brightest star of the three, Sirius is the next brightest, and the sun is the least bright of these three stars.

Now, of course, if you look up in the sky, the sun seems the brightest of all stars. It is so bright, in fact, that when the sun is in the sky that you are observing, its light blocks out the light coming from all of the other stars in the universe. Until the earth moves so that the sun is out of the sky that you are observing (e.g., at night), you cannot see any other stars. Even though the sun is a relatively dim star, then, it looks bright to us simply because it is close.

In the same way, if you knew how to identify Sirius and Rigel in the night sky, it would appear to you that Sirius is brighter than Rigel. Once again, however, this is because of distance. Rigel is so far away from the earth that only a tiny portion of its light hits the earth. Thus, even though it is a *very* bright star, it seems dim to us. Sirius is a lot closer to earth. Thus, a larger fraction of its light hits the earth. As a result, even though Sirius is not as bright as Rigel, it appears significantly brighter to us when we see it in the sky.

Now we can finally come to the neat part. As early as 1910, two brilliant astronomers, Einar Hertzsprung and Henry Russell, began to see that there was a relationship between a star's temperature and its magnitude. They plotted one versus the other and noticed that the stars they put on their chart seemed to fall into groups. When they made their research known, astronomers found their means of classifying stars. The graph that Hertzsprung and Russell developed became known as the **Hertzsprung-Russell Diagram**, which is often abbreviated as **H-R diagram**.

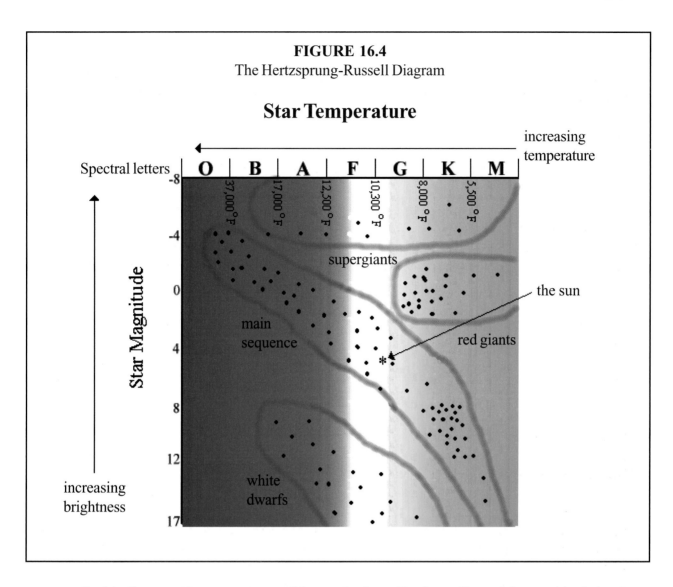

**FIGURE 16.4**
The Hertzsprung-Russell Diagram

In this diagram, the temperature of the star is plotted horizontally, and the magnitude is plotted vertically. The hotter the star, the farther to the left it is plotted, and the brighter the star, the higher it is plotted on the graph. The background of the graph tells you the color of the star. Remember, the color of a star depends primarily on its temperature. Thus, as one travels from the right side of the graph to the left side, the color goes from red (cooler stars) to blue (hotter stars). In addition, I have put the spectral letters for stars on top of the graph. Once again, a star's spectral letter depends only on its temperature. Thus, the spectral letter can be determined by a star's horizontal position on this graph.

Each of the dots in the diagram represents a star. These are only a few of the many stars that have been analyzed, but they show a distinct pattern. There is a broad band of stars that fall along a roughly diagonal path from the upper left-hand side of the graph to the lower right-hand side. We call these the **main sequence** stars. Notice that our sun is in this band. Thus, the sun is a main sequence star. Below the band of main sequence stars is a small groups of stars called the **white dwarfs**. Directly above the main sequence stars is another group called the **red giants** and above the red giants is a groups of stars called the **supergiants**. The diffuse, gray bands on the chart are simply there to help you better see these groupings of stars. In order to determine what basic kind of star an astronomer is studying, then, he or she looks at the position of the star on this chart. The group that the star falls into on this chart is the first step in the classification of the star.

What does this classification tell us about a star? Well, it turns out that each of these groups have their own, unique properties. About 90% of the stars that astronomers have studied are main sequence stars. These stars, as you might expect, are similar to the sun. They all produce a large amount of their energy from the nuclear fusion of hydrogen into helium. The more massive a main sequence star, the stronger its gravitational field. This means that the core temperature and pressure is high, and the rate of nuclear fusion is high. As a result, the more massive the main sequence star, the brighter it is.

In fact, it seems that the main difference between all main sequence stars is their individual mass. When a main sequence star is more massive, it is brighter and warmer. When it is less massive, it is fainter and cooler. Thus, if you look at the H-R diagram above, you can conclude that the main sequence stars that are basically blue in color are significantly more massive than the main sequence stars that are red in color.

Although there is a strict relationship between mass, brightness, and temperature for main sequence stars, that is not the case for red giants. Red giants, as their name implies, are huge stars. In the core of a red giant, there is nuclear fusion, but it is not the same kind of fusion as that which takes place in a main sequence star. A red giant has a core that is made mostly of helium. The core of a red giant is significantly hotter than that of a main sequence star, which results in a much brighter star. That's why red giants are high on the H-R diagram.

In this hot core, three helium atoms undergo nuclear fusion to make carbon atoms. That's the nuclear fusion which powers a red giant. Now despite the fact that a red giant's core is much hotter than that of a main sequence star, the overall temperature of a red giant is lower than most main sequence stars. That's why red giants are red.

Supergiant stars are, as the name implies, the largest stars in the universe. Astronomers have observed supergiants that, if put at the center of our solar system, would extend all of the way out to the orbit of Saturn! That's a BIG star! These stars are very rare. Despite their brightness, very few have been observed in the universe.

Based on current observations, it seems that white dwarfs are the second most common star in the universe. Remember, main sequence stars are by far the most common. However, a large number of white dwarfs have been observed as well. If you look again at the H-R diagram, you will see that the magnitude of white dwarfs is pretty high compared to most of the other stars on the diagram. This means that they are not very bright. Since we see a lot of white dwarfs despite the fact that they are not very bright, we must assume that they are relatively common in the universe.

As their name implies, white dwarfs are quite small.  Many in the universe seem to be even smaller than the planet earth.  That's quite small for a star!  Despite the fact that white dwarfs are small, they are incredibly massive.  Even a teaspoon full of the "stuff" that makes up a white dwarf would weigh several tons here on earth.  The matter in a white dwarf, then, is *very* tightly-packed.

---

**ON YOUR OWN**
Use the H-R Diagram in Figure 16.4 to solve these problems.

16.5  A star has a magnitude of 4, and its temperature indicates that it has a spectral letter of "F."  What kind of star is it?

16.6  Is the star in the problem above more or less massive than a star with a magnitude of 10 and a spectral letter of K?

16.7  Are red giants cooler or warmer than most white dwarfs?

---

## Variable Stars

In the previous section, I talked about stars that could be easily placed on the H-R diagram.  Not all stars can be easily placed on such a diagram, however, because some stars do not have a constant magnitude.  It turns out that the brightness of some stars varies and, as a result, it is not easy to place them on the H-R diagram, as their vertical position would continually change.  These are called **variable stars**, and there are two basic kinds: **pulsating variables** and **novas**.

The novas are the most spectacular variable stars in the universe.  The term "nova" comes from Latin and it means "new star."  This is not a good description for what a nova *is*, but it is a great description for what a nova *appears to be*.  Early astronomers noticed that every once in a while, a star would seem to appear at a point in the sky where there was no star before.  Thus, it looked like a new star had been born, so it was called a nova.  Modern astronomers now know that a nova is the result of an explosion within a star.  When a star explodes, it emits a fraction of its mass as a shell of gas.  That causes a temporary surge in its brightness, which causes the star to be more visible for a short time.

Although you might think of an explosion as something that would destroy a star, novas can explode many, many times.  After all, each explosion might result in only a small fraction of the nova's mass being expelled.  As a result, these explosions can occur over and over again.  It has also been theorized that some novas actually replenish their mass by attracting debris from other nearby stars, allowing a nova to explode even more often.  Most novas explode in regular intervals, some every few days, some every few years.

The extreme example of a nova is a **supernova**. A supernova is a true explosion of a star. When a supernova occurs, the star expands rapidly and brightens enormously, and then fades away permanently. The debris left over from such an explosion is a cloud of bright gases called a **nebula**. In 1054 A.D., early astronomers recorded observing a flash of light in the sky that seems to be what we would expect of a supernova. If we look at that same position in the sky today, we see the **crab nebula**.

**FIGURE 16.5**
The Crab Nebula

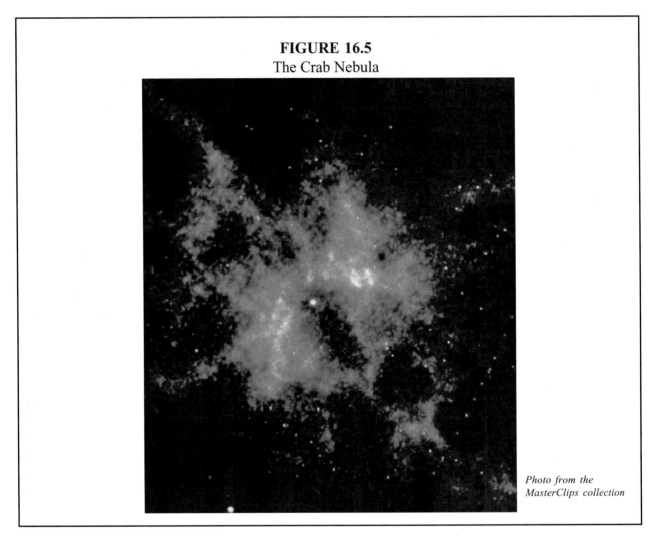

*Photo from the MasterClips collection*

Astronomers assume, therefore, that the crab nebula is the debris that was formed in the supernova explosion.

Supernovas are rare occurrences in the universe. Prior to 1987, only three had been observed in the history of astronomy, one of which is assumed to have left behind the crab nebula. On February 24, 1987, modern astronomers had their first glimpse of a supernova. Since this is the first supernova observed with modern instruments, it is the subject of a large amount of astrophysical scrutiny.

A much more common type of variable star is the pulsating variable. These stars expand and contract, much like a balloon that is constantly being inflated and deflated. The brightness of the star changes as it expands and contracts. Thus, a pulsating variable's brightness increases and decreases time and time again. Unlike a nova, the star does not eject a fraction of its mass as a result of the expanding and contracting that it does. Thus, a pulsating star has a long life time. Many pulsating stars have very regular periods of pulsation, which means that the rate at which they expand and contract is quite constant. As a result, the variation in brightness is constant as well.

A very well-studied class of pulsating stars is the Cepheid (sef' eyed) variable. These pulsating stars are yellow supergiants. The rate at which these stars expand and contract is very constant. As a result, the time that it takes for them to go from bright to dim is easily measured and does not change. Some Cepheid variables take as little as a day to go from bright to dim, while some take up to a year. These particular variable stars are instrumental in astronomers' attempts to measure long distances in the universe. I will talk about them again in a later section of this module.

For a while astronomers thought that there was a third kind of variable star, because stars that seemed to be neither novas nor pulsating variables did appear to vary in brightness with time. As more study was done, however, astronomers found that it is possible for two stars to be close enough to each other to actually orbit one another, much like the planets in our solar system orbit the sun. These are called **binary stars** because they are actually composed of two stars that are quite close to one another. If a binary star system is oriented properly relative to earth, the stars will pass in front of one another as they orbit. This results in one star obstructing our view of the second star. These systems, called **eclipsing binary stars**, vary in apparent brightness not because their magnitude changes. Instead, they vary in brightness because one of the two stars can block our view of the other. Thus, although these stars appear to be variable stars, they really are not.

---

**ON YOUR OWN**

16.8 Which kind of variable star lasts the longest: supernovas, novas, or pulsating variables?

---

## Measuring the Distance to Stars

When I was discussing the classification of stars, I mentioned that in order to measure the magnitude of a star, one must take into account the distance between earth and the star. How in the world can an astronomer measure something like that? We have not even been able to send an unmanned spacecraft to the edge of our own solar system. Other than the sun, the nearest star (Alpha Centauri) is a long way past the confines of our solar system. How, then, can we measure the distance to even the nearest star, since we have not traveled there?

Well, there are two main ways that astronomers measure the distance from the earth to a star: the **parallax method** and the **apparent magnitude method**. The first method, the parallax method, uses some rather simple arguments based on geometry, so I want to start with that method. When astronomers want to measure the distance to a star, they can observe it at two different times. Since stars are all quite far away, they do not appear to move much in the night sky. It turns out that all stars do, in fact move. Even though we think of the sun as stationary in our solar system, it is still moving in relation to other stars in the universe. Nevertheless, since the stars that we see (with the exception of the sun) are so far away, their movement is not noticeable to us. Thus, if an astronomer observes a star on one day and that same star 6 months later, the star should be in the same place in the sky.

However, despite the fact that the star should be at the same place in the sky, the *astronomer* has moved due to the orbit of the earth around the sun. This provides us with a way to measure the distance to the star. Examine Figure 16.6 to see what I mean.

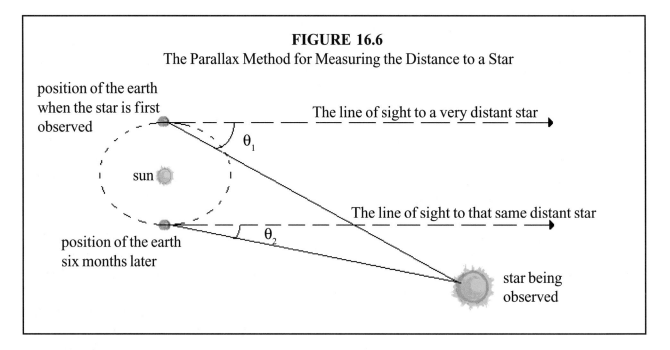

**FIGURE 16.6**
The Parallax Method for Measuring the Distance to a Star

position of the earth when the star is first observed

The line of sight to a very distant star

$\theta_1$

sun

The line of sight to that same distant star

position of the earth six months later

$\theta_2$

star being observed

When using the parallax method, an astronomer observes a very distant star and then observes the star for which he or she wants to determine the distance. The astronomer then measures the angle between the line of sight for those two stars. In the figure, that angle is denoted as $\theta_1$. If the astronomer then waits for six months, the earth will have traveled halfway around the sun. As a result, it will be in a different spot in the sky. If the astronomer then observes the same two stars again and measures the new angle between their lines of sight, he or she will have $\theta_2$. For nearby stars, $\theta_1$ will not be equal to $\theta_2$. It turns out that some rather straightforward geometry can be used to develop an exact relationship between the difference in those two angles and the distance to the star.

This method for judging distance can also be used to measure long distances on earth. Airplane navigators use it all of the time. They call it "triangulation." The nice thing about it is that the method is exact. It is a result of geometry. Thus, when astronomers use the parallax method to determine the distance to a star, the result is just as accurate as if the astronomer had used a long ruler and measured the distance directly. The bad thing about this method is that it can only be used to measure the distance to nearby stars. The farther away the star is, the less the difference between $\theta_1$ and $\theta_2$. Thus, for large distances, we cannot detect a difference in the angles and, as a result, we can no longer use the parallax method.

How far away can astronomers measure using the parallax method? Well, the first thing you have to know to answer that question is the units that astronomers use to measure distances in space. Most astronomers use **light years** as a distance unit.

<u>Light year</u> - The distance light travels in one year

Now if you think about it, that's a *long* distance unit. After all, light travels 300,000,000 meters every second. In a year, then, it travels approximately 9,500,000,000,000,000 meters, which is about the same as 6 trillion miles! That's a long way! Using that unit, the parallax method can be used to measure the distance to stars that are less than 100 light years away. If a star is farther away than that, the difference in sight line angles is simply too small for astronomers to measure. Alpha Centauri, for example, is the closest star to us, next to the sun, of course. The parallax method tells us that it is 4.3 light years away from us.

If you've read much about astronomy, you know that scientists talk about distances in the universe that are *much* longer than 100 light years. For example, astronomers tell us that Betelgeuse (bee' tul jews), a supergiant star, is 300 light years from us. They also tell us that the universe is more than 30 billion light years across. How do they get those numbers?

In order to measure distances on the order of 100 light years and beyond, astronomers use the apparent magnitude method. The idea behind this method was discovered by American astronomer Henrietta Leavitt. She studied an enormous number of Cepheid variable stars whose distances had been measured by the parallax method. Thus, these stars were all closer to the earth than 100 light years. She noticed that there seemed to be a direct relationship between their pulsation period and their magnitude. When a Cepheid variable star takes a long time to go from bright to dark, the star's average brightness is quite large; thus its magnitude is small. When the star takes a short time to go from bright to dark, the star's average brightness is low; so its magnitude is high. Astrophysicists had already predicted this relationship with a mathematical theory, and Leavitt's data provided evidence for that theory.

Armed with this information, astronomers can measure the distance to any observable Cepheid variable star, regardless of how far away it is. After all, if you have a way of calculating the magnitude of a star, and you then measure the amount of light that makes it to the earth from that star, it is very easy to determine how far away the star is. The trick, of course, is knowing the magnitude of the star to begin with. The relationship that Leavitt demonstrated for Cepheid variable stars close to the earth gave astronomers that ability. Thus, as long as there is a Cepheid star nearby, the distance to any structure in the universe can be measured using the apparent magnitude method.

Since Leavitt's discovery, other variable stars have been shown to exhibit a relationship between period and magnitude. As a result, astronomers have even more structures in the universe that they can use to measure distances. This has allowed astronomers to "map out" a significant fraction of our universe.

---

**ON YOUR OWN**

16.9 Which distance-measuring method is the most reliable: the parallax method or the apparent magnitude method?

---

Galaxies

Stars do not exist alone in space. They are grouped together in large ensembles known as **galaxies**.

Galaxy - A massive ensemble of hundreds of millions of stars, all interacting through the gravitational force, orbiting around a common center

All of the stars that can be seen with the naked eye (including the sun) belong to the same galaxy: the **Milky Way**.

Galaxies can be grouped according to their appearance. There are **spiral galaxies**, **elliptical galaxies**, and **lenticular galaxies**. All three of these kinds of galaxies have one thing in common: a bright spot in the center, which is called the **nucleus**.

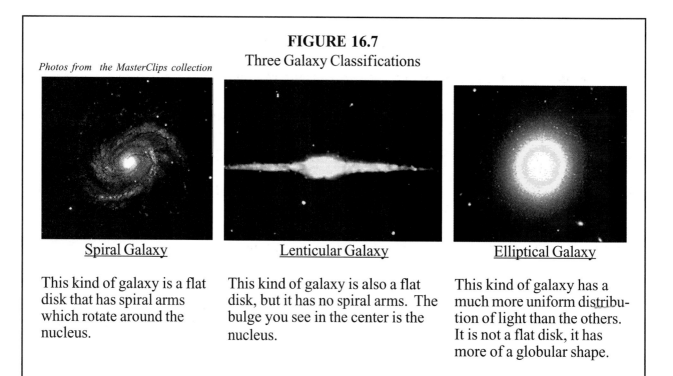

**FIGURE 16.7**
Three Galaxy Classifications

*Photos from the MasterClips collection*

Spiral Galaxy

Lenticular Galaxy

Elliptical Galaxy

This kind of galaxy is a flat disk that has spiral arms which rotate around the nucleus.

This kind of galaxy is also a flat disk, but it has no spiral arms. The bulge you see in the center is the nucleus.

This kind of galaxy has a much more uniform distribution of light than the others. It is not a flat disk, it has more of a globular shape.

If a galaxy cannot be classified as one of these three types, it is called an **irregular galaxy**.

The Milky Way, the galaxy to which our solar system belongs, is a spiral galaxy. It is about 120,000 light years across, but no more than 2,000 light years thick. That's what I mean when I say that spiral galaxies are disk-shaped. Compared to the distance across such a galaxy, the thickness of the galaxy is quite small. Our sun is on the inner edge of one of the spiral arms, called the **Orion arm**.

Lenticular galaxies look a lot like spiral galaxies. They are disk-shaped, and they also have a very prominent nucleus. Lenticular galaxies, however, do not have discernible arms. Instead, the stars rotate around the nucleus in a reasonably even distribution. Elliptical galaxies, on the other hand, are not at all disk-shaped. They have a more globular shape, and the distribution of light in the "glob" is rather uniform, except for the nucleus, which is very bright.

The interesting thing about galaxies is that they rarely exist by themselves. Most galaxies are part of a bigger group of galaxies. The Milky Way, for example, is part of a small group of about 20 galaxies, which is known as the **Local Group**. The two largest galaxies in the Local Group are the Milky Way galaxy and the Andromeda galaxy. These groups of galaxies, in turn, form large **clusters**. The Local Group is on the outer edge of a cluster of galaxies known as the **Virgo Cluster**. Galaxy clusters often group together as well into giant groups known as **superclusters**.

The distribution of these clusters and superclusters in the portion of the universe that we are able to observe is not uniform. Instead, they tend to form long, stringy, almost lacelike filaments which are arranged around large voids where few or no stars exist. One of these filaments, called the **Great Wall**, stretches across more than half a billion light years in space!

## An Expanding Universe

As early as 1912, the American astronomer Vesto M. Slipher noticed that the light which came from stars in galaxies other than the Milky Way is a bit different than what was expected. You see, there are certain wavelengths of light that are emitted by elements when they are excited. These wavelengths of light are called **spectral lines**, and each element has its own, unique patterns of spectral lines it emits when it is excited. These spectral lines are well known and well understood for most elements. Slipher found that when you looked at the spectral lines which come from a certain excited element in the star of another galaxy, the spectral lines were different than what they are when the excited element is in the sun. For each element, the spectral lines had longer wavelengths when the light came from stars in other galaxies as compared to those same spectral lines that originated in our sun!

Now remember, the wavelength of visible light determines the color of the light. Visible light with the shortest wavelengths is blue while visible light with long wavelengths is red. Slipher found that the light coming from other galaxies had longer wavelengths than one would predict. In other words, the light that came from other galaxies was redder than what it should have been. This phenomenon became known as the **red shift**.

What causes the red shift? Astronomers are not 100% sure, but they have a theory. Do you remember the Doppler effect that we studied in Module #14? The Doppler effect tells us that when moving objects emit waves, the frequency (and wavelength) of the waves that we observe is different than what we would observe when the object is stationary. If the object moves towards us, the waves get bunched up, and the observed wavelength is smaller than the actual wavelength. If the object moves away from us, then the waves get stretched out, and the observed wavelength *is larger than the actual wavelength.*

That's what Slipher saw! He saw that the light coming from most of the other galaxies he could analyze had wavelengths that were longer than they should have been. Thus, he and other astronomers theorized that the red shift was actually the Doppler effect for light. If that was the case, the conclusion was obvious. Most galaxies in the universe are actually traveling away from us. As time went on, astronomers became more and more convinced of the theory that the red shift was, indeed, a Doppler effect, and therefore, most of the galaxies in the universe are moving away from us. There are a few notable exceptions to this general rule. The Andromeda Galaxy, for example, seems to be moving towards us because the light that comes from it is bluer than it should be. For the vast majority of galaxies, however, the light that they are emitting does experience a red shift, so the conclusion that most astronomers make is that the vast majority of galaxies are moving away from us.

In 1929, the American astronomer Edwin Hubble noticed something rather interesting about the red shift. He noticed that the farther the galaxy is away from earth, the larger its red shift. Thus, light that comes from nearby galaxies has slightly larger wavelengths than expected, but the light that comes from distant galaxies has *significantly* larger wavelengths than expected. If the red shift is really the result of the Doppler effect, this could only mean one thing: *the farther away the galaxy is, the faster it is moving away from us.*

What does all of this mean? Well, you first have to understand that we are not really sure that the red shift is the result of the Doppler effect. There are other explanations for the red shift, but the majority of astronomers today believe that it is, indeed, a Doppler shift. If that is the case, it tells us that *the universe is expanding.*

Now if the universe is expanding, it could be doing so in one of two ways. Since it seems that all of the galaxies are moving away from us, it could be that our solar system is the center of the universe, and all galaxies are traveling away from us. If this is the case, then, the universe is an ever-expanding sphere in which we are the center. That's not the only way that the universe could expand, however. Perform the following experiment to see how most astronomers today believe that the universe is expanding.

---

**EXPERIMENT 16.1**
An Expanding Universe

Supplies:

- Balloon
- Two colors of markers (You need to be able to write on the balloon with the markers.)

Introduction - If almost all of the galaxies in the universe are moving away from us, that does not necessarily mean we are at the center of the universe. Perform this experiment to see why.

Procedure:

A. Take the balloon and lay it flat on a table. Use one of the markers to put several dots all over the balloon, on both sides. Leave room for one special dot.
B. When you are done with the first marker, take the other one and use it to make one special dot - the one you left the space for.
C. Bring the balloon to your mouth so that you can blow it up. Hold the balloon so that you can see the single dot that has a different color than all of the others.
D. Blow up the balloon. While you are doing that, notice how the dots move in relation to that one special dot.

---

What did you see in the experiment? You should have seen that all of the dots moved away from the special dot, regardless of where the dots were. In the minds of many astronomers, this experiment is actually an illustration of how the universe is expanding. The surface of the balloon represents space. When you blow up the balloon, space begins to expand. That's how most astronomers think the universe is expanding. The special dot on the balloon represents the Milky Way galaxy, and the other dots represent other galaxies in the universe. Because space itself (the balloon) expands, all of the galaxies (the dots) move away from all of the other galaxies, including the Milky Way (the special dot).

Please realize that if the universe is expanding in this way, it means the universe *has no center*. Think about the surface of the balloon. If you put your finger on any of the dots and then began to move your finger away from the dot while still touching the surface of the balloon, what would happen? You would eventually go all the way around the balloon and your finger would eventually reach the same dot you started at. If you believe that the universe is expanding in the way illustrated by the experiment, then that has to be your view of space. In this view, space has no center. It is continuous, but like the surface of a balloon, continues to curve on itself so that it has no real beginning or end.

In the end, then, there are two views of how the universe is expanding. It might be expanding with earth at its center and all of the galaxies rushing away from the earth. That is perfectly consistent with all of the data we have. On the other hand, it might be expanding because, as space expands, it carries *all structures away from each other*, like the dots on your balloon. Once again, this is perfectly consistent with all of the data we have. Finally, it might not be expanding at all, because we do not know for sure that the red shift is the result of the Doppler effect.

Which of these three options is right? We don't really know. The vast majority of astronomers believe that the universe is, indeed, expanding. I also think that this idea is probably right. Although there are other explanations for the red shift, the Doppler effect seems to be the best one. The majority of astronomers not only believe that the universe is expanding, but they believe that it is expanding according to the way that was illustrated in Experiment 16.1. The problem is, there is no *scientific* reason to choose that means of expansion over the first one that I presented.

As I said before, if the universe is expanding, it can do so either by the means illustrated in Experiment 16.1 *or* it could do so with earth as the center of the universe and all of the other galaxies rushing away from it. At this time, there is no scientific reason to choose one of those methods of expansion over the other. They are both 100% consistent with the data we have. Why, then, do most astronomers believe in the former rather than the latter? The answer is *philosophical*, not scientific. Most astronomers do not want to believe that there is anything special about the earth. If the earth's solar system were at the center of the universe, then than would mean there was something special about it. Since most astronomers do not want to believe that, most astronomers will only consider the mode of expansion illustrated in Experiment 16.1.

Those astronomers that believe in God, however, can be more open-minded. Perhaps God had no reason to put the earth's solar system at the center of the universe. If that's the case, then the vast majority of astronomers are right. However, it is perfectly feasible that God did, indeed, put the earth's solar system at the very center of the universe. In some ways, that might even make sense. Thus, an astronomer that believes in God can look at astrophysics with a more open mind.

Does it really matter which way the universe is expanding? Actually, it does. A creation scientist by the name of Russell Humphreys recently wrote a book entitled *Starlight and Time*. The details of this book are well beyond the scope of this course, but you might consider reading it during one of your school breaks. In this book, he develops an entire theory of the formation of the universe which is predicated on the assumption that the earth's solar system is at the center of the universe.

One of the really neat things about Dr. Humphreys' theory is that it uses Einstein's Theory of Relativity to explain an age old mystery that has puzzled creation scientists for years. A large number of creation scientists (myself included) think that the earth is only a few thousand years old. The vast majority of data in science, in our opinion, is consistent with such an assumption. At the same time, the vast majority of data is inconsistent with the idea that the earth is billions of years old. Thus, a large number of creation scientists believe that God formed the universe and the earth only a few thousand years ago.

If that is the case, then, there seems to be a problem. We can observe stars that are billions of light years away from us. If creation happened only a few thousand years ago, how can we be seeing light from those stars? It would take billions of years for the light to get here. Well, Dr. Humphreys' theory explains this seemingly unexplainable problem. Using the standard theories and tools that all other astrophysicists use, Dr. Humphreys shows that if the universe is expanding with the earth as its center, the creation could have happened only a few thousand years ago, and we would still be able to see light that took billions of years to travel here!

As I said before, the details of Dr. Humphreys' theory are beyond the scope of this course. However, the point I want to make is rather simple. The majority of scientists believe in a theory called the big bang. This theory assumes that the universe is expanding, but it assumes that the expansion takes place as illustrated in Experiment 16.1. This theory concludes that the universe is the result of random chance and is billions of years old. Dr. Humphreys' theory tells us that if we assume the universe is expanding with earth's solar system as its center, then the universe need not be the result of random chance, and it need not be billions of years old.

Which theory is right? We do not know. For all we know, they are both wrong! However, we do know that the only real difference is a *philosophical* assumption. If you assume one way, you get one theory. If you assume another way, you get another theory. From a scientific point of view, both assumptions are absolutely equal. Thus, at this point, they have equal scientific merit.

---

**ON YOUR OWN**

16.10 Assume that the universe is expanding with earth's solar system as its center. Suppose you were in a galaxy other than that of earth. Would you still see a red shift from all of the other galaxies in the universe? Why or why not?

---

<u>Summing It All Up</u>

Well, you have come to the end of your physical science course. I hope you have enjoyed it. More importantly, however, I hope that you have learned something. I hope that you have come to a deeper appreciation for the ingenuity and creative genius of God. Over and over again in this course, you learned about processes in Creation that are simply too complex and too well-designed to occur by chance. I hope that, in some cases, you have been filled with awe. The Bible says "The heavens declare the glory of God; and the firmament sheweth his handywork." (Ps. 19:1) Anyone who studies science honestly and in a reasonably unbiased manner should easily come to that same conclusion!

**ANSWERS TO THE ON YOUR OWN PROBLEMS**

16.1  <u>As time goes on, the composition will change.  The amount of hydrogen will decrease and the amount of helium will increase.</u>  Remember, nuclear fusion gives the sun its power.  That very process takes hydrogen and converts it to helium.  As time goes on, then, hydrogen will be used up and helium will be produced.

16.2  <u>The photosphere has the lowest temperature.</u>  The core is the hottest because that's where all of the energy is being produced.  As the energy travels into the outer regions of the sun, it gets more spread out.  Thus, each layer of the sun is cooler than the layer underneath.  Since the photosphere is at the top, it is the coolest, because the energy is least concentrated there.

16.3  <u>This is nuclear fusion.</u>  Two small nuclei ($^7$Li has 3 protons and 4 neutrons) join to make a big nucleus ($^{12}$C has 6 neutrons and 6 protons).  If it were fission, a large nucleus would be broken down into smaller nuclei.

16.4  <u>This would eliminate the worry of meltdown in a nuclear power plant, because there could be no chain reaction.</u>  Remember, the nuclear fission process can go out of control because *one* fission process can start *several* other fission processes.  This can cause the reaction to grow and grow until it is out of control.  If *one* fission process can start *only one additional* fission process, then the fission process would be sustained, but it could never grow.  Based on our understanding of nuclear fission at this time, however, such a fission process is thought to be impossible.

16.5  If the magnitude is 4 and the spectral letter is "F," it falls somewhere on the thick bar in the H-R diagram below:

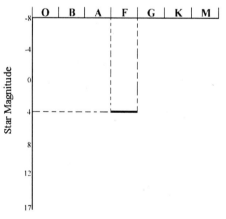

Any point on that bar is clearly in the main sequence portion of the H-R diagram, so this is a <u>main sequence</u> star.

16.6  With a magnitude of 10 and a spectral letter of "K," this star falls somewhere on the thick line shown in the H-R diagram:

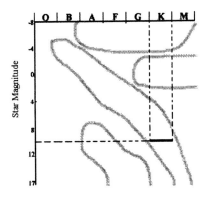

Thus, this is a main sequence star. Both stars, then, are main sequence stars. For main sequence stars, there is a direct dependence between mass and magnitude. The brighter the star, the more massive. Since a smaller magnitude means a large brightness, <u>the star in 16.5 is more massive than the star in this problem</u>.

16.7  If you look on the H-R diagram, the white dwarf group is farther to the left than the red giant group. Since temperature increases as you move to the left on an H-R diagram, <u>red giants are cooler than most white dwarfs</u>.

16.8  <u>Pulsating variables last the longest</u>. Supernovas brighten just once and then disappear forever. Novas can brighten several times, but they lose mass each time. Thus, they eventually go away as well. Pulsating variables do not lose mass when they brighten. Thus, they can live for a long time.

16.9  <u>The parallax method is the most reliable</u>. It is the direct result of geometry. The apparent magnitude method makes an assumption. It assumes that the magnitude/period relationship that exists for Cepheid variables near the earth is correct for *all* such stars. That's *probably* a good assumption, but there is no way to check it!

16.10  <u>You would still see a red shift from the other galaxies</u>. Think about it. If the universe is expanding outwards, then all objects are moving away from each other. Consider the following picture:

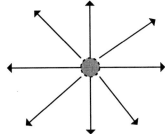

If the circle is the earth's solar system, then all galaxies would be moving away from the earth along the arrows. Notice that the arrows get farther and farther from each other. Thus, the galaxies would be moving away from one another, as well as away from the earth's solar system.

**STUDY GUIDE FOR MODULE #16**

1.  Define the following terms:

a.  Nuclear fusion
b.  Nuclear fission
c.  Critical mass
d.  Star magnitude
e.  Light year
f.  Galaxy

2.  From the inside to the outside, name the four regions of the sun.

3.  How does the sun get its power?  In which region of the sun does this process occur?

4.  What part of the sun do we see?

5.  A $^{251}$Cf nucleus is bombarded with a neutron.  It breaks down into a $^{124}$Sn nucleus, a $^{120}$Cd nucleus and 7 neutrons.  Is this nuclear fission or nuclear fusion?

6.  Two $^4$He nuclei collide and turn into a $^7$Be nucleus and 1 neutron.  Is this nuclear fusion or nuclear fission?

7.  For both nuclear fusion and nuclear fission, what can we say about the mass of the starting materials compared to the mass of what's made in the end?

8.  Why is it impossible for a nuclear power plant to have a nuclear explosion?

9.  Why is nuclear fusion considered a better option for energy production compared to nuclear fission?

10.  If nuclear fusion is a better option, why don't we use it?

11.  Using the H-R diagram on the next page, classify the following stars:

a.  Magnitude -1, Spectral Letter K
c.  Magnitude -7, Spectral Letter F

b.  Magnitude -3, Spectral Letter B
d.  Magnitude 13, Spectral Letter F

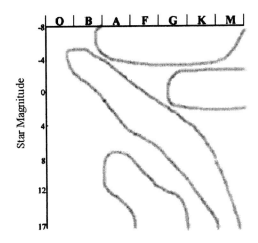

12.  Which of the stars in problem 11 is most like our sun?

13.  Order the four stars in problem 11 in terms of increasing size.

14. Order the four stars in problem 11 in terms of increasing brightness.

15.  Which of the stars in problem 11 is the coolest?

16.  What similarity exists between novas, supernovas, and pulsating variables?

17.  What is the big difference between novas, supernovas, and pulsating variables?

18.  What is a nebula?

19.  What are the two methods for measuring the distance from earth to a star?  Which of the two is the most accurate?  Which can be used to measure long distances?

20.  Why are Cepheid variables so important for measuring long distances in the universe?

21.  What are the four basic types of galaxies?  To which type does the Milky Way belong?

22. Fill in the blanks:  Stars group together to form _____, which group together to form _____, which group together to form _____, some of which group together to form _____.

23.  For the first three answers you gave in #22, give the names that apply to those to which earth's solar system belongs.

24.  Why do most astronomers believe that the universe is expanding?

25.  In what two ways could the universe be expanding?

26.  If the universe is expanding, does it matter which way?

# GLOSSARY

The numbers in parentheses refer to the page on which the definition is presented.

Absolute humidity - The mass of water vapor contained in a certain volume of air  (29)

Acceleration - The time rate of change of an object's velocity  (216)

Adiabatic cooling - The cooling of a gas that happens when the gas expands   (124)

Air mass - A large body of air with relatively uniform pressure, temperature, and humidity  (173)

Aphelion - The point at which the earth is farthest from the sun  (163)

Atmosphere - The mass of air surrounding a planet  (57)

Atmospheric pressure - The pressure exerted by the atmosphere on all objects within it  (57)

Atom - The smallest stable unit of matter in Creation  (3)

Atomic number - The number of protons in an atom  (320)

Barometer - An instrument used to measure atmospheric pressure  (60)

Beta decay - The process by which a neutron turns into a proton by emission of an electron (330)

Centripetal force - Force that is always directed perpendicular to the velocity of an object  (267)

Charging by conduction - Charging an object by allowing it to come into contact with an object which already has an electrical charge (298)

Charging by induction - Charging an object by forcing some of the charges to leave the object (299)

Cloud condensation nuclei - Small particles that water vapor condenses on to form clouds  (125)

Cohesion - The phenomenon that occurs when individual molecules are so strongly attracted to each other that they tend to stay together, even when exposed to tension (97)

Concentration - The quantity of a substance within a certain volume of space  (18)

Condensation - The process by which water vapor turns into liquid water (109)

Conventional current - Current that flows from the positive side of the battery to the negative side. This is the way current is drawn in circuit diagrams, even though it is wrong. (303)

Coriolis effect - The way in which the rotation of the earth bends the path of winds, sea currents, and objects that fly through different latitudes (170)

Critical mass - The amount of isotope necessary to cause a chain reaction (410)

Distillation - Evaporation and condensation of a mixture to separate out the mixture's individual components (112)

Earth's crust - Earth's outermost layer of rock (133)

Earthquake - A trembling or shaking of the earth as a result of rock masses suddenly moving along a fault (147)

Electrical current - The amount of charge that travels through an electrical circuit each second (300)

Electrolysis - Using electricity to break a molecule down into its constituent elements (81)

Electromagnetic wave - A transverse wave composed of an oscillating electrical field and a magnetic field that oscillates perpendicular to the electrical field (374)

Element - A collection of atoms that all have the same number of protons (322)

Epicenter - The point on the surface of the earth directly above an earthquake's focus (149)

Exosphere - The region of the atmosphere above an altitude of 460 kilometers (75)

Fault - The boundary between a section of moving rock and a section of stationary rock (147)

Firn - A dense, icy pack of snow (119)

Focus - The point along a fault where an earthquake begins (149)

Free fall - The state of an object that is falling towards the earth with nothing inhibiting its fall (221)

Friction - A force resulting from the contact of two surfaces. This force opposes motion. (244)

# PERIODIC CHART OF THE ELEMENTS

| 1A | 2A | 3B | 4B | 5B | 6B | 7B | 8B | 8B | 8B | 1B | 2B | 3A | 4A | 5A | 6A | 7A | 8A |
|---|---|---|---|---|---|---|---|---|---|---|---|---|---|---|---|---|---|
| 1<br>**H**<br>1.01 | | | | | | | | | | | | | | | | | 2<br>**He**<br>4.0 |
| 3<br>**Li**<br>6.94 | 4<br>**Be**<br>9.01 | | | | | | | | | | | 5<br>**B**<br>10.8 | 6<br>**C**<br>12.0 | 7<br>**N**<br>14.0 | 8<br>**O**<br>16.0 | 9<br>**F**<br>19.0 | 10<br>**Ne**<br>20.2 |
| 11<br>**Na**<br>23.0 | 12<br>**Mg**<br>24.3 | | | | | | 8B | 9B | 10B | | | 13<br>**Al**<br>27.0 | 14<br>**Si**<br>28.1 | 15<br>**P**<br>31.0 | 16<br>**S**<br>32.1 | 17<br>**Cl**<br>35.5 | 18<br>**Ar**<br>39.9 |
| 19<br>**K**<br>39.1 | 20<br>**Ca**<br>40.1 | 21<br>**Sc.**<br>45.0 | 22<br>**Ti**<br>47.9 | 23<br>**V**<br>50.9 | 24<br>**Cr**<br>52.0 | 25<br>**Mn**<br>54.9 | 26<br>**Fe**<br>55.8 | 27<br>**Co**<br>58.9 | 28<br>**Ni**<br>58.7 | 29<br>**Cu**<br>63.5 | 30<br>**Zn**<br>65.4 | 31<br>**Ga**<br>69.7 | 32<br>**Ge**<br>72.6 | 33<br>**As**<br>74.9 | 34<br>**Se**<br>79.0 | 35<br>**Br**<br>79.9 | 36<br>**Kr**<br>83.8 |
| 37<br>**Rb**<br>85.5 | 38<br>**Sr**<br>87.6 | 39<br>**Y**<br>88.9 | 40<br>**Zr**<br>91.2 | 41<br>**Nb**<br>92.9 | 42<br>**Mo**<br>95.9 | 43<br>**Tc**<br>(98) | 44<br>**Ru**<br>101.1 | 45<br>**Rh**<br>102.9 | 46<br>**Pd**<br>106.4 | 47<br>**Ag**<br>107.9 | 48<br>**Cd**<br>112.4 | 49<br>**In**<br>114.8 | 50<br>**Sn**<br>118.7 | 51<br>**Sb**<br>121.8 | 52<br>**Te**<br>127.6 | 53<br>**I**<br>126.9 | 54<br>**Xe**<br>131.3 |
| 55<br>**Cs**<br>132.9 | 56<br>**Ba**<br>137.3 | 57<br>**La**<br>138.9 | 72<br>**Hf**<br>178.5 | 73<br>**Ta**<br>180.9 | 74<br>**W**<br>183.9 | 75<br>**Re**<br>186.2 | 76<br>**Os**<br>190.2 | 77<br>**Ir**<br>192.2 | 78<br>**Pt**<br>195.1 | 79<br>**Au**<br>197.0 | 80<br>**Hg**<br>200.6 | 81<br>**Tl**<br>204.4 | 82<br>**Pb**<br>207.2 | 83<br>**Bi**<br>209.0 | 84<br>**Po**<br>(209) | 85<br>**At**<br>(210) | 86<br>**Rn**<br>(222) |
| 87<br>**Fr**<br>(223) | 88<br>**Ra**<br>226.0 | 89<br>**Ac**<br>(227) | 104<br>(261) | 105<br>(262) | 106<br>(266) | 107<br>(264) | 108<br>(269) | 109<br>(268) | | | | | | | | | |

| 58<br>**Ce**<br>140.1 | 59<br>**Pr**<br>140.9 | 60<br>**Nd**<br>144.2 | 61<br>**Pm**<br>(145) | 62<br>**Sm**<br>150.4 | 63<br>**Eu**<br>152.0 | 64<br>**Gd**<br>157.3 | 65<br>**Tb**<br>158.9 | 66<br>**Dy**<br>162.5 | 67<br>**Ho**<br>164.9 | 68<br>**Er**<br>167.3 | 69<br>**Tm**<br>168.9 | 70<br>**Yb**<br>173.0 | 71<br>**Lu**<br>175.0 |
|---|---|---|---|---|---|---|---|---|---|---|---|---|---|
| 90<br>**Th**<br>232.0 | 91<br>**Pa**<br>231.0 | 92<br>**U**<br>238.0 | 93<br>**Np**<br>(237) | 94<br>**Pu**<br>(244) | 95<br>**Am**<br>(243) | 96<br>**Cm**<br>(247) | 97<br>**Bk**<br>(247) | 98<br>**Cf**<br>(251) | 99<br>**Es**<br>(252) | 100<br>**Fm**<br>(257) | 101<br>**Md**<br>(258) | 102<br>**No**<br>(259) | 103<br>**Lr**<br>(262) |

# LIST OF ELEMENT NAMES AND SYMBOLS
## The list is compiled in the order that they appear on the chart

| Name | Symbol | Name | Symbol | Name | Symbol |
|---|---|---|---|---|---|
| Hydrogen | H | Strontium | Sr | Rhenium | Re |
| Helium | He | Yttrium | Y | Osmium | Os |
| Lithium | Li | Zirconium | Zr | Iridium | Ir |
| Beryllium | Be | Niobium | Nb | Platinum | Pt |
| Boron | B | Molybdenum | Mo | Gold | Au |
| Carbon | C | Technetium | Tc | Mercury | Hg |
| Nitrogen | N | Ruthenium | Ru | Thallium | Tl |
| Oxygen | O | Rhodium | Rh | Lead | Pb |
| Fluorine | F | Palladium | Pd | Bismuth | Bi |
| Neon | Ne | Silver | Ag | Polonium | Po |
| Sodium | Na | Cadmium | Cd | Astatine | At |
| Magnesium | Mg | Indium | In | Radon | Rn |
| Aluminum | Al | Tin | Sn | Francium | Fr |
| Silicon | Si | Antimony | Sb | Radium | Ra |
| Phosphorus | P | Tellurium | Te | Actinium | Ac |
| Sulfur | S | Iodine | I | Thorium | Th |
| Chlorine | Cl | Xenon | Xe | Protactinium | Pa |
| Argon | Ar | Cesium | Cs | Uranium | U |
| Potassium | K | Barium | Ba | Neptunium | Np |
| Calcium | Ca | Lanthanum | La | Plutonium | Pu |
| Scandium | Sc | Cerium | Ce | Americium | Am |
| Titanium | Ti | Praseodymium | Pr | Curium | Cm |
| Vanadium | V | Neodynium | Nd | Berkelium | Bk |
| Chromium | Cr | Promethium | Pm | Californium | Cf |
| Manganese | Mn | Samarium | Sm | Einsteinium | Es |
| Iron | Fe | Europium | Eu | Fermium | Fm |
| Cobalt | Co | Gadolinium | Gd | Medelevium | Md |
| Nickel | Ni | Terbium | Tb | Nobelium | No |
| Copper | Cu | Dysprosium | Dy | Lawrencium | Lr |
| Zinc | Zn | Holmium | Ho | | |
| Gallium | Ga | Erbium | Er | | |
| Germanium | Ge | Thulium | Tm | | |
| Arsenic | As | Ytterbium | Yb | | |
| Selenium | Se | Lutetium | Lu | | |
| Bromine | Br | Hafnium | Hf | | |
| Krypton | Kr | Tantalum | Ta | | |
| Rubidium | Rb | Tungsten | W | | |

# INDEX